COLLINS POCKET GUIDE

ALPINE FLOWERS
OF BRITAIN & EUROPE

Other Collins Pocket Guides

Birds of Britain & Europe, with North Africa and the Middle East
Hermann Heinzel, Richard Fitter and John Parslow

Trees of Britain & Europe, Alan Mitchell and John Wilkinson

Grasses, Sedges, Rushes and Ferns of Britain & Northern Europe
Richard Fitter, Alastair Fitter and Anne Farrer

Wild Flowers of Britain and Northern Europe
Richard Fitter, Alastair Fitter and Marjorie Blamey

Mushrooms and Toadstools of Britain & Europe, Stefan Buczacki

Stars and Planets, Ian Ridpath and Wil Tirion

Coral Reef Fishes of the World, Ewald Lieske and Robert Myers

Other Collins books by the same authors

Mediterranean Wild Flowers
Marjorie Blamey and Christopher Grey-Wilson

COLLINS
POCKET GUIDE

ALPINE
FLOWERS
OF BRITAIN AND EUROPE

CHRISTOPHER GREY-WILSON • MARJORIE BLAMEY

HarperCollins*Publishers*

Dedicated to the Alpine Garden Society

HarperCollinsPublishers
London Glasgow Sydney Auckland Toronto Johannesburg

For more information on other Collins Pocket Guides please contact:
CollinsNaturalHistory
77-85 Fulham Palace Road
London
W6 8JB
UK

First edition published 1979
Reprinted 1985, 1986, 1988, 1992
Second edition published 1995

ISBN 0 00 220017 1

Colour reproduction by Colourscan, Singapore
Printed in the UK by Butler & Tanner, Frome, Somerset

Contents

Notes on this new edition

The first edition of this book was published in 1979. Since then many advances have been made into the study and research of alpine plants in Europe, especially as regards classification and nomenclature. As a result a new edition of this work, rather than a reprint, was considered well worth while. The main features of this new edition are:

- the area covered by the book has been expanded to include the eastern European countries of Czechoslovakia (Czech Republic and Slovakia), Hungary, Poland and Romania, thus including the mountain masses of the Carpathians, Sudeten, Tatra, as well as the Transylvanian Alps. In addition, Iceland is now included, as well as the Dinaric Alps of Yugoslavia and the Cantabrian Mountains (Cordillara Cantabrica) of north-western Spain.
- plates formerly in black and white and located at the end of the first edition have now been re-drawn and placed in their correct position within the other colour plates, and details of fruits, leaves and flowers formerly in appendices at the rear of the volume have also been placed in their correct position in the main text. Additions and corrections have been carefully made to colour plates where author and artist felt this was necessary.
- the scientific names of plants have been brought up to date, as far as possible at the time of publication, and the synonymy of existing species expanded, where the text allows.
- the distribution of species and subspecies has been refined by a new system of coding to enable the reader to tell at a glance whether or not a species is to be found within a particular country. The new coding follows the country codes that have been internationally accepted and should be familiar to most readers.

We are always glad to receive additional information on the alpine plants of Europe, especially where extensions to existing distributions or altitudes can be confirmed. Whereas we have made every effort to include as wide a range of plants as possible, because of the limited space available, familiar weed species found on waste and disturbed land or along tracks or roadsides, as well as some local endemic species and natural hybrids, have been omitted.

Marjorie Blamey and Christopher Grey-Wilson, 1995

Introduction

What Are Alpine Plants?

The European mountains support many beautiful and often distinct plant species, variously adapted to the different habitats found in such regions.

Whereas many lowland species often reach up to alpine levels (above 1000 m in this book) few true mountain plants come much below 1500 m, at least in mainland Europe. In the extreme north of the region and in the British Isles, typical mountain species can be found well below this level for reasons not entirely understood, but probably due to a combination of factors such as climate, exposure, soil types and the effects of the last ice ages that has left pockets of mountain vegetation scattered in these areas. For instance the Spring Gentian, *Gentiana verna*, is to be found at sea level in the limestone of the Burren in western Ireland but only at alpine levels in the mountains of mainland Europe.

Typical zones of vegetation at different altitudes can be seen in most mountain areas, as is shown in the simplified diagrammatic representation overleaf. The zones often tend to merge gradually into one another and may not all be present on a particular mountain; but the various tree and shrub lines can usually be easily identified. A number of important mountain peaks are included to give an idea of the relative altitudes and zonings; these are not included for the British Isles. Generally speaking, the further north one goes the lower the different zones are found; this means that a given species is likely to be found at lower altitudes in the north of its range than the south.

The principal zones are as follows:

Sub-alpine zone This is the zone below the uppermost tree line and includes a rich flora of mixed lowland and mountain species. Meadows, woods, lanes and banks are often very floriferous, with many large herbs, shrubs and trees. Any cultivation also occurs within or below this zone. At the uppermost limit the trees (generally pine, juniper or birch) become dwarf and stunted and often rather sparse.

True alpine plant zone Above the tree line, where conditions are too rigorous to support tree growth, there is a poorer flora as regards numbers of species, but a much more highly specialised one. Dwarf and carpeting shrubs replace trees and short meadows support a rich growth of alpine plant species, often making rich splashes of colour when the spring arrives. If one walks higher still the meadows thin and the plants become even dwarfer and more highly adapted; ground or rock hugging species, which are often cushion- or tuft-forming plants with small leaves and large brightly coloured flowers. In this high alpine zone plants are frequently widely scattered but are often the most rewarding to find and see.

The main habitats in such regions are:

Alpine meadows or alpine grassland – widespread in the mountains above the tree line, especially between 1400-2800 m. They are either natural or secondary as a result of de-afforestation at the upper limit of the tree zone. Rich and often colourful alpine meadows are generally dominated by grasses and sedges but their constituent elements vary greatly from place to place and by whether they are developed on acid or basic (calcareous) rocks. Higher grassland communities up to 3000 m. can be found in parts of the Alps, Tatras and Carpathians.

Shrubberies – above the tree line, where trees are unable to grow there are often zones of bushes and related tall herbs, especially in the altitudinal range 1400-2000 m. Most widespread on calcareous soils are the

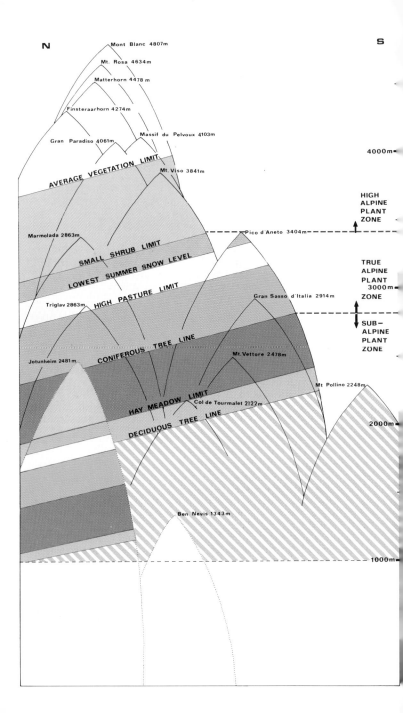

communities dominated by Dwarf Pine, *Pinus mugo*, and Alpenrose, *Rhododendron ferrugineum*, but by Green Alder, *Alnus viridis*, on more acid soils. In Scotland and Scandinavia such shrubberies are replaced primarily by low willows between 400-1200 m.

Alpine heaths – low shrubberies on acid soils dominated by ericaceous plants, often accompanied by small grasses, sedges, mosses and lichens, are found primarily between 1500-2600 m. but at lower altitudes in boreal regions. In some the Dwarf Juniper, *Juniperus communis* subsp. *alpina*, may dominate.

Snow patches – in alpine zones where late lying snow patches are slow to melt on a regular basis (especially hollows) special plant communities may develop and are characterised by a short growing season. As the snow melts so a succession of flowers open giving a halo-effect around the patches; farther away the same plants will have completed flowering and will be in fruit. Snow patches are always worth seeking out as they extend the flowering period of various species, often well into summer (e.g. *Crocus vernus, Soldanella alpina* and *Veronica alpina*).

Stream sides and wet flushes – common throughout the region and have varying associations of plants according to altitude and soil acidity, to 2500 m. Locally there may be more extensive wet areas in the form of mires developed over peat, especially in hollows close to moraines. Where the water table is more or less at the surface poor fens, dominated by various sedges, may develop.

Rock communities – these may dominate at any altitude throughout the region and will have associated plants almost up to to permanent levels of snow, certainly up to 3400 m. in the Alps. The constituent plants depend not only on whether the rocks are acid or alkaline, but also on latitude. Many of the special as well as endemic alpines are found in such habitats which can be loosely classified as follows:

1. *Moraines* – rock debris left at the sides (lateral moraines) or snout (terminal moraines) of glaciers. More extensive glacial deposits are to be found in areas previously covered by massive ice sheets, especially in boreal regions.

2. *Screes* – accumulations of rock fragments of varying sizes beneath cliffs and steep slopes. Screes are generally mobile and are being continually replenished by fresh rocky debris from above. Despite this they may harbour a great range of interesting plants, especially when screes have become stabilised and less mobile.

3. *Cliffs* – these can range from those just a few metres high to massive structures of several hundred metres or more. Cliffs harbour an interesting assortment of specialised as well as more widely dispersed plants which grow on the ledges and in suitable cracks and fissures. The rock type dominates the cliff plant communities, but aspect may also play an important role, so that some plants will only be found on shaded or north-facing cliffs.

4. *Exposed rocks* – these dominate the middle and upper alpine areas below the zone of permanent snow. Exposed rocks provide the most extreme environment for alpine plants, yet many are especially adapted to, such places and are not found elsewhere, or perhaps also on adjacent screes (e.g. *Androsace alpina, Diapensia lapponica, Edraianthus graminifolius* and *Eritrichium nanum*). They can be one of the most rewarding areas to explore, even though plants are often few and well scattered.

Habitat is specially important for many mountain plants; many are highly specialised to a particular type. Occasionally rivers, screes or

Areas of Europe over 1000 metres

moraines may bring species down to much lower altitudes than those at which they are normally found. Exploring valleys which run down from a high mountain or a glacier will often reveal interesting plants.

Mountain Flowers in Britain

We have already seen (p.9) that as one moves northwards in Europe the zones of true alpine and subalpine vegetation commence at much lower altitudes. At the same time, the number of species of plants diminishes rapidly due both to the harsher conditions, but also to the effects of the Quaternary Ice Ages which virtually wiped out the natural flora of the areas covered by glaciation. In Britain and Scandinavia this effect was most severe, but strangely, isolated pockets of alpine flora survived in both areas, though poorly represented in species numbers. Incomplete glaciation in the Alps, Pyrenees and the other mountains of Central Europe allowed the survival of many species which were quickly able to 'move back' through these mountains after the final retreat of the ice.

The mountain flora of Great Britain is best described as depauperate; it consists of about 130 species in all, of which many are local or rare and

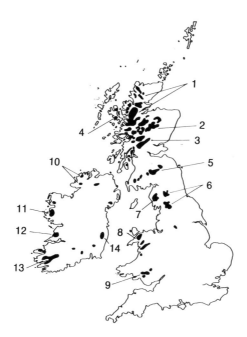

Mountain areas of Great Britain and Ireland where alpine flowers are most abundant. 1 Western Highlands, 2 Cairngorm Mountains, 3 Central Highlands, 4 Mountains of Skye, 5 Southern Highlands, 6 Pennines, 7 Lake District Mountains, 8 Snowdonia, 9 Black Mountains and Brecon Beacons, 10 Donegal Mountains, 11 Connacht Mountains, 12 Burren, 13 Kerry Mountains, 14 Wicklow Mountains

none are endemic to the area, though the following can be considered endemic to the Northern European mountain and Arctic regions:

Cerastium arcticum	*Koenigia islandica*
Cornus suecica	*Minuartia rubella*
Deschampsia cespitosa subsp.	*Rubus chamaemorus*
alpina	*Sagina nivalis*
Diapensia lapponica	*Salix lanata*
Draba norvegica	*Saxifraga cespitosa*
Erigeron borealis	*Saxifraga rivularis*

Surprisingly, both *Diapensia lapponica* and *Koenigia islandica* were only found comparatively recently in the British Isles.

Besides the northern association there is also a southern link and the following species are found both in Britain and in the Alps and Pyrenees but are excluded from the Scandinavian mountains:

Alchemilla conjuncta	*Oxytropis halleri*
Gentiana verna	*Thlaspi caerulescens*
Minuartia sedoides	*Viola lutea*
Myosotis alpestris	

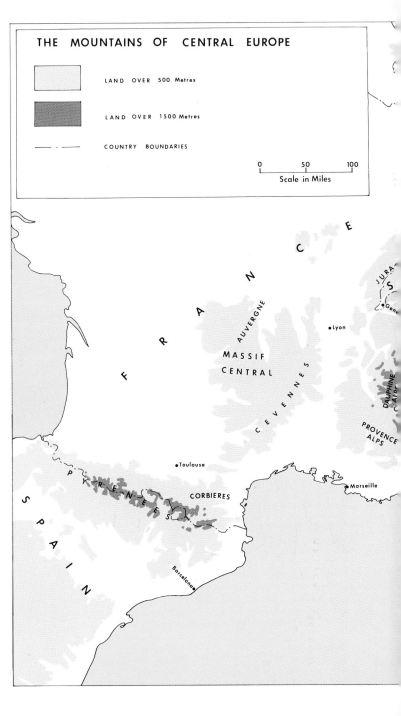

THE MOUNTAINS OF CENTRAL EUROPE

LAND OVER 500 Metres

LAND OVER 1500 Metres

COUNTRY BOUNDARIES

Scale in Miles
0   50   100

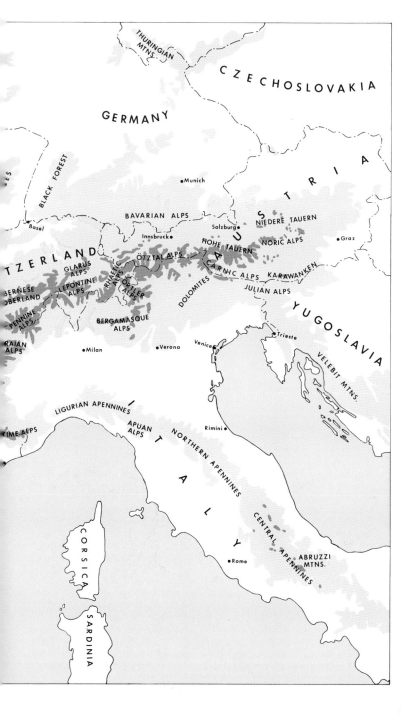

Other species, most notably *Dryas octopetala, Pinguicula grandiflora* and *Saxifraga oppositifolia,* are found throughout the mountain areas included in this book.

It is difficult to define exactly the alpine element in the northern and western European countries as the plants involved may descend right down to sea level; the spectacular Spring Gentian, *Gentiana verna,* found in the Burren in Eire is the classic example. At the same time *Primula farinosa,* which is truly alpine in the Alps and Pyrenees, never reaches alpine elevations in Britain. The closely related *Primula scotica* is another anomaly for it is restricted to the grassy cliffs in the north-west Scottish Highlands, yet it can be considered a derivative of an alpine species, *P. farinosa.*

Those wishing to study the subject in much greater detail cannot do better than read the Collins New Naturalist book on the subject – *Mountain Flowers* by John Raven and Max Walters.

The Text

The native flowering plants of the Alps, Apennines, Carpathians, Cevennes, Cordillera Cantabrica, Jura, Pyrenees, Tatras, Vosges and the mountainous regions of Britain and Northern Europe are included in the text, with the exception of grasses, sedges and rushes. The non-flowering plants, which include ferns, horsetails and their allies, are omitted as also are most introduced or alien species of flowering plants.

The less attractive and insignificant lowland species which may occasionally exceed 1000 m are also excluded to avoid overburdening the text with species which are not truly mountain plants. In Britain and Northern Europe a number of true alpine species are found well below 1000 m and this is taken into account in the text.

Area chosen. This is centred on the mountain masses of central, south-west and eastern Europe, but it also includes Northern Europe, the British Isles and Iceland. In the south-west the whole of the Pyrenees, French and Spanish, the Cordillera Cantabrica and Picos de Europa in northern Spain, the Cevennes and the Massif Central of France are included. In Central Europe the Jura, Vosges and the whole of the Alps are covered (from the Bavarian Alps of southern Germany in the north to the Maritime Alps of France and Italy in the south, as well as the Dauphine and Provence Alps. The eastern limit is the Niedere Hohen of Central Austria and the south-eastern the Karawanken Alps of south-east Austria and the Julian and Dinaric Alps of north-west and western Yugoslavia, as well as the Dolomites. The southward extension into Italy runs from the Ligurian Apennines to the Northern and Central Apennines, which floristically have much in common with the Alps (see map on pp. 14-15). The Spanish mountains south of the Cordillera Cantabrica have not been covered, i.e. the book will not be found to be comprehensive for them though the majority of their common plants are here covered, at least as regards the north of Spain.

Description. The text and illustrations have been designed to complement one another and should be read in conjunction: descriptive details are generally confined to points which cannot easily be seen from the illustrations, such as height, whether the plant is evergreen, its habitat and altitudinal range, distribution and flowering period. Important diagnostic details are stressed in *italics.* A number of assumptions are made in the descriptions: unless otherwise stated plants are erect and the flower measurements indicate diameter not length (unless otherwise stated) and the leaves are both toothed and stalked.

The characters described are, unless it has been absolutely unavoidable, ones that can be readily seen and which do not require the plant to be either picked or dug up. The use of a x10 hand lens can be a great help in accurate identification, allowing one to observe fine details of the leaves and flowers such as the hairs or glands.

Abbreviations used in the text

agg.	aggregate
ann	annual
bien	biennial
fl, fls	flower(s)
flbracts	flower bracts
flheads	flowerheads
fr	fruit
frhead	fruithead
lf, lvs	leaf, leaves
med	medium
per	perennial
sp	species
subsp.	subspecies
var.	variety

For other abbreviations used in the text, see below.

Family and generic descriptions. Notes on each family or genus are given in most cases, and include characters (only those useful for identification) common to its members. For example, the number of petals or sepals, or flower-shapes such as the composite flowers of the Daisy Family, the bell-flowers of the campanulas or the pea-shaped flowers of the Pea Family. This saves much repetition, and the notes should be borne in mind when reading species descriptions. Common names precede each species in the text. These follow, as far as it is possible, commonly used English names. Where no distinct common name exists we have derived one from the Latin epithet for the species, such as Swiss Rock-jasmine, *Androsace helvetica*. This has been done purely for convenience in order to avoid overburdening the reader with Latin names alone, although it is strictly against a botanist's best traditions.

Latin or scientific names. These follow, as far as possible, those used in *Flora Europaea* and this includes all the Dicotyledonous families and some genera of Monocotyledons. In certain instances the names do not follow *Flora Europaea* either because prior names have since been found for some species or because the author is at variance with other authorities. Important or well known Latin synonyms are included in brackets after the main name and are to be found in the Index of Scientific Names at the end of this book.

Plant Numbers. Each plant in the text has a number that corresponds with its number on the opposite plate. Closely related plants are often placed under the same number with a subsidiary letter, 11a, 11 b etc. In general the text descriptions of these subsidiary species, subspecies or varieties indicate only how it may differ from the main species, which should thus be referred to at the same time.

Aggregates. Certain groups of plants are extremely difficult to distinguish except by detailed botanical examination. Such complex groups of species have been lumped together into aggregates (agg. in the text) to save confusion. This situation arises in certain genera in particular: *Alchemilla* and *Rubus* in the Rose Family, *Cirsium, Centaurea, Hieracium* and *Senecio* in the Daisy Family. To include illustrations of all

Area covered by book. For country codes see opposite

the species involved in these complexes would have unnecessarily burdened the text.

Height. This is indicated as follows:

Tall over 60 cm (2 ft)
Medium between 30-60 cm (1-2 ft)
Short between 10-30 cm (4-12 in)
Low 0-10 cm (0-4 in)

Status. Annual, biennial or perennial status is shown in each case. Shrubs and trees are also indicated, together with a general guide to their average height (given in metres) and whether they are deciduous or evergreen.

Habit. This is often an important clue in the identification of alpine plants, thus some stress is made on the plant form - for instance tight or loose cushion habit, prostrate, creeping or tufted habit, and so on.

Hairiness or hairlessness. Indicated in most cases; the presence of hairs on a particular part of a plant is often an important clue to identification.

Leaf shape. Another important and characteristic feature of many plants. See Glossary (p.346) for definition of terms such *as pinnate* and *palmate.*

Flower shape and colour. Flower shape is usually indicated, such as bell, trumpet or saucer-shaped. Colour refers to petals, or to sepals when there are no petals present. Many plants show a remarkable variation in flower colour and many produce occasionally white or pale-coloured forms, but in such instances there are usually normal coloured flowers close-by. The plants illustrated are generally the normal form and the one most likely to be spotted in the wild; but the colour range is also indicated in the text for each species.

Flowering time. Indicated as April-June for instance. These periods give the most likely time to find a particular plant in flower, although this varies according to altitude and to location. This variation is particularly significant in mountainous regions: plants in the southern part of the range of a particular species flower earlier than those to the north and plants found at higher altitudes flower later than those from lower altitudes. Besides this, plants growing by snow patches may be considerably delayed in flowering: this is often true of certain plants, buttercups, crocuses and snowbells for instance.

One of the great joys of mountain and alpine plants is that they may be found in flower over a considerable period depending both on where they are found and at what altitude. Plants found in seed at a low altitude may often be found in flower by simply climbing further up the mountain slope.

Rarity. This is generally difficult to estimate. Certain plants occur extremely locally due to habitat conditions, but at the same time are to be found over a rather wide area. These cannot be considered as rarities. On the other hand, there are other species that are found in a very limited area only and within this they may or may not be frequent: it is the infrequently occurring ones that can be considered rare. If a plant is rare in only part of its range then this is also indicated in many instances.

Distribution and Country Codes. A system of coding (see map opposite) is used to denote the distribution of each plant in the text using the internationally accepted codes for the countries covered by this book:

A – Austria	I – Italy
B – Belgium	IRL – Ireland
CH – Switzerland	IS – Iceland
CS –Czechoslovakia (Czech Republic and Slovakia)	N – Norway
D – Germany	NL – Netherlands
DK – Denmark	PL – Poland
E – Spain	R – Romania
F – France	S – Sweden
GB – Britain	SF – Finland
H – Hungary	YU – Yugoslavian States

As well as these, prefixes in *small lettering* are added to facilitate subdivision of these areas where it is necessary:

n	north
s	south
e	east
w	west
c	central

Thus eA, nI, neYU indicates that the plant in question is to be found in the mountains of eastern Austria, northern Italy and north-eastern Yugoslavia. Such distributions may also be qualified by further information to aid the reader; for instance nE, sF; western and central Pyrenees. Such information is especially useful for species that have a limited distribution within a country or region.

Where a particular species is naturalised in part or the whole of the region then the country codes are placed in parenthesis. For example A, CH, (F, GB), H, R indicates the countries the plant in question is to be found in but it is only native in Austria, Switzerland, Hungary and Romania, being naturalised in both France and Great Britain.

Habitat. The places where plants are to be found growing is often an important clue to their identity. Some plants are found in a variety of different habitats, (e.g. meadows, open woodland and rocky places) while others are very specific (e.g. limestone rocks). Knowing the rock or soil type may help to separate closely related plants, especially in genera such as the gentians, primroses, rock-jasmines and saxifrages.

Altitude. This is in metres and a conversion table to feet is given on the final page. Where a single figure is given (to 2900 m) it implies that the plant in question is found between 1000 and 2900m, and although it may also occur below 1000 m it is the upper altitudinal limit that is the more critical. Where a particular species occurs over 1000 m then the altitudinal range is usually presented (1600-3400m). The altitudinal range is often somewhat speculative for it is dependant on existing records and it should be treated as an indicator rather than a hard and fast rule.

Identification

This book has been designed so as to be easily carried. Please *take the book to the plant* to avoid picking or spoiling specimens. Picking prevents a flower from setting seed and reproducing itself. Besides, identification is often much easier on the spot. It is also a good idea to carry a hand lens, small notebook and pencil to record details: a quick sketch of flowers, leaves and fruits can be a very useful record, as well as being a help in checking identifications.

The following points are useful to consider:

* Height and nature of plant – whether shrubby, annual, perennial, herbaceous or cushion forming and so on.
* Shape and arrangement of leaves – whether stalked or toothed, hairy or not.
* Flower shape and colour – the number of sepals and petals, stamens and styles, whether the petals are joined together or not and to what degree.
* Arrangement of flowers – solitary, in small tight clusters, in branched clusters, whether upright or drooping.
* Shape and colour of fruits – whether fleshy or dry, whether they split on ripening and if so, how many divisions.
* Habitat – whether they are growing in woodland, meadows, marshy areas or by streams and so on. If a rock plant, type of rock?
* Abundance – whether common, rare or localised.
* Locality – often important in finally determining a species or subspecies
* Altitude – to within 50 m if possible using an altimeter or maps as a guide

Remember that quite often two similar-looking species are to be found in two quite different regions or habitats; for instance one in the eastern Pyrenees and one in the Alps, or one on screes and moraines and the other in alpine meadows.

Conservation

Most mountain plants, particularly the high alpine species, do not take kindly to uprooting or to lowland gardens. Besides, there are numerous good plant firms which will supply the needs of those keen gardeners who want to grow alpines. Most of these plants are from long established stocks that have been proven in our lowland climates and are therefore the best to grow.

A good deal is said about conservation nowadays and there is a real danger that the subject might be over stressed. It is perfectly true that many species are in danger of extinction, or at least of disappearing in certain areas. Over-collecting, the use of herbicides in the past forty years and the destruction of habitats have all lead to rarity. National parks and reserves set up in many countries in recent years provide protected areas for some of the more vulnerable plants and animals. There is always the danger, however, that the visitors who turn up in such huge numbers will trample to death that which the park or reserve is intended to preserve. Habitat destruction, however it occurs, leads to a rapid decline in species.

Of course not all the species are equally threatened and it would be absurd to think that every plant in a particular reserve is endangered. However, there are plants, like the beautiful Lady's Slipper Orchid or the mysterious Edelweiss, that have declined alarmingly in the past fifty years purely because they are well known and have been over-picked. Such plants need and deserve careful protection.

Each country has its own laws relating to reserves and parks and many plants are protected by law – to PICK THESE IS AN OFFENCE. Left alone the plants will have a greater chance of survival by being able to set seed and thus reproduce in their natural environment. In this way the beauty of the mountains will be preserved for all to enjoy. In addition, in some reserves visitors may only walk along designated pathways or in certain areas so as to avoid trampling on special and often delicate alpine plant communities.

Societies to join

Alpine Garden Society: The Secretary, AGS Centre, Avon Bank, Pershore, Worcestershire WR10 3JP. The leading world-wide society for anyone interested in alpine and mountain plants, providing a quarterly bulletin, nation-wide shows, regional groups, tours to alpine regions of the world, an extensive annual seedlist, lectures and demonstrations, as well as local and international conferences.

Scottish Rock Garden Club. The SRGC Membership Secretary, 1 Hillcrest Road, Bearsden, Glasgow G61 2EB. Provides a twice-yearly journal, regional shows and lectures, conferences and an annual seed list.

Pine Family Pinaceae

Trees with needle leaves. Fruit a woody cone. Widely planted.

1 EUROPEAN SILVER FIR *Abies alba.* Evergreen pyramidal tree to 80m. Branches regularly whorled. Lvs single, grooved, whitish beneath, dark green above, leaving an oval *scar.* Cones erect, 10-20cm, with *triangular bracts* between the scales. Woods and forests, to 2100m. Fls Apr-May. T (B, GB, DK, N, S).

2 NORWAY SPRUCE *Picea abies.* Evergreen pyramidal tree to 60m. Branches regularly whorled. Lvs single, 4-sided, pointed, grass-green, falling to leave a *peg-like projection.* Cones pendent, cylindric, 10-18cm, no *bracts* protruding. Forests, to 2200m. Fls Apr-June. T (B, DK, E, GB, IRL, NL). *P. a.* subsp. *obovata* densely hairy twigs and cones 6-8cm long. A, F, CH, G; Alps – local.

3 EUROPEAN LARCH *Larix decidua.* Deciduous pyramidal tree to 35m. Twigs yellowish, hairless. Lvs single and tufted, slender pointed, pale green. Male fls yellow, female pink. Cones erect, *egg-shaped* 2-3.5cm, no *bracts* protruding. Open forests and rocky slopes, to 2500m. Fls Mar-June. A, CH, CS, D, F, H, I, PL, R (B, GB, IRL, N, S, SF, YU).

4 AUSTRIAN or BLACK PINE *Pinus nigra.* Evergreen pyramidal tree to 80m. *Bark* grey-black. Lvs in pairs, straight, deep green. Cones pendent, pointed, 5-8cm, yellowish-green. Forests, to 1800m. Fls May-June. A, I, R, YU (T). 4a *P.n.* subsp. *salzmannii* is a smaller tree. Lvs curved, bluish-green. Cones 4-6cm. sF (Cevennes and Pyrenees), E. **4b Scots Pine** *P. sylvestris* is a smaller tree than **4**, dome shaped; *bark* reddish, flaking. Lvs greyish, twisting. Cones egg-shaped, 3-6cm, brown. Forests, moors and heaths, to 2300m. Fls May-June. T (B, DK, IRL, IS, NL).

5 DWARF MOUNTAIN PINE *Pinus mugo.* Evergreen *shrub* to 3–5m, spreading, rather contorted. Bark greyish-brown scaly. Lvs paired, slightly twisted, deep green. Cones erect or slightly pendent, egg-shaped, 2-5cm, shining. Rocky and stony places, peaty bogs and screes, to 2700m. Fls May-June. A, CH, CS, sD, F, I, PL, R, YU (DK). **5A** *Pinus uncinata* similar but a small tree to 15m. Cones narrower, 5-7cm. A, CH, swD, n & cE, s & eF, I.

6 AROLLA PINE *Pinus cembra.* Evergreen pyramidal or irregular tree to 25m; bark reddish-grey. Lvs in groups of 5, slender, blue-green. Cones erect, dark *violet-brown.* Open woods and stony places, to 2700m. Fls May-June. A, CH, CS, sD, eF, nI, PL, R (IS, N, S, SF).

Cypress Family Cupressaceae

7 COMMON JUNIPER *Juniperus communis.* Evergreen shrub or small tree to 6m. Lvs in groups of 3, spine-tipped, greyish. Fls yellow, male and female on separate plants. Fr berry-like, green then blue-black when ripe. Rocky, stony places and moors, to 1500m. Fls June-July. T. **7a** *J.c.* subsp. *hemisphaerica* is a rounded shrub. Lvs broader with *a white band* down the centre. To 2500m. Fls May-June. A, CH, s & eF, H, I, YU. **7b Dwarf Juniper** *J.c.* subsp. *alpina* (= *J. nana*) is *prostrate;* lvs suddenly narrowed to a short point. To 3600m. June-July. T.

8 FRENCH ALPINE JUNIPER *Juniperus thurifera.* Evergreen pyramidal tree to 20m. Lvs scale-like in opposite pairs, overlapping, *not spiny,* deep green. Cone globose, 7-8mm, green then dark purple when ripe. Rocky and stony places, to 1400m. Fls Apr-June. nE, s & seF. **8a Savin** *J. sabina* is a low spreading shrub with tiny leaves. Cones 4-6mm, bluish-black when ripe. Rocky places, meadows and woods, to 2300m. A, CS, D, E, F, I, PL, YU.

Yew Family Taxaceae

9 YEW *Taxus baccata.* Evergreen pyramidal tree or shrub to 20m. Lvs single, in 2-rows, dark green. Fls yellowish, male and female on separate plants. Fr in a succulent *reddish-pink cup.* Woods and rocks slopes, usually on limestone, to 1800m. Fls. Mar-Apr. T – except far north.

Ephedra Family Ephedraceae

10 EPHEDRA *Ephedra distachya.* Low, twiggy, pale green shrub to 0.5m. Lvs tiny, in opposite pairs sheathing the curved twigs. Fls tiny, greenish, male and female on separate plants. Fr globose 6-7mm with *fleshy red scales.* Sandy and dry places, stream banks, to 1100m. Fls May-June. CH, CS, E, F, H, I, R, YU . **10a** *E.d.* subsp. *helvetica* has erect, deep green, twigs. A, CH, eF, I, wYU.

Willow Family Salicaceae

Deciduous trees and shrubs with alternate lvs. Bud scales solitary (Willows) or several overlapping (Poplars). Stipules often present, small or large. Fls in upright catkins in Willows or drooping catkins in Poplars, petalless, male and female on separate plants, often appearing before, or with the young lvs; male with prominent yellow or orange stamens; female green. Fr a small capsule containing many woolly-white seeds.

1 NET-LEAVED WILLOW *Salix reticulata.* Prostrate mat-forming undershrub. Lvs rounded or oval, 10-30mm, *untoothed,* long-stalked, shiny green above, whitish andconspicuously *net-veined beneath.* Catkins long-stalked; with lvs. Damp rocks and screes, 1200-2500m. June-Aug. T, except H, IRL. **1a Least or Dwarf Willow** S. *herbacea** has smaller, *slightly toothed,* lvs, 6-20mm, shiny green *beneath;* catkins short-stalked. Damp meadows and rocks, 1200-2800m. T; except H. **1b Polar Willow** S. *polaris* like 1a but lvs untoothed and broadly elliptical; fr hairy. To 1700m. July. N, S, SF.

2 RETUSE-LEAVED WILLOW *Salix retusa.* Prostrate mat-forming undershrub. Lvs oblong, *often notched,* 8-20mm, untoothed, short-stalked, shiny green above and beneath, hairless, veins *inconspicuous.* Catkins with lvs, short-stalked. Damp meadows and rocks, 1200-3000m. July-Aug. A, CH, CS, D, E, F, I, PL, R, YU. **2a** S. *serpyllifolia* is *more compact* and tightly pressed to the ground; Lvs 4-10mm, overlapping. A, CH, eF, sG, nI, YU.

3 FINELY-TOOTHED WILLOW *Salix breviserrata.* Prostrate or dwarf under- shrub. Branches crooked. Lvs oval, finely toothed, 10-20mm, shiny green above and beneath, *hairy on margins.* Catkins stalked, dark-purplish; with lvs. Damp meadows stream sides and moraines, 1700-3000m. June-July. A, CH, sD, nE, eF, nI. **3a** S. *alpina* is always prostrate with *untoothed* lvs. To 2500m. A, CS, sD, nI, PL, R, wYU. **3b Whortle-leaved Willow** S. *myrsinites* like 3 but *dead lvs* persisting until end of following season. To 1750m. May-June. nGB, N, S, SF.

4 SILKY WILLOW *Salix glaucosericea.* Knotted shrub 1-2m. Lvs lance-shaped, broadest above middle, 5.5-7.5cm, *silkily hairy,* pale green above and bluish-green beneath. Catkins long; with lvs. Damp and stony places, 1700-2550m. June-July. A, CH, eF, nI. **4a** S. *glauca* has broader lvs with *tangled hairs.* To 1750m. IS, N, S, SF.

5 ALPINE WILLOW *Salix hegetschweileri.* Shrub 0.5-3m tall. Lvs oval, broadest above middle, hairless, slightly toothed, blunt ended, shiny green above, bluish-green beneath. Catkins short-stalked. Wet stony places, stream sides, 1500- 2200m. May-June. A, CH, eF, nI, . **5a Tea-leaved Willow** S. *phylicifolia* has lvs tapered *at both ends.* To 1750m. B, S. **5b** S. *bicolor* like 5 but lvs *silkily-hairy* when young. GB, IRL, IS, N, S, SF.

6 PYRENEAN WILLOW *Salix pyrenaica.* Low shrub to 0.5m. Twigs reddish-brown. Lvs oval-elliptical, 10-30mm, *rounded at* base, untoothed, slightly hairy, always hairy-margined. Catkins long and loose appearing with lvs. Damp meadows and rocks, to 2500m. July. nE, sF (Pyrenees).

7 APUAN WILLOW *Salix crataegifolia.* Prostrate or upright shrub to 1m. Twigs *dark purple.* Lvs broadly-elliptical, 65-115mm, finely toothed, bright green above, silkily-hairy beneath at first. Rocky places, on limestone, to 1800m. May-June. nI (Apuan Alps).

8 AUSTRIAN WILLOW *Salix mielichhoferi.* Shrub to 2m. Twigs hairy at first, blackish to brownish-green. Lvs lance-shaped or oval, scarcely toothed, dull green, conspicuously net-veined beneath. Catkins short-stalked appearing with Lvs. Rocky places to 2100m. June-July. A, I.

9 HAIRLESS WILLOW *Salix glabra.* Erect *hairless* shrub to 1.5m. Twigs dark brown. Lvs broadly elliptical or oval, toothed, *waxy green* above and greyish beneath. Catkins long-stalked appearing with lvs. Damp places 1300 to 2100m. June-July A, eCH, seD, nI, wYU.

Willow Family *(contd.)*

1 LAGGER'S WILLOW *Salix laggeri.* Shrub 1-3m tall. Twigs knotted, brown or black-ish, white-felted when young. Lvs narrow-elliptical to oblong, untoothed, deep green above, downy-white beneath, stipules arrow-shaped. Catkins large. Rocky places and banks to 2000m. May-June. A, CH, eF, nl. **1a** *S. appendiculata* has *grey-brown,* hairy twigs and broader lvs, sometimes toothed, with conspicuous net-veins beneath, to 2300m. Apr-June. A, CH, swCS, D, F, nl, wYU.

2 MOUNTAIN WILLOW *Salix arbuscula.* Shrub to 2m. Twigs *hairless,* ridged under the bark. Lvs elliptical-lance-shaped, 5-40mm, *pointed,* toothed, shiny green above, greyish often hairless beneath, stipules inconspicuous. Catkins short-stalked, scales with rusty hairs. Damp meadows, stony places and moraines, to 1300m. May-June. nGB (Scotland), N, S, SF. **2a** *S. foetida* has smaller, deeply toothed Lvs, with con-spicuous *white glands.* On acid rocks, 1700-2800m. June-July. A, CH, s & eF, n & cl. **2b** *S. waldsteiniana* has larger lvs than 2, scarcely toothed; catkins *long-stalked.* On limestone rocks, 1700-2800m. A, CH, sD, nl, nYU.

3 LARGE-STIPULED WILLOW *Salix hastata.* Variable shrub to 1.5m. Twigs greenish or brownish, shiny, hairless. Lvs broadly oval or elliptical, untoothed or finely toothed, dull pale green, hairless. *Stipules large,* oval, not persistent. Catkins large, long-stalked with long white hairs. Wet meadows, rocky places and stream banks, to 2500m. May-Aug. T, except GB, IRL, H, IS.

4 SWISS WILLOW *Salix helvetica.* Shrub 0.5-2 m. Twigs thin, grey-brown becoming chestnut brown. Lvs oval, broadest above middle, 15-40mm, untoothed, shiny greenish above, *white-felted* beneath. Catkins stalkless. Wet meadows and rocky places, 1700-3000m. June-July. A. **4a Downy or Lapland Willow** *S. lap-ponum* has lvs *greyish hairy* above and beneath, rather crowded at tips of twigs; cat-kins stalkless. Wet heaths, stream sides and stony places, to 2600m. May-July. A, CH, CS, eF, nl, PL.

5 BLUE-LEAVED WILLOW *Salix caesia.* Prostrate or upright shrub to 1 m, *hairless.* Twigs brown, dull when young. Lvs elliptical or oval, 10-15mm, untoothed, dull blu-ish-green above and beneath. Catkins reddish-brown with violet anthers. Damp meadows and rocks, stream sides, 1700-2500m. June-July. A, CH, eF, nl.

6 WOOLLY WILLOW *Salix lanata.* Variable shrub to 3m. Twigs *thickly felted.* Lvs broad-oval, 10-25mm, untoothed, *yellowish-hairy* at first, then grey-hairy becoming almost hairless. Catkins yellow-hairy. Damp and stony places, to 1750m. May-July. B, S. **6a** *S. glandulifera* has lvs broadest above the middle with a *glandular margin.* nGB (c Scotland), IS, N, S, SF.

A number of larger willows reach above 1500m, though they are more charac-teristically lowland species.

7 ASPEN *Populus tremula.* Spreading tree to 20m, suckering freely. Bark smooth, greyish-brown. Buds slightly sticky. Lvs *rounded,* blunt-toothed, green, soon hair-less, trembling in breeze on long thin stalks. Catkins drooping, reddish or purplish, *before lvs.* Damp woods and heaths to 2100m. Mar-May. T.

8 BLACK POPLAR *Populus nigra.* Spreading tree to 30m. Bark rugged, blackish. Buds sticky. Lvs ace *of spades,* pointed, toothed, deep green, hairless, long-stalked. Cat-kins drooping, before lvs. Moist places, often by river banks, to 1800m. Mar-Apr. T, but widely planted (B, DK). **8a White Poplar** *P. alba** has 3-5-lobed lvs which are *white-downy* beneath. Damp woods, occasionally above 1200m. T, but widely planted (B, CH, DK, GB, NL).

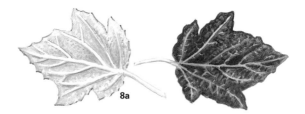

Birch Family Betulaceae

Deciduous trees or shrubs with alternate lvs. Male and female fls *catkins,* separate but on the same tree.

1 SILVER BIRCH *Betula pendula.* Narrow erect tree to 30m. Bark *silvery-white,* papery, peeling, brown and fissured below. Twigs hairless. Lvs diamond-shaped, teeth of different sizes. Catkins yellowish, male pendant, female shorter, erect. Woods, heaths and sandy places, to 2000m. Mar-May. T, except IS. **1a Downy Birch** *B. pubescens* subsp. *carpatica* is shorter, often a shrub, *bark* greyish or brownish, not fissured below; twigs *downy;* lvs uniformly toothed. T.

2 DWARF BIRCH *Betula nana.* Dwarf shrub to 1 m, sometimes almost prostrate. Twigs hairless. *Lvs* rounded with deep, blunt teeth, downy when young. Catkins as 1 but much smaller, *before* the lvs. Bogs and moors, to 2200m. Mar-May. A, CH, CS, D, F, GB, IS, N, PL, R, S, SF.

3 GREEN ALDER *Alnus viridis.* Dense shrub to 4m. Twigs hairless. Lvs elliptical or rounded, double-toothed, bright green. Catkins yellowish, with the lvs, male pendant, female brownish, like miniature fir-cones. Meadows, woods and rocky places, 1500-2300m. Apr-May. A, CH, CS, D, F, H, I, PL, R, YU. **3a Alder** *A. glutinosa.* Like 3 but often a small tree to 20m. Bark dark brown, rugged; lvs *roundish,* blunt-tipped; catkins appearing before lvs. Damp places, riverbanks, to 1800m. Feb-Mar. T, except IS. **3b Grey Alder** *A. incana* is similar to 3 but taller, young twigs hairy; lvs oval, more pointed, *greyish below.* Drier places, to 1600m. A, CH, CS, D, F, H, I, N, PL, S, SF, YU (E, GB, IRL, NL).

Hazel Family Corylaceae

4 HAZEL *Corylus avellana.* Deciduous shrub to 6 m. Bark smooth brown. Lvs oval or roundish, pointed, toothed, downy. Male fls in hanging catkins, pale yellow; female tiny erect, bud-like with red styles; before lvs. Fr a nut partly enclosed in a leafy husk. Woods and scrubby areas, to 1800m. Jan-Mar. T, except IS.

Beech Family Fagaceae

Containing the well-known Beech and Oak. Male and female fls separate but on the same tree. Widely planted.

5 BEECH *Fagus sylvatica.* Spreading deciduous *tree* to 30m. Bark smooth grey. *Buds* scaly, pointed, red-brown. Lvs oval, pointed, veins prominent at *edge,* silky hairy below when young. Fls greenish, male in hanging *tassels,* female erect, with young lvs. Fr a pyramidal brown nut ('mast') enclosed in a bristly husk. Woods, often as pure stands, to 1900m. Apr-May. T (IRL).

6 SESSILE or DURMAST OAK *Quercus petraea* (= *Q. sessiliflora*). Deciduous *tree* to 35m. Bark grey, finely Fissured. Twigs *hairless.* Lvs oval-lobed, *tapered* at the base, long-stalked. Catkins pale greenish-yellow, male long, female in short clusters. Acorns *scarcely stalked,* cup hairless. Woods, to 1800m. Apr-May. T, except IS. **6a Pyrenean Oak** *O. pyrenaica* is a smaller tree with *downy* lvs and stems. Woods and rocky slopes, to 1400m. E, F. **6b Pedunculate Oak** *Q. robur* has oblong lvs, the basal lobes overlapping the *short stalk;* twigs and lvs almost hairless; acorns *long-stalked.* Woods, often as pure stands, to 1400m. T, except IS.

7 DOWNY or WHITE OAK *Quercus pubescens.* Deciduous tree or shrub to 20m. Bark dark grey, rugged. Twigs thickly downy. Lvs oblong-lance-shaped, 6-12cm long, lobed, stalked, downy below when young. Catkins pale greenish-yellow, male long, female in short clusters. Acorn cups dowry. Woods, to 1500m. A, B, CH, CS, D, F, H, I, R YU. **7a** *Q.p.* subsp. *palensis* is smaller, often *shrub-like,* the lvs *only* 4-7cm long. sF, nE.

3   **3a**   **3b**

Nettle Family Urticaceae

Lvs opposite, armed with stinging hairs. Individual fls small; male and female separate, on the same or on different plants.

1 COMMON NETTLE *Urtica dioica.* Variable med/tall tufted per armed with strongly *stinging* hairs. Lvs dull green, heart-shaped, toothed and stalked. Fls pale green, in long drooping catkin-like spikes, male and female on separate plants. Woods, banks and waste places, often near farms and cow sheds, to 3150m. June-Sept. T. **1a**. *U. kioviensis* is bright green, the stems not hairy. A, CS, sD, H, R.

2 ANNUAL NETTLE *Urtica urens.* Short/med *annual* armed with weakly stinging hairs. Lvs clear green, oval, heart-shaped or narrowed at the base, short-stalked. Fls greenish, in short erect or spreading spikes, male and female separate but *on the same* plant. Cultivated ground and waste places, to 2700m. June-Sept. T.

Sandalwood Family Santalaceae

Semi-parasitic perennials growing on the roots of various herbs and shrubs. Lvs alternate, untoothed. Fls small, whitish, cup or bell-shaped, 4-5 lobed, with sepals, each with a bract and two shorter bracteoles; stamens 4-5, style 1. Fr a small green nut.

3 ALPINE BASTARD TOADFLAX *Thesium alpinum.* Short, usually slightly branched, per. Lvs linear to narrow-oblong, one-veined. Fls *4-lobed,* in one sided spikes, rarely branched; bracts 2-3 times longer than the fls. Dry meadows and stony places, to 2800m. May-Aug. T, except GB, IRL, IS, N, NL, SF, . **3a Pyrenean Bastard Toadflax** *T. pyrenaicum* has 5-lobed fls usually in *two-sided,* zig-zagged spikes; fls 3-4mm long. A, B, CH, CS, E, F, n & cl, PL, YU. **3b** *T.p.* subsp. *grandiflorum* (= subsp. *alpestre*) like 3a but fls larger, 5-5.5mm long. A, nel, wYU.

4 BAVARIAN BASTARD TOADFLAX *Thesium bavaricum.* Short/med per, stems usually unbranched. Lvs dark green, lance-shaped, 3-5 veined. Fls in lax-branched spikes; bracts as long or up to twice as long as the fls. Dry meadows and scrub, to 1250m. June-Aug. A, CH, CS, sD, eF, H, I, R, YU. **4a** *T. linophyllon* has narrow elliptical, 1-3-veined lvs, often rather yellowish-green. Same distribution plus PL.

5 BRANCHED BASTARD TOADFLAX *Thesium divaricatum.* Short, rather robust stemmed, *much branched,* per. Lvs linear, one-veined. Fls 5-lobed, in branched clusters; bracts *shorter than* the fls. Dry meadows and scrub, to 2150m. June-Aug. E, s & eF, I, YU.

Mistletoe Family Loranthaceae

6 MISTLETOE *Viscum album.* Woody, regularly branched *parasitic* shrub occurring in rounded masses on various trees. Lvs *opposite,* elliptical or oblong, broadest above the middle, yellowish-green, untoothed. Fls inconspicuous, green, 4-petalled, male and female on separate plants. Fr a juicy *white berry,* sticky. Parasitic on dicotyledonous trees, apples and poplars in particular. Feb-Apr. T, except IRL, IS, SF. **6a** *V.a.* subsp. *abietis* is parasitic on Silver Fir and other firs. A, CH, sD, sF, H, I, YU. **6b** *V.a.* subsp. *austriacum* is parasitic on pines and larch. A, CH, CS, sD, I, YU.

Birthwort Family Aristolochiaceae

7 ASARABACCA *Asarum europaeum.* Low creeping, patch-forming, downy stemmed per. Lvs kidney or heart-shaped, untoothed, long-stalked, shiny. Fls dull brownish-purple, bell-shaped, 12-15mm, 3-lobed, solitary and hidden amongst the lvs. Woods on calcareous soils, to 1300m. T, except northern Scandinavia, IRL, IS (DK, GB, NL, N, S). **7a** *A.e.* subsp. *italicum* has lvs as wide as long, the lower surface hairless or almost so. n & cl, YU; Crna Gora. **7b** *A.e.* subsp. *caucasicum* is like 7a but upper leaf surface minutely pimply. swCH, eF, nwI.

1

♀fl

♂fl

fr

2

♀fl

3

fl

4

5

6

fl

7

fr

Dock Family Polygonaceae

DOCKS or SORRELS *Rumex.* Mostly hairless perennials with alternate lvs and sheaths (ochrea) at the lf-bases, forming a tube round the stem (ochrea). Fls small, green, in whorls forming long branched spikes, the lower accompanied by a small lf; 3 petals and 3 sepals all alike and often reddish, the inner 3 enlarging and hardening to become the valves round a 3-sided nut. Each species has a characteristic shaped fr important in identification.

1 SHEEPS SORREL *Rumex acetosella.* Variable low/short slender per. Lvs *arrow-shaped,* the basal lobes sometimes divided, spreading or forward pointing, often very narrow. Fls greenish, on erect stems, branched from the middle, male and female usually on separate plants. Dry meadows and heaths, on acid soils, to 2400m. May-Aug. T.

2 RUBBLE DOCK or FRENCH SORREL *Rumex scutatus.* Short/med tufted per, branched from the base. Lvs green or bluish-green, helmet-shaped, as long as broad, with spreading basal lobes. Fls few on erect branched stems, stamens and stigmas in the same fl. Fr 4.5-6mm. Rocky places and screes, to 2500m. May-Aug. T, except H, IRL, IS, N. SF,(GB, S).

3 SNOW DOCK *Rumex nivalis.* Low/short tufted per, not more than 20cm tall. Lvs small, *often all basal,* the outermost oblong, without basal lobes, the inner often arrow-shaped; stem lvs not more than two. Fls reddish, in lax spikes, seldom branched, male and female on separate plants. Fr 3mm. Snow patches in limestone areas, 1600-2750m. July-Sept. A, CH, sD, nI, YU.

4 MOUNTAIN DOCK *Rumex alpestris* (= *R. amplexicaulis, R. arifolius, R. montanus*). Med/tall coarse per with leafy stems. Basal lvs oval-heart-shaped, twice as long as broad, strongly veined. Fls greenish, in loose *branched clusters,* male and female on separate plants. Fr 2.5-3mm. Meadows and woods, often on acid soils, to 2500m. June-Sept. T, except GB, IRL, IS.

5 APENNINE DOCK *Rumex nebroides* (= *R. gussonei*). Short tufted, *often* loosely cushion-forming per. Basal lvs narrow arrow-shaped, twice as long as broad, the basal lobes forward pointing; stem lvs few, very narrow. Fls greenish, in short branched clusters. Fr 2.5-3mm; nut dark brown. Limestone crevices and screes, to 2000m. June-Aug. sF; eastern Pyrenees, I, YU.

6 COMMON SORREL *Rumex acetosa.* Short/tall acid tasting per. Lvs arrow- shaped; 2-4 times as long as broad, the basal lobes *backward pointing,* the upper lvs clasping the stem; ochrea with a fringed margin. Fls in slightly branched clusters, male and female on separate plants. Fr 3-3.5mm; nut *shiny black.* Meadows and woods, to 2100m. May-Aug. T-rarer in the south.

7 MONKS RHUBARB *Rumex alpinus.* Tall coarse per, stems often reddish. Basal lvs heart-shaped, as long as broad, long-stalked, upper lvs narrower; ochrea papery. Fls yellowish-green, in crowded branched clusters, stamens and stigmas in the same fls. Fr 4.5-6mm, valves untoothed. Meadows, often around farms and cattle sheds on nitrogen-rich soils, to 2500m. June-Aug. A, CH, CS, sD, E, s & eF, I, PL, R, YU (GB).
7a Northern Dock *R. longifolius* has broad lance-shaped lvs, 3-4 times longer than broad, wavy-margined. Often by streams. D, DK, E, F, GB, IS, N, S, SF (CS, PL). **7b** *R. nepalensis* has oblong-oval Lvs, heart-shaped at the base; fr valves with hooked teeth. Mountain woodland clearings. c & sI, YU.

basal
lf

1

2

3

fr

fr

fr

4

fr

fr

fr

5

6

7

fr

Dock Family (contd.)

1 ICELAND PURSLANE *Koenigia islandica* A tiny, often reddish, ann. Lvs *broadly-elliptical*, deep green and somewhat fleshy. Flowers tiny, greenish, 3-parted, solitary or clustered. Damp muddy and bare ground, pool margins, to 1500m. nGB, IS, N, S, SF.

2 KNOTGRASS *Polygonum aviculare.* Low, erect or prostrate, hairless ann. Lvs lance-shaped or oval, larger on main stem. Ochrea *silvery-transparent.* Fls greenish, pink or white, 1-6 together at base of upper lvs. Stony and bare ground, to 2300m. June-Oct. T.

3 BISTORT *Polygonum bistorta.* Short/tall, almost hairless, per, patch-forming. Lvs narrow *oval-triangular,* the stalks winged in upper part. Fls bright pink in dense oblong clusters 10-15mm broad. Damp grassy places, to 2500m. June-Oct. T, except IS and most of Scandinavia.

4 ALPINE BISTORT *Polygonum viviparum.* Low/med hairless, tufted, per. Lvs oblong to narrow-lance-shaped, tapered at base, margin *rolled under.* Fls pale pink or white in slender spikes 5-10mm broad; lower part of spike with small brownish-purple *bulbils.* Grassy and rocky places, to 2300m. June-Aug. T, only mountains in S.

5 ALPINE KNOTGRASS *Polygonum alpinum.* Short/med hairless per. Lvs oblong-lance-shaped, tapered at both ends. Fls white or pink, in thin *branched spikes.* Damp meadows and rocky places, to 2200m. July-Aug. A, CH, E, sF, I, R, YU (D, GB).

6 MOUNTAIN SORREL *Oxyria digyna.* Short hairless, tufted, per. Lvs mostly basal, *kidney-shaped,* long-stalked. Fls tiny, greenish, 4-petalled, in branched spikes. Fr a drooping winged nut. Damp rocks and stream sides, often on granite, to 3500m. July-Aug. T.

Pink Family Caryophyllaceae

Lvs in opposite pairs, rarely toothed. Fls with 4-5 petals and sepals; sepals separate or joined into a tube; stamens 8-10. Fr a dry capsule, splitting with the same number of teeth as styles or twice as many.

7 PURPLE LYCHNIS *Lychnis flos-jovis.* Short/tall hairy per. Lvs lance to spoon-shaped, pointed, the upper unstalked. Fls bright pink to purplish or scarlet, rarely white, 14-18mm, in dense heads; petals notched. Meadows, rocks and screes, to 2100m. June-July. A, CH, D, I (CS).

8 RAGGED ROBIN *Lychnis flos-cuculi.* Med/tall roughly-hairy per. Lvs oval-spoon-shaped, the upper pointed and unstalked. Fls bright pink, 30-40mm, in loose branched clusters; petals *4-lobed,* ragged. Damp meadows and marshy places, to 2500m. May-June. T.

9 STICKY CATCH FLY *Lychnis viscaria.* Short/tall tufted per, *sticky* below upper lf junctions. Lvs lance-shaped, mostly basal, hairless. Fls red or purplish, 20mm, in *whorled' clusters;* petals, notched. Dry meadows and rocky places to 1800m. May-June. T, except IS, rare in south-west.

10 ALPINE LYCHNIS *Lychnis alpina.* Low/short tufted, hairless per. Lvs linear or narrow spoon-shaped, mostly basal. Fls pale purple, rarely white, 8-12mm, in compact heads; petals notched. Meadows, rocky and stony places, to 2000-3100m. June-Aug. T, except CS, H, IRL, PL, R, YU, rare in the Apennines.

11 CORN COCKLE *Agrostemma githago.* Tall, greyish-hairy ann. Lvs narrow lance-shaped, pointed. Fls dull purple with a whitish centre, 30-80mm, petals slightly notched; sepals forming a tube with 5 narrow lobes projecting beyond petals. Cornfield weed usually, to 2000m. May-Aug. T (IS).

12 PETROCOPTIS *Petrocoptis pyrenaica.* Low/short loosely tufted, per; thin stemmed. Lvs thin, oval-lance-shaped, green. Fls white or very pale purplish, 10-15mm; petals slightly notched. Calyx whitish, 5-8mm long. Rocky places and banks, 1300-2800m. May-Aug. nE, sF; western Pyrenees. **11a** *P. hispanica* has thicker bluish-green Lvs. nE; west-central Pyrenees and Jaca Region. **11b** *P. crassifolia* is like 11a but calyx larger, 9-13mm. nE; central Pyrenees, Bielsa region. **11c** *P. pardoi* has pink or red, unnotched petals. neE.

Pink Family *(contd.)*

CATCHFLIES and CAMPIONS have showy fls with 5 separate, often notched, long-clawed petals; sepals joined into a tube with 5 teeth. Styles 3, protruding (except 1).

1 NORTHERN CATCHFLY *Silene uralensis* subsp. *apetala* (= *S. wahlbergella, Melandrium apetalum*). Short, unbranched, slightly hairy per. Lvs narrow-oblong. Fls solitary, 14-18mm, petals reddish-purple, *completely surrounded* by the *inflated,* whitish sepal-tube. Damp meadows and stony places, to 1900m. June-July. N, S., SF. **1a** *S. furcata* has *sticky,* branched stems. N, S, SF.

2 NOTTINGHAM CATCHFLY *Silene nutans.* Variable med unbranched, hairy per, sticky above. Lvs oblong-spoon-shaped, stalked, the upper narrower and unstalked. Fls half drooping, petals white above, pink or greenish beneath, deeply cleft, *rolled back;* sepal-tube narrow, 9-12mm, hairy. Meadows, stony places and banks, to 2200m. May-Aug. T, except IRL, IS. **2a Italian Catchfly** *S. italica* has *erect* fls; petals less recurved. T, except IRL, IS, N, S, SF (D, GB).

3 SPANISH CATCHFLY *Silene otites.* Variable short/med bien or per, stickily hairy at base. Lvs oblong-spoon-shaped, the lower long-stalked. Fls small, 3-5mm, *greenish-yellow,* in whorled clusters; styles and stamens on different plants. Dry, often sandy, places, to 2000m. June-Sept.T, except IRL, IS.

4 LARGE-FLOWERED CATCHFLY *Silene elisabethae.* Low/short tufted per. Lvs mostly in basal rosettes, lance-shaped, hairless or slightly hairy along margins. Fls large, reddish-purple or pink, 25-35mm, usually *solitary;* petals *notched and toothed.* Limestone rocks and screes, 1500-2500m. July-Aug. nl; southern Alps.

5 HEART-LEAVED CATCHFLY *Silene cordifolia.* Short tufted hairy per. Lvs *oval-heart-shaped.* Fls white or pink, 10-15mm, in clusters of 1-4; petals deeply notched. Rocks and screes, 1200-2400m. July-Aug. seF, nwl; Maritime Alps. **5a Eared Catchfly** *S. auriculata* is taller with lvs densely hairy along *margins;* fls smaller, with white petals with two small lobes at base. To 2000m. nl; Apuan Alps.

6 BLADDER CAMPION *Silene vulgaris.* Very variable med branched, greyish, often hairless per. Lvs oval to linear, often wavy-edged, 10-25mm broad. Fls white, 15-18mm, petals deeply notched; sepal-tube inflated, *bladder-like.* Meadows, rocks and banks, to 3100m. May-Sept. T. **6a** *S. uniflora* subsp. *glareosa* is more *prostrate;* fls with scales in throat. Calcareous screes. A, CH, CS, nE, s & eF, nl, wYU. **6b** *S.u.* subsp. *prostrata* is like 6a but lvs oval, not lance-shaped, and fls *without* throat scales. sA, sCH, nE, s & eF, nl, YU. **6c. Red Campion** *S. dioica* has larger bright pink fls; sepal-tube hairy, not inflated. T (IS).

7 VALAIS CATCHFLY *Silene vallesia.* Low/short, stickily-hairy, mat-forming per. Lvs oblong-lance-shaped to linear. Fls 1-3 clustered, 14-16mm, petals pale pink above, reddish beneath, deeply cleft, *curling in at tip.* Rocks and screes, to 2100m. July-Aug. sCH, seF, nl, swYU .

8 NARROW-LEAVED CATCHFLY *Silene campanula.* Low/short slender, hairless per. Lvs *linear,* pointed. Fls solitary or 2, petals white above, reddish-purple beneath, notched; sepal-tube 7-8mm, hairless. Damp limestone rocks, to 2200m. July-Aug. seF; nwl; Maritime Alps.

9 TUFTED CATCHFLY *Silene saxifraga.* Rather like 8 *but sticky* hairy below and forming *rounded tufts.* Fls whitish or greenish above, greenish or reddish beneath; sepal-tube 8-13mm, hairless. Limestone rocks and screes, to 2400m. May-Aug. sA, sCH, E, s & eF, I, R, YU.

10 PYRENEAN CATCHFLY *Silene borderei.* Low *mat-forming* per. Lvs mostly basal, narrow-spoon-shaped, hairy margined, covered in *raised dots,* upper Lvs linear. Fls pink in clusters of 1-4; petals deeply cleft; sepal-tube 8-10mm, hairy. Rocks, 2000-2200m. Aug. nE, sF; west and central Pyrenees.

11 MOSS CAMPION *Silene acaulis* (incl. subsp. *longiscapa*). Low per forming moss-like cushions, hairless, bright green. Lvs tiny, linear. Fls solitary, pink, 5-10mm, on stalks 1-6 mm long; petals notched; capsule 6-13mm long. Damp rocks and screes, short turf, to 3700m. June-Aug. T. **11a** *S.a.* subsp. *bryoides* (= *S.a.* subsp. *exscapa*) has flowering stems very short, not more than 0.5mm long; capsule 3-5mm long. A, CH, CS, sD, E, s & e F, I, YU.

12 &13, see p.38.

Pink Family *(contd.)*

12 ROCK CAMPION *Silene rupestris.* Short, hairless, branched, greyish per. Lvs elliptical, broadest towards tip. Fls small, white or pink, in *large clusters;* petals notched; sepal-tube 4-6mm, hairless. Rocks and screes, often on acid rocks, to 2900m. June-Sept. T, except GB, IRL, IS, H, P, YU. 12-13, see p.37.

13 ALPINE CATCHFLY *Silene alpestris* (= *Heliosperma alpestre*). Short, thin stemmed, branched, almost hairless per, sticky above. Lvs oblong-lance-shaped to linear. Fls white, 8-10mm; petals *4-6-toothed;* sepal-tube 5-7mm, short-hairy. Limestone rocks, to 2500m. June-Aug. A, nI, wYU. **13a** *S. pusilla* (= *S. quadrifida*) is a frail plant with white, pale pink or lilac fls, 6-8mm. A, CH, CS, sD, E, s & eF, I, PL, R, YU.

1 ALPINE GYPSOPHILA *Gypsophila repens.* Sprawling hairless per. Lvs bluish-green, narrow lance-shaped. Fl stems upright from prostrate stems. Fls 8-10mm, white, pale pink or lilac, *petals* longer than sepals, notched. Rocky, stony and grassy places and banks, on limestone, to 2900m. May-Sept. A, CH, CS, nE, s & eF, I, PL, YU.

SOAPWORTS *Saponaria.* Tufted or sprawling perennials with solitary or clustered fls. Calyx cylindrical with 5 short teeth. Petals with a long narrow claw. Styles 2.

2 SPOON-LEAVED SOAPWORT *Saponaria bellidifolia.* Short/med tufted, generally hairless, per; fl stems upright, unbranched. *Lvs spoon-shaped,* stalked, the upper narrower, few. Fls 7-8mm, yellow in tight clusters, petals notched; *stamen stalks* yellow. Rocks and pastures, to 2000m. June-July. nE, s & eF, I, R, Yu.

3 YELLOW SOAPWORT *Saponaria lutea.* Low hairy cushion per; fl stems upright, unbranched. Basal lvs narrow lance-shaped, stem lvs linear, few. Fls 8mm, yellow, in tight clusters, petals blunt-tipped; *stamen stalks* violet-black, protruding. Limestone rocks, 1500-2600m. July-Aug. swCH, eF, nl.

4 TUFTED SOAPWORT *Saponaria caespitosa.* Low/short, scarcely hairy cushion per. Basal lvs narrow lance-shaped, stem lvs smaller, few. *Fls* 8-14mm, purplish, in small clusters, petals round-tipped. Rocks and screes, to 2100m. July-Aug. nE, sF; central Pyrenees.

5 DWARF SOAPWORT *Saponaria pumilio* (= *Silene pumilio).* Low almost hairless, cushion per, *stems short, leafless.* Lvs linear, tufted. *Fls solitary,* 14-18mm, rose-red rarely white, petals broad, notched. Meadows on acid soils, 1900-2600m. Aug-Sept. A, nel, R.

6 ROCK SOAPWORT *Saponaria ocymoides.* Low/short sprawling, hairy per. Lvs ovallance to spoon-shaped. Fls 610mm, pink or purplish, in *branched clusters,* petals blunt. Grassy, rocky or stony places, to 2000m. Mar-Oct. A, CH, D, E, F, I, YU (CS).

7 TUNIC FLOWER *Petrorhagia saxifraga* (= *Kohlrauschia saxifraga).* Short/med generally hairless per. *Lvs linear,* pointed, upright. Fls 5-8mm, white or pink, solitary *or* in a loose branched head, petals notched. Dry stony and sandy places, to 1300m. June-Aug. T, except B, IRL, IS, N, NL, PL, S (GB, S). **7a** *P. prolifera* (= *Kohlrauschia prolifera)* is larger with unbranched, *dense,* fl-clusters; fls pink or purplish. Generally on calcareous soils. May-Sept. T, except GB, IRL, IS, N, SF.

PINKS *Dianthus.* Tufted perennials with stiff stems and greyish or grey-green linear lvs. Fls solitary or clustered. Calyx tubular, surrounded at base by several paired epicalyx-scales. Petals long-clawed, broad at top, serrated or deeply cut along margin. Styles 2, often protruding. Calyx details, see p.41.

8 PAINTED PINK *Dianthus furcatus.* A variable low/med densely-tufted, hairless per. *Lvs* linear, flat, soft. Fls 1-3, pink or whitish, 10-20mm, petals serrated; epicalyx scales reaching halfway up the calyx. Dry meadows, rocky and stony places, to 2300m. June-Aug. swCH, s & eF, nwI.

9 SEQUIER'S PINK *Dianthus seguieri.* A variable med, loosely tufted, hairless per. Lvs green, narrow lance-shaped, 1-2mm broad. Fls pink or purplish with a ring of *dark spots* near the centre, 14-20mm, throat hairy, solitary or 2-4 clustered; epicalyx scales as long as the calyx. Meadows and stony places, to 1600m. June-Sept. CH, CS, sD, neE, s & eF, nI

10-11, see p.40

10 SWEET WILLIAM *Dianthus barbatus.* Short/med, almost hairless per. Lvs lance-shaped. Fls purple, pink or reddish, often spotted, 20-34mm, in *dense flat-topped clusters;* epicalyx-scales green, pointed. Meadows and woodland clearings, to 2500m. June-Aug. A, CS, nE, sF, H, I, PL, R, YU; widely cultivated. **10a** *D. b.* subsp. *compactus* has the lower lvs stalked and purplish-brown epicalyx scales. A, CH, CS, sD, I, R, wYU. Nos **11** text on p. 40.

11 FRINGED PINK *Dianthus monspessulanus.* Short/med, loosely tufted per. Lvs green linear, 1-3mm broad, thin and flexible. Fls pink or white, 20-30mm, in lax branched clusters of 2-5, petals deeply *fringed,* fragrant; epicalyx-scales half as long as the calyx. Meadows, stony places and woods, to 2000m. May-Aug. CH, nE, s & eF, nl, YU. **11a** *D.m.* subsp. *marsicus* is shorter with larger, usually solitary, fls 30-40mm. c & sl; Apennines. **11b** *D. sternbergii* is like 11a but lvs and stems bluish-green; fls usually solitary. A, nl, wYU. **11c** *D. superbus* like 11 but petals fringed over *half-way,* the central part *oblong;* fls often solitary. To 2400m. T, except B, GB, IRL, IS. See p.39.

The genus *Dianthus* is extremely complicated and the species often difficult to distinguish. In Europe alone there are some 121 species, though many are in the Mediterranean region. Calyx characters are often a useful guide to accurate identification and the following drawings of species found on p.41 should help.

In addition the following species may also be found in the region:

D. arenarius is like *D. plumarius* but the petals have a greenish or purplish spot near the base. CS, eD, PL, SF.

D. callizonus is like *D. alpinus* but the stems with at least 5 pairs of lvs (not up to 4). Fls carmine pink, 20-30mm. R; southern Carpathians.

D. graniticus is like *D. petraeus* but calyx only 10-15mm long and fls always solitary, the petal limb bearded in part. scF; Cevennes and Auvergne.

D. nitidus is similar to *D. alpinus* but taller and with smaller flowers which are often borne in pairs. CS, PL; western Carpathians.

D. petraeus is somewhat like *D. gratianopolitanus* but flowers smaller, 10-20mm, solitary or grouped, the petal limbs generally not bearded. R, YU; not in the Alps.

D. trifasciculatus is like *D. collinus* and *D. furcatus* but the outer epiclayx scales are longer than the calyx and leaf-like. Lvs with 7-9 veins. Fls pink, 20-24mm, the limb bearded at the base. CS, R, YU.

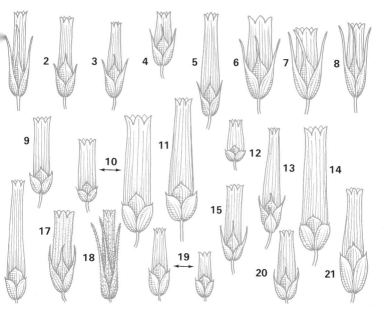

Dianthus calyces with accompanying flower bracts

Pink Family (contd.)

1 ALPINE PINK *Dianthus alpinus.* Low/short, tufted, hairless per. Lvs narrow-oblong, the lowest 3-5mm broad, *blunt,* deep glossy-green. Fls purplish-red with *white spots,* occasionally white, 30-36mm, solitary; petals serrate-edged. Limestone rocks, to 2500m. June-Aug. A; north-eastern Alps.

2 GLACIER PINK *Dianthus glacialis.* Low, tufted, almost hairless per. Lvs linear, 1-2mm broad, fleshy. Fls purple-red, 15-18mm, solitary, *surrounded* by the Lvs; petals serrate-edged. Meadows and stony places, on acid rocks, 1900-2900m. July-Aug. A, CH, CS, nI, PL, R. **2a** *D. g.* subsp. *gelidus* has lf-margin hairy at the base and larger fls. R.

3 THREE-VEINED PINK *Dianthus pavonius* (= *D. neglectus).* Low, tufted, hairless per. Lvs linear grassy, pointed, 3-veined. Fls pinkish-purple, 20-24mm, usually solitary; epicalyx-scales *as long* as the calyx. Meadows and stony places, 1200-3000m. July-Aug. seF, nwI; possibly also in the eastern Alps.

4 CHEDDAR PINK *Dianthus gratianopolitanus* (= *D. caesius).* Low/short hairless, *bluish-green,* tufted per. Lvs linear, 1-2mm broad, more or less flat. Fls pink or purplish, 15-30mm, usually solitary, fragrant; calyx brownish-purple, the epicalyx-scales *very short.* Meadows and stony places, to 2200m. May-July. B, GB (Cheddar Gorge, rare), CS, D, F, PL.

5 WOOD PINK *Dianthus sylvestris.* Variable low/short per; stems branched usually, except in high alpine forms. Lvs *green,* linear, grassy, the basal only 1 mm broad and usually *recurved.* Fls pink, 15-25mm, rarely slightly fragrant, solitary or two together; epicalyx-scales short. Meadows and stony places, 1400-2800m. July-Aug. A, CH, sS & eF, H, I, YU.

6 SHORT PINK *Dianthus subacaulis.* Low/short neat, densely tufted, hairless per. Lower lvs narrow lance-shaped, blunt, 1 mm broad, the stem lvs shorter and *pressed against* the stem. Fls small pale pink, 6-12mm, solitary; epicalyx-scales short. Meadows, rocky and stony places, to 1700m. June-Aug. P. **6a** *D. pungens* has narrower, 0.5mm, and longer, lvs and darker fls. E, c & sF.

7 PYRENEAN PINK *Dianthus pyrenaicus.* Short/med, loosely tufted per, with trailing, slightly woody, stems. Lvs narrow lance-shaped, green, *sharply pointed.* Fls small, pale pink, 6-8mm, *in branched clusters;* epicalyx-scales short. Meadows and rocky places, to 1500m. sF, nE; Pyrenees. **7a.** *D. p.* subsp. *catalaunicus* has blue-green lvs and deep pink fls, 12-16mm. sF, nE.

8 COMMON PINK *Dianthus plumarius.* Short/med bluish-green, loosely tufted per. Lvs linear, 1 mm broad, pointed. Fls white to bright pink, 24-36mm, usually solitary, fragrant; petals *deeply and narrowly lobed;* epicalyx-scales very short. Meadows and rocky places, usually limestone, to 2000m. Apr-Aug. A, CS. H, PL, YU. **8a** *D. serotinus* is more slender with cream-coloured fls in groups of 2-5. Sandy habitats. CS, H, R, YU.

9 MAIDEN PINK *Dianthus deltoides.* Short/med, loosely tufted, bluish-green per, stems *rough-hairy.* Lvs linear, often broadest above the middle, edges rough-hairy. Fls deep or pale pink (or rarely white) with *a darker band* near the centre and white spots, 15mm; epicalyx-scales half as long as the calyx. Dry grassy places and open woods, to 2000m. June-Oct. T, except IRL, IS.

10 DEPTFORD PINK *Dianthus armeria.* Short/med stiff-hairy, green ann/bien. Lvs oblong, blunt, flat and thin, the upper linear. Fls small, pink or reddish, 10-12mm, in *branched* clusters; epicalyx-scales *as long* as the hairy sepal-tube. Dry sandy and waste places, to 1250m. June-Aug. T, except IRL, IS, N, nS, SF.

11 TALL PINK *Dianthus giganteiformis* (= *D. pontederae).* Short/tall rather slender per. Lvs linear, 2-4mm broad, flat, pointed. Fls purple, 6-10mm, in dense *clusters;* epicalyx-scales brown, pointed, half as long as the 10-13mm long calyx. Rocky and grassy places, to 1400m. A, CS, H, R, YU. **11a** *D. giganteus* is *more* robust with larger fls, 10-16mm; calyx 17-20mm long. R, nYU.

12 CARTHUSIAN PINK *Dianthus carthusianorum.* Variable low/med hairless, tufted per. Lvs linear, pointed, 1-5mm broad. Fls deep pink to purple, 20-30mm, in *dense clusters;* calyx and epicalyx-scales *purplish brown,* scales half as long as the calyx. Dry grassy and stony places, open woods, to 2500m. May-Aug. T, except DK, GB, IRL, IS, N, SF (sS).

Pink Family (contd.)

STITCHWORTS *Stellaria*. Annuals or perennials. Fls white, in branched clusters, each with 5 separate sepals and 5 deeply notched or cleft petals (usually cleft over halfway to the base); stamens normally 10; styles 3. Fr capsule with 5 teeth.

1 WOOD STICHWORT *Stellaria nemorum*. Short/med patch-forming per, stems hairy *all round*. Lvs oval, pointed, lower long-stalked, the upper stalkless. Fls 18-24mm, petals cleft almost to the base, twice as long as the sepals. Damp woods, to 2400m. May-July. T, except IRL, IS.

2 COMMON CHICKWEED *Stellaria media* agg. Variable low/short often sprawling annual, stems hairy all round or with a single line of hairs. Lvs oval, pointed, all but the uppermost stalked. Fls 6-10mm, petals cleft almost to the base, equalling *sepals*, sometimes absent. Cultivated and bare ground, a common weed, to 2500m. In fl most of the year except at higher altitudes. T.

3 GREATER STICHWORT Stellaria *holostea*. Short/med, straggling, rather rough, *square-stemmed* per. Lvs lance-shaped, long-pointed, stalkless. Fls 15-30mm, petals cleft to *halfway*, about twice as long as the sepals. Woods, hedgerows and banks, usually on heavy soils, to 2000m. Apr-June. T, except IS and the far north.
3a Lesser Stichwort *S. graminea* has smooth stems and lvs; fls smaller, 5-12mm, petals usually equalling the sepals. May-Aug. T (IS).

4 BOG STICHWORT *Stellaria uliginosa* (= *S. alsine*). Low/short rather sprawling, patch-forming, hairless per, stems square. Lvs elliptical to oval lance-shaped, smooth, usually stalkless. Fls small, 4-5mm, the petals shorter than the sepals. Wet places, often by streams and pools, to 2300m. May-Aug. T, except IS and the far north.

5 LONG-LEAVED STICHWORT *Stellaria longifolia*. Low/short patch-forming hairless per, stems square, *rough*. Lvs narrow lance-shaped, rough-edged. Fls small, 4-8mm, in clusters, the petals equalling the sepals. Damp wooded places, to 2100m. June-July. A, CH, CS, D, nl, N, PL, R, S. **5a** *S. crassipes* is lower with oval lvs and fls 8-10mm, solitary. June-July. cN, S. **5b** *S. borealis* (= *S. calycantha*) like 5a but lvs often narrower and *yellowish-green*. Fls tiny, 3-5mm, petals shorter than the sepals, or absent. A, CH, CS, D, nl, N, PL, R, S.

PEARLWORTS *Sagina*. Small insignificant, mossy, tufted or cushion-forming annuals or perennials, with slender stems and Lvs. Fls 4-5 parted; sepals separate; petals usually white, *not notched*, sometimes absent. Fr capsule with 4-5 teeth.

6 KNOTTED PEARLWORT *Sagina nodosa*. Low/short tufted per. Lvs linear, diminishing in size up the stem, the upper *with tufts* of lvs at the nodes. Fls 5-10mm, solitary or *2-3* together; petals 5, *2-3* times longer than sepals. Damp, often sandy places, usually on calcareous soils. July-Sept. T.

7 CUSHION PEARLWORT *Sagina caespitosa*. Low per forming small cushions. Lvs linear. Fls 6-8mm, *amongst* the cushion of lvs; petals 5, *longer than* the violet-edged sepals. Damp rocky places, gravels, by snow patches, to 1570m. June. IS, N, S. **7a** *S intermedia* has smaller fls, 3-8mm, the petals 4-5, shorter than the sepals. June-Aug. IS, N, S. **7b** *S. glabra* is laxer than 7, the fls 5-10mm, on short stalks; sepals *not* violet-edged. Meadows and stony places, on acid soils, 1600-2700m. July-Aug. s & eF, CH, nl.

8 ALPINE PEARLWORT *Sagina saginoides* (= *S. linnaei*). Low loosely tufted, hairless per. Lvs linear, *bristle-tipped*; stem lvs shorter. Fls 5-7mm, solitary or two together, petals 5, equalling sepals. Damp places, to 2750m. June-Aug. T, except B, DK, sGB, IRL, NL.

9 PROCUMBENT PEARLWORT *Sagina procumbens*. Low hairless, mat-forming per, spreading outwards from a *central leafy rosette*. Lvs linear, bristle-tipped. Fls tiny, greenish-white, 2-4mm, solitary; petals 4 or absent, smaller than the sepals. Damp bare places, to 2800m. May-Sept. T. **9a** *S. apetala* is a variable low/short *annual* without a basal leafy rosette; petals often absent. T-except S.

10 KNAWEL *Scleranthus perennis* Variable short, more or less erect, almost hairless, rather spiky-looking per. Lvs lance-shaped to linear, pointed, often hairy-edged. Fls small, in clusters, petal-less; sepals fused in the lower half, membraneous-edged. Fields and waste places, on acid soils, to 2250m. May-Oct. T- except IRL, IS and the far north. **10a** *S. p.* subsp. *polycnemoides* forms dense *low cushions* with shorter lvs. nE, sF; eastern Pyrenees.

Pink Family (contd.)

MOUSE-EAR CHICKWEEDS *Cerastium*. Tufted perennials. Fls white, in small loose clusters, or solitary, petals 5 shallowly or deeply cleft, but seldom beyond halfway; sepals separate from one another; stamens 5 or 10; styles usually 5 *(3 in Starwort Mouse-ear)*. Fr capsule with as many teeth as styles.

1 STARWORT MOUSE-EAR *Cerastium cerastoides* (= *C. trigynum*). Low loosely matted per, hairless except for a *single line of hairs* down the stem, rooting at the nodes. Lvs pale green, linear to oblong. Fls 9-15mm, solitary or *2-3* together, the petals deeply cleft, styles 3; bracts lf-like. Damp rocky and grassy places, 1500-3000m. July-Aug. T, except B, DK, sGB, IRL, H.

2 SNOW IN SUMMER *Cerastium tomentosum*. Low/short mat forming, *white-woolly* per. Lvs lance-shaped. Fls 15-25mm, in loose clusters, the petals twice as long as the sepals, deeply cleft. Grassy and rocky places, banks, to 2250m. May-July. I; Apennines, but widely cultivated elsewhere (A, CH, CS, D, DK, F, GB, IRL, NL, S).

3 NARROW-LEAVED MOUSE-EAR *Cerastium lineare*. Low/short, slender, tufted, hairy per. Lvs linear to elliptical, those of non-flowering shoots *in loose rosettes,* hairy only along edges. Fls 16-20mm, solitary or 2-3 together, the petals deeply cleft, sepals hairy; bracts leaf-like. Rocky places, to 1600-2100m. July-Aug. seF, nwI; southwestern Alps.

4 JULIAN MOUSE-EAR *Cerastium julicum*. Low densely tufted hairy per. Lvs narrow oblong to elliptical, hairy along edges at base only, *margin rolled under*. Fls 14-18mm, solitary or *2-3* together, the petals deeply cleft, sepals hairy; uppermost bracts with membranous edges. Rocky and grassy places, 2100-2250m. July-Aug. sA, nel; south-eastern Alps.

5 ITALIAN MOUSE-EAR *Cerastium scaranii*. Short tufted per, hairy. Lvs oval to elliptical, hairy on *both sides*. Fls 12-20mm, solitary or in clusters of 2-7, the petals shallowly notched; bracts with membranous edges. Rocky places, to 2000m. May-July. I; Apuan Alps southwards.

6 FIELD MOUSE-EAR *Cerastium arvense* agg. Variable low/short tufted or loosely matted per, sparsely hairy. Lvs narrow lance-shaped. Fls 12-20mm, in clusters of 3-7, rarely solitary, the petals deeply cleft, twice as long as the sepals; bracts with *thin membranous edges.* Fr *curved.* Dry fields and rocky places, to 3100m. Apr-Sept. T, except IS (N, S).

7 ALPINE MOUSE-EAR *Cerastium alpinum*. Low mat-forming greyish-green hairy per, hairs *long and soft.* Lvs oblong or elliptic, *broadest* above the middle. Fls 18-25mm, in clusters of 2-5 or solitary, the petals deeply cleft; bracts with membranous edges. Grassy and rocky places, mainly on acid rocks, 1800-2850m. June-Aug. T, except B, IRL, NL. **7a** *C.a.* var. *lanatum* has *white-woolly* Lvs and stems. T range of the species. **7b** *C.a.*var. *squalidum* like 6a but with *glandular hairs* mixed in the wool, especially of the peduncles. A, CH, CS, nE, sF, nI, R; possibly elsewhere.

8 ARCTIC MOUSE-EAR *Cerastium nigrescens* subsp. *arcticum.* Low/short greyish, hairy per, hairs *short* and stiff. Lvs elliptical, broadest above the middle. Fls 20-30mm, solitary or *2-3* together, the petals shallowly cleft; bracts green and leaf-like. Rocky places and screes, to 1700m. June-Aug. nGB, IS, N, S, SF. **8a Glacier Mouse-ear** *Cerastium uniflorum* has broader, soft, bright green lvs and smaller fls, often rather creamy-white. On granites and schists, 1900-3400m. July-Aug. A, Ch, CS, sD, eF, nI, PL, wYu.

9 BROAD-LEAVED MOUSE-EAR *Cerastium latifolium*. Low loosely tufted per, glandular hairy. Lvs *oval to oval-elliptical,* pointed. Fls 15-20mm, solitary or 2-3 together, the petals shallowly cleft, twice as long as the sepals; bracts green and leaf-like. Rocky places, moraines and screes, on limestone, 1500-3500m. July-Aug. A, CH, CS, sD, I, PL, R. **9a** *C. pyrenaicum* has petals hairy-edged at base, scarcely longer than sepals. neE, sF (eastern Pyrenees).

1   2   3

4   5   6

7   8   9

Pink Family (Contd.)

1 BELL-FLOWERED MOUSE-EAR *Cerastium pedunculatum.* Low loosely tufted, slightly hairy per. Lvs lance-shaped, *stiff.* Fls 7-8mm long, *bell-shaped,* usually solitary, the petals deeply cleft. Acid rocks, moraines and screes, 2000-3800m. July-Sept. A, CH, eF, nI.

2 CARINTHIAN MOUSE-EAR *Cerastium carinthiacum.* Low/short loosely matted, almost hairless, per. Lvs shiny-green, oval to lance-shaped, pointed. Fls 10-18mm, in clusters of 2-7; bracts with wide membranous edges. Rocky places, usually on calcareous or dolomitic rocks, to 2400m. June-Aug. A, eCH, nI, wYU. 2a *C.c.* subsp. *austroalpinum* is more densely *glandular-hairy.* A, s & eCH.

3 SLOVENIAN MOUSE-EAR *Cerastium subtriflorum.* Low/short tufted hairy bien/per. Lvs elliptical to oval or lance-shaped, *Stalkless.* Fls 12-20mm, in clusters of 3 or more, the sepals with membranous edges; lowest bracts leaf-like. Rocky places, 1600-2200m. July-Sept. neI, nwYU; Giulie and Julian Alps.

4 COMMON MOUSE-EAR *Cerastium fontanum.* Variable low/short hairy per with leafy non-flg shoots. Lvs lance-shaped, stalkless. Fls 5-14mm; petals deeply cleft, equalling sepals; lower bracts leaf-like, the upper membranous edges. Grassy places and bare ground, to 2400m. Apr-Nov. T.

5 GREY MOUSE-EAR *Cerastium brachypetalum,* Variable low/short hairy, often greyish, ann. Lvs oval to elliptical, the lowermost spoon-shaped. Fls 6-10mm, in loose clusters, the petals deeply cleft, shorter or slightly longer than the sepals; fl stalks *bent* just below fls; all bracts leaf-like. Dry open places, often on calcareous soils, to 1300m. Apr-Nov. T, except IRL, IS.

6 STICKY MOUSE-EAR *Cerastium glomeratum.* Low/short stickily-hairy, often yellowish, ann. Lvs oval to elliptical, broadest above the middle. Fls 5-8mm, often not opening fully, in *tight clusters;* petals deeply cleft, about as long as the sepals; all *bracts lf-like.* Bare ground, waste places, to 1300m. Apr-Oct. T, except SF.

7 LITTLE MOUSE-EAR *Cerastium semidecandrum.* Low/short semi-prostrate or erect, glandular-hairy, ann. Lvs elliptical to oval, the lowermost broadest above the middle. Fls 5-9 mm, in small clusters, the petals slightly notched, *shorter than* the sepals; sepals and bracts with membranous edges. Dry, often stony, places, to 1550m. Mar-May. T, except IS.

8 DWARF MOUSE-EAR *Cerastium pumilum.* Variable low, more or less erect, glandular-hairy ann, often reddish tinged. Lvs elliptical, broadest above the middle, the upper ones oval. Fls 6-9mm, in loose clusters, the petals often *purplish tinged,* about as long as the sepals; bracts and sepals with *membranous* edges. Dry grassy and bare places, on calcareous soils, to 1300m. Apr-June. T, except IRL, IS and far north.

9 SEA MOUSE-EAR *Cerastium diffusum* (= C. *tetrandrum*). Variable low/short glandular-hairy ann. Lvs oval to elliptical, the lowermost spoon-shaped. Fls 6-14mm, in loose clusters, the petals shallowly notched, *shorter than* the sepals; bracts usually all leaf-like. Dry grassy and stony places, to 1300m. Mar-July. T, except IS.

GENERIC DIFFERENCES

White-flowered members of the Caryophyllaceae:

Arenaria: petals not notched; styles 3, occasionally 5; fruit capsule with 6 or 10 teeth.

Cerastium: petals shallowly to deeply notched; styles usually 5, occasionally 3-4; fruit capsule with usually 10, occasionally 6 or 8 teeth.

Minuartia: petals not notched; styles usually 3, sometimes 5; fruit capsule with 3 or 5 teeth.

Moehringia: petals 4-5; styles 2-3; fruit capsule with 4 or 6 teeth

Stellaria: petals deeply notched to bifid; styles 3; fruit capsule with 6 teeth.

Pink Family (Contd)

SANDWORTS *Minuartia*. Like *Arenaria* but the fr capsule has the same number of teeth as styles. Lvs often bristle-tipped or awl-like and forming moss-like tufts.

1 SICKLE-LEAVED SANDWORT *Minuartia recurva* (= *Alsine recurva*). Low densely tufted per, slightly glandular-hairy. Lvs *sickle-shaped* 4-10mm, 3-veined. Fls white 7-9mm, solitary or in clusters of 2-8. Grassy and stony places, usually on acid soils, to 1900m. A, CH, E, F, I, IRL, R, YU.

2 APENNEAN SANDWORT *Minuartia graminifolia*. Low/short dense cushion per, glandular-hairy. Lvs narrow lance-shaped, stiff, 10mm long or more. Fls white, 10-16mm, in clusters of 2-7 on 4-14cm stems. Rocky places, 1400-2000m. July-Aug. I, R, YU. **2a** *M.g.* subsp. *clandestina* is *hairless* with shorter lvs. YU. **2b** *M. cerastiifolia* like *2*, but lvs less *than* 10mm long, distinctly keeled beneath and fls 6-10mm. nE, sF; west-central Pyrenees.

3 ROCK SANDWORT *Minuartia rupestris* (= *Alsine rupestris*). Low loosely tufted or creeping per, glandular-hairy, stems *often rooting* at the nodes. Lvs small lance-shaped, 2-4mm, hairy-edged. Fls white 7-9mm on 1-3cm stems. Rocks and screes, 1900-2500m. A, sD, eF, nI, wYU. 3a *M. r.* subsp. *clementei* (= *M. lanceolata*)* is more robust with *larger* lvs with 5-7cm fl stems carrying 2-3 fls. seF, nwI; Cottian Alps.

4 *Minuartia cherlerioides* (= *M. aretioides*). Very low dense cushion-forming per. Lvs tiny, 1.5-3mm, Oblong-elliptical, blunt, *hairless,* 3-veined. Fls white, 4-7mm, solitary on very *short* stalks; petals slightly shorter than the 3-veined sepals. Limestone rocks and screes, 2000-2500m. A, eCH, sD, nI, wYU. **5a** *M. c.* subsp. *rionii* has *hairy-edged* lvs. Acid rocks and screes. A, CH, sD, nI.

5 BERGAMASQUE SANDWORT *Minuartia grignensis*. Low *hairless* per. Lvs crowded towards base of plant, linear, 5-15mm, 3-veined. Fls small white, 5-7mm, in branched clusters of up to 12; petals slightly longer than the *3*-veined sepals. Lime-stone dolomitic cliffs, 1300-1900m. nI; Bergamasque Alps.

6 AUSTRIAN SANDWORT *Minuartia austriaca* (= *Alsine austriaca*). Low/short loose, cushion-forming per, hairless or slightly glandular-hairy. Lvs *narrow lance-shaped to linear*, 10-20mm, hairless. Fls large white, 12-20mm, solitary or 2-3 together; petals slightly notched about twice as long as sepals. Calcareous rocks and screes, 1900-2100m. A, sD, nI, wYU. **6a** *M. villarsii* has slightly broader Lvs and smaller, 8-15mm, fls. nE, s & eF, nI.

7 VERNAL SANDWORT *Minuartia verna* (= *Alsine verna*). Very variable low/short, loose cushion-forming, glandular-hairy per. Lvs linear, pointed, keeled below, to 20mm long. Fls white, 68mm, with *purplish anthers,* in clusters of 2-7, sometimes solitary; petals slightly longer than sepals. Grassy and stony places, screes, to 3000m. May-Sept. T, except DK, IS, NL. **7a** *M. v.* subsp. *collina* has fls in clusters of 6 or more, *anthers yellow,* the petals slightly shorter than the sepals. eA, CS, H, neI, R.

8 *Minuartia capillacea* (= *Alsine liniiflora*). Short, loose cushion-forming, glandular-hairy per. Lvs linear, *stiffly-pointed* 10-20mm, hairy-edged, 1-3 veined. Fls white, 14-22mm, solitary or in clusters of 2-6, petals about twice as long as sepals. Calcareous rocks and screes, to 2000m. eF, CH, nI, wYU. **8a** *M. laricifolia** is more delicate with smaller, 5-12mm, lvs and fls; sepals and fl-stalks *downy.* Acid rocks and screes, 1300-2000m. July-Aug. A, nE, sF, CH, nI, wYU. **8b** *M.l.* subsp. *kitaibelii* has hairless sepals and fl stalks. Calcareous rocks and screes. A, CS, neI, PL, R, wYU.

9 NORTHERN SANDWORT *Minuartia biflora*. Low slender, slightly hairy, per, forming loose tufts. Lvs linear, 4-10mm, l-veined. Fls white, rarely pale lilac, 7-12mm, solitary or 2-3 together; petals *slightly longer* than sepals. Damp open places, often by snow patches, 2000-2800m. June-Aug. A, CH, nI, IS, N, S, SF.

10 MOSSY CYPHEL *Minuartia sedoides* (= *Alsine sedoides*). Low hairless per forming dense *flattish yellowish-green* cushions. Lvs small, 3-8mm, narrow lance-shaped, closely overlapping, 3-veined. Fls greenish, 48mm, solitary, almost stalkless; petals absent. Grassy and stony places, rock ridges, moraines, 1800-3800m. A, CH, CS, sD, nE, F, nGB (Scotland), nI, PL, R, YU.

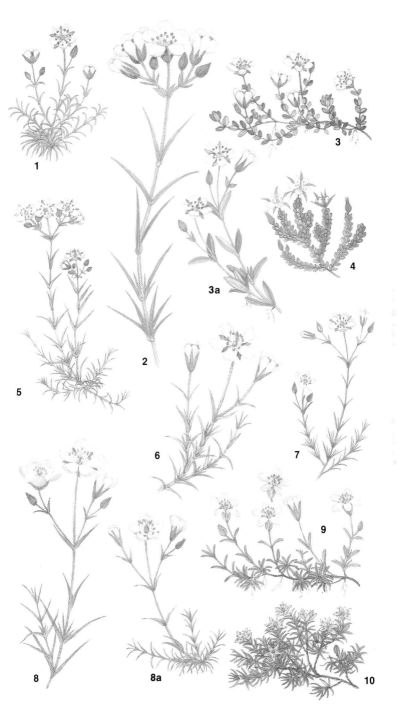

Pink Family *(contd.)*

SANDWORTS *Arenaria* and *Moehringia*. Fls in small loose clusters or solitary, white, rarely pale purplish-pink; petals not notched, stamens 10, styles 3-5. Fr a capsule splitting with twice as many teeth as styles.

1 PINK SANDWORT *Arenaria purpurascens,* Low mat-forming per, stems hairy in the upper half. Lvs oblong or lance-shaped, pointed, l-veined, hairy at base. Fls *pale purplish-pink,* sometimes white, 7-14mm, in clusters of 2-4; sepals hairless. Damp rocky places, 1800-2800m. July-Aug. nE, s & seF; Pyrenees and Cordillera Cantabrica.

2 IMBRICATE SANDWORT *Arenaria tetraquetra.* Low almost hairless per, forming dense flat cushions. Lvs oval, blunt, *closely overlapping.* Fls white, 5-9mm, solitary, with 4 or 5 petals and sepals. Dry places, 1800-2700m. July-Aug. E, sF. **2a** *A.aggregata* has narrower, *pointed,* lvs and fls in dense clusters of 3 or more. E, s & seF, nwl (Maritime Alps). **2b** *A.a.* subsp. *erinacea* (= *A. erinacea)* usually has solitary fls. eE.

3 LARGE-FLOWERED SANDWORT *Arenaria grandiflora.* Low/short hairy per, forming loose cushions. Lvs *narrow lance-shaped,* pointed. Fls white, 8-15mm, solitary or 2-3 together, stalks downy; sepals hairy. Dry rocky and stony places, to *2000m.* May-Aug. A, CH, CS, E, F, I.

4 CARNIC SANDWORT *Arenaria huteri.* Low hairy tufted per. Lvs oblong, *broadest above* the middle. Fls white, 15-20mm, solitary or 2-3 together; sepals hairy. Dolomitic rock crevices, to 2000m. June-Aug. nel; Carnic Alps.

5 TWO-FLOWERED SANDWORT *Arenaria biflora.* Low sprawling, usually hairless per; stems *rooting at the lower nodes.* Lvs *oval* or almost rounded, l-veined. Fls white, 5-mm, two together or solitary. Damp places, often over granite rocks or by snow patches, 1700-3200m. June-Aug. A, CH, s & seF, H, I, R, YU.

6 NORWEGIAN SANDWORT *Arenaria norvegica.* Low loosely tufted ann/per, almost hairless. Lvs oblong, broadest above the middle, usually dark green. Fls white, 5-6mm, stalked, solitary or 2-3 together; anthers white. Open stony places and screes on calcareous soils, to 1450m. June-July. nGB (subsp. *anglica* in northern England); IS, N, S, SF. **6a** *A. humifusa* is more mat-forming with short fl-stalks and *pale purple anthers.* N (rare), S.

7 CILIATE-LEAVED SANDWORT *Arenaria ciliata.* Variable low per with rough-edged stem. Lvs elliptical to spoon-shaped, hairy on edges, at least in the lower half. Fls white, 6-10mm, in clusters of 2-7; anthers white. Meadows and rocky places on calcareous soils, 1400-3200m. July-Aug. A, CH, CS, D, E, F, I, IRL, N, P, R, SF, YU

8 CADI SANDWORT *Arenaria ligericina.* Low/short tufted, *glandular-hairy per.* Lvs narrow-elliptical or oblong, pale green. Fls white, 6-9mm, In loose clusters of 3-10, limestone rocks, to 2000m. July-Aug. eE, sF; eastern Pyrenees and Sierra del Cadi.

9 SOUTH-EASTERN SANDWORT *Moehringia diversifolia.* Low/short almost hairless per, with thin stems. Lvs oval or spoon-shaped, the lower stalked. Fls small, white, 3-4mm, on *downy stalks,* solitary or in clusters of 2-5. Acid rocks and screes, to 1800m. May-July. seA.

10 *Moehringia dielsiana.* Low hairless, fragile per. Lvs narrowly-oblong or spoon-shaped, pointed, blue-green. Fls white, 10-12mm, usually solitary, long. stalked. Cliff crevices, 1300-1400m. June-July. nl; Bergamasque Alps. **10a** *M. papulosa* often has pendent stems and small 4-5 parted fls. cl; central Apennines. **10b** *M. tommasinii* always has 4-parted fls. Limestone rocks. nel, nwYU; Istrian Peninsula.

11 NARROW-LEAVED SANDWORT *Moehringia bavarica.* Low/short sprawling or erect, hairless, *bluish-green,* per. Lvs *linear,* appearing veinless. Fls white, 5-8mm, solitary or in small clusters, 5-petalled. Limestone rocks to 1600m. May- July. A, nl, YU; from Monte Baldo eastwards. **11a** *M. insubrica* (= *M. bavarica* subsp. *insubrica*) has *shorter* lvs and smaller fls. nl; Brescian Alps.

12 MOSSY SANDWORT *Moehringia muscosa.* Variable low hairless per with sprawling weak stems. Lvs *linear,* pointed, 1-3 veined. Fls white, 4-8mm, in clusters of 3-6, usually 4-petalled. Shaded damp rocks and mossy places, to 2350m. May-Sept. A, CH, CS, D, F, F, H, I, PL, R, YU. **12a** *M. glaucovirens* has smaller, 5-petalled fls, usually solitary or 2-3 together. Shady limestone rocks. nl.

13 CREEPING SANDWORT *Moehringia ciliata.* Low *creeping,* mat-forming per; stems hairless. Leaves linear, with a few hairs at base. Fls small, white, 4-5mm, solitary or *2-3* together, 5-petalled. Limestone screes to 3000m. June-Aug. A, CH, sD, s & e F, nl, wYU.

Buttercup Family Ranunculaceae

Alpine species generally perennial, occasionally annuals or woody climbers. Fls with numerous stamens and normally five, but sometimes more, petals or petal-like sepals. Fls sometimes with nectary spurs or honey lvs, which secrete nectar. Fr a collection of dry achenes or follicles, rarely a berry.

1 STINKING HELLEBORE *Helleborus foetidus.* Med/tall foetid per. Lvs all on the stem, hand-like with 7-11 narrow lance-shaped, toothed, segments, stalked, uppermost lvs undivided. Fl lantern-shaped, 1-3cm, petal-less, sepals yellowish- green, edged purple, in clusters. Woods and scrub on calcareous soils, to 1600m. Jan-Apr. B, CH, c & sD, F, GB, n & cE, n & cI

2 GREEN HELLEBORE *Helleborus viridis.* Short/med per with two root-lvs that do not overwinter. Lvs hand-like with 7-13 narrow-elliptical lobes, toothed; stem lvs smaller, stalkless. Fls broad open-cups, 4-5cm, sepals apple-green, scentless, overtopped by lvs. Woods, scrub and rocky places, usually on limestone, to 1600m. Mar-Apr. A, B, CH, D, nE, F, GB, nI; the form in western Europe is subsp. *occidentalis.* **2a** *H. dumetorum* has smaller, scented fls held *above the* lvs. Mar-May. A, H, R, YU. **2b.** *H. bocconei* is like 2 but lf *segments* 5-7 and fls yellowish-green, 5-7cm. c & sI. **2c** *H. odorus* is like 2b but lvs hairy beneath, the stem lvs markedly smaller than the basal. H, n & cI, R, YU.

3 CHRISTMAS ROSE *Helleborus niger.* Low clump-forming per with *overwintering* basal lvs. Lvs hand-like with 7-9 elliptical toothed segments. Fls large, saucer-shaped, 5-8cm, white with yellow anthers. Woods and scrub on limestone, to 1900m. Jan-Apr. A, CH, sD, n & cI, wYU (CS, F). **3a.** *H. n.* subsp. *macranthus* has broader, somewhat bluish-green lf segments and larger fls, 8-11cm. n & cI, n & wYU.

4 WINTER ACONITE *Eranthis hyemalis.* Low hairless per, rootstock a small tuber. Lvs palmately lobed, all from roots and *appearing* as fls fade. Fls solitary cups, 2-3cm, with 5-7 yellow sepals, surrounded by a *ruff* of green leafy bracts. Damp woods, scrub and banks, to 1500m. Jan-Mar. I, YU; widely planted and often naturalised elsewhere (B, CH, CS, D, GB, NL, H, R).

5 CALLIANTHEMUM *Callianthemum anemonoides.* Low hairless per. Basal lvs 2-pinnate, segments oblong, pale green, stalked; stem lvs similar, stalkless. Fls 3-3.5cm, white with an orange central ring; sepals 5, *petals* 5-20. Fr 5mm long. Open coniferous woods on calcareous soils, to 2100m. Mar-May. A; north-east Alps. **5a** *C. kernerianum* is *smaller* with fls 2.5cm across. Rocky limestone slopes, to 1500m. May-July. nI; southern Alps, local. **5b** *C. coriandrifolium* is similar to 5 but petals *broader* and fr *achenes* only 3mm long. Turf and stony places on neutral or acid soils, often by melting snow, 1800-3000m. July-Aug. A, CH, CS, nE, s & eF, nI, PL, R, wYU.

6 LOVE-IN-A-MIST *Nigella arvensis.* Short upright, branched, ann. Lvs grey-green, *feathery* with many thread-like segments. Fls 2-3cm, long stalked with 5 blue 'clawed' petals, often green-veined. Weed of cornfields and waste places. June-July. A, B, CH, CS, D, F, H, I, NL, PL, R, YU.

7 GLOBEFLOWER *Trollius europaeus.* Short/tall hairless per. Basal lvs palmate, deeply cut, stalked; upper lvs smaller, stalkless. Fls large 3-5cm, almost *spherical,* with up to ten yellow sepals curving in at the top. Damp meadows and open woods, to 2800m. May-Aug. T, except B, IS, NL. **7a** *T. e.* subsp. *transsilvanicus* is not more than 20cm tall usually with recurved, not straight, stigmas. A, nI, YU, H, R.

1, fruit

2, fruit

Buttercup Family *(contd.)*

1 RUE-LEAVED ISOPYRUM *Isopyrum thalictroides.* Low short slender, hairless per. Basal lvs stalked, trifoliate, leaflets 3-lobed, grey-green; stem lvs stalkless. Fls saucer-shaped, 10-20mm, with five oblong white sepals. Damp shady woods, to 1200m - rarely higher. Mar-May. A, CS, E, s & eF, H, I, PL, R, YU.

2 BANEBERRY *Actaea spicata.* Medium hairless rhizomatous per, strong smelling. Lvs, *'umbellifer-like'*, 2-pinnate or 2-trifoliate, dark green above, paler below, stalked; upper lvs smaller. Fls in small oblong clusters, with 4 small petals and 4 long stalked stamens, *all* white. Fr a large shiny *black berry.* Damp woods, to 1900m. May-July. Poisonous. T, except IRL, IS. **2a** *A. erythrocarpa* 3-ternate lvs and *red* berries. S, SF.

3 MARSH MARIGOLD *Caltha palustris.* Short/med hairless per, much dwarfed at high altitudes, often creeping. Lvs large, *heart-shaped,* toothed, dark green, shiny. Fls open cups, 1.5-5cm, with five golden yellow sepals, *no* petals. Fr pod-like clusters, conspicuous. Marshes, bogs and wet pastures, to 2500m. Mar-July. T.

MONKSHOODS *Aconitum.* Perennials with stout leafy stems and tuberous brown rootstocks. Fls with five petal-like sepals, *the* upper one forming a hood or helmet, often spur-like. Fr consisting of 2-5 follicles as in *Aquilegia* and *Delphinium.* Very Poisonous.

4 WOLFSBANE *Aconitum lycoctonum* subsp. *vulparia* (= *A. vulparia*). Tall hairless per. Lvs palmately cut to middle, segments 4-6, deep green. Fls pale yellow, in branched spike-like racemes; *helmet* long and narrow. Meadows, woods and stony places, to 2400m. June-Aug. A, B, D, nE, F, NL, CH, CS, nl, PL, R, wYU. **4a** *A. l.* subsp. *neapolitanum* (= *A. lamarckii*) has pale green *lvs* with 7-8 segments and denser, many flowered racemes. July-Aug. sA, sCH, E, s & eF, I. **4b Northern Wolfsbane** *A.l.* subsp. *lycoctonum* (= *A. septentrionale*) has hairy violet fls, the hood thicker at the base than 4. To 1300m. N, S, SF.

5 YELLOW MONKSHOOD *Aconitum anthora.* Med/tall hairless per. Lvs palmately cut to middle, segments narrow, lobed and pointed. Fls yellowish, *sometimes* blue, few in a loose cluster; helmet rounded, as broad as high. Dry meadows and rocky places often on limestone, to 2200m. July-Sept. A, CH, CS, E, s & eF, H, I, PL, R, YU.

6 VARIEGATED MONKSHOOD *Aconitum variegatum.* Med/tall hairless per. Lvs palmately cut to the middle, segment deeply lobed and toothed. Fls blue streaked with white, rarely all white, in loose racemes; helmet oblong, twice as high as broad. Meadows, woods and clearing to 2000m. July-Sept. A, CH, CS, sD, E, s & eF, H, I, PL, R, YU. **6a** *A. v.* subsp. *paniculatum* (= *A. paniculatum*) has stickily-hairy fl stems and violet or mauve fls in a loose, branched, cluster; helmet as broad as high. Damp meadows and woods, to 2400m. A, CH, eF, nl.

7 COMMON MONKSHOOD *Aconitum napellus* subsp. *vulgare.* Very variable med/tall hairless per to 1.7m. Lvs palmately cut for two thirds to the middle, not crowded below the fls, with linear segments. Fls violet, deep blue or reddish-violet, in dense usually unbranched spike-like, hairy, racemes; helmet rounded, as broad as high. Damp meadows and woods, to 2500m. July-Sept. A, CH, sD, nE, s & e F, nl, wYU. **7a** *A. n.* subsp. *tauricum* (= *A. tauricum*) has broad segmented lvs crowded below the fls and racemes usually *hairless.* A, nel, R, wYU. *A. n.* subsp. *napellus* is confined to south-western Britain.

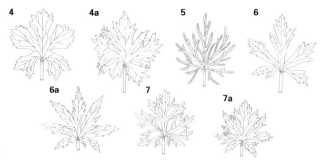

Buttercup Family *(contd.)*

LARKSPURS *Delphinium.* Fls in spike-like racemes; with 5 petal-like sepals, the upper with a long narrow spur pointing backwards. Fr of 3-5 follicles. Poisonous.

1 MOUNTAIN LARKSPUR *Delphinium montanum.* Short/med velvety-hairy per, stems erect. Lvs *long-stalked,* palmately cut almost to the middle, lobes oblong, toothed. Fls pale blue, 12-20mm, sepals *narrow* oblong. Fr hairy. Meadows and stony places to 2000m. June-Aug. nE, sF; central and eastern Pyrenees. **1a D. dubium** is taller with short lf stalks and dark blue fls, 16-23mm. seF, nl.

2 ALPINE LARKSPUR *Delphinium elatum.* Rather similar to 1 but stems with *straight* not curved hairs. Fls deep or dirty blue or bluish-violet, 14-17mm, sepals *broad* oval or rounded; spur longer than sepals. Fr *usually* hairless. Meadows and stony places, to 2000m. June-Aug. A, CH, CS, eF, I, PL, R, YU. **2a** *D.e.* subsp. *helveticum* has a spur *equal* in length to the sepals. wA, CH, eF. **2b** *D.e.* subsp. *austriacum* like 2a but fls *larger,* 17-21mm. A.

ANEMONES *Anemone.* Perennials with basal lvs and a whorl of short stalked or stalkless lvs on the stem below the fls. Fls solitary or clustered, cup or saucer shaped; sepals 5 or more, 'petal-like'. Fr a cluster of achenes *not* feathered.

3 WOOD ANEMONE *Anemone nemorosa.* Low hairless per. Stem Lvs 3, *stalked,* palmately-lobed to the middle; basal lvs similar, appearing after the fls. Fls solitary white, often flushed pink, 20-35mm, with 6-7 sepals. Woods, to 1800m. Mar-May. T, except IS, N, PL, R. **3a** *A. trifolia* similar to 3 but stem lvs *trifoliate.* Woods and rocky places, to 1900m. May-July. A, E, F, H, I, SF, YU.

4 YELLOW ANEMONE *Anemone ranunculoides.* Short hairy per. Stem lvs like 3 but *almost* stalkless. Fls solitary or two, *yellow,* 15-20mm, with 5-8 petals. Woods, to 1500m. Mar-May. T, except GB, IRL, IS. **4a** *A. r.* subsp. *wockeana* is smaller and forms dense patches. CS, D, PL.

5 NARCISSUS-FLOWERED ANEMONE *Anemone narcissifolia* (= *A. narcissiflora*). Low/med hairy per. Lvs palmately-lobed to the middle. Fls white, often pink flushed below, 20-30mm in *umbels* of 3-8, with 5-6 sepals. Meadows, usually on limestone, 1500-2600m. June-July. A, CH, CS, sD, E, s &eF, I, PL, R, YU.

6 SNOWDROP WINDFLOWER *Anemone sylvestris.* Short/med hairy per. Lvs palmately-lobed almost to the middle. Fls solitary white, 30-70mm, with only 5 sepals, hairy beneath. Dry woods on limestone, to 1200m. Apr-June. A, CH, CS, sD, eF, H, I, PL R, sS, YU.

7 MONTE BALDO ANEMONE *Anemone baldensis.* Low hairy per. Basal lvs trifoliate, leaflets each 3-lobed and toothed; stem lvs similar but smaller. Fls solitary, white, sometimes bluish outside, 25-40mm, *with* 8-10 pointed sepals. Rocky places and screes, 1800-3000m. July-Aug. A, CH, eF, nl, wYU; often local.

8 BLUE WOOD ANEMONE *Anemone apennina.* Low hairy per. Stem lvs 3, trifoliate, toothed; basal lvs similar, appearing after the fls. Fls solitary, blue, rarely white, 25-35mm, with 8-14 oblong sepals. Open woods and scrub to 1200m. Mar-Apr. c & sI, YU (A, B, D, DK, F, GB, NL, S).

3

Buttercup Family (contd.)

PASQUE FLOWERS *Pulsatilla*. Tufted hairy perennials usually with ferny Lvs and large leaves, upright or nodding fls, stalked with a ruff of feathery leafy bracts below; sepals usually five or six, petal-like, hairy outside. Fr clustered, with long silky plumes, often persisting into late summer. Poisonous.

1 ALPINE PASQUE FLOWER *Pulsatilla alpina*. Med hairy per. Lvs 2-pinnate, hairy above; basal and stem lvs *stalked*. Fls large, white often flushed bluish-purple outside, upright cups, 4-6cm. Meadows over limestone, to 2700m. May-July. A, CH, sD, n & cE, c, s & eF, I, wYU. **1a** *P.a.* subsp. *apiifolia* (= *P. sulphurea*)* has *pale yellow* fls. Meadows generally over acid rocks, to 2700m. Similar distribution.

2 WHITE PASQUE FLOWER *Pulsatilla alba*. Low hairy per. Lvs 2-pinnate, more or less *hairless* above; basal and stem lvs *stalked*. Fls large, white, sometimes bluish-flushed, upright cups, 2.5-4.5cm. Meadows, generally over acid rocks, to 2200m. May-July. A, CS, sD, nE, sF, PL, R, wYu.

3 SPRING PASQUE FLOWER *Pulsatilla vernalis*. Low/short hairy per. Lvs evergreen, pinnate, *much less* divided than 1 and 2, leaflets oblong, toothed; stem lvs stalk- less, linear. Fls white, flushed pink, violet or blue on the outside, deep cups, 4-6cm, at first drooping, later upright. Meadows and stony places, often by melting snow, 1300-3600m. Apr-July. A, CH, CS, DK, nE, s & eF, nI, sN, PL, sS, SF, YU.

4 SMALL PASQUE FLOWER *Pulsatilla pratensis*. Low/short hairy per. Lvs 2-pinnate, feathery; stem lvs stalkless, narrowly-elliptic, pointed. Fls dark purple, sometimes pale violet or greenish-yellow, greyish hairy outside, 3-4cm, *always* drooping; sepals with recurved tips. Meadows, to 2100m. Apr-May. A, CS, D, DK, H, sN, PL, R, sS, nwYU. **4a** *P. montana* is similar but with bluish to dark violet fls, sepals not *recurved* and opening more. Meadows and open woods, to 2150m. Apr-May. CH, seF, nI, R, YU. **4b** *P. rubra**has dark red-brown, purplish-brown or reddish black fls. n & eE, c & sF.

5 COMMON PASQUE FLOWER *Pulsatilla vulgaris*. Low hairy per. Lvs 2-pinnate, feathery, covered with long hairs at first, later almost hairless; stem lvs stalkless, linear. Fls large, dark to pale purple, bell-shaped 5.5-8.5cm, erect at first, then drooping, anthers bright yellow. Meadows, often on limestone, to 1200m. May- June. A, B, CH, CS, D, F, sGB, H, PL, R, sS, YU. **5a** *P. v.* subsp. *grandis* has lvs *appearing* after the fls, with about 40 lobes. A, CH, CS, sD. **5b Haller's Pasque Flower** *P. halleri* is similar to 5 but lvs less divided (with only 5 primary segments, not 7-9), mature lvs and stems densely woolly-hairy. To 3000m. June-July. A, CH, CS, PL, nI, YU. **5c** *P. h.* subsp. *styriaca* like 5b but with *longer* lf blades, 5-11cm instead of 3-7cm. eA; Steiermark. **5d** *P. h.* subsp. *slavica* usually has only 3 primary leaf divisions. R; western Carpathians.

6 HEPATICA *Hepatica nobilis* (= *H. triloba*, *Anemone hepatica*). Low evergreen, slightly hairy per. Lvs 3-lobed, heart shaped at base, stalked, green above, purplish below. Fls solitary saucers, 15-25mm, purple, bluish-violet or pink, rarely white, with 6-9 sepals and 3 sepal-like bracts. Woods, scrub, rocky and grassy places, often on limestone, to 2200m. Mar-Apr. T, except GB, IRL, IS, NL (B). **6a** *H. transsilvanica* has blunt-toothed leaf lobes and larger fls, 25-40mm. Mountain woods. cR.

4b

Buttercup Family *(contd.)*

CLEMATIS *Clematis.* Perennials or woody climbers with opposite, usually 1-2-pinnate lvs. Fls with 4 petal-like sepals and numerous stamens. Fr clustered, with long hairy plumes giving 'old man's beard' appearance.

1 TRAVELLER'S JOY *Clematis vitalba.* Deciduous scrambling or climbing woody perennial, sometimes with very long stems. *Lvs* pinnate, leaflets toothed, often with twisting 'tendril-like' stalks. Fls greenish-white, fragrant, 15-20mm with many conspicuous stamens, in large clusters. Fr* in dense greyish *clusters,* typical Old Man's Beard. Woods, scrub and hedges, to 2100m. June-Sept. T, except nGB, IS, N, SF (DK, IRL, P, S).

2 ERECT CLEMATIS *Clematis recta.* Tall erect per, *not* woody. Lvs pinnate, leaflets *untoothed oval.* Fls white, upright, 15-20mm, in terminal branched clusters. Open woods and dry hills, rarely above 1100m. May-June. A, CH, CS, D, E, F, H, I, PL, R, YU (B).

3 SIMPLE-LEAVED CLEMATIS *Clematis integrifolia.* Med/tall erect per, stems usually unbranched. Lvs oval, pointed, untoothed, not pinnate. Fls nodding purple bells, 3-5cm, solitary or 2-3. Meadows, rarely over 1000m. June-Aug. A, CS, H, I, R, YU.

4 ALPINE CLEMATIS *Clematis* (= *Atragene*) *alpina.* Deciduous climbing or scrambling per. *Lvs* 2-pinnate with twisting 'tendril-like' stalks. Fls large, *solitary, nodding,* 2.5-4cm, violet or purplish, with white, 'petal-like' staminodes inside. Rocky mountain woods and meadows, 1900-2900m. June-July. A, CH, CS, D, eF, H, I, R, YU. **4a.** *C. a.* subsp. *sibirica* has white or cream fls. sN, PL, SF.

5 PYRENEAN PHEASANT'S-EYE *Adonis pyrenaica.* Short/med per, stems pale green not scaly at base. Lvs 2-3-pinnate, feathery. Fls large, 40-60mm, with *twelve* or more shiny golden-yellow petals; sepals hairless. Rocky and stony places and screes, to 2400m. June-July. nE, s & seF. **5a** *A. vernalis* is similar but stems scaly at base and with larger fls; sepals hairy. Dry meadows and rocks, rarely much above 1200m. Apr-May. A, CH, CS, sD, E, F, H, I, PL, R, S, YU. **5b** *A. volgensis* has linear-lance-shaped, toothed, leaflets and more numerous petals (H, R). Hybrids between 5a and 5b occur in the wild.

6 APENNINE PHEASANT'S-EYE *Adonis distorta.* Low per with *curved* stems and lf-segments; stems *not* scaly at base. Lvs 2-3-pinnate, basal ones *long* stalked. Fls *smaller* than 5 and 5a, 30-45mm, petals yellow, shiny, sepals hairy. Rocky and stony places usually on limestone, 2000-2900m. cl; central Apennines.

7 PHEASANT'S-EYE *Adonis annua.* Low/short hairless ann. Lvs 3-pinnate, feathery, the lower unstalked. Fls open cups, 15-25mm, with 5-8 scarlet petals; anthers numerous black or purplish; sepals *hairless.* Fr achenes 3–5-5mm long. Cornfields and waste places, often on calcareous soils, to 1500m. May-Aug. Ch, E, s & eF, I, YU (GB). **7a** *A. aestivalis* has red fls and achenes 3–5-5mm long; lower lvs *stalked.* A, B, CH, CS, D, E, F, H, I, PL, R, YU. **7b** *A. flammea* is similar to 7 but fls 20-30mm, sepals *hairy;* achenes with a *black* beak. As 7a, except for B.

8 MOUSETAIL *Myosurus minimus.* Low/short hairless ann. Lvs linear, in a basal tuft, rather fleshy. Fls small solitary, long stalked, with 5-7 greenish yellow petals *and* sepals. Fr *head* greatly elongated 'mouse-tail' like. Damp cultivated and bare ground, rarely above 1400m. Mar-May. T, except IRL, IS.

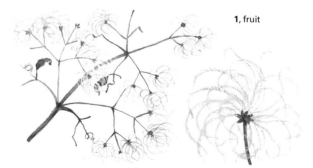

1, fruit

Buttercup Family (contd.)

BUTTERCUPS *Ranunculus*. Fls open cups, shiny yellow or white, rarely pinkish, with *both* sepals and petals, distinguishing them from anemones, globe flowers and marsh marigolds. Fr a cluster of dry seeds (achenes).

1 MULTI-FLOWERED BUTTERCUP *Ranunculus polyanthemos*. Short/med hairy per, much branched. Basal lvs rununcula in outline, cut to middle into 5 lobes, lobes *narrow,* toothed, stem lvs similar but smaller. Fls golden-yellow, 18-25mm, sepals erect. Meadows and grassy places, to 1250m. May-Oct. CS, c & eD, N, PL, S, SF. **1a** *R. p.* subsp. *polyanthemoides* is taller, the basal lvs only 3-lobed, the central lobe very long. A, B, CH, CS, D, DK, F, sN, NL, PL, R, S, SF, YU.

2 WOOD BUTTERCUP *Ranunculus serpens* subsp. *nemorosus* (= *R. nemorosus*). Short/med hairy per, branched. Basal lvs *pentagonal* in outline, 3-lobed, lobes *broad* toothed; stem lvs scarcely toothed. Fls golden-yellow, 15-20mm, sepals erect. Meadows and grassy places, to 2000m. Apr-Oct. T, except GB, IRL, IS, N, SF and far north. **2a** *R.s.* subsp. *serpens* similar but bien with shorter stems *rooting* at the nodes. A, CH, c & sD, nl. **2b** *R.s* subsp. *polyanthemophyllus* is taller than 2, the basal lvs rounded in outlined, the central lobe often short-stalked. A, CH, sD, eF, nl, wYU. **2c Creeping Buttercup** *R. repens**. Rather like 2a but creeping with rooting *runners;* basal lvs *triangular* in outline with a stalked central lobe. To 2500m. T.

3 WOOLLY BUTTERCUP *Ranunculus lanuginosus*. Med very hairy per. Basal lvs rounded in outline, 3-lobed, lobes broad, *less* deeply cut than 1, & 2; stem lvs similar but smaller. Fls orange-yellow, 20-30mm, sepals erect. Damp meadows and woods, to 1600m. May-Aug. T, except B, GB, IRL, IS, N, NL, S. **3a Meadow Buttercup** *R. acris** has 3-7-lobed lvs, the end lobe *unstilted, lobes* narrowed at base; fls smaller golden yellow. To 2500m. Apr-Oct. T, except CH, GB, IRL, IS.

4-8 are very similar and often confused. Fls solitary or two to three clustered; sepals erect.

4 GOUAN'S BUTTERCUP *Ranunculus gouanii*. Low/short hairy per. Basal lvs 3-5-lobed, lobes oval, broadest above middle, toothed; stem lvs *untoothed* linear lobes, *clasping* stem at base. Fls golden-yellow, 20-40mm, sepals *densely* hairy. Meadows and rocky places, to 2800m. May-Aug. nE, sF; Pyrenees and Cordillera Cantabrica. **4a** *R. ruscinonensis* is smaller, stem lvs *not* clasping. nE, sF; central and eastern Pyrenees.

5 CARINTHIAN BUTTERCUP *Ranunculus carinthiacus*. Low/short per with *hairless* lvs. Basal lvs 3-5-lobed, lobes narrow, oblong or oval, toothed; stem lvs similar, *not* clasping. Fls golden-yellow, 8-22mm, sepals scarcely hairy. Meadows, woods and screes, to 2800m. May-Aug. A, sD, E, s & eF, I, wYU.

6 MOUNTAIN BUTTERCUP *Ranunculus montanus*. Short per with hairy or hairless lvs. Basal lvs 3-5-lobed, lobes oval, toothed; stem lvs narrower, *half-clasping* stem. Fls-golden-yellow, 10-30mm, sepals with short hairs. Achene with *slender* hooked beak. Meadows, woods, screes and snow patches, to 2800m. May-Aug. A, sD, s & eF, nl, nwYU. **6a** *R. venetus* has densely hairy lvs and a *stout* beak to the achenes. nl; south-eastern Alps.

7 GRENIER'S BUTTERCUP *Ranunculus grenierianus*. Low/short per with very *hairy* lvs. Basal lvs 3-5-lobed, lobes oval, toothed; stem lvs with linear or lance- shaped lobes *broadest* near the base. Fls golden-yellow, 8-22mm, sepals hairy. Achenes with along hooked beak. Meadows, acid screes, to 2800m. May-Aug. A, CH, sD, eF, nl. **7a** *R. oreophilus* like 7; the stem lvs linear; achenes with *a short* beak. A, CH, CS, sD, eF.

8 HOOKED BUTTERCUP *Ranunculus aduncus*. Similar to 6. Lvs *always* hairy, *lower* clasping stem at their base. Fls golden-yellow, 12-25mm, sepals with long hairs. Meadows, to 2800m. June-July. wCH, eF, nwl.

2c   basal growths   3a

Buttercup Family (contd.)

1 BULBOUS BUTTERCUP *Ranunculus bulbosus* agg. Short/med very hairy per, stem base *swollen*. Basal and lower lvs 3-lobed, lobes oval, toothed, central one *stalked;* upper lvs with linear-lance-shaped lobes. Fls golden-yellow, 20-30mm. Sepals hairy, *turned down*. Fl stalks furrowed. Meadows and grassy places, to 2500m. Apr-July. T, except IS, S and far north. **1a** *R. sardous* is *annual,* hairier, the stem scarcely swollen; fls smaller, *pale yellow*. T, except IRL, IS (N).

2 PYGMY BUTTERCUP *Ranunculus pygmaeus*. Tiny low, scarcely hairy, per. Basal lvs *kidney-shaped* in outline with 3-5 blunt lobes. Fls yellow, 5-10mm. Short turf and by snow patches, 1800-2800m. July-Aug. A, CH, CS, nI, IS, N, PL, S, SF. **2a** *R. hyperboreus* is creeping with 5-lobed lvs and *3-petalled fls*. To 2100m. IS, N, S, SF. **2b** *R. nivalis* * is taller than 2, with *larger* stem lvs and fls 12-15mm. Short grassy places by snow patches, to 1550m. July. c & nN, nS, SF.

3 THORE'S BUTTERCUP *Ranunculus thora*. Short hairless per. Lvs waxy, lowest *large, kidney-shaped,* toothed, unstalked, upper lvs much smaller. Fls yellow, 10-20mm, solitary or two to five clustered; sepals hairless. Meadows and rocky places on limestone, to 2200m. May-July. A, CH, CS, nE, c & sF, I, PL, R, YU.

4 HYBRID BUTTERCUP *Ranunculus hybridus*. Similar to 3 but with *two* large lower lvs, kidney-shaped, toothed and lobed towards the top. Fls yellow, 12-25mm, solitary or two to three. Achenes short beaked. Stony places on limestone, to 2500m. June-July. A, sD, nl, wYU. **4a** *R. brevifolius* is smaller with several large lower lvs and achenes long beaked. cI, YU.

5 ALPINE BUTTERCUP *Ranunculus alpestris*. Low hairless, tufted, per. Lvs *shiny-green,* basal rounded in outline, 5-lobed, long stalked; stem lvs with 3 linear lobes, stalkless. Fls white, 20mm, two or three clustered. Sepals hairless. Damp meadows, stony places and snow patches, 1300-3000m. June-Oct. A, CH, CS, E, c & eF, I, PL, R, YU. **5a** *R. a.* subsp. *traunfellneri* (= *R. traunfellneri*) * is smaller, basal lvs matt-green, 3-lobed; fls 15mm, solitary. A, nel, nwYU.

6 CRENATE BUTTERCUP *Ranunculus crenatus*. Low hairless per. Basal lvs *round-heart-shaped,* 3-lobed at top, long stalked; stem lvs linear-lance-shaped. Fls white, 20-25mm, solitary or two, petals notched or un-notched. Damp rocks and screes, 1700-2400m. June-July. A, n & cI, R, YU. **6a** *R. bilobus* has *distinctly veined* lower lvs and *more* notched petals. Limestone rocks, to 2000m. nel.

7 ACONITE-LEAVED BUTTERCUP *Ranunculus aconitifolius*. Short/med slightly hairy per. Lvs 3-5-lobed, lobes oblong-oval, central one cut to the middle; upper lvs stalkless. Fls white, 10-20mm, in *branched* clusters; *sepals* reddish-purple, falling as fls open. Meadows and woods, to 2600m. May-Aug. A, CH, CS, sD, n & cE, c & sF, I, YU. **7a** *R. platanifolius* * is larger, the lvs 5-7-lobed, central lobes *not* cut to middle. Scrub and dry meadows, to 1600m. May-Aug. T, except GB, IRL, NL, IS and far north.

8 SEQUIER'S BUTTERCUP *Ranunculus seguieri*. Short downy per. Basal lvs long stalked, 3-5-lobed, each lobe with *angular-pointed* segments; stem lvs similar but smaller. Fls white, 20-25mm, solitary or two, petals slightly *notched*. Achenes downy. Damp meadows, stony places and screes on limestone, 1800-2400m. June-July. A, nE, s & eF, n & cI, nwYU.

9 GOLDILOCKS BUTTERCUP *Ranunculus auricomus*. Short, slightly hairy, per. Lower lvs only slightly lobed. Fls few, yellow, petals 5 *often distorted* and of differing sizes, sometimes absent; sepals purple tinged. Woods and hedges, to 2100m. Apr-May. T.

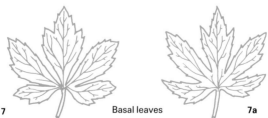

7   Basal leaves   **7a**

Buttercup Family (contd.)

1 GLACIER CROWFOOT *Ranunculus glacialis.* Low/short hairless per. Lvs thick, 3-lobed, lobes short stalked, with angular teeth; upper lvs linear. Fls white *becoming* pink or purplish tinted, 25-40mm, solitary or two to three; *sepals* with purple-brown hairs. Rocky debris, moraines and screes, often near snow patches, on acid rocks, 2300-4250m. July-Oct. T, except B, DK, nF, GB, IRL, NL, IS and far north.

2 LESSER SPEARWORT *Ranunculus flammula.* Variable short/med hairless per, erect or creeping, often rooting at lf junctions, but *without* runners. Lvs shiny-green, lance shaped, slightly toothed, the lower stalked. Fls yellow, 7-20mm, in branched clusters. Wet meadows and stream banks, to 2000m. June-Oct. T. **2a Creeping Spearwort** *P. reptans* * is more slender with *runners* and rooting at all nodes, the lvs narrow, spoon-shaped or elliptic; fls 5mm. T, except B, IRL, NL.

3 GREATER SPEARWORT *Ranunculus lingua.* Med/tall hairless per with long *runners.* Lvs oblong-lance-shaped, toothed, stalked or unstalked. Fls golden-yellow, 30-50mm, stalks *not* furrowed. Wet meadows and marshes to 1200m. June-Sept. T, except IS and far north.

4 PYRENEAN BUTTERCUP *Ranunculus pyrenaeus.* Low/short more or less hairless per. Lvs bluish-green, linear to lance-shaped, *untoothed,* stalkless. Fls white, 10-20mm, solitary or two to three; *sepals* whitish, hairless. Damp meadows and slopes on limestone, 1700-2800m. May-July. E, sF; Pyrenees only. **4a.** *R. keupferi* (= *R. pyrenaeus* subsp. *platagineus*) is more robust with yellowish-green, not whitish, sepals and fls 10-30mm. A, eF, CH, nI.

5 PARNASSUS-LEAVED BUTTERCUP *Ranunculus parnassifolius.* Low hairy or hairless per. Lvs shiny-green. *oval-heart-shaped,* or broad lance-shaped, ribbed, untoothed, hairy above. Fls white often pink or red tinged, 20-30mm, solitary or up to 5; sepals hairy. Rocks and moraines on limestone, often by snow patches, 1900-2900m. July-Aug. neE, sF; eastern Pyrenees. **5a** *R. p.* subsp. *heterocarpus* has 0-5 unequal, white, petals per fl. A, CH, sD, nE, s & eF, n & cI. **5b** *R. p.* subsp. *cabrerensis* has basal lvs hairy beneath. nwE. **5c** *R. p.* subsp. *favargeri* is like 5 but lvs densely hairy along veins above. nwE, swF.

6 AMPLEXICAULE BUTTERCUP *Ranunculus amplexicaulis.* Low/short hairless per. Basal lvs oval-lance-shaped, pointed, stalked; stem lvs stalk less, *clasping* stem at base. Fls white, 20mm; sepals greenish, hairless, soon *falling.* Meadows, to 2500m. June-July. n & cE, sF.

MEADOW-RUES *Thalictrum.* Perennials with 2-4-pinnate, ferny, lvs and racemes or clusters of feathery fls. Fls with four tiny petals, no sepals and a bunch of conspicuous, coloured, stamens. Fr a cluster of dry, one seeded, achenes.

7 SMALL MEADOW-RUE *Thalictrum simplex.* Short/tall hairless per. Basal lvs 2-3-pinnate, leaflets oval to linear, toothed or not. Fls yellow, *drooping* at first but becoming erect, in short-branched clusters. Meadows, to 2000m. July-Aug. T, except GB, IRL, IS, NL and far north.

8 LESSER MEADOW-RUE *Thalictrum minus.* Variable med/tall hairless per. Basal lvs 2-4-pinnate, leaflets rounded or oval, toothed in upper half. Fls yellowish, *drooping* at first but becoming erect, in long-branched clusters. Rocky and dry grassy places, to 2850m. May-July. T, except IS.

9 STINKING MEADOW-RUE *Thalictrum foetidum.* Short slightly hairy, *foetid,* per. Lvs ash-grey, 3-4-pinnate. Fls yellow, *drooping,* in long-branched clusters. Rocks and stony places, usually on limestone, 1500-2400m. June-Aug. A, CH, CS, E, s & eF, H, I, R, YU.

2a

7   8

9

Meadow-rue fruits

Buttercup Family *(contd.)*

1 GREAT MEADOW-RUE *Thalictrum aquilegifolium.* Med/tall hairy per. Lvs 2-3-pinnate, leaflets oval, *broadest* near the top, toothed. Fls with pale greenish-white petals, and lilac or whitish stamens, in larger branched clusters. Damp woods and meadows, to 2500m. May-July. T, except B, GB, IRL, IS, N, NL and far north.

2 LARGE-FRUITED MEADOW-RUE *Thalictrum macrocarpum.* Med hairless per with lvs like 1. Fls with greenish petals and yellowish stamens, few in branched clusters. Fr achenes large, 8-10mm, *long-beaked.* Damp limestone rocks, to 2200m. June-Sept. nE, sF; west and central Pyrenees. **2a** *T. tuberosum* is tuberous rooted, with fls 15-15mm and *white or cream* petals and small achenes. Dry rocky places, to 2000m. n & eE, sF; Pyrenees southwards.

3 ALPINE MEADOW-RUE *Thalictrum alpinum.* Short/low, rather insignificant, hairless per, *unbranched.* Lvs 2-pinnate. Fls with purple petals, stamens *violet* with yellow anthers. Damp meadows, stony and rocky places, 1900-2900m. June- July. T, except B, CS, D, DK, NL, PL, nS.

COLUMBINES *Aquilegia.* Tufted perennials, with usually branched stems and 2-trifoliate lvs. Fls drooping, with 5 coloured sepals and petals, the petals with long backward-pointing spurs. Fr a cluster of follicles like Delphinium. Poisonous.

4 COMMON COLUMBINE *Aquilegia vulgaris.* Med/tall per, stems usually hairy, leaflets dull green, hairy *beneath.* Fls violet-blue or purplish, rarely white, 3-5cm, spurs *hooked;* stamens yellow, *scarcely* protruding. Woods, meadows and rocky places, usually on limestone, to 2000m. May-July. T, except IS (DK, N, S, SF). **4a** *A. transsilvanica* has sepals 22-40 (not 18-25)mm long. R. **4b** *A. viscosa* has stems sticky with glands, fls blue to whitish and spurs 15-23mm long. neE, sF.

5 DARK COLUMBINE *Aquilegia atrata.* Med/tall per, stems hairy. Leaflets hairless. Fls *dark* purple-violet, 3-4cm, spurs hooked; stamens yellow, *protruding* well beyond petals. Woodland clearings and rocky places on limestone, to 2000m. May-July. A, CH, sD, eF, n & cI, nwYU. **5a** *A. nigricans* has *larger* fls, 5-6cm and leaflets *hairy* beneath. A, H, I, PL, R, YU. **5b** *A. n.* subsp. *subscaposa* has bright blue fls. R.

6 EINSEL'S COLUMBINE *Aquilegia einseleana.* Short/med. slightly hairy per. Leaflets hairless or with a few hairs above. Fls violet-blue or purplish, 2.5-3.5cm, spurs straight; stamens *not* protruding. Grassy and stony places and woods, on limestone, to 1800m. June-July. A, c & eCH, sD, nI, wYU. **6a** *A. thalictrifolia* has *stickily hairy* stems and lvs and larger fls. To 1600m. nI.

7 BERTOLONI'S COLUMBINE *Aquilegia bertolonii.* Short per, stems sometimes unbranched, stickily hairy in upper half. Fls blue-violet or dark blue, 2.5-3.5cm, sepals *downward* pointing; spurs straight or curved. Woods and rocky places, to 1700m. June-July. seF, nwI; Maritime Alps and Ligurian Apennines.

8 PYRENEAN COLUMBINE *Aquilegia pyrenaica* (incl. *A. aragonensis*). Short, more or less hairless per, stems usually branched. Fls bright blue or lilac, 3-5cm, spurs long, slender and curved. Rocky and stony places, 1800-2500m. July-Aug. E, sF. **8a** *A. p.* subsp. *discolor* is shorter, not more than 15cm, with inner petals often white or bicoloured. nwE; Cordillera Cantabrica. **8b** *A. p.* subsp. *guarensis* has stems glandular-hairy throughout and lvs 1-, not 2-ternate; fls blue or bluish-white. nE, sF; central Pyrenees.

9 ALPINE COLUMBINE *Aquilegia alpina.* Short/tall- hairy per. Fls *large,* bright blue, 5-8cm, spurs long, straight or curved. Meadows, woods and rocky places, to 2600m. July-Aug. A, CH, eF, nI; particularly in the western Alps.

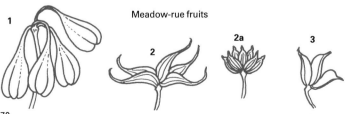

Meadow-rue fruits

Paeony Family Paeoniaceae

1 PEONY *Paeonia officinalis.* A variable med robust, clump-forming per. Basal lvs large, shiny green above, 2-3-trifoliate. Fls solitary, very large open cups, shiny red or pinkish, 7-13cm, petals 5-8; stamens many, pale yellow. Meadows and woods, to 1700m. May-June. CS, E, c & sF, H, I, R, YU (D). **1a** *P. mascula* (= *P. corallina*) has most leaflets *undivided* and broader; fls pink to red E, c & sF, I, R, YU (GB).

Barberry Family Berberidaceae

Fls in short racemes with four to six petals, each with a honey petal (nectar producing) within.

2 BARRENWORT *Epimedium alpinum.* Short tufted per. Lvs 2-trifoliate, leaflets oval or heart-shaped, *spiny-margined.* Fls dull red with four pale yellow honey petals, 9-13mm. Damp woods and shady places, to 1300m. Mar-May. A, n & cI, YU (B, D, DK, F, GB, NL).

3 BARBERRY *Berberis vulgaris.* Deciduous shrub to 4m, stems with 3-pointed *spines.* Lvs oval, spiny-margined. Fls yellow, 6-8mm, in drooping racemes. Fr a bright red, oblong, berry, edible. Rocky hill slopes, generally on limestone, to 2300m. Apr-June. T, except IS and far north (DK, GB, IRL, N, S, SF).

Fumitory Family Fumariaceae

Often included in the Poppy Family *Papaveraceae.* Thin stemmed annuals or perennials, hairless, with 2-pinnate Lvs. Fls in short spike-like racemes, two-lipped, spurred. Corydalis has oblong fr capsules, fumitory rounded ones.

4 YELLOW CORYDALIS *Pseudofumaria lutea* (= *Corydalis lutea*). Short hairless per with leafy branched, stems. Lvs green above, greyish beneath. Bracts tiny oblong, *untoothed.* Fls golden-yellow, 12-20mm, spur short. Rocks, walls and shady places, to 1700m. May-Oct. c & sCH, nI (very widely naturalised in the region). **4a** *P. alba* (= *Corydalis acaulis, C. ochroleucus*) has lvs *greyish* above and beneath and fls *white* with a yellowish-green apex. I, YU (B, D, F, NL).

5 BULBOUS CORYDALIS *Corydalis cava* (= *C. bulbosa* of gardens). Low/short, tuberous-rooted, per, stems *without* a scale below the lowest lf. Bracts large, *untoothed.* Fls dull purple or whitish, 1-30mm, spur down curved. Woods, hedgerows and cultivated land to 2000m. Mar-May. T, except GB, IRL, IS, N (NL). **5a** *C. intermedia* has stems with an *oval scale* below the lowest lf and fls purple, rarely white, 10-15mm, in racemes of 2-8. Woods and pastures, generally on limestone, to 2000m. Mar-Apr. T, except B, CH, CS, D, F, H, I, PL, R, YU. **5b** *C. pumila* is similar to 5a but with *toothed bracts.* T, except IRL, IS, N and far north.

6 SOLID-TUBERED CORYDALIS *Corydalis solida* (= *C. bulbosa*). Short, tuberous rooted, per with an oval *scale* below the lowest lf. Bracts large, *toothed.* Fls purplish, 15-25mm, in racemes of 10-20, spurs slightly curved. Woods, hedgerows and cultivated ground, to 2000m. Mar-May. T, except IRL, IS (BR, DK, N).

7 SARCOCAPNOS *Sarcocapnos enneaphylla.* Low much branched, *cushion forming,* per. Lvs pinnate, leaflets heart-shaped. Fls long-stemmed, white or yellowish with a purple tip, 8-10mm, spurs short. Shady limestone and basic rocks, to 1200m. Apr-June. n, c & eE, sF; eastern Pyrenees and mts of northern Spain.

8 COMMON FUMITORY *Fumaria officinalis* agg. Weak bluish-green scrambling ann. Leaf-segments flattened. Fls purplish-pink, darker at tip, 7-9mm, in long- *stalked* racemes. Bracts *more* than half the length of the fl stalk. Waste and stony places and cultivated land to 1500m. Apr-Oct. T. **8a** *F. schleicheri* has *shorter* bracts and deep pink fls, 5-6mm in racemes of 12 or more. To 1700m. A, Ch, CS, D, F, H, I, PL, R, YU. **8b** *F. vaillantii* is similar to 8a but the racemes short-stalked with 5-12 fls; fls pale pink *tipped* with blackish-red. To 2100m. May-Oct. T, except IRL, IS, N and far north.

1, seed

1, fruit

1

2

3

4

5

6

7

8

Poppy Family Papaveraceae

Annuals or perennials with 1-2-pinnate Lvs and large, solitary fls with four, rather crumpled-looking, silky petals. Sepals two, falling as fls open. Fr a capsule with pores at the top.

1 COMMON or CORN POPPY *Papaver rhoeas.* Med/tall rather bristly ann. Lvs 1-2-pinnate. Fls deep scarlet, sometimes with a dark centre, 5-8.5cm. Fr almost round, *hairless.* Cultivated land, banks and waste places, to 1800m. May-July. T, except IS. **1a Long-Headed Poppy** *P. dubium** has *smaller* pale scarlet fls, 3-5.5cm, and fr *oblong* in outline. T, except IS, N.

2 PRICKLY POPPY *Papaver argemone.* Short/med bristly ann. Lvs 1-2-pinnate. Fls pale scarlet, often with a black centre, 3.5-4.5cm, petals not overlapping. Fr oblong-club-shaped in outline, *bristly.* Fields and waste places, to 1700m. May- July. T, except IS, N. **2a** *P. hybridum** has almost globular-shaped fr covered by many yellowish bristles; fls crimson. E, F, I, sN, YU (D, GB, IRL).

3 PYRENEAN POPPY *Papaver lapeyrousianum* (= *P. suaveolens, P. s.* subsp. *endressii*). Low bristly tufted per. Lvs 1-2-pinnate, *scarcely* bristly. Fls yellow or red, 20-30mm. Fr oval in outline, bristly. Rocky places, screes and moraines on limestone, 1800-2500m. July-Aug. E, sF.

4 RHAETIAN POPPY *Papaver rhaeticum.* Short tufted bristly per. Lvs 1-2-pinnate; leaflets *not* opposite, oval-lance-shaped, blunt. Fls golden-yellow, sometimes red or white, 4-5cm. Limestone rocks, screes and moraines or river gravels, 1500-3050m. July-Aug. sA, sCH, nE, s & eF, nI, nwYU. **4a** *P. sendtneri* is smaller with sharply pointed leaflets and white fls, 3-4cm, 2000-2700m. A, CH, n & cI, nwYU.

5 ALPINE POPPY *Papaver burseri.* Short tufted per, almost hairless. Lvs 1-2-pinnate; leaflets usually *opposite,* lance-shaped or linear, sharply pointed. Fls white, 3-4cm. Limestone rocks, screes, moraines and river gravels, 1200-2000m. July-Aug. nA, sD, nCH. **5a** *P. kerneri* has yellow fls. eA, nwI, nwYU. *P. burseri, P. kerneri, P. rhaeticum* and *P. sendtneri* are sometimes placed in a single variable species called *P. alpinum.*

6 ARCTIC POPPY *Papaver radicatum* Variable low/short tufted hairy per; juice white or yellow. Lvs pinnately-lobed. Fls pale to deep yellow, sometimes pinkish, 2-4cm. Fr oblong, *softly* hairy. Screes and gravels, to 1850m. June-Aug. Faeroes, IS, N, S (A and perhaps elsewhere as a garden escape). **6a** *P. lapponicum* has 30 stamens or more, not less (as in 6) and narrow oval, rather than rounded, fl buds. N.

7 GREATER CELANDINE *Chelidonium majus.* Med/tall slightly hairy per, branched. Lvs greyish, alternate, pinnate, end leaflet 3-lobed. Fls bright yellow, 1.5-2cm, in *umbel-like* clusters of 3-8. Fr a long narrow capsule. Banks, hedges and waste places, to 1700m. May-Oct. T, except Is and far north (IRL).

8 WELSH POPPY *Meconopsis cambrica.* Med tufted, slightly hairy per. Lvs pinnate, basal ones long-stalked, but stem lvs short-stalked. Fls solitary, yellow, 4-7cm. Fr narrow-oblong in outline with a *short beak* on top, hairless. Woods, rocky and shady places, to 2000m. June-Aug. wGB, IRL, w & sF, nE (DK, N and probably elsewhere in the region).

fruit   fruit

1a   2a

2

3

4

8

5

6

7

Cress Family Cruciferae

Annual or perennial herbs, rarely small shrubs. Lvs usually alternate, often tufted or in basal rosettes in high alpine species. Inflorescence a raceme or panicle, or fls in rounded, stalked or unstalked clusters, or solitary. Fls with 4 separate sepals and 4 petals and usually 6 stamens; petals usually even but sometimes two larger, often clawed. Fr a linear rounded or heart shaped, 2-parted capsule, very variable in shape and often split to reveal a central hyaline membrane.

The characters of the fruits are very characteristic of particular genera and are a great aid to accurate identification; the fruits vary greatly in diversity and form from genus to genus. Often both flowers and fruits can be found on the plant at the same time and essential characters can usually be observed in immature fruits, especially with the aid of a x10 hand lens. The accompanying outline drawings present the major fruit types found in alpine representatives of the family.

Other specific generic characters are as follows:

Flowers zygomorphic (with two long and two short petals): *Iberis.*

Fruits pendent: *Isatis.*

Fruits flattened, two-lobed and winged: *Biscutella.*

Fruit small with a notched apex: most *Aethionema* species, *Capsella, Iberis, Thlaspi.*

Fruits large and flat, at least 25mm long: *Lunaria.*

Fruits small and elliptical or rounded, not notched: *Alyssum, Cochlearia, Draba, Erophila, Petrocallis, Ptilotrichum.*

Fruits long and linear: *Arabis, Brassica, Cardamine, Erysimum, Matthiola, Sisymbrium.*

Crucifer Fruits, scale c. x 1⅓

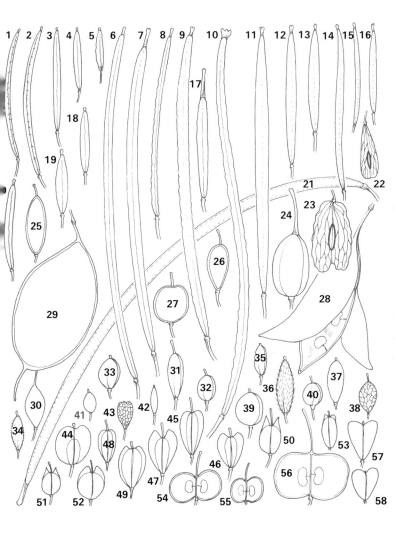

Cress Family (contd.)

1 LONDON ROCKET *Sisymbrium irio.* Short/med hairy or hairless ann. Lower lvs pinnately-lobed with a large end lobe, stalked; upper lvs smaller, scarcely lobed. Fls yellow, 4-6mm, in branched clusters. Fr *linear,* 25-65mm, hairless, over-topping fls when young. Waste places and fields, to 1400m. May-Sept. T, except B, IS, N, S, SF (CS, GB, IRL, NL, H). **1a False London Rocket** *S. loeselii* is hairier with larger fls; fr not *overtopping* fls. T, except IRL, IS, N, S, SF (B, CH, DK, E, F, GB, NL, S).

2 AUSTRIAN ROCKET *Sisymbrium austriacum* (= *S. pyrenaicum*). Short/tall hairy or hairless bien/per. Lvs pinnately-lobed or unlobed, stalked. Fls yellow, 7-10mm. Fr linear, 15-50mm, *rather twisted.* Fields and waste places to 1600m. May-Sept. A, B, CH, CS, D, E, F, I (NL). **2a** *S.a.* subsp. *chrysanthum* has shorter contorted fr, 7-15mm. n & cE, sF; central and eastern Pyrenees.

3 MURBECKIELLA *Murbeckiella pinnatifida* (= *Sisymbrium pinnatifidum*). Low/short per with *branched* hairs. Basal lvs toothed or untoothed, upper pinnately-lobed. Fls *white,* 5-6mm, in loose racemes, petals *notched.* Fr linear, 10-30mm, hairless. Rocky places to 3000m. June-Aug. n & cE, sF, CS, I. **3a** *M. zanonii* has *all lvs* pinnately-lobed; fls larger, 7-10mm and fr longer. nI; northern Apennines.

4 TANSY-LEAVED ROCKET *Hugueninia tanacetifolia* (= *Sisymbrium tanacetifolium*). Med hairy or hairless, rather greyish, per. Lvs *2-pinnately-lobed,* the lower long-stalked. Fls yellow, 3-6mm, many, in loose clusters. Fr narrow- oblong, 6-15mm. Rocky and grassy places and stream sides, 1700-2500m. June-Aug. sCH, eF, nwI; south-western Alps. **4a** *H.t.* subsp. *suffruticosa* is hairier with *less-lobed* lvs. nE, sF; Pyrenees and northern Spain.

5 ALPINE BRAYA *Braya alpina.* Low tufted, hairy per. Basal lvs lance-shaped, slightly toothed or untoothed, *stem lvs* one or few. Fls white or purplish, 4-6mm, in small clusters, petals *blunt-ended.* Fr broad-linear, 5-11mm, hairless. Dry rocky and stony places, usually on limestone, 2000-3000m. July-Aug. CH, I, wYU. **5a** *B. linearis* is taller with the lower lvs linear. Gravels on calcareous soils. N, S, except the far north. **5b** *B. purpurascens* usually has *no* stem lvs. IS, N.

6 ALPINE WOAD *Isatis allionii.* Short hairless or slightly hairy per. Lvs greyish, *clasping stem* at base, untoothed, stalkless. Fls yellow, 5-6mm, in branched clusters. Fr elliptical *brown,* 15-25mm, often notched at top. Stony places, to 2350m. July-Aug. eF, cI. **6a Woad** *I. tinctoria* is taller and bien, with smaller fls, 4mm; fr dark brown when ripe. Waste ground, grassy and rocky places, to 2000m. T, except IRL, IS.

TREACLE-MUSTARDS *Erysimum.* Anns or pers with branched hairs and narrow Lvs. Fls yellow in small elongated clusters, sepals upright. Fr a long linear pod.

7 WOOD TREACLE-MUSTARD *Erysimum sylvestre.* Short/med tufted, silver-grey, per. Lvs linear to narrow-lance-shaped, sometimes slightly toothed. Fls lemon-yellow, 12-16mm. Fr 40-90mm, grey-green with a short 1-2mm beak. Rocky, stony places and gravels to 1600m. May-Aug. A, nI, nwYU. **7a** *E. rhaeticum* (= *E. helveticum*) is greener; fr with a longer beak, 2-3mm. To 2800m. A, eF, CH, nI.

8 DECUMBENT TREACLE-MUSTARD *Erysimum humile* (= *E. decumbens; E. dubium, E. ochroleucum*). Short/med green or greyish per. Lvs oblong or narrow-lance-shaped, untoothed. Fls pale yellow, 14-20mm. Fr 35-80mm, grey-green, with a 2-6mm *beak.* Rocky and stony places, usually on limestone, to 2300m. May-June. CH, eF.

9 HAWKWEED-LEAVED TREACLE-MUSTARD *Erysimum hieracifolium* (= *E. strictum, E. marschallianum*). Med/tall green or greyish bien/per. Lvs linear or oblong, margin wavy, *toothed.* Fls small yellow, 7-9mm, petals *hairy* on back. Fr 30-55mm, grey or greenish, beak short, 1-2mm. Woods, rocky and stony places, usually on limestone, to 1700m. May-Aug. T, except GB, IRL, IS and far north. **9a** *E. virgatum* has narrower *untoothed* lvs; *larger* fls, 10-12mm. A, CH, D, nI, nwYU.

10 HOARY TREACLE-MUSTARD *Erysimum incanum.* Short/med grey-green *annual.* Basal lvs pinnately-lobed, upper lance-shaped. Fls very small yellow, 3-4mm, petals hairy on back. Fr 30-55mm. grey. Rocky and stony places, to 1800m. n & cE, sF; Pyrenees to central Spain.

Cress Family (contd.)

1 ALPINE DAME'S VIOLET *Hesperis inodora.* Med/tall downy-white bien/per. Lvs lance-shaped, coarsely toothed, the upper ones *half-clasping* the stem. Fls white, 15-25mm, in loose branched racemes, *not* fragrant. Fr long, linear, to 100mm. Rocky and waste places, to 1500m. May-July. seF; Maritime Alps.

2 DAME'S VIOLET *Hesperis matronalis.* Med/tall *hairy* green bien/per. Lvs lance-shaped, lobed and toothed, the upper short-stalked or unstalked, *not* clasping. Fls violet-purple, 15-20mm, very fragrant. Pod long, linear, to 100mm, curving upwards. Rocky and waste places, roadsides, hedges, to 1400m. May-Aug. T (B, CH, D, DK, GB, IRL, N, IS, NL, S, SF). 2a *H.m.* subsp. *candida* has *white* fls. A, CH, CS, sD, nE, sF, R, wYU. **2b** *H. laciniata* has more deeply lobed lower lvs and *yellow fls* suffused with purple. To 1500m. E, sF, I, YU.

3 SAD STOCK *Matthiola fruticulosa* (= *M. tristis*). Short/med slightly to *densely white hairy*, per. Lvs linear or oblong, untoothed, wavy-margined or lobed. Fls purple-red, occasionally yellow, 15-25mm, in loose spikes. Fr linear, 25-120mm. Rocky places, often on limestone, to 2000m. May-Aug. CH, s & eF, I, YU.

BITTERCRESSES *Cardamine.* Annuals or perennials with simple or pinnate lvs. Fls white or purple, rarely pale yellow; inner two sepals slightly pouched at base. Stigma slightly two-lobed. Fr a linear pod. Petal length includes the 'claw'.

4 SEVEN-LEAFLET BITTERCRESS *Cardamine* (= *Dentaria*) *heptaphylla.* Short/med per. Lvs pinnate with 3-5 pairs of narrow toothed leaflets, slightly hairy. Fls white, pink or purplish, in a loose raceme, petals 14-20mm long. Woods, particularly of Beech, to 1800m May-July.CH, sD, sF, E, I. **4a** *C. pentaphyllos* (= *Dentaria pentaphyllos*)* has *palm-like* lvs with 3-5 leaflets, and rather larger fls. Woods and rocky places, to 2200m. A, CH, D, c & eF, E, I, wYU.

5 KITAIBEL'S BITTERCRESS *Cardamine kitaibelii.* Short/med hairless per. Lvs *pinnate* with 2-6 pairs of lance-shaped, toothed lflets. Fls *pale yellow,* in loose racemes; petals 12-16mm. Woods, to 1900m. Apr.-June. CH, I, wYU.

6 DROOPING BITTERCRESS *Cardamine* (= *Dentaria*) *enneaphyllos.* Short hairless per. Lvs trifoliate, in a whorl of two to four, leaflets oval-lance-shaped, toothed. Fls pale yellow or white in a drooping cluster; petals 12-1 6mm. Woods, to 2150m. Apr-July. A-except France and Switzerland. A, CS, sD, H, I, PL, RM, YU.

7 TRIFOLIATE BITTERCRESS *Cardamine trifolia.* Short, slightly hairy, per. Lvs mostly *basal, trifoliate,* leaflets rounded or oblong, slightly lobed, purplish beneath. Fls white or pink, with yellow anthers; petals 9-11mm. Moist woods and shady places, often on limestone, to 1400m. Apr-June. A, CH, CS, D, F, H, I, PL, YU.

8 ASARUM-LEAVED BITTERCRESS *Cardamine asarifolia.* Short/med hairless per. Lvs *kidney-shaped,* slightly toothed, long stalked, the upper sometimes trifoliate. Fls white with violet anthers; petals 6-10mm. Damp pastures and stream sides, to 2000m. July-Aug. CH, nE, s & eF, n & cI.

9 LARGE BITTERCRESS *Cardamine amara.* Short/med slightly hairy per, basal lvs *not* in a rosette. Lvs pinnate with 1-5 (-7) pairs of oval, toothed, leaflets. Fls white, rarely purplish, with violet anthers; petals 7-9mm. Damp pastures and woods, stream sides, to 2000m. Apr-June. T, except IS and far north. 9a *C. a.* subsp. *opizii* (= *C. opizii*) has 5-9 *pairs* of leaflets and smaller fls. A, CH, sD, nI, wYU.

10 RADISH-LEAVED BITTERCRESS *Cardamine raphanifolia.* Med/tall hairless per with a basal rosette. Lvs pinnate with 1-5 pairs of rounded leaflets; upper lvs *with narrow* leaflets. Fls reddish-violet, rarely white, with yellow anthers; petals 8-12mm. Damp pastures and stream sides, to 2500m. May-July. E, s & eF, I, YU.

4a

Cress Family (contd.)

1 CUCKOO FLOWER or LADY'S SMOCK *Cardamine pratensis.* Med hairless per, with basal lvs forming a rosette. Lvs pinnate with 1-7 pairs of leaflets, stem lvs dissimilar from basal. Fls white tinged with violet or pink, anthers yellow; petals 8-13mm, slightly notched. Damp pastures and woods, stream sides, to 2600m. Apr-July. T, except IS. **1a** *C. p.* subsp. *crassifolia* is smaller, without a distinct lf rosette; fls purplish, petals 8-13mm; lvs with 1-3 pairs of leaflets. nE, sF; Pyrenees. **1b Coral-root Bittercress** *C. bulbifera* has small brownish-purple *bulbils* at base of upper lvs. Rarely above 1500m. T, except IS, NL, IRL .

2 IVY-LEAVED BITTERCRESS *Cardamine plumieri.* Low/short slightly hairy bien/per. Lower lvs ivy-like with 3-5 lobes, upper pinnate. Fls white, petals 6-8mm, often slightly notched. Damp rocky places, to 2200m. June-Aug. seF, I.

3 MIGNONETTE-LEAVED BITTERCRESS *Cardamine resedifolia.* Low/short hairless per. Lower lvs *spoon-shaped,* some above trifoliate, the upper with 3-7 lobes. Fls white, petals 5-8mm. Damp rocky places, to 3500m. June-Aug. A, CH, CS, E, c, s & eF, I, PL, R, YU.

4 ALPINE BITTERCRESS *Cardamine bellidifolia.* Low hairless per. Lvs mostly in a basal rosette, *all spoon-shaped,* untoothed. Fls white in clusters of 2-5, petals 3. 5-5mm. Fr purplish-brown. Damp meadows and gravels, usually on acid soils, to 2100m. July-Aug. N, S, SF. **4a** *C.b.* subsp. *alpina* has 2-3 stem lvs and shorter brown fr. To 3000m. A, CH, sD, E, F, nl.

5 TALL ROCKCRESS *Cardaminopsis arenosa.* Low/tall slightly hairy ann/per. Lvs *pinnately lobed,* the upper ones narrower, toothed. Fls white, becoming pink or lilac, 8-10mm, in loose racemes. Fr linear 10-45mm long, strongly flattened. Sandy soils, usually calcareous, to 1400m. Apr-June. T, except GB, IRL, IS and far north. **5a** *C. petraea* is smaller with the upper lvs untoothed. A, CS, D, GB, IRL, IS, I, N, PL, R, S. **5b** *C. halleri** like 5a but basal lvs *simple or pinnate* with rounded leaflets. A, CH, CS, c & sF, sD, I, PL, R, YU (B).

6 PERENNIAL HONESTY *Lunaria rediviva.* Tall roughly-hairy per, branched. Lvs oval, pointed, sharply toothed, the upper stalked. Fls pale purple to violet, 15-20mm, *fragrant.* Fr elliptical, 4-9cm, very flattened, pointed at both ends, splitting to leave a shiny silvery membrane. Damp woods and shady places, often on calcareous soils, to 1400m. May-July. A, B, CH, CS, D, DK, E, H, I, PL, R, S, YU.(T).

7 HONESTY *Lunaria annua* Hairy bien forming a lax leaf rosette in the first season, elongating in the second. Lvs deep green, oval to lance-shaped or heart-shaped, the lower stalked, the upper short-stalked or unstalked; margin toothed. Fls purple, occasionally pink or white, 20-30mm, borne in simple or branched racemes. Fr large and conspicuous, round or oval, 2-7cm with more rounded frs, splitting to leave a shiny silvery membrane. Introduced in many areas, but seldom exceeding 1200m. I, YU, R (naturalised T except IRL, IS, DK).

ROCKCRESSES *Arabis.* Annuals or perennials with undivided lvs, often in basal rosettes and with few stem lvs. Fls white or pinkish, the inner *2* sepals often pouched at the base. Fr a long, parallel-sided, rather flattened pod.

8 BLUE ARABIS *Arabis caerulea.* Low/short tufted, hairy or hairless, per. Lvs oval, broadest above middle, toothed at apex, stalked. Fls pale blue 5-6mm, in small clusters. Damp rocks and moraines, on limestone, to 3500m. July-Aug. A, CH, sD, F, nI, nwYU.

Cress Family *(contd.)*

1 HAIRY ROCKCRESS *Arabis hirsuta.* Low/med hairy bien/per; stems rather stiff, branched above. Basal lvs in a rosette, oval, only slightly toothed, *tapered* to the base; stem lvs smaller, oval to lance-shaped, *clasping* the stem. Fls white, 3-4.5mm, numerous. Pod slender, erect, 15-35mm, closely pressed to the stem. Wet or dry calcareous rocks, to 2050m. May-Aug. T, except Faeroes and IS. **1a** A. *allionii* is shorter with *hairless* stems; fls 5-6mm. Wet rocks. A, CS, sD, seF, I, PL, YU. **1b** A. *brassica* (= A. *pauciflora*) is both hairless and glaucous; Pods spreading. A, B, CH, CS, D, E, F, I, Yu.

2 CORYMBOSE ROCKCRESS *Arabis ciliata.* (= A. *corymbiflora*). Low/short hairy bien/per; stems stiff, mostly unbranched. Basal lvs in a rosette, oval, broadest above the middle, toothed; stem lvs oval to elliptical, *rounded* at base. Fls white, 3-5mm, in *compact* clusters. Pod slender 12-22mm, erect. Rocky slopes and gravels, to 2700m. May-July. **2a** A. *serpyllifolia** has the lower lvs long-stalked; stems and lvs bear starry hairs. A, CH, CS, sD, nE, s & eF, I, PI, R, YU (DK).

3 COMPACT ROCKCRESS *Arabis vochinensis.* Low tufted per with branched hairs. Basal lvs in compact rosettes, oblong, broadest above the middle, blunt, *untoothed;* stem lvs oblong, narrowed at the base. Fls white, 6-8mm, in lax clusters. Pod 8-15mm long. Rocky places, to 2200m. eA, nel, nwYU; south-east Alps.

4 ANNUAL ROCKCRESS *Arabis recta.* Short hairy ann. Lvs oval to oblong, untoothed, the lowermost stalked and withered at flowering time; stem lvs clasping the stem, *arrow-shaped* at base. Fls tiny, white, 3-4mm, petals *erect.* Pod slender, 10-35mm, less than 1 mm wide. Rocky places, to 1500m. Apr-June. T, except DK, GB, IRL, IS, N, S, SF (B). **4a** A. *nova* is taller, often bien, fls 4-5mm; pod 25-70mm, *over* 1mm wide. A, CH, nE, s & eF, nI, nwYU. **4b Towercress** A. *turrita** is a med softly hairy biennial/per often with reddish stem and *very long pods,* all *twisted* to one side and curving downwards, 80-140mm long. T, except DK, IRL, IS, N, NL, S, SF (GB).

5 SCOPOLI'S ROCKCRESS *Arabis scopoliana.* Low tufted per, *hairless except* on lf edges. Lvs oval or oblong, broadest above the middle, *narrowed* into the stalk, untoothed, mostly in basal rosettes. Fls white, 7-11mm, in compact clusters. Pod short, 6-10mm. Rock crevices and screes, to 2200m. May-July. nwYU; Slovenian Alps, possibly in Italian Alps.

6 BRISTOL ROCKCRESS *Arabis scabra* (= A. *stricta*). Low/short, rather horny-stemmed, tufted per. Lvs mostly in basal rosettes, oblong, toothed and stalked, thick, *glossy dark green* above. Fls *cream,* 4-8mm. Pod slender, 35-50mm long. Dry grassy and rocky places, to 1400m. Mar-May. wCH, swGB (rare), nE, s & seF.

7 DWARF ROCKCRESS *Arabis pumila.* Low/short tufted, hairy per. Lvs *mostly* in basal rosettes, oval, broadest above the middle, narrowed into the stalk, with several teeth or untoothed. Fls white, 6-7mm, in small clusters. Pod slender, 20-40mm. Damp rocky places, gravels, to 2850m. June-July. A, CH, sD, eF, I, nwYU; Alps and Apennines.

8 SOYER'S ROCKCRESS *Arabis soyeri.* Short/med *almost hairless* tufted per. Lvs mostly in basal rosettes, *glossy* dark green above, oval, broadest above the middle, stalked and finely toothed; stem lvs clasping. Fls white, 5-7mm, in small clusters. Pod slender, 25-50mm. Damp places on calcareous soils, 1800-2800m. June-Aug. nE, sF; Pyrenees. **8a** A.s. subsp. *coriacea* (A. *jacquinii*) has stem lvs *not* clasping. A, CH, sD, eF, nI, PL, R, YU; Alps and western Carpathians.

9 ALPINE ROCKCRESS *Arabis alpina.* Low/med somewhat creeping, mat-forming, starry-haired, grey-green per. Basal lvs oblong, deeply *toothed,* stalked, the stem lvs clasping, unstalked. Fls white, 8-10mm, in loose clusters, with spreading petals. Pod 20-35mm. Damp rocks and gravels, streamsides, often on calcareous soils, to 3000m. Apr-Aug. T, except IRL, NL (B).

10 CEVENNE ROCKCRESS *Arabis cebennensis.* Med/tall hairy per, stems branched in the upper half. Lvs oval, coarsely toothed, stalked. Fls pale or deep violet, sometimes white, 7-10mm. Pod long, 30-45mm. Rocky places, to 1550m. May-July. sF; especially the Cevenne. **10a** A. *pedemontana* is short, *smaller* in all its parts and almost hairless; fls always white, 6-7mm. nwI; Cozie Alps. Both species very close to *Cardaminopsis.*

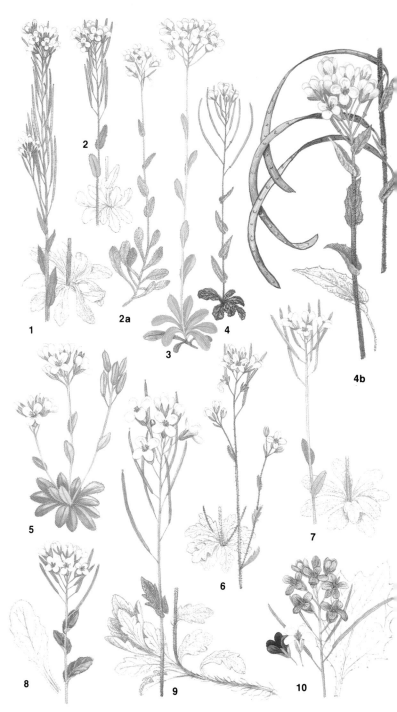

Cress Family (contd.)

ALYSSUMS *Alyssum.* Perennials with star-shaped hairs and untoothed lvs. Fls yellow in compact clusters, sometimes elongating in fruit. Fr oblong or rounded, somewhat inflated, with a persisting style.

1 ALYSSOIDES *Alyssoides utriculata.* Short/med starry-haired per, with a woody stock and *rosettes of lvs.* Lvs oblong-spoon-shaped, stalked except on stems, untoothed. Fls yellow, 8-14mm. Fr rounded, inflated, long beaked. Rocks and crevices, to 1500m. Apr-June. eF, I, R, YU.

2 WULFEN'S ALYSSUM *Alyssum wulfenianum.* Low/short prostrate or semierect, grey or *whitish* per. Lvs oval-oblong, untoothed, starry-haired. Fls yellow, 5-7mm, in rounded clusters. *Fr elliptical, inflated,* long beaked. Dry rocky places, to 2000m. June-Aug. A, nl, wYU; south-eastern Alps. **2a** *A. ovirense* is greener with more rounded lvs and hairy-backed petals. To 2700m. A, nl, wYU; south-eastern Alps.

3 MOUNTAIN ALYSSUM *Alyssum montanum* (= *A. thessalum*). Low/short prostrate or semierect, *often whitish,* per. Lvs oblong or spoon-shaped, starry-haired, the upper narrower. Fls yellow, 5mm, in elongated clusters; petals *notched.* Fr rounded, inflated, long beaked. Rocky places and gravels, to 2500m. May-July. A, CH, CS, D, E, F, H, I, PL, R, YU.

4 PYRENEAN ALYSSUM *Alyssum pyrenaicum* (= *Ptilotrichum pyrenaicum*). Low/short *silvery,* cushion-forming, sub-shrub. Lvs oval-lance-shaped, narrowed at base, untoothed. Fls white, 5-7mm, in dense rounded clusters. Fr oval, flattened, hairy, long-beaked. Limestone cliffs, to 1500m. June-July. sF; eastern Pyrenees. **4a** *A. laeprousianum* (= *Ptilotrichum lapeyrousianum*) has hairless, short beaked, frs borne in lax racemes. neE, sF; eastern Pyrenees. **4b** *A. ligusticum* is like 4a but frs in dense compact racemes. seF, nwl.

5 DIFFUSE ALYSSUM *Alyssum diffusum.* Low loosely tufted, grey-green per with straggling non-flowering leafy stems. Lvs oval to elliptical, often broadest above the middle, the upper lvs narrower. Fls mid-yellow, 5-7mm, in clusters greatly elongating in fr, petals *slightly notched.* Pod rounded, 4-6mm. Rocky and stony places, to 2400m. May-July. E, s & seF, I. **5a** *A. cuneifolium* is more closely tufted with *grey or whitish* stems and lvs. Fl clusters short and compact. Pod more elliptical, grey-hairy.neE, sF, I.

6 ITALIAN ALYSSUM *Alyssum argenteum.* Short/med erect hairy per *with* long non-flowering leafy shoots. Lvs elliptical, broadest above the middle, greenish above, grey beneath, the basal lvs *much smaller.* Fls yellow, 3-5mm, in loose clusters. Pod oblong, 3.5-6mm, hairy. Rocky places, to 1250m. June-July. nw I; south-western Alps.

7 ALPINE ALYSSUM *Alyssum alpestre.* Low spreading *whitish* or sometimes grey-hairy per, with numerous non-flowering Leafy rosettes. Lvs elliptical, broadest above the middle or spoon-shaped. Fls yellow, 3-4mm, in loose clusters. Pod elliptical, 2.5-4.5 mm, *rather* assymetrical. Grassy and rocky places, 1500-3100m. June-Aug. CH, eF, I; south-western and central Alps. **7a** *A. serpyllifolium* has *larger* lvs and smaller, *2-3* mm, fls. Pod broader. E, sF; Pyrenees and Spain.

8 SHEPHERD'S PURSE *Capsella bursa-pastoris.* Very variable low/med ann/bien, hairy or hairless. Lvs mostly in a basal rosette, lance-shaped, pinnately-lobed, toothed or not; upper lvs clasping the stem. Fls white, 2-3mm, in lax racemes, petals *twice* as long as the green sepals. Pod small, *triangular heart-shaped,* 6-9mm long. Fields and waste places, a frequent weed, to 2000m. Flowering most of the year except at higher altitudes. T. **8a** *C. rubella* has *reddish* tinged petals E, F, GB, I, YU (A, D, CH).

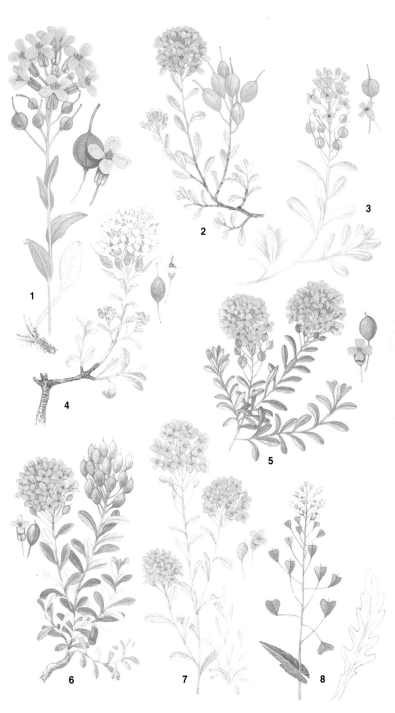

1

2

3

4

5

6

7

8

Cress Family (contd.)

WHITLOW-GRASSES *Draba*. Low tufted perennials, sometimes annual. Lvs toothed or untoothed, margins sometimes with stiff bristles. Fls rather small in loose upright racemes or small clusters, yellow or white. Fr a round or elliptical-oblong pod with a short beak.

1 YELLOW WHITLOW-GRASS *Draba azoides*. Low tufted hairless per, with lfless stems. Lvs linear-elliptical in rosettes, margin bristly. Fls yellow 45mm, clustered at end of 5-15cm long stems, petals oblong, *blunt*. Fr elliptical, with a l.5-3mm *beak*. Rocky and stony places, usually on limestone, to 3600m. Apr-July. T, except DK, IRL, IS, N, S, SF; in GB confined to south-west Wales. **1a** *D. hoppeana* is dwarfer, the fr beak only 1mm long, 2200-3600m. July-Aug. A, CH, sD, eF, I. **1b** *D. aspera** is like 1 but lvs *not more* than 1mm broad and fr beak longer, 3.5-7mm. sF, c & sI, YU. **1c** *D. alpina* like 1 but lvs broader, oval-lance-shaped, *slightly* hairy, hairs branched. To 1650m. July. IS, N, S, SF.

2 WOOLLY-FRUITED WHITLOW-GRASS *Draba lasiocarpa*. More robust than 1 with lfless stems to 20cm. Lvs oblong, pointed, 3-4mm broad, margin bristly. Fls deep yellow, petals *rounded*. Fr oblong with a short beak 1-1.5mm. Rocky and stony places, to 2000m. A, CS, H, R, YU.

3 SAUTER'S WHITLOW-GRASS *Draba sauteri*. Low per, forming loose cushions. Lvs linear or narrow lance-shaped, in rosettes, margin bristly. Fls yellow, clustered on *short* lfless 1-3cm long stems. Fr short-oblong, beak 0.5mm. Limestone rocks and gravels, 1900-2900m. July-Aug. A, seD; north-east Alps.

4 ENGADINE WHITLOW-GRASS *Draba ladina*. Low tufted per, slightly hairy. Lvs lance-shaped or elliptical, *covered in* star shaped hairs, margin slightly bristly. Fls pale yellow, in small clusters, on leafless stems 1-5cm long. Fr oblong, beak 1 mm. Limestone rocks, 2600-3050m. July-Aug. eCH; centred on the Engadine.

5 STARRY WHITLOW-GRASS *Draba stellata*. Low tufted, starry-haired, per; stems leafy. Lvs oval, broadest above middle; stem lvs one or two, often toothed. Fls white or cream, clustered. Fr elliptical, beak 1-2mm. Limestone rocks, to 2500m. June-Aug. A; north-east Alps.

6 CARINTHIAN WHITLOW-GRASS *Draba siliquosa* (= *D. carinthiaca*). Low/short starry-haired per, forming loose cushions, stem leafy. Lvs lance-shaped, margin bristly at base. Fls white, clustered. Fr narrow-oblong, erect, hairless, *unbeaked*. Rocks and screes, usually on limestone, 1500-3600m. June-Aug. A, CH, CS, sD, nE, s & eF, I, R. **6a** *D. norvegica* often has one fl at the base of the inflorescence; fr often hairy, *spreading*. neA, Faeroes, nGB, IS, N, S, SF.

7 AUSTRIAN WHITLOW-GRASS *Draba dubia*. Low/short starry-haired per, stems usually lfy. Lvs narrow oval, all untoothed. Fls white, in small clusters. Fr oblong-elliptical, hairless, beak short, 0.5mm. Rocks and screes, 1300-3200m. May-July. A, CH, CS, D, E, F, I, PL, YU; only in west Carpathians. **7a** *D. kotschyi* is laxer with broad oval lvs, the *upper* toothed. R; south and east Carpathians. **7b** *D. tomentosa* like 7 but stems and fr *starry-hairy*. Limestone rocks and screes, to 3500m. June-Aug. A, CH, CS, sD, eF, I, PL, YU.

8 BALD WHITE WHITLOW-GRASS *Draba fladnizensis* (= *D. wahlenbergii*). Low tufted per, *stems leafless*, hairless. Lvs oblong-oval, margin bristly. Fls white, in small clusters. Fr elliptical, beak short, 0.5mm. Rocky and grassy slopes, prefering acid soils, 1600-3400m. June-Aug. A, CH, CS, D, F, I, IS, N, R, SF. **8a** *D. dorneri* has basal lvs *acutely* tipped and hairless above except for the margins. R; southern Carpathians.

9 TWISTED WHITLOW-GRASS *Draba incana*. Short erect hairy bien, stems leafy. Lvs lance-shaped, blunt, sometimes toothed, *short-stalked*. Fls white, 3-4mm, in loose clusters, *petals notched*. Fr oblong-lance-shaped, *twisted*. Rocky and stony places, usually on limestone, to 2600m. May-July. A, CH, DK, E, F, nGB, IRL, IS, N, SF. **9a** *D. nivalis* is sometimes per with pale bluish-green lvs; stems *usually lfless*. Fls creamy white. To 1920m. June. IS, N, S, SF.

10 WALL WHITLOW-GRASS *Draba muralis*. Short, slightly hairy, ann; stems erect, leafy. Lvs broad-oval, upper partly-clasping the stem. Fls tiny, white, 2mm, petals notched. Fr oblong-elliptical, hairless. Rocks and walls, to 1300m. Apr-June. T, except Faeroes and IS; often casual. **10a** *D. nemorosa* has *pale yellow* fls and hairy fr. T-except B, DK, GB, IRL, IS, NL.

Cress Family (contd.)

1 SPRING WHITLOW-GRASS *Erophila* (=*Draba*) *verna*. Variable low/short, slightly hairy ann, stems lfless. Lvs lance-shaped or elliptic, sometimes toothed, in a basal rosette. Fls white or pinkish, 3-5mm, petals *cleft to* middle. Fr elliptical, 5-10mm, on long stalks. Waste places, sandy or stony ground, to 1700m. Mar-May. T, except Faeroes. **1a** *E. v.* subsp. *spathulata* has fr broader and not more than 5mm long. Similar distribution.

2 PYRENEAN WHITLOW-GRASS *Petrocallis* (=*Draba*) *pyrenaica*. Low densely tufted, greyish~hairy, per. Lvs wedge-shaped, lobed at tip, bristle margined. Stems lfless. Fls pale lilac or pink, rarely white, 6-7mm, petals *rounded,* in small clusters. Limestone rocks and screes, 1700-2900m. June-Aug. A, CH, CS, sD, nE, s & eF, I, ?R, YU.

3 COMMON SCURVY-GRASS *Cochlearia officinalis* subsp. *pyrenaica.* Variable short/med, hairless, bien or per. Lvs heart- or kidney-shaped, slightly *fleshy,* lower long stalked and in a rosette, upper *clasping* the stem. Fls white, 8-10mm, in loose clusters. Fr elliptical or oval in outline, 3-7mm. Dry banks, grassy and stony places, to 2200m. Apr-Aug. T, A, B, CH, CS, D, DK, E, F, N, NL, PL, R, S. **3a** *C. o.* subsp. *scotica* is low, rarely more than 10cm tall and often with pale lilac fls; fr 2.5-3.5mm. Rocks and wet flushes. n & swGB, n & wIRL; in GB confined to Scotland and Scilly Isles. **3b** *C. tatrae* has oval or heart-shaped basal lvs and *pale yellow* fls. Granitic rocks. CS, PL; western Carpathians. **3c** *C. aragonenesis* has upper stem lvs *linear,* not oval or oblong and white or violet fls; fr narrow elliptical. Limestone rocks. neE.

4 KERNERA *Kernera saxatilis.* Variable low/short hairless per, usually branched. Basal lvs lance or spoon-shaped, toothed or not, stalked, in a rosette; upper lvs oval, often half~clasping the stem. Fls white, 3-5mm, many in racemes, petals rounded. Fr rounded. Rocky and grassy places on limestone, to 2000m. A, CH, CS, D, E, F, I, PL, R, YU.

5 ALPINE SCURVY-GRASS *Rhizobotrya* (= *Kernera*) *alpina.* Rather like a compact form of 3. Low cushion per with short stems. Lvs oblong-spoon-shaped, blunt, long-stalked. Fls tiny, white, 2mm, each with a small bract at base of fl stalk, borne in tight clusters. Fr oval. Dolomitic rocks, 1900-2800m. neI; Dolomites.

6 CHAMOIS CRESS *Pritzelago* (= *Hutchinsia*) *alpina.* Low tufted per; stems lfless, hairy. Lvs *pinnate,* hairless, shiny. Fls white, 4-5mm, petals rounded, in small clusters. Fr 4-6mm, oval, pointed. Limestone rocks and screes, to 3400m. May-Aug. A, CH, sD, nE, s & eF, I, PL, R, YU. **6a** *P. a.* subsp. *brevicaulis* has *hairless* stems, smaller fls and blunt-ended, 3.5-4mm, fr. Basic or acid rocks. A, CH, eF, nI, YU. **6b** *P. a.* subsp. *auerswaldii* has flexuous and *leafy* flowering stems. nE; Cordillera Cantabrica.

7 HYMENOLOBUS *Hymenolobus pauciflorus.* Low, slender, slightly hairy ann or bien. Lvs spoon-shaped, *3-lobed* or *unlobed.* Fls tiny, white, 2-3mm, in loose clusters. Fr 2-4mm, rounded or elliptical in outline. Rocky and stony places, waste ground, to 1600m. May-Aug. A, CH, , eE, c & eF, I.

8 AETHIONEMA *Aethionema saxatile.* Low/short hairless ann or per, branched. Lower lvs oval or oblong, blunt, *untoothed,* the upper narrower and pointed. Fls white, purplish or lilac, 3-5mm, in small clusters, petals rounded, 1.8-3.2mm. Fr 5-9mm, rounded, *winged.* Rocks and screes, usually limestone, to 2300m. Apr-July. CH, CS, D, E, F, H, I, R, YU. **8a** *A. s.* subsp. *ovalifolium* has larger fls with the sepals at least 1.7mm long and petals 3-5mm. Limestone cliffs. E, swF. **8b** *A. thomasianum* is more compact with very crowded racemes; fr 10-12mm. Rocky slopes, often on Schist. nwI; Aosta Valley.

2

Cress Family (contd.)

PENNYCRESSES *Thlaspi*. Perennials or biennials, rarely annual, Stem lvs usually clasping. Fls in rounded clusters, elongating in fruit. Fr heart-shaped, flattened usually winged.

1 SMALL-FLOWERED PENNYCRESS *Thlaspi brachypetalum*. Short/med hairless, bluish green, bien. Lvs elliptical or oblong, toothed or untoothed; basal ones in a rosette, stalked. fls white, 3-5mm, petals equal in length to sepals; anthers *whitish*. Woods and pastures, usually on acid soils, to 2000m. Apr-July. CH, nE, s & eF, nI. **1a** *T. caerulescens* has petals longer than sepals and reddish or dark violet *anthers*. T, except IRL (DK, IS, N, S, SF). **1b** *T. dacicum* has petals markedly longer than the sepals and anthers *yellow*. R; eastern and southern Carpathians. **1c** *T. stenopterum* is like 1b but with narrowly winged fr. n & cE.

2 APENNEAN PENNYCRESS *Thlaspi stylosum*. Very low cushion-forming per. Lvs mostly in basal rosettes, elliptical-spoon-shaped, untoothed, fleshy. Fls *purplish*, 8mm; anthers violet. Rocks and screes, to 2000m. Apr-June, c & sI; central and southern Apennines.

3 EARLY PENNYCRESS *Thlaspi praecox*. Short, hairless, greyish-green, per; more or less cushion-forming. Lvs oblong or oval, toothed or not, often *violet beneath*. Fls white, 7-9mm; sepals usually violet-tipped, Grassy and stony places, shaded limestone rocks, to 2250m. Mar-May. A, eF, I, YU. **3a** *T. goesingense* is a larger, greyer plant; fl stems *often* branched. A, H, YU.

4 MOUNTAIN PENNYCRESS *Thlaspi montanum*. Short mat-forming, hairless, per with erect fl stems. Lvs oval or rounded, not or slightly toothed, greyish, the basal ones in rosettes, stalked. Fls white, 7-9mm; anthers pale yellow. Fr wings more than 1 mm wide, *notch deep*. Grassy and rocky places, screes and cliff ledges. June-Aug. A, B, CH, CS, D, eF, nI, YU.

5 ALPINE PENNYCRESS *Thlaspi alpinum*. Low/short, mat or cushion~forming, hairless, per. Lvs oval to oblong, blunt, untoothed, the basal ones in rosettes, stalked. Fls white, 7-9mm; anthers yellow. Fr wings less than 1 mm wide, *notch shallow*. Grassy and rocky places, screes, to 3000m. June-Aug. A, CH, eF, nI. **5a** *T. alpestre* (= *T. kerneri*) has *pointed* stem lvs and smaller fls. s & seA, nI, wYU; south-eastern Alps. **5b** *T. kovatsii* has smaller fls, the petals not more than 5mm long. R, neYU.

6 ROUND-LEAVED PENNYCRESS *Thlaspi cepaeifolium*. Variable low tufted, hairless, per with *long rooting runners*. Lvs rounded or oblong, fleshy, rarely toothed; basal ones not in rosettes. Fls pink, mauve or violet, 8-10mm, honey-scented. Fr 7-10mm, keeled, *not winged*. Rocks and screes, to 3000m. June-July. A, nI, nwYU; south-east Alps. **6a** *T.c.* subsp. *rotundifolium* is larger, *with* basal lf rosettes; lower lvs *opposite*. A, CH, eF, nI, YU.

CANDYTUFTS *Iberis*. Like Pennycresses but fls with upper two petals small and lower two large. Fr heart-shaped, flattened, winged.

7 SPOON-LEAVED CANDYTUFT *Iberis spathulata* (= *I. nana*). Low hairy per, sometimes ann. *Lvs fleshy*, spoon-shaped, generally untoothed. Fls purplish to white, in flat-topped clusters. Fr narrowly winged, 4-5mm. Rock crevices, screes and gravels, 1500-2800m. June-Aug. nE; eastern Pyrenees. **7a** *I. s.* subsp. *nana* (= *I. nana*) *is* hairless with *slightly* toothed lvs. nwI; Maritime Alps and Ligurian Apennines.

8 DAUPHINE CANDYTUFT *Iberis aurosica*. Low/short hairless per. Lvs rather fleshy, *narrow* oblong-spoon-shaped, sometimes with 1-2 teeth at tip. Fls purple or lilac, borne in flat-topped clusters. Rocks and gravels, usually on limestone, to 2600m. July-Aug. nE, seF; southern Pyrenees and south-west Alps.

9 ANNUAL CANDYTUFT *Iberis stricta*. Med hairless ann, stems slender, branched. Lvs linear, pointed, toothed. Fls small pink to lilac, in flat-topped clusters. Fr oval, 3-5mm. Calcareous soils and rocks to 1300m. June-Aug. seF; Haute Alps. **9a** *I.s.* subsp. *leptophylla* has more or less untoothed lvs and rounded frs. seF, nwI; south-west Alps and Ligurian Apennines. **9b** *I. amara* has lvs *pinnately lobed* and flowers white, pink or purple. Dry slopes and arable land. B, CH, E, F, sD, sGB, NL, I (A, CS, H, PL, R).

10 ALPINE CABBAGE *Brassica repanda*. Very variable short/med hairless per, forming small tufts. Lvs all basal, spoon-shaped or oval, toothed or pinnately lobed. fls yellow, 8-15mm, in clusters of 2-12. Fr linear, narrowing into the beak, to 5cm long. Rocky and gravelly places, to 2500m. Apr-Aug. E, s & seF, I. **10a** *B. gravinae* has *leafy* stems and smaller fls, 8-12mm. c & sI; Apennines.

Cress Family *(contd.)*

1 BUCKLER MUSTARD Biscutella laevigata. Variable short/med bristly-hairy, sometimes hairless, per. Lvs mostly in a basal tuft, lance-shaped, lobed or toothed, occasionally entire, stalked; stem lvs narrow-lance-shaped, untoothed. Fls yellow, 5-10mm, in branched clusters. Fr flattened, with *two rounded* lobes and a thin beak in between. Grassy and rocky places, open woods, to 2600m. May-Aug. A, B, CH, CS, E, F, H, I, PL, YU. **1a** *B. brevicaulis* is a smaller plant rarely more than 20cm tall with fr 6-9mm wide, not 9-12mm. seF, nwI; south-west Alps.

2 SCAPOSE BUCKLER MUSTARD *Biscutella scaposa.* Med hairy per, stems branched or not. Lvs in a basal tuft, lance or spoon-shaped, lobed or more, lobed and toothed; stem lvs *tiny or absent.* Fls yellow, 5mm. Fr as 1. Grassy and rocky places, to 1600m. May-July. c & nwE, sF. **2a** *P. flexuosa* has flexuous stems and *semi-clasping* stem lvs. nE, sF; central and eastern Pyrenees.

3 ROSETTED BUCKLER MUSTARD *Biscutella brevifolia.* Short, slightly hairy, per. Lvs in a *dense basal rosette,* oblong-lance-shaped, 1-5cm long, pinnately-lobed usually, blunt-tipped. Fls yellow, 5-6mm. Fr as 1. Rocky places to 1600m. May-July. nE, sF; central Pyrenees. **3a** *B. intermedia* has *broader,* scarcely lobed, lvs. n & cE, sF.

4 CHICORY-LEAVED BUCKLER MUSTARD *Biscutella cichoriifolia.* Med hairy per. Lvs mostly in a basal tuft, oblong, lobed and toothed, long-stalked; stem lvs *clasping.* Fls yellow *larger* than 1-3, 12-20mm, in dense clusters, elongating in fr. Fr as 1. Rocky and dry places, to 1800m. May-July. CH, E, s & eF, I, YU.

5 LEPIDIUM *Lepidium villarsii.* Short/med slightly hairy, grey-green, per. Lvs broadly elliptical, stalked, *untoothed,* the upper lvs more triangular, stalkless. Fls *white,* 4-6mm, anthers violet. Fr small, oblong, winged and notched at top. Mountain grassland, to 2500m. June-Aug. eF; French Alps. **5a** *L. v.* subsp. *reverchonii* has fr *narrowed* at the top into the style, rarely with a slight notch. neE.

6 COINCYA *Coincya richeri* (=*Brassicella* or *Rhynchosinapis richeri*). Med hairless, branched per. Lvs oblong, elliptical or spoon-shaped, toothed or not, long stalked. Fls yellow, 18-25mm, in dense *flat-topped* clusters, elongating in fr. Fr linear, more than 40mm, with a tapered beak. Grassy and rocky places, to 1750-2500m. June-Aug. seF, nwI; south-west Alps. **6a Wallflower Cabbage** *C. monensis* subsp. *recurvata* (= *Brassica* or *Rhynchosinapis cheiranthos*)* is *hairy* with pinnately-lobed lvs. Rocky, waste and dry places to 1500m. June-Aug. B, D, E, F, n & nwI (GB, NL).

Mignonette Family *Resedaceae*

Annuals or Perennials with alternate lvs. Fls tiny, in long spikes, with 4-8 sepals and petals; petals cut into narrow lobes; stamens numerous. Fr a capsule, open at top.

7 CORN MIGNONETTE *Reseda phyteuma.* Short/med downy ann or bien. Lvs spoon-shaped, often with 1-2 lobes on either side. Fls whitish, 5-7mm. Fr drooping. cultivated and waste ground, banks, to 1600m. June-Sept. CH, E, F, H, I, PL, R, YU (A, CS, S). **7a Wild Mignonette** *R. lutea* has 1-2-pinnate lvs and *yellow* fls; fr erect. To 2000m. T, except IS, N, S, SF. **7b Weld** *R. luteola* is hairless with *unlobed* lvs and yellowish-green fls. Fr erect. T, except IS, N; widely naturalised.

8 PYRENEAN MIGNONETTE *Reseda glauca.* Short/med tufted, hairless, per. Lvs *linear,* generally untoothed, bluish-green. Fls whitish, 6-7mm, in long loose spikes. Fr erect. Meadows and rocky places, screes, to 2500m. July-Aug. nE, sF; Pyrenees and Cordillera Cantabrica.

9 SESAMOIDES *Sesamoides clusii* (= *S. pygmaea, Reseda sesamoides*). Low/short hairless per with arched stems, forming small hummocks. Lvs lance-shaped, untoothed, the basal ones in dense rosettes. Fls whitish, 4-5mm, in long spikes. Fr *star-shaped.* Meadows, rocks and damp screes, to 2000m. May-Sept. n & nwE, c, s & eF, nwI. **9a** *S. purpurascens* (= *Reseda purpurascens*) forms laxer leaf-rosettes; calyx lobes triangular and stamens 10-15, not 7-12. E, sF, nwI

6a

Sundew Family Droseraceae

Insectivorous plants. Lvs in basal rosettes, covered in long sticky reddish hairs. Fls 5-6 parted, in long leafless spikes.

1 COMMON SUNDEW *Drosera rotundifolia*. Low per with solitary spreading rosettes. Lvs rounded, 5-8mm across, stalked. Fls white, 5mm, in 5-10-fld spikes. Peat or sphagnum bogs or moors, always acid, to 2000m. June-Aug. T.

2 LONG-LEAVED,SUNDEW *Drosera anglica*. Low/short per with solitary, *erect,* rosettes. Lvs *narrow oblong,* 20-30mm long, tapered at base into stalk. Fls white, 6mm, in 3-fld, long-stalked spikes. Bogs, moors and wet heaths, sometimes slightly calcareous, to 1900m. July-Aug. T, except southern Apennines. **2a** *D. intermedia** is similar, but rosettes *grouped* and lvs oblong, 7-8mm long, stalked; fl-spikes *short-stalked.* T, except IS and southern Apennines.

Stonecrop Family Crassulaceae

Succulent annuals or perennials with thick, generally untoothed, lvs. Fls usually starry, 5-parted or more; stamens alternating with petals or twice as many. Fr consisting of separate carpels, equal in number to the petals.

3 MUCIZONIA *Mucizonia sedoides*. Low *hairless ann*, forming dense tufts. Lvs alternate, oblong, 2-4mm, overlapping. Fls purplish pink, erect bells, 6-7mm, in crowded clusters; petals 5, *fused together* to the middle. Rocky places, gravels and screes on acid soils, 2000-3000m. June-Aug. E, sF.

HOUSELEEKS *Sempervivum*. Perennials with dense succulent leafy rosettes, forming mats by production of runners, stem lvs alternate. Fls 8-16 parted, starry with narrow pointed petals; stamens twice as many petals.

4 WULFEN'S HOUSELEEK *Sempervivum wulfenii*. Short per with rosettes 40-50mm across. Lvs oblong-spoon-shaped, hairy margined, otherwise hairless, bluish-green. Fls lemon-yellow, 20-22mm, petals with a *purple spot* at base. Rocky places, acid rocks usually, 1700-2700m. July-Aug. A, eCH, nI, wYU.

5 LARGE-FLOWERED HOUSELEEK *Sempervivum grandiflorum* (= *S. gaudinii*). Short per with flat rosettes 20-50mm across, smelling of resin. Lvs oblong, narrowed at base, *hairy all over*, dark green with a red-brown tip. Fls yellow, 20-36mm; petals with a purple spot at base. Acid rocks, to 2500m. July-Oct. sCH, nI. **5a** *S. pittonii* is smaller with grey-green rosettes, *not* resin-scented; fls greenish yellow. A; Steiermark.

6 COBWEB HOUSELEEK *Sempervivum arachnoideum*. Low mat-forming per. Rosettes small, 5-15mm, covered in a *cobweb* of whitish hairs. Fls reddish-pink, 14-18mm. Acid rocks, screes and alluvium, to 3100m. July-Sept. A, CH, sD, eF, nI. **6a** *S. a.* subsp. *tomentosum* has rosettes 15-25mm across. wCH, nE, s & eF.

7 MOUNTAIN HOUSELEEK *Sempervivum montanum*. Low mat or tuft-forming per. Rosettes small, 5-20mm, hairy, resin-scented. Lvs oval, broadest above the middle, *dull green*. Fls red-purple, 24-30mm. Acid rocks and screes, 1500-3200m. July-Aug. A, CH, CS, E, s & eF, I, PL, R (N). **7a** *S. m.* subsp. *burnatii* has *rosettes* 30-80mm across. wCH, eF, nwI; south-west Alps. **7b** *S. m.* subsp. *stiriacum* has rosettes 20-45mm across; *lvs red-tipped.* eA.

8 DOLOMITIC HOUSELEEK *Sempervivum dolomiticum*. Low tufted per with globular rosettes, 20-40mm. Lvs oblong-lance-shaped, pointed, *slightly hairy*, bright green with a brownish tip. Fls deep pink, 18-20mm; petals with a central red-brown stripe. Dolomitic and basal rocks, 1600-2500m. July-Sept. nel; south-east Alps including the Dolomites. **8a** *S. cantabricum* has larger dark green rosettes lvs, red tipped, and fls reddish-purple. nE; Cordillera Cantabrica.

9 COMMON HOUSELEEK *Sempervivum tectorum* (incl. *S. andreanum*). Variable short/med per with large flattened rosettes, 30-80mm across, blue-green tinged with red. Lvs oblong- lance-shaped, fine-pointed, *margin white-hairy,* otherwise hairless. Fls dull pink or purple, 18-20mm, in large clusters. Grassy and rocky places, screes. to 2800m. July-Oct. A, CH, sD, nE, s & eF, I, wYU (S).

10 LIMESTONE HOUSELEEK *Sempervivum calcareum*. Like 9 but lf-rosettes more globular and the lvs broader, *blue-green*, tipped with purple-brown. Fls pale pink, 14-16mm. Limestone rocks, to 1800m. July-Sept. seF, nwl; south-west Alps.

Stonecrop Family (contd.)

1 HEN-AND-CHICKENS HOUSELEEK Jovibarba globifera (= J. sobolifera). Low/short succulent per with short runners. Lvs in globular rosettes, incurving, hairy margined, otherwise hairless, greyish-green, red-tipped; stem lvs more pointed, overlapping. Fls narrow yellow bells, 15-17mm; petals 6, margin toothed. Sandy and grassy places, usually on acid soils, to 1500m. July-Sept. A, CH, CS, sD, E, F, H, I, PI, R, YU. **1a** J. g. subsp. allionii has pale yellowish-green, finely-hairy lvs and greenish white fls. Rocks and screes, to 2000m. seA, swCH, seF, nw and nel. **1b** J. g. subsp. arenaria like 1 but rosettes more open, bright green, the stem lvs narrower, long-pointed. To 1500m. A, nel, nwYU. **1c** J. g. subsp. hirta like 1, but rosettes dark green and more open, lvs not red-tipped. To 1900m. sA, E, I, YU.

STONECROPS Sedum. Fleshy perennials or annuals. Lvs usually alternate, rarely toothed, spaced along stem, not crowded into basal rosettes. Fls 5-8 parted, starry, in branched clusters. Fr usually 5-parted, thus distinguishing them from saxifrages.

2 ORPINE Sedum telephium. Variable short/tall, often red tinged per. Lvs large, up to 7cm, flattened, rounded to narrow-oblong, toothed. Fls purplish-red, yellowish-green on whitish, 8-10mm, in dense flattish clusters. Woods, rocks and shady places, to 1800m. July-Sept. T, except Faeroes and IS.

3 REDDISH STONECROP Sedum anacampseros. Short, hairless, rather sprawling, per. Lvs flattish, elliptical-oval, bluish-green, untoothed. Fls deep red inside, bluish-lilac outside, 8-9mm, in dense rounded clusters. Acid rocks, 1400-2500m. July-Aug. CH, nE, s & eF, I (N).

4 CREAMISH STONECROP Sedum ochroleucum (= S. anopetalum). Short/med per. Lvs linear-cylindrical, pointed, 8-20mm. Fls cream to greenish white, 12-14mm, 5-8-parted, erect in bud, in loose clusters; sepals hairy. Rocky places, walls and banks, to 2300m. June-July. E, sF, CH, I, R, YU. **4a** S.o. subsp. montanum has bright yellow 5-parted fls. A, sF, CH, nE, H, I, YU.

5 ROCK STONECROP Sedum rupestre (= S. reflexum). Like 4 but fl clusters drooping in bud. Fls yellow, usually 7-parted; sepals hairless. To 2000m. June-July. T, except IS and northern Scandinavia.

6 BITING STONECROP or WALLPEPPER Sedum acre. Low hairless, mat-forming, evergreen per. Lvs oval-cylindrical, blunt, 3-6mm. Fls bright yellow, 10-1 2mm, in clusters of 2-4. Rocky and sandy places, banks, to 2300m. June-July. T. **6a** S. sexangulare* has linear-cylindric lvs in 5-6 regular rows. T, except E, IRL, IS, N, S, SF (GB). **6b** S. urvillei (= S. sartorianum) has dead lvs persisting, whitish with a black tip. A, CS, H, R, YU. **6c** S. alpestre is dwarfer with lvs broadest above the middle; fls 6-7mm. A, CH, CS, D, E, F, I, PL, R, YU.

7 WHITE STONECROP Sedum album. Low/short, bright-green, often red-tinged, mat-forming per. Lvs cylindric, rather flattened above, 4-12mm. Fls white, 5-parted, 4-8mm, in loose, flat-topped clusters. Rocky places and walls, to 2500m. June-Aug. T, except Faeroes and IS (IRL).

8 ENGLISH STONECROP Sedum anglicum. Low mat-forming evergreen, greyish or reddish, hairless per. Lvs cylindrical-rounded, 3-5mm. Fls white or pink, 6-9mm, few to a cluster. Acid rocks and banks, to 1800m. June-Sept. E, F, GB, IRL, N, S.

9 THICK-LEAVED STONECROP Sedum dasyphyllum. Like 8 but smaller. Lvs mostly opposite, downy, often slightly sticky. Fls white, streaked with pink, 5-6mm. Acid rocks and walls and banks, to 2500m. June-Aug. A, CH, D, E, s & eF, I, R, YU (B, DK, GB, IRL, NL).

10 WHORLED-LEAVED STONECROP Sedum monregalense. Low/short downy stemmed per. Lvs cylindric-oblong, 6mm, opposite or in whorls of 4, hairless. Fls white, in loose clusters; petals with hairy mid-vein. Shady rocks, to 1200m. June. Aug. seF, I; south-west Alps and Apennines.

11 CHICKWEED STONECROP Sedum alsinifolium. Low hairy per. Lvs alternate, rhombic or spoon-shaped, rather thin, 10-15mm. Fls white, 8-10mm, in loose leafy clusters. Shady rocks and caves, to 1450m. June-Sept. nwl. **11a**. S. magellense is hairless, with racemes of fls, not branched. cl, YU; not Alps.

12 HAIRY STONECROP Sedum villosum. Low reddish, downy per, sometimes bien. Lvs alternate, narrow-oblong, flattened above, 4-7mm. Fls pink, 5-8mm, long-stalked, in loose clusters. Wet places, to 2450m. June-Aug. T, except B, DK, IRL, c & sl, NL.

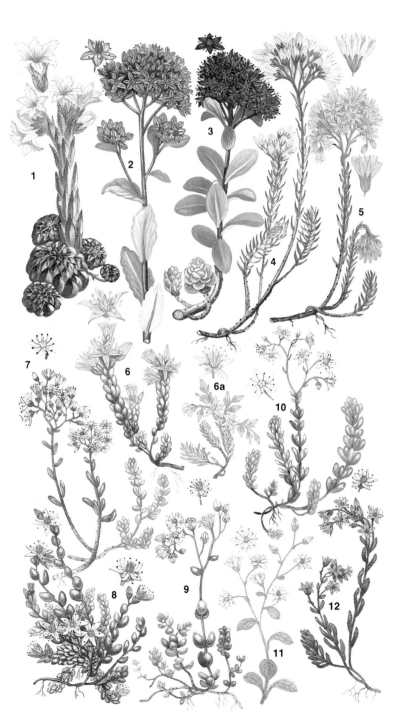

Stonecrop Family *(contd.)*

1 PINK STONECROP *Sedum cepaea. Short* hairy per/ann, stems thin. Lvs *opposite or whorled,* oblong to oblong-spoon-shaped, flat, lower stalked. Fls pale pink, 8-10mm, five-parted, in loose, branched clusters. Shady places, to 1250m. June-July. CH, E, s & eF, I, R, YU (D, NL).

2 DARK STONECROP *Sedum atratum.* Low hairless ann, stems erect, often reddish. Lvs alternate, oblong or club-shaped, often reddish. Fls cream, red-lined, five-six-parted, in dense *flat-topped* clusters. Rocky and stony places, often on limestone, to 3200m. June-Aug. A, CH, CS, D, s & eF, nl, PL, R, Y; rare in east of range. **2a** *S.a.* subsp. *carinthiacum* is taller and greener, with *greenish-yellow* fls. eA, CS, nel, PL, R, YU.

3 ANNUAL STONECROP *Sedum annuum.* Low, branched, hairless, ann/bien, often red-tinged. Lvs alternate, narrow-oblong. Fls yellow, five-parted, in loose branched clusters. Rocky and stony places, to 2900m. June-Aug. T, except B, DK, GB, IRL. **3a** *S. rubens*** has narrower, longer, lvs and *white or pink* fls. T, except A, CS, DK, GB, IRL, H, IS, PL. **3b** *S. hispanicum* like 3a but plant *often hairy;* fls six-nine parted. To 2250m. A, CH, H, I, R, YU (D, S).

4 ROSEROOT *Rhodiola rosea.* Low/short hairless, grey-green, per; stems often purple-tinged. Lvs alternate oval to oblong, *toothed,* thick. Fls dull-yellow, four- parted, in dense, *flat-topped,* clusters; male and female fls on different plants. Fr orange. Meadows, rocks and screes, on acid and limestone rocks, to 3000m. May-Aug. T.

Grass of Parnassus Family Parnassiaceae

5 GRASS of PARNASSUS *Parnassia palustris.* Short hairless tufted per. Lvs heart-shaped, untoothed, long-stalked; stem lf *solitary,* stalkless, *clasping.* Fls solitary, white, 15-30mm, five petals with transparent veins. Damp grassy places and marshy areas, to 2500m. June-Sept. T, except the far north. **5a** *P. p.* subsp. *obtusiflora* has no stem lf or, if present, near the stem base and *not* clasping. Arctic and subarctic Europe.

Gooseberry Family Grossulariaceae

Deciduous shrubs with alternate, palmately-lobed, toothed lvs. Fls small, 5-petals and sepals. Fr an edible berry, developed below fls.

6 ROCK REDCURRANT *Ribes petraeum.* Bush to 3m. Lvs rounded in outline, 3-5-lobed, hairy or hairless. Fls bell-shaped, pinkish, in *horizontal or drooping* racemes. Berry dark purple-red. Woods, stream banks and rocky places, to 2450m. Apr-June. A, CH, CS, E, s & eF, H, I, PL, YU.

7 WILD GOOSEBERRY *Ribes uva-crispa* (= *R. grossularia*). Spiny shrub to 1.5m. Lvs 3-5-lobed, hairy of hairless. Fls with pinkish-green sepals and white petals, in clusters of one to three. Berry large green, yellowish or purple tinged, *stiff-hairy.* Woods, banks and rocky places, to 1800m. T, except IS; widely naturalised.

8 MOUNTAIN CURRANT *Ribes alpinum.* Bush to 2m. Lvs 3-lobed, usually hairless. Fls greenish in *erect* racemes, male and female on different plants. Berry scarlet, hairless, rather tasteless. Open woods and rocky places, usually on limestone, to 1900m. Apr-May. T, except B, DK, IRL, IS, NL.

9 REDCURRANT *Ribes rubrum* and **BLACKCURRANT** *R. nigrum* (9a)* are frequently naturalised in the area, especially in the Alps. The former is readily recognised by its hairless drooping-racemes of pale green fls, followed by strings of *red* berries, the latter by drooping racemes of reddish or brownish-green fls, followed by *black,* aromatic berries. Both species have edible fr. Both T, except IS; widely naturalised in the region from cultivated plants.

3a, colour forms

Saxifrage Family Saxifragaceae

Perennials, sometimes annuals, often cushion-forming with simple or deeply lobed lvs, frequently in basal rosettes; stem lvs, when present, alternate except where stated; lvs sometimes lime-encrusted. Fls with 5 sepals and petals, 10 stamens and 2 stigmas. Fr a many seeded *capsule, 2-parted.*

1 HAWKWEED SAXIFRAGE *Saxifraga hieracifolia.* Short/med hairy per. Lvs large, 3-7cm, all in basal rosettes, oval or oblong, slightly toothed, thick-stalked. Fls *greenish* tinged with purple-red, 4-7mm, in slender leafless spikes. Damp rocks, moraines and streamsides, to 2400m. July-Aug. A, CS, sF, N, PL, R.

2 STARRY SAXIFRAGE *Saxifraga stellaris.* Variable low/short, densely tufted, sparsely hairy per, with leafless stems. Lvs in basal rosettes, oblong or rather spoon-shaped, toothed, short-stalked. Fls white, 10-15mm, each petal with *two yellow spots,* in lax clusters, anthers pink; sepals downturned. Damp places, streamsides and marshes, to 1900m. June-Aug. T, except B, DK, NL. **2a** *S. s.* subsp. *alpigena* is more loosely tufted, with *smaller* fls, 7-10mm. To 3000m. A, CH, CS, D, E, s & eF, n & cl, R, YU. **2b** *S. foliolosa* is like a small version of 2 but usually with a solitary lf rosette. Fls usually replaced by small *bulbils.* IS, N, S, SF.

3 FRENCH SAXIFRAGE *Saxifraga clusii.* Low/short hairy per. Lvs in a loose rosette, oval, irregularly toothed. Fls white, 10-16mm, in branched clusters; *petals* two short and three long, each with two yellow spots. Shady and damp places, streamsides, on acid rocks, to 2600m. June-Aug. E, sF.

4 ARCTIC SAXIFRAGE *S. nivalis* is a low per with leafless, hairy, stems; lvs thick, in basal rosettes, coarsely toothed, purplish beneath. Fls white or pink, 6mm, in *rounded heads.* Rock crevices, usually basaltic, to 2100m. Faeroes, GB, IRL, IS, N, PL, S, SF. **4b Slender Saxifrage** *S. tenuis* is smaller than 3a and slenderer. Fls distinctly stalked, borne in loose clusters. To 1700m. Faeroes, IS, N, S, SF.

5 SPOON-LEAVED SAXIFRAGE *Saxifraga cuneifolia.* Short, loosely tufted per with lfless stems. Lvs fleshy, *spoon-shaped,* usually slightly toothed, hairless, stalks broad and hairy-edged. Fls white, 5-8mm, in small clusters; sepals downturned. Woods and shady rocks, to 2300m. June-Aug. A, CH, E, sF, I, R, YU.

6 WOOD SAXIFRAGE *Saxifraga umbrosa.* Short/med tufted, somewhat hairy, per. Lvs rather leathery, oval-oblong, toothed, often hairless; stalks broad and flat, hairy margined. Fls white, each petal with a few *pale red spots and two yellow spots,* 8-10mm, in loosely branched clusters; sepals downturned. Woods, usually on limestone, to 1850m. June-July. nE, sF; west and central Pyrenees (A, DK, GB). **5a** *S. hirsuta* has kidney-shaped or rounded lvs, hairy on *both surfaces*; lf stalks long and slender, rounded in section. Fls with *numerous* red spots. Shady places and streamsides., 1500-2500m. May-July. nE, sF, swIRL (GB). **5b** *S. h.* subsp. *paucicrenata* has oblong-elliptic lvs with *short* stalks. Limestone rocks and screes. nE, swF; mainly western Pyrenees. Hybrids occur between 5 and 5a where they grow together and are known as *S.* x *geum.*

7 ROUND-LEAVED SAXIFRAGE *Saxifraga rotundifolia.* Variable short/med loosely tufted, slightly hairy, per, with *leafy stems.* Lvs round to kidney-shaped, toothed, the lower long-stalked. Fls white, 12-20mm, each petal yellow spotted at base and red spotted near the tip, in laxly branched clusters; sepals erect. Damp or shady places, to 2500m. June-Oct. A, Ch, CS, sD, c & sF, I, R, YU (B, GB).

8 ROUGH SAXIFRAGE *Saxifraga aspera.* Low/short, loosely matted per, almost hairless, with sprawling leafy stems. Lvs oblong-lance-shaped, pointed, with *bristly edges,* unstalked. Fls white or cream, the centre yellow, sometimes red spotted, 10-16mm, in loose clusters of 2-5. Rocky and stony places, often acid, to 2400m. July-Aug. A, CH, nE, I. **7a Mossy Saxifrage** *S. bryoides* has shorter shoots which form *dense mats*; lvs incurved; fls solitary. Acid rocks, 2000-4000m. A, CH, CS, sD, nE, s & eF, H, I, PL, R.

9 MARSH SAXIFRAGE *Saxifraga hirculus.* Short loosely tufted, red-brown-hairy per, stems leafy in the lower half. Lvs lance-shaped, blunt, untoothed. Fls *bright yellow,* sometimes red spotted, 20-30mm, solitary or in clusters of 2-4. Wet places, bogs, to 1500m. June-Sept. T, except B; extinct in NL.

10-13, see p. 104.

10 RUE-LEAVED SAXIFRAGE *Saxifraga tridactylites*. Low/short stickily-hairy ann, often reddish. Lower lvs spoon-shaped, stalked, untoothed, withered at flowering time; upper lvs 3-5-lobed. Fls white, 4-6 mm, in lax leafy clusters; petals *notched*. Walls and bare places, usually on limestone, to 1550m. June-Sept. T, except Faeroes and IS.

11 BIENNIAL SAXIFRAGE *Saxifraga adscendens* (= *S. controversa*). Low/short tufted, hairy bien. Basal lvs in a *dense rosette*, all lvs 2-5-lobed, stalkless. Fls white, rarely yellowish, 6-10mm, in small clusters; petals notched. Pastures, damp rocks and screes, 1800-3500m. June-Aug. A, CH, CS, E, F, I, N, PL, R, S, SF, YU. **10a** *S. a.* subsp. *parnassica* is smaller , not more than 15cm tall; fr capsules *rounded*, not oblong. c & sl; Apennines. **10b** *S. petraea* has the lower lvs cut into *numerous* narrow lobes; fls 14-18mm, with notched petals. nel, nwYU.

12 COBWEB SAXIFRAGE *Saxifraga arachnoidea*. Short tufted per covered with *sticky cobweb-hairs*. Lvs rhombic or oval, 3-7-lobed. Fls greenish-white or yellowish, 6mm, long-stalked, in small clusters. Limestone caverns and underhangs, to 1700m. July-Aug. nI; vicinity of Lake Garda.

13 FRAGILE SAXIFRAGE *Saxifraga paradoxa*. Low/short rather fragile, almost hairless, per. Lvs thin and shiny, kidney-shaped, 5-7-lobed usually, stalked. Fls pale green in lax clusters; petals *slightly shorter* than sepals. Shady crevices in acid rocks, rarely much above 1000m. seA, nwYU; Karnten and Steiermark.

Saxifraga is a large an important alpine genus with many diverse forms. Sectional differences can often help in accurate identification and these are outlined on p. 112. In addition, drawings of important leaf characters combined with text descriptions and distributions should enable the reader to identify most of the species within the region. The leaf drawings are to be found on pages 105, 109 and 113.

Hybrids are sometimes found in the wild and often reveal unusual characters, or characters intermediate between the parent species. In most instances the parent plants are likely to be found close at hand.

Habitat differences may also aid identification; whereas some species prefer shade and moisture other prefer exposed cliffs and rock crevices, moraines or screes.

Saxifrage leaves, scale 1-8 x ⅔, 9-18 x 3

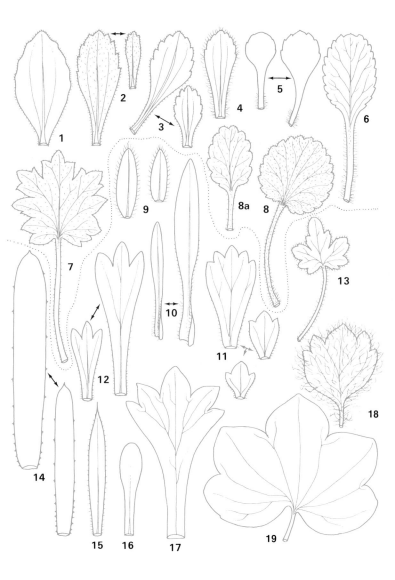

Saxifrage Family (contd.)

1 YELLOW MOUNTAIN SAXIFRAGE *Saxifraga aizoides.* Low/short leafy, loosely tufted per. *Lvs fleshy,* narrow-oblong, 10-25mm, sometimes slightly toothed, stalkless. Fls bright yellow or orange, sometimes red spotted, in a lax head. Damp and stony places, stream-sides, to 3150m. June-Sept. T, except B, DK, NL, S.

2 AWL-LEAVED SAXIFRAGE *Saxifraga tenella.* Low, almost hairless per, forming dense mats. Lvs *linear-pointed,* 8-10mm, hairy on edges, stalkless. Fls creamy-white, 6mm, in small clusters; fl stems hairless, few leaved. Shady rocks and screes, usually limestone, to 2400m. July-Aug. A, nI, nwYU; south-east Alps. **2a** *S. glabella* has narrow, spoon-shaped lvs, entirely hairless; fls white, 5mm. cI, sYU; central Apennines and Balkans.

3 NEGLECTED SAXIFRAGE *Saxifraga praetermissa.* Low/short mat-forming, slightly hairy per, with sprawling leafy shoots. Lvs oblong to almost rounded, to 10mm, 3-5-lobed; lobes pointed. Fls white, 9-10mm, solitary, or 2-3 together, on slender stems. Damp or shady screes, often acidic, snow patches, 1500-2500m. July-Sept. nE, sF; Pyrenees and Picos de Europa. **3a** *S. cuneata* is smaller, rarely over 15cm tall; lvs hairless except sometimes on the margins, rather sticky. Shady rocks, screes, walls, limestone. nE, swF; mainly western Pyrenees. **3b** *S. wahlenbergii* is hairless and forming a mat or low cushion; lf segments blunt; flowering stems not more than 7cm long. Damp grassy places, 1000-2500m. CS, PL; western Carpathians.

4 WATER SAXIFRAGE *Saxifraga aquatica.* Med rather stout per, forming rounded tufts with *erect leafy stems.* Lvs shiny, 15-40mm broad, divided into *numerous* pointed segments, stalked, slightly hairy. Fls white, 12-18mm, in branched clusters. Stream margins and damp places, 1500-2200m. July-Aug. nE, sF; central and east Pyrenees. Hybrids *(S. x capitata)* occur between 3 and 4 where they grow together.

5 HAIRLESS MOSSY SAXIFRAGE *Saxifraga pentadactylis.* Low/short hairless per, forming rounded cushions. Lvs slightly sticky, 3-5-lobed; stems sparsely leafy. Fls white, 8-9mm, on stems up to 17cm tall. Acid rocks, screes, 1800-2900m. July-Aug. nE, sF; Pyrenees and northern Spain. **5a** *S. p.* subsp. *losae* has rigid lvs with the stalk no longer than the blade, often broad. neE. **5b** *S. hypnoides** has widely spaced lvs, entire or 3-lobed, borne on slender lateral shoots; fls pure white, *drooping* in bud. Mountain rocks and screes, streamsides and grassy places. B, neF, GB, IRL, IS, N. **5c** *S. fragilis* (= *S. corbariensis*) is like 5 but has lvs with 3 main lobes, each cut into further segments; fls *larger,* 15-25mm. Shaded limestone rocks and screes, rarely much above 1000m. neE, sF; particularly in the Corbieres.

6 GERANIUM-LIKE SAXIFRAGE *Saxifraga geranioides.* Low/short stickily-hairy per, forming rounded cushions of lvs. Lvs deeply divided into 11 or more narrow primary segments, hairy. Fls white, 22-24mm, *slightly scented,* in close corymbose clusters, on sparsely leafy stems. Acid rocks and screes, to 2950m. July-Aug. nE, sF; eastern Pyrenees and mountains of north-east Spain. **6a** *S. moncayensis* has less than 11 primary segments and flowers about *half the size,* borne in a lax panicle. Shady rocks, usually siliceous, 1000-1600m. neE. **6b** *S. vayredana* is like 6a but lvs with a strong *spicy* smell and flowers fewer, rarely more than 9. Similar habitats, to 1600m. neE.

7 SCENTED-LEAVED SAXIFRAGE *Saxifraga intricata* (= *S. nervosa*). Low hairy per forming loose, but rather hard, cushions. Lvs dark green with 3-5 narrow lobes, covered in short hairs, *scented.* Fls white, 8-10mm, in small clusters. Exposed siliceous rocks, to 2700m. May-Aug. nF, sF; central and east Pyrenees, Cordillera Cantabrica.

8 PIEDMONT SAXIFRAGE *Saxifraga pedemontana.* Low/short, somewhat hairy per, forming fairly dense cushions. Lvs slightly fleshy, 5-11-lobed, broad stalked, with long hairs. Fls fairly large, white, 18-26mm, in close clusters. Shaded silicaceous rocks, 1500-2800m. June-Aug. sw,cA. seF, nwI; south-west Alps. **8a** *S. p.* subsp. *prostii* (= *S. proostii*) has lvs more rounded in outline and with *narrower* stalks. sF; Cevennes.

9-13, see p.108

9 SCREE SAXIFRAGE *Saxifraga androsacea.* Low, slightly hairy cushion per. Lvs *all basal,* forming small rosettes, each with 3 short lobes or unlobed, hairy on edges. Fls white, 10-12mm, 1-3 together; petals slightly notched. Damp screes and snow patches, 1500-3550m. May-July. A, CH, CS, sD, E, sF, I, PL, R, YU. **9a** *S. seguieri* has lvs always unlobed and hairy all over; fls smaller, 5-6mm, *dull yellow.* July-Aug. A, eF, CH, n.l. **9b** *S. depressa* is taller than 9, with more elongated leafy shoots and fls 8-10mm in clusters of 3-8; stems *often* leafless. Shady rocks and screes, mostly on porphyritic rocks, 2000-2850m. nel; Dolomites. **9c** *S. italica* is like 9b but *smaller* overall; flower 1-3 on almost leafless stalks. Limestone rocks and screes. cI; central Apennines.

10 EASTERN SAXIFRAGE *Saxifraga sedoides.* Low loose, mat-forming hairy per. Lvs lance or spoon-shaped 8-9mm, *unlobed*; stems usually leafless. Fls small, dull yellow, 4-6mm, solitary or 2-3 together; sepals *as long* as petals. Shady limestone screes and snow patches, June-Sept. c & nA. **10a** *S. s.* subsp. *hohenwartii* has stems with 3-5 lvs. s & eA, c & nel, YU. **10b** *S. aphylla* is a more compact plant and lvs usually with a *3-toothed* apex; fls greenish yellow. Screes and snow hollows, generally limestone, 2100-2800m. A, CH, sD, nl.

11 BERGAMASOUE SAXIFRAGE *Saxifraga presolanensis.* Low/short dense cushion-forming, stickily-hairy, per. Lvs in dense columns, the lowest dead and whitish but *persisting*, upper pale green, narrow spoon-shaped, 12-15mm. Fls greenish-yellow, 6-7mm, in clusters of 2-4; petal narrow, notched. Shaded limestone cliffs and rocks, 1750-2000m. Aug. snl; Bergamasque Alps. **11a** *S. muscoides* has shorter shoots with narrow lance-shaped lvs, hairy but scarcely sticky. Fls white or pale lemon-yellow, with *broad* petals, not notched. Rocks and screess, rarely on limestone, 2200-4200m. June-Aug. A, CH, eF, I. **11b** *S. facchinii* is like 11a but with very small, 4mm, dull yellow fls tinged with red, *usually solitary* and among the lvs on short stalks. Limestone rocks and screes, 2200-3250m. July. nel; Dolomites.

12 MUSKY SAXIFRAGE *Saxifraga exarata.* Variable slightly hairy per, in fairly dense cushions. Lvs 3-1 5mm, *usually 3-lobed,* but sometimes 5-lobed or unlobed, lobes rounded, *not grooved.* Fls dull yellow or cream, rarely deep reddish, 5-8mm, solitary or 2-7 clustered on almost Ifless stems; petals oblong, not touching. Rocks, and stony places, 1200-4000m. July-Aug. wA, CH, e & seF, nl. **12a White Musky Saxifrage** *S. e.* subsp. *moschata* Variable low hairy per, forming fairly dense soft cushions. Lvs 3-5-lobed, broad-stalked, the lobes blunt and *grooved.* Fls white or pale yellow, rarely pink, 7-8mm, in clusters of 3-8. Rocky and stony places, to 3600m. June-Aug. A,Jura,Ap. Often confused with 12 but distinguished by the larger, usually white petals, and the grooved lvs; the two hybridise readily. **12b** *S. hariotii* has 3-lobed pointed lvs, *shiny green* and with grooved lobes, almost hairless. Limestone rocks and stony meadows, 1600-2300m. nwE, swF; western Pyrenees.

13 CEVENNE SAXIFRAGE *S. cebennensis* is rather like 12a but an altogether larger plant with more compact, pale green cushions and lvs with *long hairs.* Fls pure white, 12-15mm, on leafy stems bearing 3-4 fls usually. Shaded limestone rocks. sF; Cevennes.

Saxifrage leaves, scale 1-4 x 2; 5-18 x 4

1 *S. exarata*, p. 108
2 *S. cebennensis*, p. 108
3 *S. pubescens*, p. 110
3a *S. p.* subsp. *iratiana*, p. 110
4 *S. cespitosa*, p. 110
5 & 5b *S. oppositifolia*, p. 110
5a *S. o.* subsp. *blepharophylla*, p. 110
5c *S. o.* subsp. *speciosa*, p. 110
5d *S. o.* subsp. *rudolphiana*, p. 110
6 *S. retusa*, p. 110
7 *S. biflora*, p. 110

8 *S. diapensioides*, p. 110
9 *S. tombeanensis*, p. 110
10 *S. vandelii*, p. 110
11 *S. burseriana*, p. 110
12 *S. squarrosa*, p. 112
13 *S. aretioides*, p. 112
14 *S. caesia*, p. 112
15 *S. valdensis*, p. 114
16 *S. porophylla*, p. 114
17 *S. media*, p. 114
18 *S. marginata*, p. 112

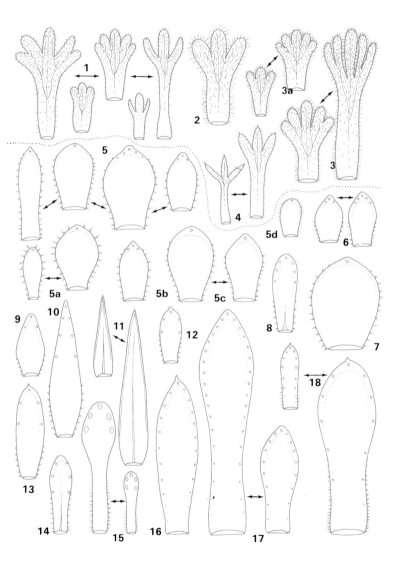

Saxifrage Family (contd.)

1 HAIRY SAXIFRAGE Saxifraga pubescens. Low loose cushion-forming per, with large leafy rosettes. Lvs 10-20mm long, 5-lobed, sometimes 3-lobed, long-stalked. Fls white, 8-12mm, with rounded petals. Rocky and stony places, to 2800m. June-Aug. neE, sF; eastern Pyrenees. **1a** S.p. subsp. iratiana* is lower with denser cushions and smaller lvs, 4-10mm, overlapping along the stem. Fls often red-veined. 2400-2800m. nE, sF; central Pyreneess. **1b** S. cespitosa is more compact, the lvs usually 3-lobed, with pointed lobes; fls dull white or creamish. Faeroes, GB, IS, N, S, SF.

2 BULBOUS SAXIFRAGE Saxifraga bulbifera. Low short hairy bulbous per; stems unbranched. Lvs kidney-shaped, blunt-toothed, the lower long-stalked; each lf with a small bulbil at its base. Fls white, 8-12mm, in small clusters. Grassy, rocky and shady places, to 1400m. May-June. A, CH, CS, E, H, I, R, YU.

3 MEADOW SAXIFRAGE Saxifraga granulata. Med, erect, hairy, bulbous per. Lvs most basal, kidney-shaped, blunt-toothed, long-stalked, rarely with stem lvs; no stem bulbils. Fls white, 10-18mm, in loose branched clusters; petals oblong. Meadows, avoiding lime, to 2200m. Mar-July. T, except Faeroes and IS.

4 DROOPING SAXIFRAGE Saxifraga cernua. Low, erect, thin-stemmed bulbous per. Lvs kidney-shaped with 5-7 pointed lobes, the lower long-stalked, the upper lvs and bracts with small bulbils at base. Fls white, 7-12mm, usually solitary or absent. Rocky, often shaded places, 1800-2500m. July. A, CH, CS, GB, nl, IS, N, PL, R, S, SF. **4a** S. rivularis has bulbils only at the basal lvs; lvs 3-5-lobed. July-Aug. Faeroes, nGB, IS, N, S, SF.

5 PURPLE SAXIFRAGE Saxifraga oppositifolia (incl. S. latina and S. murithiana) Low mat-forming per, with long trailing stems covered with small, 2-6mm, unstalked opposite lvs, bluish-green or green; each lf oval, broadest towards the top, with 1-5 lime pores, hairy in the lower half. Fls solitary, pale pink to deep purple, 10-20mm, almost stalkless, anthers bluish. Rocky and stony places and screes, often on limestone, to 3800m. B, DK, NL; rare in the Pyrenees. **5a** S.o. subsp. rudolphiana is very compact with small, 2mm long, closely overlapping lvs; fls 9-12mm, with rather pointed petals. A, CS, nel, R, YU. **5b** S.o. subsp. blepharophylla is compact with blunt spoon-shaped lvs, 3-4mm, with a margin of long hairs. A; mainly Austrian Alps, perhaps in Yugoslavia. **5c** S. o. subsp. paradoxa has mostly alternate, not opposite, lvs and rather large fls. nE, sF; Pyrenees. **5d** S.o. subsp. speciosa like 5 but lvs broad, with a horny, unhairy, apex; fls large, purple, 14-20mm. cl; Abruzzi mountains.

6 RETUSE-LEAVED SAXIFRAGE Saxifraga retusa. Rather like some compact forms of 5, but lvs curved back from middle and deep shiny green. Fls small, purplish-red, 8mm, in clusters of 2-3; petals narrow, oval, anthers orange. Rocky and stony places, on acid rocks, 2000-3000m. June-Aug. A, CH, CS, nE, s & eF, I, PL, R; absent from parts of the south-west Alps. **6a** S. r. subsp. augustana has long flowering stems, 2-5cm, carrying 2-5 fls, each 10mm. Limestone rocks. swCH, seF, nwl; south-west Alps.

7 TWO-FLOWERED SAXIFRAGE Saxifraga biflora. Low loose, matted, cushion per. Lvs broad-oval or rounded, 5-9mm, with a single lime pore, but not lime encrusted. Fls reddish-purple or whitish with a yellow centre, 16-20mm, in clusters of 2-8; petals separate from each other. Damp screes, moraines and river gravels, 2000-3200m. June-Aug. A, Ch, sD, eF, nl.

8 COLUMNAR SAXIFRAGE Saxifraga diapensioides. Low cushion per, stems columnar with overlapping lvs. Lvs oblong, thick, 4-6mm, untoothed, bluish-green. Fls white, 14-16mm, in clusters of 2-6. Limestone rocks, 1500-2900m. July-Aug. swCH, eF, nwl; south-west Alps. **8a** S. tombeanensis* has shorter lance-shaped lvs, with an incurved, pointed, tip, 3-5mm long. Fls 18-22mm. To 2300m. May-June. nl; Italian Alps. **8b** S. vandellii has narrow lance-shaped lvs, 8-11mm; fls 14-16mm across. Limestone cliffs. nl; Italian Alps.

9 ONE-FLOWERED CUSHION SAXIFRAGE Saxifraga burseriana. Low dense, bluish cushion per. Lvs lance-shaped, 5-12mm, pointed, mostly in basal rosettes. Fls white, 14-28mm, solitary on leafy, reddish, stems. Limestone rocks and screes, to 2200m. Mar-July. A, sD, nl, wYU.

10-11, see p.112

10 YELLOW SAXIFRAGE *Saxifraga aretioides*. Low dense, hard, cushion per; stems columnar with overlapping lvs, branched. Lvs narrow-oblong, 5-7mm, with a short incurved, pointed, tip. Fls *bright yellow*, 10-16mm, in clusters of 3-5. Rocky places to 2300m. June-Aug. nE, sF; Pyrenees and Cordillera Cantabrica.

11 BLUE SAXIFRAGE *Saxifraga caesia*. Low cushion per with flattish grey- or bluish-green lf rosettes. Lvs oblong-spoon-shaped, curved backwards, 3-6mm, lime en-crusted. Fls white, 8-11mm, in clusters of 2-5 on long *slender stems*. Limestone rocks and screes, to 3000m. July-Sept. A, CH, CS, sD, nE, F, I, Pl, YU. **11a** *S. squarrosa* has greener, harder cushions; lvs smaller, narrow oblong, recurved *only* at the tip. Lime-stone rocks, to 2700m. A, I, wYU; south-east Alps. **11b** *S. marginata* has lvs flat or curved only at the tip and *larger* flowers, the petals 7-12mm long, not 3-6mm, white or occasionally pale pink. Rocks and cliffs, often limestone. c & sI, R, YU; Apennines and southern Carpathians.

Prime Divisions of the Genus *Saxifraga*

The important alpine genus *Saxifraga* is divided into a number of useful sections as follows:

Section Ciliatae: plants cushion or mat-forming with entire deciduous leaves; flow-ering stems with some leaves and with yellow or orange flowers, usually in mid to late summer; *S. hirculus*.

Section Cotylea: tufted shade-loving plants with rounded, long-stalked leaves and erect panicles of flowers; *S. rotundifolia*.

Section Gymopera: tufted evergreen, shade-loving, plants with rosettes of leath-ery, toothed leaves. Flowers in airy panicles, white or pink, the petals often spot-ted: *S. cuneifolia, S. hirsuta, S. spathularis, S. umbrosa*.

Section Ligulatae: plants with evergreen green, grey-green or silvery rosettes of untoothed, often lime-encrusted leaves. Flowers white or pink, borne in large spray-like panicles; *S. callosa, S. cochlearis, S. cotyledon, S. crustata, S. floru-lenta, S. hostii, S. longifolia, S. mutata, S. paniculata, S. valdensis*.

Section Mesogyne: delicate deciduous plants with pale leaves often with bulbils at their base. Flowers white: *S. carpatica, S. cernua, S. hyperborea, S. rivularis*.

Section Micranthes: plants tufted with most of the leaves in basal rosettes, toothed. Flowering stems usually branched and carrying many small starry flowers, white or greenish-white; *S. clusii, S. foliolosa, S. hieracifolia, S. nivalis, S. stellaris, S. tenuis*.

Section Porphyrion: plants cushion- or mat-forming, often dense, with close-set un-toothed leaves which usually bear lime pores at the tip; leaves opposite in subsec-tion Oppositifolia (O) flowers with prominent petals (subsection Kabschia, K) or petals hidden within prominent red-glandular sepals (subsection Engleria, E); *S. aretioides* (K), *S. biflora* (O), *S. burseriana* (K), *S. caesia* (K), *S. diapensioides* (K), *S. marginata* (K), *S. media* (E), *S. oppositifolia* (O), *O. porophylla* (E), *S. retusa* (O), *S. squarrosa* (K), *S. tombeanensis* (K), *S. vandellii* (K).

Section Saxifraga: a large section which includes the mossy saxifrages. Mostly evergreen perennials forming soft mats or cushions, which are often divided: *S. adscendens, S. aphylla, S. aquatica, S. androsacea, S. arachnoidea, S. bulbif-era, S. cebennensis, S. cespitosa, S. cuneata, S. depressa, S. exarata, S. facchinii, S. geranioides, S. glabella, S. granulata, S. hariotii, S. hypnoides, S. moncayen-sis, S. intricata, S. italica, S. muscoides, S. paradoxa, S. pedemontana, S. pentadac-tylis, S. petraea, S. praetermissa, S. pubescens, S. sedoides, S. tenella, S. tridactylites, S. vayredana, S. wahlenbergii*.

Section Trachyphyllum: plants mat-forming with bristly narrow leaves *S. aspera, S bryoides*.

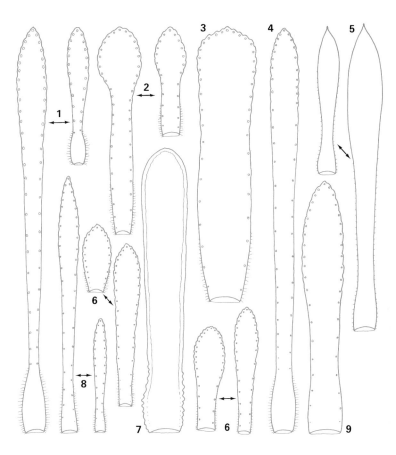

Saxifrage leaves, scale x 1½

1 *S. callosa*, p. 114
2 *S. cochlearis*, p. 114
3 *S. cotyledon*, p. 114
4 *S. longifolia*, p. 116
5 *S. florulenta*, p. 116

6 *S. paniculata*, p. 116
7 *S. mutata*, p. 116
8 *S. crustata*, p. 114
9 *S. hostii*, p. 114

Saxifrage Family (contd.)

1 THICK-LEAVED SAXIFRAGE *Saxifraga callosa* (= *S. lingulata*). Variable low clump-forming per. Lf rosettes large, untidy. Lvs long-linear or spoon-shaped, pointed, 25-90mm, greyish, lime encrusted. Fls white, 11-16mm, petals often *red-spotted* at base, in loose panicles. Limestone rocks and cliffs, to 2500m. June-Aug. seF, I; Maritme Alps and Apennines. **1a** *S. cochlearis* similar but smaller and more delicate with lvs narrow-spoon-shaped, blunt, 8-40mm long. To 1900m. seF, nc & neI; Maritime Alps and Ligurian Apennines. **1b** *S. valdensis* like 1a but smaller and densely cushioned. Lvs linear to oblong-spoon-shaped, 4-12mm; fls *plain* white, in flattish clusters. To 2800m. July-Aug. seF, nwI; south-west Alps.

2 ENCRUSTED SAXIFRAGE *Saxitraga crustata.* Short tufted per; lf rosettes rather flat. *Lvs strap-shaped,* pointed, 15-60mm, greyish and lime encrusted. Fls white, 8-11mm, petals sometimes red-spotted at base, in narrow *short-branched* panicles. Limestone rocks, to 2200m. June-Aug. A, nI, w & cYU.

3 PYRAMIDAL SAXIFRAGE *Saxifraga cotyledon.* Short/med per. If rosettes large, flattish. Lvs broad-oblong with *a point at flat tip,* 20-60mm, finely toothed, *not* lime encrusted. Fls white, 11-18mm, petals sometimes purple spotted, in *broad* panicles, branched from base of stem. Acid rock crevices, 1500-2600m. July-Aug. A, CH, sD, nE, I, IS, N, S. The disjunct populations from the Alps, Pyrenees, Scandinavia and Iceland differ in minor ways from each other.

4 HOST'S SAXIFRAGE *Saxitraga hostii.* Med tufted per with large lf rosettes, dark-green. Lvs oblong or oval, broadest above the middle, 20-100mm, toothed, tip often *down-curved, not* lime encrusted. Fls white, 9-15mm, petals red-spotted in panicles at top of stems. Limestone rocks, to 2500m. May-July.c & eA, wYU; possibly also in CS, H (N). **4a** *S.h.* subsp. *rhaetica* has narrower lvs, tapered to *a sharp point.* nI; Italian Alps.

5 REDDISH SAXIFRAGE *Saxifraga media.* Low/short bluish-green per. Lvs in dense rosettes, 7-20mm, narrow-oblong, pointed, *pink at base.* Fls and most of the inflorescence pinkish-purple, 4-6mm in slender spikes, petals short *surrounded by* a *deep* red hairy calyx. Rocks, usually limestone or shale, to 2510m. June-Aug. neE, sF; eastern Pyrenees. **5a** *S. porophylla** has flatter rosettes and lvs 6-16mm. c & sI; Apennines.

1
2
3
4

Saxifrage Family *(contd.)*

1 PANICULATE or LIVELONG SAXIFRAGE *Saxifraga paniculata* (= *S. aizoon*). Variable short/med per, rather like a small version of *S. hostii* but lf rosettes *more* rounded and *lime encrusted.* Lvs oblong or oval, broadest above middle, *finely toothed.* Fls white or cream, rarely pale pink or red-spotted, 8-11mm, in loose panicles *at top* of stems. Rocky, stony places and screes, to 2700m. May-Aug. T, except B, DK, GB, IRL, NL, S, SF.

2 ORANGE SAXIFRAGE *Saxifraga mutata.* Med per. If rosette loose, large. Lvs broad-strap-shaped, blunt, 10-70mm, shiny dark-green, not lime encrusted. Fls *starry orange,* 9-15mm; in large loose panicles, to 50cm long. Damp stony places, on limestone, to 2200m. June-Aug. A, CH, CS, eF, H, nl; Alps to the Tatras. **2a** *S. m.* subsp. *demissa* has numerous racemes from each rosette, each up to 20cm long. R; southern Carpathians.

3 PYRENEAN SAXIFRAGE *Saxifraga longifolia.* Med per, with a *single large* leafy rosette, long lived but dying after flowering and fruiting. Lvs linear-strap-shaped, pointed, 30-80mm, greyish, lime encrusted. Fls white, 9-11mm, in large narrow-panicles, to 60cm long, with many fls. Limestone cliffs and rocks, to 2400m. May-Aug. n & eE, sF; Pyrenees and eastern Spain.

4 THE ANCIENT KING *Saxifraga florulenta.* Med per with a single, many-leaved rosette, long lived but dying after flowering and fruiting. Lvs narrow-oblong, broadest above middle, very regularly arranged, green, *not lime encrusted.* Fls flesh-pink, 5-7mm, in long pointed, spike-like, racemes. Granite cliffs and crevices, 1900-3250m. July-Sept, but rarely *seen* in fl. seF, nwl; central Maritime Alps where it is rare and protected.

3, basal rosettes

4, basal rosettes

Rose Family Rosaceae

A large family of trees, shrubs and herbs. Lvs alternate, often pinnate, usually with stipules at base of lf stalk. Fls small or large, clustered, spiked or solitary. Petals and sepals usually five; petals separate from each other; sepals fused to basal cup (receptacle). Stamens many. Fr variable; dry with separate fruitlets (achenes) or fleshy, hip or berry-like, often large and edible (apple, pear, strawberry etc.)

1 HAIRY SPIRAEA *Spiraea decumbens* subsp. *tomentosa.* Rather sprawling *deciduous* shrub to 0.5m, thin-stemmed. Lvs oblong, toothed, stalkless, grey-hairy below. Fls white, 5-7mm, in rounded clusters. Limestone rocks and screes, to 1600m. June-July. A, I, YU; south-east Alps.

2 ELM-LEAVED SPIRAEA *Spiraea chamaedryfolia* (= *S. ulmifolia*). Densely branched deciduous shrub to 2m, pointed, toothed towards top, *hairless.* Fls white, 8-10mm, in dense rounded clusters. Woodland and scrub, to 1200m. May-June. A, CS, I, R, YU (F, D, H).

3 GOATSBEARD SPIRAEA *Aruncus dioicus* (= *A. vulgaris, Spiraea aruncus*). Tall hairless per with large pinnate lvs; *no stipules.* Fls white, 5mm, in dense branched finger-like spikes, forming a pyramid. Damp and shady places, usually on acid soils, to 1700m. May-Aug. A, B, CH, CS, D, E, F, H, I, PL, R, YU.

4 DROPWORT *Filipendula vulgaris.* Short/med per rather like 3, but lvs with *stipules* at base. Lvs with 8 or more pairs of leaflets. Fls pale cream, purplish beneath, 8-16mm, in branched *flat-headed* clusters. Dry grassy meadows on limestone, to 1500m. June-Sept. T, except Faeroes, IS and far north. **4a Meadowsweet** *F. ulmaria* is a taller plant, the lvs with *not more* than 5 pairs of leaflets. Fls creamy, 4-8mm, *fragrant.* Wet meadows, marshes and woods, to 1500m. June-Sept. T.

5 ROCK BRAMBLE *Rubus saxatilis.* Short/med hairy per, prostrate, prickly, with annual erect stems. Lvs trifoliate; lflets oval-elliptical, toothed. Fls white, 8-10mm, with *narrow erect petals,* in loose clusters. Fr shiny red, with 2-6 large fleshy segments, edible. Woods, scrub and shady rocks, to 2400m. May-June. T.

6 RASPBERRY *Rubus idaeus.* Tall erect or arching per, with biennial stems, armed with weak prickles. Lvs pinnate, with 5-7-toothed leaflets, *white-hairy* beneath. Fls white, 10mm, with oblong, erect petals, in loose, branched clusters. Fr red or orange with many small fleshy segments, edible. Woods, heaths and banks, to 2300m, but widely cultivated. June-Aug. T, except Faeroes, IS.

7 BLACKBERRY or BRAMBLE *Rubus fruticosus* agg. A large and complicated group with over 40 species in the area but mostly at rather low altitudes. Scrambling, often thicket-forming shrub, much-branched, usually with straight or curved *prickles.* Stems often very long and angled, rooting at the tip. Lvs prickly, pinnate with 3-5 toothed leaflets. Fls white or pink, 15-30mm, in stout branched clusters. Fr reddish at first but becoming *purple-black* when ripe, with many fleshy segments, edible. Woods, scrub, banks, rocky and waste places, seldom above 1700m. May-Nov. T.

8 DEWBERRY *Rubus caesius.* Weak sprawling shrub; *stems round,* slightly prickly. Lvs trifoliate, leaflets 2-3-lobed, toothed, hairy. Fls white, 20-25mm, in small branched-clusters. Fr bluish-black with a waxy bloom, with few segments, larger than 7, edible. Damp places, generally on limestone, to 1200m. May-Sept. T, except Faeroes, IS.

9 ARCTIC BRAMBLE *Rubus arcticus.* Short creeping per, not prickly. Lvs trifoliate, leaflets oval-elliptical, toothed. Fls *bright red,* sometimes pink, 15-25mm, solitary. Fr dark red. Grassy places and thickets on moors, to l150m. July. N, S, SF.

10 CLOUDBERRY *Rubus chamaemorus.* Low/short downy, creeping, per. Lvs *palmately-lobed.* Fls white, 15-20mm, solitary; male and female on separate plants. Fr orange when ripe. Moors and bogs, to 1400m. June-Aug. CS, D, DK, GB, IRL, N, PL, S, SF.

Rose Family *(contd.)*

ROSES *Rosa.* Deciduous shrubs with thin, much branched, stems armed with thorns and/or bristles. Lvs pinnate, with toothed lflets and stipules. Fls large and showy, solitary or clustered, often sweetly scented; petals 5, notched; many stamens. Fr a berry-like hip.

1 FIELD ROSE *Rosa arvensis.* Scrambling shrub to 1 m; stems green, thorns hooked. Leaflts 5-7, slightly hairy, dull green above. Fls white, 25-45mm, styles *joined* into a column. Hip round or oval, red; sepals lobed, *falling.* Woods, scrub and hedges, to 2000m. June-Aug. A, B, CH, CS, D, E, F, GB, H, I, IRL, NL, YU.

2 BURNET ROSE *Rosa pimpinellifolia.* Suckering shrub to 1 m; stems with *straight thorns* and stiff bristles. Leaflets 5-11, hairless. Fls white, sometimes pink, 16-36mm, solitary. Hip rounded, *purple-black;* sepals unlobed, persisting. Dry open places and rocks, to 2000m. May-Aug. T, except E, nN, nS, SF.

3 CINNAMON ROSE *Rosa majalis* (= *R. cinnamomea*). Patch-forming shrub to 2m; stems reddish-brown, thorns slender, slightly curved. Leaflets 5-7, hairy, *bluish-green* above. Fls purplish-pink, 32-50mm, solitary. Hip round or oval, red; sepals unlobed, persisting. Scrub, often along stream banks, to 2200m. May-July. T, except GB, IRL, IS (B, DK, NL). **3a Blue-leaved Rose** *R. glauca* (= *R. rubrifolia*)* has bluish-green or purplish, hairless lvs and fls usually in *clusters* of two to five. Stony places and woodland edges, to 2100m. June-Aug. A, CH, CS, E, F, H, I, PL, R, YU.

4 ALPINE ROSE *Rosa pendulina* (= *R. alpina).* Shrub to 2m; stems yellowish- green or purplish, *no thorns* usually. Lflets 7-11, slightly hairy, bright or yellowish-green. Fls deep purplish-pink, 26-46mm, solitary. Hips *narrow pear- shaped,* red, hairy; sepals unlobed, persisting. Woods and open places, to 2600m. May-Aug. T, except DK, GB, IRL, IS, N, NL, S, SF.

5 PROVENCE ROSE *Rosa gallica.* Patch forming shrub to 0.75m; stems with bristles and hooked prickles. Leaflets 3-7, *hairy beneath,* dull bluish-green. Fls deep pink, 50-80mm, usually solitary. Hip round to elliptic, bright red, bristly; sepals lobed, *falling.* Dry open places and banks, to 2000m. May-Aug. T, except DK, GB, IRL, IS, N, NL, S, SF (E).

6 STYLED ROSE *Rosa stylosa.* Scrambling shrub to 3 m; stems with stout hooked thorns. Leaflets 5-7, hairy beneath, green. Fls white, sometimes pink, 26-56mm, solitary or clustered; styles *joined* into a column. Hip oval or round, red; sepals lobed, falling. Woods, scrub and hedgerows, to 2000m. June-July. A, CH, D, E, F, GB, H, I, IRL, R.

7 MOUNTAIN ROSE *Rosa montana.* Shrub to 3m; stems bluish-green or purplish with hooked or nearly straight thorns. Leaflets 7-9, *hairless,* bluish-green. Fls pale pink, becoming whitish, 25-40mm, usually solitary. Hip oval to narrow-pear-shaped, red; sepals lobed, persisting. Rocks and screes to 2000m. June-July. A, CH, E, sF, I. **7a** *R. jundzillii* has pale to deep pink fls and smaller hips; sepals *falling.* A, CH, CS, D, F, H, I, PI, R, YU.

3a

Rose Family (contd.)

1 WHITISH-STEMMED BRIAR *Rosa vosagiaca* agg. Suckering shrub to 2m; stems with many hooked thorns, reddish, *whitish-bloomed* when young. Leaflets 5-7, usually bluish-green, *hairy.* Fls bright pink, 25-50mm, solitary or clustered. Hip rounded or pear-shaped, deep red and smooth with *persisting erect sepals.* Scrub and lightly wooded areas, to 2200m. June-Aug. T, except B, Faeroes, GB, IRL, IS.

2 DOG ROSE *Rosa canina.* Suckering shrub to 2m or more; stems green with many hooked thorns. Leaflets 5-7, bluish-green or green, *hairless.* Fls pink or white, 30-50mm, solitary or clustered; styles hairy or hairless. Hips rounded or oval, red and smooth, with *downturned or no* sepals. Scrub, banks and grassy places, to 2200m. June-Aug. T, except Faeroes, IS.

3 BLUNT-LEAVED DOG ROSE *Rosa obtusifolia.* Suckering shrub to 2m; stems green with short hooked thorns. Leaflets 5-7, bluish-green or green, *hairy,* gland- dotted beneath. Fls pink or white, 20-35mm, solitary or clustered. Hips rounded or oval, red and smooth, with *down-turned or no* sepals. Scrub, banks and grassy places, to 2200mm. June-Aug. T, except E, F, N. NL, SF.

4 DOWNY ROSE *Rosa tomentosa* agg. Variable shrub to 2m, stems pale green arching with *straight or slightly curved* thorns. Leaflets 5-7, soft, densely downy, with a resinous smell. Fls pink, sometimes white, 30-45mm, solitary or clustered. Hips rounded or pear-shaped, *hairy;* sepals pinnately-lobed, downturned, not persisting. Scrub and hedgerows, to 2200m. May-July. T, except IS, SF and far north.

5 APPLE ROSE *Rosa villosa* agg. Like 4, but with slender straight thorns. Leaflets 5-7, downy, bluish-green with a resinous smell. Fls pink, 30-45mm, solitary or clustered. Hip rounded to pear-shaped, hairy, with *erect persisting* pinnately-lobed sepals. Scrub, hedgerows and banks, to 2200m. June-July. A, CH, D, F, NL, H, I, PL, R, YU (CS, DK, sN, sS).

6 SWEET BRIAR *Rosa rubiginosa.* Shrub to 3 m; stems with hooked thorns *mixed with* short bristles, especially below the fls. Leaflets 5-7, yellowish-green often tinged with red or brown, sticky beneath with brown hairs, sweet smelling. Fls *deep pink*, 18-28mm, solitary or in clusters of 2-3; fl stalks hairy. Hips rounded or elliptical, bright red, smooth or hairy; sepals pinnately-lobed, *erect and persisting.* Scrub, dry banks and stony places, to 2100m. June-July. T, except E, Faeroes, IS. **6a** *R. elliptica* has no bristles and *smooth fl stalks;* fr smooth. June-Sept. T, except DK, N, NL, S, SF.

7 FIELD BRIAR *Rosa agrestis.* Shrub to 2m; stems arching, with hooked thorns. Leaflets 5-7, dull green, stickily-hairy beneath. Fls white, 22-38mm, solitary or 2-3 clusters; fl stalks *hairless.* Hips rounded or elliptical, red, smooth; sepals downturned but *not persisting.* Hedgerows, woodland margins and banks, to 2200m. May-July. T, except Faeroes, IS, N, N, SF. **7a** *R. micrantha** has *hairy fl-stalks* and hairy or smooth hips. T, except DK, IS, N, S, SF.

7a

Rose Family (contd.)

1 AGRIMONY *Agrimonia eupatoria.* Low/tall downy per with *pinnate Lvs;* stipules present. Leaflets *deep* green above, *whitish* beneath. Fls golden-yellow, 5-8mm, in long spikes. Fr grooved, covered with small erect hooks. Dry and grassy places, usually on limestone, to 1800m. June-Aug. T, except Faeroes, IS and far north. **1a Fragrant Agrimony** *A. procera* is larger and aromatic. Lvs green above and beneath; fls 8-10mm; *fr hardly* grooved, with some hooks bent back. T, except Faeroes, IS, nSF and far north. **1b** *A. pilosa* has *pale* yellow fls; mature fr only 4-5mm (not 6-12mm). PL, R, SF (CS).

2 BASTARD AGRIMONY *Aremonia* (= *Agrimonia*) *agrimonioides*). Low/short hairy per like 1 but stem lvs often trifoliate. Fls yellow, 7-10mm, in short leafy clusters. Fr without hooks. Woods, shrub and waste places, to 1900m. May-June. A, CS, D, H, I, R, YU (CH, GB).

3 GREAT BURNET *Sanguisorba officinalis.* Short/tall hairless per. Lvs pinnate, with 3-7 pairs of leaflets, bluish-green below. Fls tiny, dull crimson, in *dense oblong heads* 10-30mm long, no petals; stamens four, protruding. Damp grassy places and woods, to 2300m. June-Sept. T, except parts of the north (SF). **3a Salad Burnet** *S. minor** has *greyish lvs* with 3-12 pairs of leaflets; *fls greenish,* the upper with red styles, lower with yellowish anthers, in dense *rounded* heads. To 2200m. T, except Faeroes, IS.

4 ITALIAN BURNET *Sanguisorba dodecandra.* Med/tall hairless per. Lvs pinnate, with 4-10 pairs of leaflets, pale green below. Fls tiny, greenish-yellow to whitish in *dense oblong heads* 40-70mm long; stamens four to fifteen, protruding. Meadows and streambanks, to 2000m. nI; Sondrio District (PL).

5 MOUNTAIN AVENS *Dryas octopetala.* Low evergreen, carpeting, downy, subshrub. Lvs oblong-oval or heart-shaped, toothed, stalked, deep green above, whitish beneath. Fls white, 20-40mm, solitary, with *seven or more petals.* Fr with long *feathery styles,* bunched. Meadows and rocks, usually on limestone, to 2500m. May-Aug. T, except B, DK, sI, NL.

AVENS or GEUMS *Geum.* Perennials with pinnate, trifoliate or tri-lobed lvs. Fls yellow or pinkish, with 5-7 petals. Fr with hairy, hooked or unhooked styles.

6 CREEPING AVENS *Geum reptans.* Low hairy per with long *reddish-runners.* Lvs pinnate, Lflets toothed. Fls bright yellow, 25-40mm, solitary; petals oval or rounded. Styles not hooked. Rocks, gravels and moraines, 1500-2800m. July-Aug. A, CH, CS, D, F, I, PL, R, YU. **6a Alpine Avens** *G. montanum** has *no* runners and lvs with a very large oblong end leaflet. Fls golden-yellow, petals often slightly notched. A, CH, CS, D, E, F, I, PL, R, YU.

7 WATER AVENS *Geum rivale.* Short downy per. Lvs pinnate, with 3-6 pairs of leaflets; upper lvs trifoliate. Fls solitary *nodding-bells,* 8-15mm, cream or pale pink with brownish-purple sepals. Styles hooked. Damp meadows, woods and stream- sides, to 2100m. May-July. T.

8 PYRENEAN AVENS *Geum pyrenaicum.* Short hairy per, no runners. Basal lvs pinnate, with 4-6 pairs of leaflets, the end leaflet *very large, rounded.* Fls bright yellow, 18-24mm, solitary; petals rounded. Styles jointed near top, not hooked. Stony meadows, to 1800m. July-Aug. nE, sF; Pyrenees.

9 HERB BENNET *Geum urbanum.* Short/med downy per. Lower lvs pinnate; upper trifoliate or trilobed with *lf-like stipules* up stems. Fls pale yellow, 10-15mm, petals oval or oblong. Styles *hooked at tip.* Woods and shady places, to 1850m. May-Sept. T, except Faeroes, IS. **9a** *G. aleppicum* has fls about 20mm with *rounded,* spreading petals. CS, H, PL, R (SF). **9b** *G. heterocarpum* is a softly hairy plants, flowers 9-10mm and tip of style covered in *deflexed bristles.* eF, cI.

3a

2

3

4

5

7

8

6

6a

9

Rose Family (contd.)

1 WALDSTEINIA *Waldsteinia ternata*. Short creeping hairy per with rooting *runners*. Lvs trifoliate, leaflets toothed, narrowed to the base. Fls white, 13-15mm, in loose clusters. Styles *falling* off in fr. Rocky and grassy places, seldom exceeding 1000m. A, CS,R, YU (SF). **1a** *W. geoides* has *no* runners, whilst the basal leaves are 5-7-lobed. CS, H, R, YU (D).

CINQUEFOILS *Potentilla* are usually creeping perennials with digitate or pinnate lvs. Fls white, sometimes white or purple, usually 5-petalled, stamens numerous; calyx and epicalyx present. Fr a cluster of dry achenes, styles not persisting.

2 SHRUBBY CINQUEFOIL *Potentilla fruticosa*. Much branched, grey-hairy deciduous shrub, to 1m, but often dwarf at high altitudes. Lvs pinnate, leaflets 5-7 oblong to elliptic, untoothed. Fls yellow, 16-24mm, solitary or in loose clusters. Rocky places, river banks, on calcareous soils, to 2600m. June-Aug. E, F, GB, nel, IRL, S (N).

3 MARSH CINQUEFOIL *Potentilla palustris* (= *Comarum palustre*). Short/med, slightly hairy, creeping per. Lvs pinnate, leaflets 5-7 oblong, toothed. Fls purplish, starry, 20-30mm; sepals *much larger* then the linear, deep, purple, petals. Wet meadows, bogs and moors, preferring acid soils, to 2100m. May-July. T.

4 SILVERWEED *Potentilla anserina*. Short creeping per with long rooting runners. Lvs pinnate *silvery* at least beneath, leaflets toothed. Fls yellow, 14-20mm, solitary, with oval petals. Damp grassy places and banks, to 2400m. May-Aug. T.

5 ROCK CINQUEFOIL *Potentilla rupestris*. Short/med hairy per; no runners. Lvs *pinnate*, leaflets oval to almost rounded, toothed. *Fls white*, 16-28mm, solitary or clustered. Rocky and wooded slopes, to 2200m. May-June. T, except DK, IRL, IS, NL and northern Scandinavia.

6 CUT-LEAVED POTENTILLA *Potentilla multifida*. Short/med downy per. Lvs pinnate, leaflets 5-9 pinnately cut into *linear lobes*, green above, greyish-silky beneath. Fls yellow, 10-14mm, in clusters. Meadows and rocks, usually on acid soils, 2000-3000m. July-Aug. CH, s & eF, nl (SF).

7 PENNSYLVANIAN CINQUEFOIL *Potentilla pennsylvanica*. Short/tall *greyish-hairy* per. Lvs pinnate, leaflets 7-19 oblong, coarsely toothed or lobed. Fls yellow, 16-24mm, in large clusters. Rocky and grassy places, to 1500m. May-July. c & sE, seF, nwl.

8 SNOWY CINQUEFOIL *Potentilla nivea*. Low/short tufted per, stem often downy-white. *Lvs trifoliate*, leaflets oval, toothed, green above, densely white-downy beneath. Fls yellow, 12-18mm, in small clusters. Rocky places and screes, usually limestone, 1600-2600m. June-Aug. A, F, CH, nl, N, S, SF. **8a** *P. chamissonis* is taller, the lvs sometimes with more then three leaflets, the stalks with straight, not curled, hairs. N, S, SF; Arctic Europe.

9 HOARY CINQUEFOIL *Potentilla argentea*. Variable short/med per; stems usually downy, erect or sprawling. Lvs *digitate*, leaflets 5, pinnately-lobed, toothed, lower leaflets with 2-7 teeth, dark green above, densely *white-hairy* beneath. Fls yellow, 8-12mm, in branched clusters. Rocky and stony places, open woods, to 1950m. June-Aug. T, except Faeroes, IRL, IS. **9a** *P. neglecta* has larger fls, 12-16mm, and lower lvs with 9-11 teeth to each leaflet. T, except Faeroes, IRL, IS. **9b** *P. calabra* like 9 but leaflets grey-green or whitish above. c & sl; central and southern Apennines. **9c** *P. collina* has lvs white or silvery beneath with hairs; styles club-shaped, *not* linear. A, CH, CS, D, DK, F, H, I, PL, R, S.

4

Rose Family (contd.)

1 LARGE-FLOWERED CINQUEFOIL *Potentilla grandiflora*. Short/med hairy per. Lvs trifoliate; leaflets oval or rounded, toothed, green above, grey-hairy beneath. Fls yellow, 22-32mm, in branched clusters, petals slightly notched. Meadows and rocky places, on acid soils, to 3100m. June-Aug. A, CH, nE, s & eF, nI. **1a** *P. delphinensis* has lvs with *5-leaflets,* green above and below. On calcareous soils, 1500-2800m. July-Aug. seF; Cottian and Dauphine Alps.

2 PYRENEAN CINQUEFOIL *Potentilla pyrenaica*. Short/med per, hairs *pressed* against stems. Lvs digitate, leaflets 5, oblong, toothed, green above and beneath. Fls yellow, 22-32mm, in branched clusters. Meadows and rocky places to 2300m. July-Aug. nE, sF; Pyrenees and northern Spain.

3 THURINGIAN POTENTILLA *Potentilla thuringiaca*. Short/med very hairy per. Lvs digitate, *leaflets* 5-9 oblong to lance-shaped, toothed. Fls yellow, 15-22mm, in branched clusters. Meadows and rocky places to 2500m. Apr-Aug. CH, CS, D, F, I, R (N, S, SF).

4 DWARF CINQUEFOIL *Potentilla brauniana* (= *P. dubia*). Low tufted per, slightly hairy, with *numerous* non-flowering leaf-rosettes. Lvs small, trifoliate; leaflets oblong to oval, slightly toothed, hairless above. Fls yellow, 7-11mm, solitary or in clusters of 2-3, petals longer than sepals; epicalyx segments blunt. Grassy and rocky places, often by snow patches, on limestone, 1800-3150m. July-Aug. A, CH, D, E, s & eF, I, YU. **4a** *P. frigida* is taller and much *hairier,* the petals shorter or as long as the sepals. Acid rocks, 2400-3700m. A, CH, nE, s & eF, nI. **4b** *P. norvegica* is often ann and has few, if any, non-flowering leaf-rosettes. T, except IS (B, CH, F, GB, NL, YU).

5 GOLDEN CINQUEFOIL *Potentilla aurea*. Low mat-forming hairy per. Lvs digitate; leaflets 5, oblong, toothed, the end tooth *much smaller* than the adjacent ones, margin silkily-hairy, stipules oval to lance-shaped. Fls golden yellow, often orange in the centre, 14-24mm, in loose, long-stemmed, clusters; petals broad, notched. Grassy and rocky places, usually on acid soils, 1400-2600m. June-Sept. A, CH, CS, D, E, s & eF, I, PL, R, YU. **5a Alpine Cinquefoil** *P. crantzii* * is not mat-forming; leaflets with end tooth *equal* to the adjacent ones, margin not silkily-hairy. To 3000m. T, except B, IRL, NL. **5b** *P. tabernaemontani* like 5 but shoots rooting down, stipules of lower *lvs linear.* To 3000m. T, except IRL, sI, IS. **5c Creeping Cinquefoil** *P. reptans* has fl stems rooting at lf joints and *solitary fls.* To 1700m. T, except Faeroes, IS. **5d Tormentil** *P. erecta* * has 4-*petalled* fls. To 2500m. T.

6 GREY CINQUEFOIL *Potentilla cinerea*. Low mat-forming, densely grey *starry-haired,* per; stems often rooting down. Lvs with 3-5 oblong or lance-shaped, toothed, leaflets, grey-green above, grey beneath. Fls yellow, 10-16mm, solitary or in clusters of 2-6. Dry meadows and rocky places, to 1600m. Apr-July. T, except GB, IRL, IS, N, NL, SF.

7 LAX POTENTILLA *Potentilla caulescens*. Low/short hairy per. Lvs digitate; leflets 5-7, oblong, toothed. *Fls* white, 14-22mm, in branched clusters; petals narrow, slightly notched or not. Limestone rock crevices, to 2400mm. July-Aug. A, sD, E, s & eF, I, YU.

8 EASTERN CINQUEFOIL *Potentilla clusiana*. Low tufted hairy per. Lvs digitate; leaflets 5, oblong, broadest above the middle, with 3-5 *teeth* at the blunt apex. Fls white, 20-22mm, solitary or in clusters of 2-3; petals broad, notched. Limestone or dolomite rocks and screes, 1200-2400m. July-Aug. A, sD, nI, nwYU.

9 ALCHEMILLA-LEAVED CINQUEFOIL *Potentilla alchimilloides*. Short hairy per. Lvs digitate; leaflets 5-7, oblong-elliptical with 3 small teeth at the apex, hairless above but *silvery hairy* beneath. Fls white, 18-22mm, in branched clusters; petals notched, longer than sepals. Rocks and screes, to 2200m. July-Aug. nE, sF; Pyrenees. **9a** P. *valderia* is taller and grey-hairy; leaflets toothed in upper half, petals *shorter* than sepals. seF, nwI; Maritime Alps. **9b** *P. haynaldiana* has *long hairs* on stems and lf stalks. R; southern Carpathians. **9c** *P. nivalis* has lvs *green* and glandular beneath; filaments hairless, not hairy. n & eE, s &s eF.

Rose Family (contd.)

1 PINK CINQUEFOIL Potentilla nitida. Very low dense cushion-forming *silvery-grey* per. Lvs trifoliate; leaflets oblong, broadest above the middle and toothed only at the apex. Fls *pink* or sometimes white, 22-26mm, solitary or 2-together. Limestone rocks and screes, 1200-3150m. June-Sept. A, seF, nI, nwYU; south-west and south-east Alps, northern Apennines.

2 CREAMY CINQUEFOIL Potentilla gammopetala. Short hairy per. Lvs with 3-5 green leaflets, oval, toothed in the upper half. Fls *cream or pale yellow*, 14-17mm, in branched clusters; petals as long as sepals and epicalyx, giving a *starry* effect. Acid rocks, usually gneiss, 1800-2100m. July-Aug. CH, nI; central Alps. **2a** P. apennina is small, all lvs trifoliate and *silvery-hairy*; leaflets narrow, toothed only at the apex; fls white with a *cup-like* epicalyx. Rocks and screes, 1600-2200m. cI; central Apennines.

3 TUFTED POTENTILLA Potentilla saxifraga. Low/short *densely tufted* hairy per. Lvs with 3-5 linear to lance-shaped leaflets, 3-toothed at apex, green and almost hairless above, silvery-hairy beneath. Fls white, 9-12mm, in small clusters; petals longer than sepals; styles hairy and persisting in fr. Limestone crevices, to 1200m. May-June. seF, nwI; Maritime Alps. **3a** P. micrantha has leaves toothed all along margins of 3 leaflets and hairless non-persistent styles. A, CH, CS, E, s & eF, H, I, R, YU. **3b** P. montana is like 3a but leaflets *only* toothed in the upper part and fls rather larger, the petals 6-9mm. E, w & cF.

4 CARNIC CINQUEFOIL Potentilla carniolica. Low hairy per. Lvs trifoliate; leaflets oval, broadest above the middle, toothed, green above and grey-hairy beneath. Fls *small*, white, rarely pink, 6-8mm, solitary or 2-4 clustered. Calcareous rocks, to 1600m. Apr-June. nwYU.

5 SIBBALDIA Sibbaldia procumbens. Very low, stiffly-hairy, tufted per. Lvs trifoliate; leaflets oval, broadest above the middle, 3-toothed at apex. Fls *small* yellow, 5mm, petals *shorter* than the sepals, sometimes absent; stamens five. Damp grassy and rocky places, often by snow patches, 2000-3200m. July-Aug. T, except B, E, IRL, I, NL, R, YU.

6 WILD STRAWBERRY Fragaria vesca. Low/short hairy per with *long runners* rooting at intervals. Lvs trifoliate in basal tufts, bright green; leaflets sharply toothed. Fls white, 15mm, clustered on a stalk not longer than the lvs; flstalks with *closely pressed* hairs. Fr the familiar small red wild strawberry, edible. Grassy places, woodland and scrub, to 2400m. May-June. T, except Faeroes. **6a Hautbois Strawberry** F. moschata* is larger with the main flstalks *much* longer than the lvs, seldom with runners; fls 20mm; fr without seeds at base. To 1800m T, except Faeroes, IRL, IS. **6b** F. viridis* like 6 but runners *short* and hairs of the fl stalks spreading; fr without seeds at base. To 1900m. T, except GB, IRL, IS, NL.

LADY'S MANTLES Alchemilla. A very confusing group with over fifty species in the area and here treated as aggregates for convenience. Tufted perennials. Lvs palmate with shallow or deep, usually toothed, lobes. Fls tiny green or yellowish, clustered, 4-parted with sepals and epicalyx, but no petals. Fr a single achene.

7 CUT-LEAVED LADY'S MANTLE Alchemilla pentaphyllea. Low slightly hairy per, stems often sprawling. Lvs small, not more than 3cm across, with 3-5 *deeply cut* wedge-shaped segments, separated almost to lf centre. Fls greenish-yellow, in 1-2 whorled clusters. Stony and gravelly north-facing slopes, often by snow patches, on acid soils, 1850-3000m. July-Aug. A, eF, CH, nI.

8 ROCK LADY'S MANTLE Alchemilla saxatilis. Very low slightly hairy per. Lvs 5-lobed, the central lobe *separated* to the lf centre; lobes finely toothed at the apex, *hairless* above. Fls in whorled clusters on a long stalk. Acid rocks, to 2200m. CH, sD, E, s & eF, nI, YU. **8a** A. transiens often has 6-7-lobed lvs which are more distinctly toothed. CH, E, s & eF, nI, nwYU.

9 ALPINE LADY'S MANTLE Alchemilla alpina. Variable low/short creeping hairy per. Lvs 5-7-lobed, the central one separated to the lf centre; lobes oblong, toothed at the apex, green above, *silvery-hairy beneath*. Fls pale green, in branched clusters on stems as long as lvs. Meadows, stony places and open woods, on acid soils, to 2600m. June-Aug. T, except B, CS, DK, NL, PL, R, YU. **9a** A. basaltica has fl stems *much longer* than the lvs. Acid rocks. CH, nE, c, s & EF. **9b** A. subsericea* like 9 but lvs greyish and only slightly hairy beneath. wA, CH, nE, s & eF, I.

Rose Family (contd.)

1 HOPPE'S LADY'S MANTLE *Alchemilla hoppeana* agg. Low/short hairy per. Lvs 7-9-lobed, usually hairless above but slightly to silvery-hairy beneath; lobes elliptical, oblong to linear, *joined* near the lf centre, toothed in the upper half. Fls pale green, in whorled clusters, branched. Meadows, rocky and stony places, on limestone, to 2600m. June-Aug. A, swD, eF. **1a** *A. plicatula* has the middle lobe *separated* to the lf centre. A, CH, sD, E, F, I, R, YU. **1b** *A. conjuncta* has lvs dull blue-green and shiny above, hairy beneath CH, eF (GB). **1c** *A. grossidens* has dull green lvs that are only *sparsely* hairy beneath; teeth 2-3mm, not 1mm. A, CH, sD, eF, nl.

2 INTERMEDIATE LADY'S MANTLE *Alchemilla splendens* agg. Low/short hairy per. Lvs 7-11-lobed, hairy or hairless above; lobes usually cut *halfway* to lf centre, each with 10 or more teeth. Fls greenish, in branched, separated, clusters. Meadows, rocky places and woodland margins, to 2500m. June-Sept. CH, nE, s & eF.

3 SMALL LADY'S MANTLE *Alchemilla glaucescens* egg. Low/short softly hairy per; stems with spreading hairs. Lvs *not more* than 6cm wide, 5-9-lobed, hairy above *and beneath;* lobes cut under halfway to lf centre, each with 8-10 teeth. Fls greenish, in dense clusters, branched. Meadows, rocky and stony places, to 2500m. June-Sept. T, except E, IS.

4 LADY'S MANTLE *Alchemilla vulgaris* agg. Very variable low/med, often rather densely hairy per; stems with spreading hairs. Lvs *often* more than 6cm wide, 7-11-lobed, green on both sides; lobes cut under halfway to lf centre, each with 12 or more teeth. Fls pale green, 3-5mm, in loose branched clusters. Damp meadows and open woods, to 3100m. June-Sept. T.

5 DECEPTIVE LADY'S MANTLE *Alchemilla fallax* agg. Low/short per, stems and lf stalks *hairless* or hairs *pressed* to the surface. Lvs 7-9-lobed, hairless above, slightly hairy beneath; lobes cut under halfway to lf centre, each with 10 or more teeth. Fls greenish, 3-6mm, in branched clusters. Meadows and rocky places, to 3100m. June-Sept. A, CH, sD, E, s & eF, I, YU.

6 HAIRLESS LADY'S MANTLE *Alchemilla fissa.* Low/short, delicate, *hairless* per. Lvs small, 5-7-lobed; lobes cut halfway or more to lf centre, each with 8-12 *large* teeth. Fls pale green, 3.5-5 mm, in small clusters. Wet rocks and by snow patches, to 2500m. A, C, CS, nE, s & eF, PL.

7 WILD COTONEASTER *Cotoneaster integerrimus.* Deciduous shrub, rarely more than 1 m tall, often prostrate; young twigs downy, but soon becoming hairless. Lvs oval to almost rounded, 2-5cm, *untoothed,* deep green above, *grey-downy* beneath. Fls pink in drooping clusters of 2-4; calyx hairless or slightly hairy along margin. Fr a small red berry. Dry rocky and stony places, open woods, to 2800m. Apr-June. T, except IRL, Is and far north. **7a** *C. nebrodensis* * is taller with larger lvs and reddish fls *in larger groups* of 3-12; calyx hairy *all* over. Rocky and stony places, to 2400m. Apr-May. T, except B, GB, IRL, IS, NL, and far north (DK, N, S). **7b** *C. niger* is a larger shrub to 2m with shiny reddish brown twigs, reddish or reddish white flowers and *black* fr. CS, DK, H, N, PI, R, YU.

7a

Fruiting branch

Rose Family *(contd.)*

1 WILD PEAR *Pyrus pyraster.* Small/medium deciduous tree to 20m; branches *usually spiny,* twigs grey to brown. Lvs rounded to oval, finely toothed, stalked, hairless when mature. Fls white, 25-35mm, in clusters. Fr globular to pear-shaped, yellowish, brown or blackish, *hard.* Woods and scrub to 1700m. Apr. T, except IRL, IS, NL and far north. **1a Cultivated Pear** *P. communis* is usually non-spiny and with *reddish-brown* twigs; fr larger, soft, sweet tasting. Widely cultivated, but often naturalised in hedgerows, to 1600m. T, except much of the north.

2 SOUTHERN PEAR *Pyrus nivalis* (= *P. communis nivalis*). Small/med deciduous tree to 20m; branches usually non-spiny, twigs white-hairy when young, becoming blackish. Lvs oval, broadest above the middle, usually untoothed, grey-hairy. Fls white, 24-28mm, in clusters. Fr globular, yellowish-green with purple dots. Sunny slopes and dry open woods, to 1600m. Apr. A, CH, CS, eF, H, I, R, YU. **2a** *P. austriaca* has *lance-shaped lvs,* finely toothed towards the apex, hairless above when mature. A, Ch, CS, H, R. **2b** *P. amygdaliformis* has *narrower* lvs than 2a, sometimes 3-lobed, and smaller 12-14mm fls. To 1700m. sF, E, c & sl, YU.

3 WILD CRAB *Malus sylvestris.* Small deciduous tree to 10m; branches rather spiny. Lvs oval or elliptical, pointed, toothed, stalked, hairless when mature. Fls white or pink, 30-40mm, in clusters. Fr globular, a yellowish-green apple, sometimes red-flushed. Open woods and hedgerows, to 1600m. May. T, except Faeroes, IS and far north.

4 FALSE MEDLAR *Sorbus chamaemespilus.* Small deciduous shrub to 1.5m. Lvs elliptical to oval, toothed, green above and beneath. Fls *pink,* 5-7mm long, in small dense clusters; petals narrow, erect. Fr globular, scarlet, 10-13mm. Open woods, stony places and cliffs, to 2500m. May-July. A, Ch, CS, D, E, F, I, PL, R, YU.

5 MOUNTAIN ASH or ROWAN *Sorbus aucuparia.* Small slender deciduous tree to 15m; branches smooth, silvery-grey. Lvs pinnate, leaflets oblong, toothed, green above, greyish-hairy beneath at first. Fls creamy-white, 8–10mm, in dense clusters. Fr a small orange or scarlet berry. Woods, scrub and rocky places, to 2400m. May-June. T, except Faeroes.

6 WHITEBEAM *Sorbus aria.* Small/med deciduous tree to 25m; branches grey, smooth. Lvs oval to elliptical, widest below the middle, shallowly-lobed, toothed, stalked, green above, *white-hairy beneath.* Fls white, 10-15mm, in dense flattish clusters. Fr 8-15mm, oblong in outline, scarlet when ripe. Dry woods and rocky places, usually on lime, to 1700m. May-June. T, except Faeroes, N, NL, S, SF. **6a** *S. torminalis* has more lobed lvs, *green beneath* at maturity; fr brown, finely dotted. T, except Faeroes, IRL, IS, N, S, SF. **6b** *S. mougeotii* like 6 but with *more prominently lobed* lvs, grey-hairy beneath and globular red frs. CH, nE, s & eF, ?nI. **6c** *S. austriaca* has more rounded lvs than 6b and frs with many *large dots.* A, CS, H, R, YU.

7 AMELANCHIER *Amelanchier ovalis.* Deciduous shrub to 3m; bark blackish. Lvs oval, often broadest above the middle, toothed, white-downy beneath when young. Fls white, 16-20mm, in *short-spiked clusters;* petals narrow, pointed. Fr a small bluish-black berry. Open woods and rocky places, usually on limestone, to 2400m. Apr-June. T, except GB, IRL, IS, N, NL, S, SF.

8 HAWTHORN or MAY *Crataegus monogyna* (= *C. oxyacantha*). Shrub or small tree to 10m; branches spiny. Lvs oval to rhombic, deeply 3-5 lobed more than halfway to the midrib; stipules *untoothed.* Fls white, 8-15mm, in broad clusters; styles one. Fr a dark to bright red berry (haw), 6-10mm. Hedges and thickets, to 1700m. May-June. T, except Faeroes, IS and far north. **8a** *C. macrocarpa* is a spreading shrub with finely toothed lf lobes and toothed stipules; fr 12-15mm, styles 2-3. A, CH, CS, eF, sD, nI. **8b** *C. laevigata* like 8 but lvs *less deeply lobed,* the lobes finely toothed. Fr 8-1 2mm; styles 2-3. T, except Faeroes, IRL, IS and northern Scandinavia.

Rose Family (contd.)

1 MARMOT PLUM *Prunus brigantina* (= *P. brigantiaca*). Small spreading deciduous tree or shrub, to 6m; young twigs *glossy, hairless*. Lvs *oval* to elliptical, pointed, toothed, glossy above, hairy on veins beneath. Fls white, 15-20mm, in clusters of 2-5, appearing with the young lvs. Fr a glossy yellow plum, 25-30mm. Dry stony slopes, scrub, 1200-1800m. Apr.-May. eF, nwl.

2 BLACKTHORN or SLOE *Prunus spinosa*. Dense deciduous spiny shrub to 4m; bark black, young twigs usually hairy. Lvs oval, broadest above the middle, finely toothed, dull green. Fls white, 10-15mm, *usually solitary,* before the lvs. Fr a small bluish-black plum, 10-15mm. Scrub and hedges, to 1600m. Mar-May. T, except Faeroes, IS and far north.

3 WILD CHERRY or GEAN *Prunus avium*. Med spreading tree to 20m; bark reddish-brown, twigs hairless. Lvs oblong pointed, toothed, often reddish, sparsely hairy beneath. Fls white, 14-22mm, in clusters of 2-6. Fr a bright red, *usually bitter,* cherry, 9-12mm. Woods and hedges, to 1700m. Apr-May. T, IS and far north. Various varieties are frequently cultivated.

4 ST. LUCIE'S CHERRY *Prunus mahaleb*. Deciduous shrub or small tree, to 10m; *young twigs* glandular-hairy. Lvs oval, toothed, usually hairless beneath, *with glands along* the edges. Fls white, 8-12mm, in clusters of 3-10. Fr a black bitter cherry, 8-10mm. Open woods, thickets and dry slopes, to 1700m. Apr-May. T, except GB, IRL, IS, NL, SF (N, S). Sometimes cultivated.

5 BIRD CHERRY *Prunus padus*. Deciduous tree to 17m; young shoots hairless; bark brown, peeling, foetid. Lvs elliptical-oblong, almost hairless, finely toothed, dull green. Fls white, 10-16mm, in long *arching or drooping spikes,* heavy-scented. Fr a shiny black cherry, 6-8mm. Woods, hedges and moors, to 2200m. May. T, except IS and far north.
5a *P.p.* subsp. *borealis* is a shrub to 3m with *hairy* young shoots; fls scarcely scented. A, CH, CS, sD, PL, R, YU.

Pea Family Leguminosae

A large and highly distinctive family. Lvs usually trifoliate or pinnate, sometimes simple, alternate, occasionally with spines or tendrils. Fls 5-petalled, the upper the 'standard', often broad and erect, overlapping the two side petals or 'wings' which lie on either side of the lower two united-petals or 'keel', which conceals the 10 stamens and style; sepal tube with 5 short or long teeth. Fr a pod, splitting when ripe in most instances.

6 LABURNUM *Laburnum anagyroides*. Deciduous shrub or small tree to 7m; bark smooth, twigs greyish.green with *hairs pressed* to the surface. Lvs trifoliate, leaflets untoothed, grey-green beneath. Fls golden-yellow, in drooping stalked spikes. Pod 40-60mm, flattened, pressed-hairy. Woods and scrub, often on limestone, to 2000m. Apr-May. A, CH, CS, F, H, I, R, YU (GB, IRL). Frequently cultivated. **6a Alpine Laburnum** *L. alpinum* has *hairless* green twigs and hairless pods; lvs pale green beneath. A, CH, CS, F, I, YU.

7 LUGANO BROOM *Cytisus emeriflorus* (= *Genista glabrescens*). Small shrub to 60cm; branches rigid, angular, often rather gnarled, young twigs hairy. Lvs trifoliate, leaflets lance-shaped, *silvery-hairy beneath.* Fls yellow 1-4 in leafy clusters. Pods 25-35mm, hairless. Thickets and stony places, to 1850m. June. sCH, nl; southern Alps.

8 ARDOIN BROOM *Cytisus ardoini*. Small shrub to 80cm; young twigs downy with 8-10 *winged ridges*. Lvs trifoliate, leaflets oblong, hairy above and beneath. Fls yellow, in clusters of 1-3 on short side shoots. Pod 20-25mm, densely hairy. Calcareous rocks, to 1500m. Apr-May. seF; Maritime Alps. **8a** *C. sauzeanus* has 5-angled twigs, the pod usually hairy only along the edges. seF. **8b** *C. decumbens* like 8a but with *simple* oblong or lance-shaped lvs and hairy pods. CH, c & eF, I, YU.

9 PYRENEAN BROOM *Cytisus purgans* (= *Sarothamnus purgans, Genista purgans*). Bluish-green shrub to 1m, usually less; twigs ridged, scarcely leafy, hairy when young. Lvs sparse, trifoliate, unstalked, simple on fl stems. Fls deep yellow, *vanilla-scented,* solitary or paired at stem tips. Pod black when ripe, 15-30mm, hairy. Dry stony slopes, on acid rocks, to 1900m. May-July. nE, sF. **9a** *C. sessilifolius* is hairless, *all* the lvs trifoliate; fls in clusters of 3-12. Woods and scrub to 2300m. neE, sF, I.

Pea Family *(contd)*

1 PURPLE BROOM *Chamaecytisus purpureus* (= *Cytisus purpureus*). Small almost hairless, subshrub, to 30cm. Lvs trifoliate, leaflets oblong, pointed. Fls *lilac-pink or purplish*, 15-25mm, in clusters of 2-3, forming leafy spikes. Pod 15-25mm, hairless. Scrub and rocky places, on lime, to 1400m. May. A, nl, nwYU; south and south-east Alps.

2 HAIRY BROOM *Chamaecytisus hirsutus* (= *Cytisus hirsutus, Cytisus pumilus*). Spineless hairy subshrub, to 1 m, usually less; stems more or less erect. Lvs *trifoliate*, leaflets oval to elliptical. Fls yellow or pinkish-yellow, 20-25mm, the standard sometimes brown spotted, in clusters of 1-4. Pod linear, 25-40mm, hairy. Grassy places and scrub, often on acid soils, to 1900m. Apr-June. A, CH, CS, F, H, I, PL, R, YU. **2a** *C. polytrichus* forms *low mats*, not more than 30cm tall; pod densely hairy. eF, I, R, YU. **2b** *C. ciliatus* is like 2 but leaflets *larger*, 20-30mm, not 6-20mm. A, CS, H, R, YU. **2c** *C. leiocarpus* has mature lvs *hairless* and calyx hairless or almost so. R, neYU. **2d** *C. austriacus* has plain deep yellow fls in heads with a *ruff* of lvs below. CS, H, R, YU.

3 DYER'S GREENWEED *Genista tinctoria*. Variable small to medium spineless deciduous shrub to 1 m, but often less, slightly hairy. Lvs elliptical to lance-shaped, not *trifoliate*. Fls yellow, 8-15mm, in leafy stalked spikes. Pod 25-30mm, *hairless*. Meadows, scrub and open woods, to 1800m. May-Aug. T, except Faeroes, IRL, IS. **3a** *G. lobelii* is a *spiny* much-branched shrub with simple lvs; fls borne singly at each bract. Limestone rocks. eE, seF. **3b Black Broom** *Lembotropis nigricans* has *trifoliate* lvs and smaller fls in leafless spikes. A, CH, CS, D, H, I, PL, R, YU.

4 SILVERY BROOM *Genista sericea*. Much branched hairy shrub, to 40cm. Lvs narrow-elliptical, not *trifoliate*, green and hairless above, *but silvery-hairy* beneath. Fls yellow, 10-14mm, in clusters of 2-5. Pods hairy. Rocky slopes, to 1300m. May-July. nel, YU. **4a** *G. cinerea* is erect with long *spikes* of fls; bracts in groups up the spike. To 1900m. Apr-July. E, sF, I. **4b** *G. pilcsa* like 4a but *bracts alternate* up the spike. Woods, heaths and open places. Apr-Oct. T, except Faeroes, IRL, IS, N, S, SF.

5 GERMAN GREENWEED *Genista germanica*. Small *spiny shrub*, to 60cm, hairy. Lvs lance-shaped, hairy beneath. Fls yellow, 10-12mm, in short spikes, the standard shorter than the keel petal. Pod *short oval*, 5-8mm, hairy. Grassy places, scrub and heath, to 2300m. May-Sept. A, B, CH, CS, D, F, H, NL, n & cI, R, wYU.

6 SOUTHERN GREENWEED *Genista radiata* (= *Cytisanthus radiatus*). Small bushy shrub to 50cm, *spineless*. Lvs opposite *trifoliate*, leaflets linear-lance-shaped, silvery-hairy beneath. Fls yellow, 8-14mm, in small clusters. Pod short oval, 5-6mm. Rocky places, woods and scrub on lime, to 2200m. May-July. A, CH, eF, n & cl, R, nwYU.

7 SPANISH GORSE *Genista hispanica*. Rather like 5 but more densely spiny. Lvs lance-shaped, often broadest above the middle, hairy beneath. Fls yellow, 6-8mm, in dense, almost *rounded, clusters*, the standard as long as the keel petal. Pod short oval, 5-6mm, almost hairless. Rocky and stony places, to 1500m. Apr-Sept. eP. **7a** *G.h.* subsp. *occidentalis* has *larger* fls, 8-11mm. nE, swF; western Pyrenees and northern Spain.

8 WINGED GREENWEED *Chamaespartium sagittale* (= *Genista sagittalis, Genistella sagittalis*). Low spineless subshrub to 30cm, with prostrate branches giving rise to erect *green-winged* fl branches, slightly hairy. Lvs small, elliptical, sparse. Fls yellow, 10-12mm, in dense terminal clusters. Pod oblong, 14-20mm, hairy. Open woods, grassy and rocky places, to 1950m. May-July. A, B, CH, CS, D, E, F, H, I, R, YU (PL).

9 ECHINOSPARTUM *Echinospartum horridum*. (= *Genista horrida*). Low densely spiny shrub, to 40cm, *branches opposite*. Lvs trifoliate, leaflets oblong, broadest above the middle, silvery-hairy beneath. Fls yellow, 12-16mm, *solitary or two* together at stem tips; calyx slightly inflated. Pod oblong, 9-14mm, silkily-hairy. Limestone rocks, stony meadows, to 1800m. Jurie-Sept. nE, sc & sF.

Pea Family (contd.)

1 HEDGEHOG BROOM *Erinacea anthyllis* (= *E. pungens*). *Spiny* cushion shrub to 50cm, thickly branched. Lvs and branches opposite; lvs small solitary or trifoliate, *quickly falling*. Fls blue-violet, 16–18mm, in groups of two to three. Pod linear-oblong, hairy. Dry rocky slopes, usually on limestone, to 2000m. May-June. E, sF (mainly eastern Pyrenees).

2 GORSE *Ulex europaeus*. Dense evergreen shrub to 2.5m, hairy. Lvs stiff *furrowed spines*. Fls golden yellow, 14-18mm, in spiny clusters, almond-scented; calyx 2-lipped, greenish-yellow, hairy. Pod oval-oblong, hairy. Heaths, banks and grassy places, to 1200m. Fls most of the year. CH, D, E, GB, IRL, NL, I (A, B, CS, DK, N, S). **2a** *U. minor* is small, often prostrate, with shorter and smaller, paler, fls. July-Nov. E, wF, sGB.

3 BLADDER SENNA *Colutea arborescens*. Deciduous shrub to 4m, hairy, much branched. Lvs pinnate. Fls deep yellow, often red-marked, 20-24mm, in loose racemes. Pod large, *inflated,* papery brown when ripe. Dry slopes and open woods, often on limestone, to 1600m. June-Aug. A, CH, CS, D, E, F, H, I, R, YU (B, GB).

MILK VETCHES *Astragalus*. Perennials, often tufted, with pinnate lvs, usually with a terminal leaflet, sometimes spiny. Fls in loose racemes or dense clusters at base of lvs; keel-petal blunt-tipped; calyx with short teeth.

4 WILD LENTIL *Astragalus cicer*. Short/med straggling, hairy, per. Leaflets 10-15 pairs, lance-shaped or oval. Fls *pale yellow*, in dense rounded, long-stalked clusters. Pods rounded, inflated, pointed, *black and white* hairy. Meadows and scrub, to 1800m. June-July. A, B, CH, CS, E, F, H, I, PL, R, YU.

5 PURPLE MILK-VETCH *Astragalus danicus*. Short slender hairy per. Leaflets 6–13 pairs, oval or oblong, *blunt*. Fls purple or bluish-violet, in dense rounded, long-stalked clusters, *white* hairy. Meadows, usually on limestone, 1800-2400m. May-July. A, CS, D, DK, F, GB, IRL, I, PL, S.

6 PURPLE VETCH *Astragalus purpureus*. Short slender hairy per. Leaflets 7-15 pairs, elliptical-oblong, *notched*. Fls purplish, sometimes whitish, 16-18mm long, in dense rounded, long-stalked clusters. Pods oval, inflated, white hairy. Stony places and scrub, usually on limestone, to 1800m. May-July. E, s & eF, I, YU.

7 PALLID MILK-VETCH *Astragalus frigidus* (=*Phaca frigida*). Short *almost* hairless per, unbranched. Leaflets 3-8 pairs, broad-elliptical. Fls *yellowish-white*, 12-14mm long, in loose, long-stalked clusters. Pod brownish, elliptical, black or white-hairy at first. Meadows and stony places, usually on limestone, 1700-2800m. July-Aug. A, CS, CH, D, Faeroes, F, I, N, PL, R, S.

8 MOUNTAIN LENTIL *Astragalus penduliflorus*. Short/med hairy per, branched. Leaflets 7-15 pairs, elliptic or oblong-lance-shaped. Fls yellow, in loose, long-stalked clusters. Pod oval, *inflated,* black-hairy at first. Meadows, woods and stony places, to 2850m. July-Aug. A, CH, CS, D, E, F, I, PL, R, YU.

9 ALPINE MILK-VETCH *Astragalus alpinus* (=*Phaca alpina, P. astragalina*). Rather like a slender version of 5. Leaflets 7-12 pairs, elliptic, blunt or pointed. Fls whitish with *a bluish-violet* keel, 10-14mm long, in loose, long-stalked clusters. Pod oblong, *blackish-hairy*. Meadows rocky and stony places, 1900-3100m. July-Aug. T, except B, DK, Faeroes, IRL, IS, NL; GB confined to Scotland. **9a** *A. a.* subsp. *arcticus* has purplish violet fls and fr 8-11 (not 10-15) mm long. Arctic Europe; not IS.

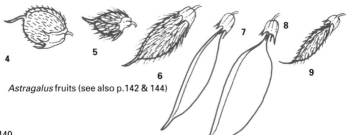

Astragalus fruits (see also p.142 & 144)

Pea Family *(contd.)*

1 SPRAWLING MILK-VETCH *Astragalus depressus.* Variable low tufted, hairy, per. Leaflets 6-14 pairs, oblong or heart-shaped, broadest above the middle. Fls whitish or bluish-purple, 10-12mm long, in *short-stalked* clusters. Pod linear-lance-shaped, hairless. Sunny, dry, limestone rocks, to 2700m. May-July. CH, E, s & eF, I, R, YU.

2 NORWEGIAN MILK-VETCH *Astragalus norvegicus* (= *A. oroboides*). Short erect per, hairless or almost so. *Leaflets* 5-8 pairs, oblong-oval, notched. Fls pale violet, 10-12mm long, in dense, long-stalked clusters. Pod egg-shaped, blackish-hairy. Meadows, 1900-2500m. July-Aug. A, CS, N, S, ?R.

3 SOUTHERN MILK-VETCH *Astragalus australis* (= *Phaca australis*). Low/short hairy per, more or less erect. Leaflets 4-8 pairs, narrow-elliptic to oval-lance-shaped. Fls yellowish-white, often with violet tips, 10-15mm long, in loose, long-stalked racemes. Pod oblong-oval, *inflated,* hairless. Meadows and stony places, 1800-3100m. May-July. A, CH, CS, D, E, s & eF, I, PL, R, YU.

4 WILD LIQUORICE *Astragalus glycyphyllos.* Med/tall straggling per, slightly hairy. Leaflets 4-6 pairs, oval or broad-elliptical, blunt. Fls pale cream, 11-15mm long, in dense, *short-stalked* racemes. Sepal tube *hairless.* Pod linear-oblong, slightly *curved,* hairless. Grassland, open woods and scrub, to 2000m. June-Aug., except Faeroes, IS and far north.

5 STEMLESS MILK-VETCH *Astragalus exscapus.* Low tufted, very *hairy* per. Leaflets 12-19 pairs, elliptic oval. Fls bright yellow, 20-30mm long, in clusters *amongst* lvs. Sepal tube very hairy. Pod oblong, hairy. Meadows and open woods, usually on limestone, to 2200m. May-July. A, CH, CS, D, E, H, I, R.

6 *Astragalus centralpinus.* Med/tall erect per, stems very *hairy.* Leaflets 20-30 pairs, elliptic to oval-lance-shaped. Fls yellow, 15-20mm long, in oblong *unstalked* clusters. Sepal tube very hairy. Pod oval, hairy. Grassy places, to 1500m. July-Aug. eF, nwI; south-west Alps.

7 MOUNTAIN TRAGACANTH *Astragalus sempervirens.* Low/short-spiny, tufted, per; greyish-hairy. Leaflets 4-10 pairs, linear-oblong, broadest above the middle. Fls white to pale purple, in short-stalked clusters *amongst* lvs. Pod egg-shaped, very hairy. Rocky places and gravels, usually on limestone, to 2750m. May-Aug. E, s & eF, I.

8 AUSTRIAN MILK-VETCH *Astragalus austriacus.* Short/med, more or less erect, slightly hairy per. Leaflets 5-10 pairs, linear. Fls blue and violet, 5-8mm long, in loose, long-stalked racemes. Pod linear-oblong, pointed, hairy. Dry grassy and rocky places, scrub, usually on limestone, to 1700m. June-Aug. A, CS, neE, s & eF, H, I, R, YU **8a** *A. sulcatus* has lvs sparsely hairy beneath, *linear* calyx teeth and pale lilac fls. eA, CS, H, R. **8b** *A. arenarius* has stipules *fused* together (not separate at each node), and larger purple or lilac, occasionally white or yellowish, fls, 13-17mm long.

9 TYROLEAN MILK-VETCH *Astragalus leontinus.* Low/short pale-green, hairy per. Leaflets 5-10 pairs, oval to narrowly-elliptic. Fls violet or pale-purplish, 13-18mm long, in *rounded,* long-stalked clusters. Pod oblong-egg-shaped, hairy. Meadows and rocky places, usually on limestone, to 2650m. July-Aug. A, CH, eF, nI, nwYU.

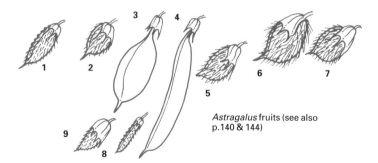

Astragalus fruits (see also p.140 & 144)

Pea Family (contd.)

1 FALSE VETCH *Astragalus monspessulanus*. Low/short tufted, slightly hairy, per, stemless. Leaflets 10-20 pairs, rounded to oblong, blunt. Fls purplish-violet, sometimes whitish, 20-30mm long, in loose, long-stalked clusters. Pod linear, curved and pointed, almost *hairless* (see p.142). Meadows and stony ground, usually on limestone, to 2600m. Apr-Aug. CH, E, s & eF, I, R, YU. **1a** *A. spruneri* has mainly 5-8 pairs of *leaflets* and white, pale purple or violet fls. seR, eYU.

2 INFLATED MILK-VETCH *Astragalus vesicarius*. Low hairy per. Leaflets 5-10 pairs, linear-lance-shaped to oblong. Fls whitish with a purple or violet *standard,* 17-23mm long, in loose, long-stalked, clusters. Pod oblong, pointed, *very hairy*. Meadows and stony places to 2000m. A, CS, E, s & eF, H, I, R, YU. **2a** *A.v.* subsp. *pastellianus* is taller with *yellowish* fls. nel; Italian Alps.

MILK-VETCHES *Oxytropis* is similar and often confused with *Astragalus* but *keel* of fls ending in a small point, not blunt. Fls in dense-rounded, long-stalked, clusters.

3 NORTHERN MILK-VETCH *Oxytropis lapponica*. Low tufted, hairy, per. Leaflets 8-14 pairs, lance-shaped or oblong; stipules joined together. Fls violet-blue, 8-12mm long. Pod narrow-oblong, with *short hairs*. Meadows, stony places and screes, 1800-3050m. July-Aug. A, CH, s & eF, I, N, S, SF, YU. **3a** *O. deflexa* has stipules separate not partly fused and whitish fls. nN.

4 MOUNTAIN MILK-VETCH *Oxytropis jacquinii* (= *Astragalus montanus* in part). Low/short, slightly hairy, tufted per. Leaflets 14-20 pairs, lance-shaped or narrow-oval; stipules *hardly* joined. Fls purplish-violet, 10-13mm long. Pod oval, pointed, slightly inflated, *short-stalked,* slightly hairy. Meadows and stony places, usually on limestone, 1500-2900m. July-Aug. A, Ch, sD, eF, nl; Alps and Jura. **4a** *O. carpatica* is stemless with *bright blue* fls, 10-16mm long. CS, PL, R; Carpathians.

5 GAUDIN'S MILK-VETCH *Oxytropis gaudinii* (= *Astragalus triflorus* var. *gaudinii*). Low sprawling, stemless, *silvery-hairy* per. Leaflets 10-12 pairs, lance-shaped. Fls lilac-blue, 10-15mm long. Pod narrow-oblong; stipules joined. Meadows and stony places, 1800-3100m. July-Aug. wCH, eF, nwl; south western Alps. **5a** *O. amethystea* has *13-20 pairs* of leaflets, pale purplish fls and oval, densely-hairy, pods. neE, eF; eastern Pyrenees and south-western Alps. Forms natural hybrids with 4 where the two overlap in distribution.

6 SAMNITIC MILK-VETCH *Oxytropis pyrenaica* (= *O. montana samnitica*). Low tufted, downy per, stemless. Leaflets 12-20 pairs, oblong-elliptic to lance-shaped. Fls purplish or bluish-violet, 10-12mm long. Pod narrow-oval, pointed, slightly hairy. Limestone rocks to 3000m. July-Aug. A, CH, E, s & eF, I, R, YU. **6a** *O. triflora* (= *Astragalus triflorus*) is more slender with *less than 12* pairs of leaflets and only 3-5 fls to a cluster. A, nel; eastern Alps.

7 MEADOW or YELLOW MILK-VETCH *Oxytropis campestris* (= *Astragalus campestris*). Low, tufted, downy per, stemless. Leaflets 10-15 pairs, elliptical or lance-shaped. Fls pale yellow, 15-20mm long. Pod oval, pointed, hairy. Meadows and rocky places, to 3000m. July-Sept. T, except B, DK, Faeroes, IS, IRL, NL and northern Scandinavia. **7a** *O.c.* subsp. *tiroliensis* has *pale violet* or *whitish* fls. A, eCH, nl. **7b** *O. c.* subsp. *sordida* has yellowish or pale violet fls *and* an oblong-cylindrical, not oval, fr. N, SF.

8 FOUCAUD'S MILK-VETCH *Oxytropis foucaudii*. Low hairy per, stemless. Leaflets 12-16 pairs, oval-lance-shaped. Fls lilac, 10-14mm long. Pod narrow-elliptical, very *hairy*. Meadows and rocky places, to 2600m. July-Aug. nE, sF.

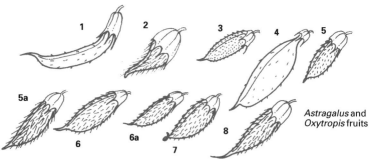

Astragalus and *Oxytropis* fruits

Pea Family *(contd.)*

1 SILKY MILK-VETCH *Oxytropis halleri* (= *0. sericea, Astragalus sericeus*). Low *silky-hairy* per, stemless. Leaflets 10-14 pairs, oval-lance-shaped. Fls bluish-purple, 15-20mm long. Pod oval to narrow-elliptical, densely short-hairy. Dry meadows and stony places, usually on acid soils, 1500-2950m. July-Aug. A, CH, CS, nE, s & eF, nGB, nI, PL, R. **1a** *O.h.* subsp.*velutina* has *much hairier* stalks and pale purplish fls. wA, eCH; central Alps.

2 WOOLLY MILK-VETCH *Oxytropis pilosa* (= *Astragalus pilosus*). Short/med tufted per, *densely long-hairy,* with a stem. Leaflets 9-13 pairs, oblong. Fls *pale yellow,* 12-14mm long. Pod oval or oblong, pointed, very hairy. Grassy, stony places and gravels, to 2600m. June-Aug. A, CH, CS, sD, eF, H, I, PL, R, S, YU.

3 STINKING MILK-VETCH *Oxytropis fetida* (= *Astragalus fetidus*). Low/short stemless, tufted per, *stickily-hairy,* unpleasant smelling. Leaflets 15-25 pairs, lance-shaped or oblong. Fls yellowish, 12-22mm long. Pod oblong, slightly curved, hairy. Grassy slopes and screes, 1800-3000m. July-Aug. CH, eF, nl.

VETCHES *Vicia.* Perennials, sometimes annual, climbing or scrambling; stems not winged. Lvs pinnate, ending in a clasping tendril or leaflet. Fls in loose, stalked or unstalked, one-sided clusters, rarely solitary. Pods narrow-oblong, splitting and brown when ripe.

4 SILVERY VETCH *Vicia argentea.* Short, *silvery-hairy* per. Lvs ending in a leaflet; leaflets 7-9 pairs, linear, blunt. Fls white with violet veins, 18-25mm long, in stalked-clusters. Pod oblong, brown-hairy. Meadows, stony places and screes, 1600- 2300m. July-Aug. nE, sF.

5 TUFTED VETCH *Vicia cracca.* Clambering per to 1 m, slightly hairy. Lvs with *tendrils;* leaflets 6-15 pairs, linear to oblong. Fls bluish-violet, 8-12mm, in stalked clusters of 10-30. Pod oblong, brown, *hairless.* Meadows, scrub, banks and hedges, to 2200m. June-Aug. T. **5a** *V. incana* has *densely hairy* stems and clusters of 20-40 fls. A, CH, CS, E, s & eF, I, YU. **5b** *V. tenuifolia* has *larger* purple, pale lilac or bluish-lilac fls 12-18mm. T, except IRL, IS, N, nS, SF (GB, NL). **5c** *V. onobrychioides* like 5 but fls much larger, 17-24mm, violet with a paler keel. CH, E, s & eF, I, YU. **5d Wood Vetch** *V. sylvatica* * is *hairless* with white, purple-veined fls, 12-20mm. Woods. T, except B, IS, NL.

6 PALE VETCH *Vicia oroboides.* Short/med, slightly hairy, per. Lvs *not ending* in a tendril or leaflet; leaflets 1-4 pairs, oval, pointed. Fls pale yellow, 14-19mm long, in short-stalked clusters. Pod oblong, hairless, *black.* Meadows and woods, to 1600m. May-July. A, neI, H, YU.

7 PYRENEAN VETCH *Vicia pyrenaica.* Low/short almost hairless, per. Lvs ending in a *tendril;* leaflets 3-6 pairs, rounded or oblong. Fls bright violet-purple, 16-25mm long, solitary. Pod oblong, hairless, black. Pastures and screes, 1400-2500m. June.Aug. E, sF

8 BUSH VETCH *Vicia sepium.* Variable med/tall downy per. Lvs ending in a *branched tendril;* leaflets 3-9 pairs, oval to oblong. Fls dull bluish-purple, 12-15mm long, in *short-stalked* clusters. Pod oblong, hairless, black. Fields, scrub and hedgerows, to 2150m. Apr-Oct. T, except Faeroes. **8a** *V. grandiflora* has stipules *toothed* at the base and yellow fls 23-35mm long, sometimes purple-tinged. A, CS, H, I, R, YU (D, PL).

9 HAIRY TARE *Vicia hirsuta.* Short, slender, hairy *ann.* Lvs ending in a branched tendril. Leaflets 4-10 pairs, linear to oblong. Fls *small,* dirty-white, tinged purple, 2-5mm, in short-stalked clusters. Pod oblong, black, downy. Grassy and waste places, to 1800m. May-Aug. , except Faeroes (IS). **9a** *V. tetrasperma* has *pale purple* fls, 4-8mm and brown, *hairless* pods. T.

The **Common Vetch**, *Vicia sativa,* and **Broadbean**, *V. faba,* are often cultivated to 2200m. T, except Faeroes, IS and far north.

Milk-vetch fruits (see also p.144)

1 2 3 5d

146

Pea Family (contd.)

PEAS Lathyrus. Similar to vetches but stems *winged* or *angled;* Lvs often with fewer leaflets and fls larger, usually in one sided, stalked clusters.

1 SPRING VETCHLING Lathyrus vernus. Short/med, tufted, usually hairless, per, *stems angled.* Lvs without tendrils; leaflets 2-4 pairs, oval or lance-shaped, pointed. Fls reddish-purple, becoming blue, 13-20mm long. Pod oblong, hairless, brown. Woods and scrub, usually on limestone, to 1900m. Apr-June. T, except Faeroes, GB, IRL, IS. **1a** L. venetus has more *rounded* leaflets and pods covered in *brown glands.* A, CS, H, R, YU.

2 YELLOW PEA Lathyrus laevigatus. Short/med hairless per. Lvs without tendrils; leaflets 2-6 pairs, elliptical, or oval. Fls *yellow,* 15-25mm long. Pod hairless, brown. Meadows and woods, usually on limestone, to 2300m. June-July. A, CH, CS, D, nE, F, I, PL, R, YU. **2a** L.l. subsp. *occidentalis* is slightly hairy with narrower leaflets. A, CH, sD, nE, S & eF, nI, nwYU. **2b Yellow Vetchling** L. aphaca* las large leafy stipules and a tendril but *no leaflets;* fls small, solitary. T, except DK, IRL, IS, N, S, SF (B, Ch, D, GB, NL).

3 SLENDER VETCH Lathyrus filiformis (= L. canescens). Short/med hairless per; stems ridged. Lvs *without* tendrils; leaflets 2-4 pairs, linear-lance-shaped, pointed. Fls bright reddish-purple, 14-22mm long. Pod hairless, brown. Limestone rocks, to 1450m. May-July. eE, sF, nI. **3a** L. bauhinii has *larger* fls, 20-27mm long. CH, sD, nE, s & eF, YU.

4 FELTED VETCH Lathyrus pannonicus agg. Variable short/med hairy per; stems narrowly winged or ridged. Lvs without tendrils; leaflets 1-4 pairs, linear to oblong-lance-shaped. Fls pale cream, *tinged* reddish-purple, 12-18mm long. Pod hairless, pale brown. Grassland and scrub, to 1200m. Apr-June. A, CS, D, F, H, I, PL, R, YU.

5 BITTER VETCH Lathyrus montanus (= L. macrorrhizus). Short/med hairless per; stems winged. Lvs without tendrils; leaflets 2-4 pairs, linear to elliptic. Fls crimson, *turning* greenish-blue, 10-16mm long. Pod hairless, red brown. Pastures, woods and scrub, usually on acid soils, to 2200m. Apr-June. T, except Faeroes, IS and far north.

6 MEADOW VETCHLING Lathyrus pratensis. Short/tall scrambling, hairless or downy per; stems angled. Lvs with tendrils; leaflets *one pair,* linear or lance-shaped. Fls yellow, 10-16mm. Pod sometimes hairy, black. Grassland and scrub, to 2150m. May-Aug. T. **6a** L. hallersteinii has *leaflets* 8-15mm wide, not 2-9mm. R, eYU.

7 CIRRHOSE VETCH Lathyrus cirrhosus. Tall scrambling, hairless, per; stems winged. Lvs with tendrils; Lflets 2-3 pairs, elliptic or oblong-lance-shaped. Fls pink, 12-17mm long. Pod hairless, pale brown. Dry grassy places, scrub and banks, to 1600m. May-July. nE, sF; Pyrenees and Cevennes.

8 BROAD-LEAVED EVERLASTING PEA Lathyrus latifolius. Variable clambering per to 3m, hairy or hairless; stems *broad winged.* Lvs with tendrils; lflets *one pair,* oval to elliptic. Stipules broad. Fls large purple-pink, 20-30mm. Pod hairless, brown. Scrub and hedgerows, to 1500m. July-Sept. T, except DK, IRL, IS N, S, SF (B, GB, D). **8a** L. heterophyllus has 2-3 pairs of leaflets on upper lvs and *smaller* fls, 12-22mm. To 1900m. A, CH, CS, D, E, I, c & sS, PL. **8b** L. sylvestris similar to 8 but with *narrower* lvs and stipules and smaller fls, 13-20mm. T, except Faeroes, IRL, IS and far north. **8c** L. tuberosus* like 8 but stems angled, not *winged* and fls small, bright crimson, 12-20mm. T, except IRL, N, SF (DK, GB, S).

9 BROWN VETCH Lathyrus setifolius. Short/med hairless ann. Leaflets linear. Fls *solitary,* orange-red or brownish, 8-11mm long, on long slender stalks. Grassy places and banks, to 1300m. May-July. E, sF, I, R, YU.

The **Chickling Pea,** Lathyrus sativus, is commonly cultivated up to 1800m.

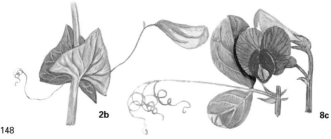

2b   8c

Pea Family (contd.)

RESTHARROWS *Ononis.* Perennials or small shrubs, often glandular-hairy and spiny. Lvs trifoliate or single on same plant. Fls pink, sometimes yellow. Pod oval or oblong, hairy, splitting.

1 ROUND-LEAVED RESTHARROW *Ononis rotundifolia.* Med hairy, much-branched, subshrub. Leaflets elliptic to rounded, *blunt,* toothed. Fls pink or whitish, 16-20mm long, in long-stalked clusters of one to three. Woods and rocky places, usually on limestone, to 1750m. May-Aug. A, CH, E, s & eF, n & cI.

2 SHRUBBY RESTHARROW *Ononis fruticosa.* Med/tall *erect,* hairy, subshrub. Leaflets oblong-lance-shaped, *pointed,* saw-toothed, *hairless.* Fls pink, 10-20mm long, in stalked clusters of one to three. Dry rocky places, to 1600m. May-Aug. nE, s & eF: central Pyrenees, northern Spain and French Alps.

3 MT. CENIS RESTHARROW *Ononis cristata* (= O. *cenisia*). Low/short, often mat-forming, hairy, subshrub. Leaflets oblong, toothed. Fls pink, 10-14mm long, solitary, on slender stalks. Meadows, rocky places and screes, usually on limestone, to 1800m. June-Sept. n & eE, s & seF, cI.

4 YELLOW RESTHARROW *Ononis striata.* Low/short downy per. Leaflets rounded to oblong, broadest above the middle, toothed. Fls yellow, 10-13mm long, solitary or in small, short-stalked clusters. Limestone rocks, to 1800m. June-Aug. E, sF, I; not Alps. **4a** O. *aragonensis** has *larger leaflets and fls,* 12-18mm, in loose terminal clusters. Meadows and rocks, to 2500m. June-July. n & eE, sF; Pyrenees mainly. **4b Large Yellow Restharrow** O. *natrix** is taller than 4a, much-branched and *stickily hairy.* Fls deep yellow, often veined red or purple, 14-16mm long. Dry rocky places on limestone, to 2100m. May-July. CH, sD, E, s & eF, I, YU.

5 SPINY RESTHARROW *Ononis spinosa.* Variable short/med erect or sprawling, hairy per; *stems stiffly-spiny.* Leaflets narrow oval, blunt or pointed, toothed. Fls pink or purplish, 6-20mm long, usually solitary. Meadows, dry slopes and waste places, often on limestone, to 1800m. Apr-Sept. T. except Faeroes, IRL, IS, SF. **5a Restharrow** O. *repens* is lower and more spreading with *spineless or softly spiny* stems; leaflets *notched* at tip. T, except northern Scandinavia (SF).

6 TALL MELILOT *Melilotus altissima.* Med/tall hairless bien/per. Lvs trifoliate; leaflets oblong-oval, blunt, toothed. Fls yellow, 5-7mm long, in slender, stalked, spikes. Pod oblong, pointed, downy, black when ripe. Damp waste places and fields, to 2000m. June-Sept. T, except IS, SF and far north (GB, IRL). **6a Common Melilot** M. *officinalis* has brown *hairless* pods; fls with keel shorter than wings. To 2000m. T, except Faeroes, IS (DK, GB, IRL, N, S, SF).

7 WHITE MELILOT *Melilotus alba.* Med/tall hairless bien. Lvs trifoliate; leaflets oval to oblong, toothed. Fls white, 4-5mm, in stalked spikes. Pod *hairless,* greyish-brown when ripe. Fields and waste places, to 1850m. July-Oct. T, except Faeroes, IRL, IS and far north (B, GB).

8 PYRENEAN MEDICK *Medicago hybrida.* Short hairless per. Lvs trifoliate; leaflets broad-oval to rounded, pointed, finely toothed. Fls *small,* yellow, 2-3mm long, in stalked clusters of two to five. Pod oblong, *curved,* pointed, black when ripe. Woods and rocky places, on limestone, to 1800m. June-Aug. sF; northern Pyrenees and Corbieres. **8a Black Medick** M. *lupulina* is *hairy* with ten to fifteen fld racemes; pod *kidney-shaped,* black. To 2300m. T, except far north (Faeroes, IS).

9 SPRAWLING MEDICK *Medicago suffruticosa.* Low/short slightly downy per, rather sprawling. Lvs trifoliate; leaflets oval or heart-shaped, broadest above middle, toothed. Fls yellow, 3-6mm long, in stalked clusters of three to eight. Pod *twisted* into 2-4 spirals with a hole in the middle. Rocky places, to 2300m. July-Aug. eE, sF; Pyrenees and Corbieres. **9a Lucerne** M. *sativa* is very variable with *larger* fls, 6-11mm long, blue, purplish or yellow; pod curved or spiralled. To 1800m. T, except Faeroes, IS and far north.

4b Large Yellow Restharrow   **9a** Lucerne

Pea Family (contd.)

CLOVERS *Trifolium*. Perennials, sometimes annuals with trifoliate lvs, usually stalked; leaflet margins slightly toothed. Fls in dense rounded or oblong clusters; wings longer then keel petal. Pod small, often more or less covered by the dead fl remains.

1 ALPINE CLOVER *Trifolium alpinum*. Low tufted hairless per. Leaflets lance- shaped or linear. Fls *large,* pink or purplish, rarely cream, 18-25mm long, in 3-12-fld clusters. Meadows and pastures, on acid soils, 1700-2500m. June-Aug. A, CH, nE, s & eF, I.

2 MOUNTAIN CLOVER *Trifolium montanum*. Short/med unbranched per; stems woolly. Leaflets oval, lance-shaped or elliptical, hairless above. Fls *white or yellowish,* 7-9mm, in dense rounded clusters. Dry grassy places, open woods, often on limestone, to 2600m. May-July. T, except DK, GB, IRL, IS, NL.

3 WHITE or DUTCH CLOVER *Trifolium repens*. Low/short creeping, more or less hairy per; stems rooting at lf joints; leaflets bright green, often with a *white crescent* zone, oval or elliptical. Fls white or pale pink, rarely purple, 7-10mm long, in dense rounded clusters, *sweetly scented*. Meadows, grassy and waste places, to 2750m. May-Oct. T; frequently cultivated.

4 PALE CLOVER *Trifolium pallescens*. Low tufted *hairless* per. Leaflets bright green, elliptical or oval, broadest above the middle. Fls yellowish-white or pink, *becoming dark brown,* 6-10mm long, in dense rounded clusters, sweetly scented; angle between sepal teeth sharp. Damp pastures and screes, on acid rocks, 1800-2700m. July-Sept. A, CH, E, s & eF, I, R, YU. **4a** *T. thalii* has *dull green* lvs and white or red fls in oval clusters. Meadows and pastures on limy soils, to 3100m. A, CH, sD, nE, s & eF, I. **4b Alsike Clover** *T. hybridum* like 4 but taller *with* white and pink fls; angles between sepal teeth blunt. To 2150m. T, except Faeroes, IS; widely naturalised in northern and western Europe.

5 BROWN CLOVER *Trifolium badium*. Short tufted hairy or hairless per. *Uppermost lvs opposite;* leaflets elliptical or diamond-shaped. Fls golden yellow, *becoming bright chestnut-brown,* 7-9mm long, in dense rounded clusters. Meadows and damp stony places, usually on calcareous soils, 1400-2800m. July-Aug. A, CH, CS, E, s & eF, I, PL, R, YU.

6 LARGE BROWN CLOVER *Trifolium spadiceum*. Rather like 5. Leaflets oblong. Fls golden yellow, becoming very dark brown, 6 mm long, in *dense oblong clusters*. Grassy places, on acid soils, to 2200m. June-Aug. A, CH, CS, D, nE, I, N, S, SF, YU.

7 CRIMSON CLOVER *Trifolium incarnatum*. Short/erect hairy *ann.* Leaflets rounded to oblong, broadest above the middle. Fls *blood-red,* pink or white, 10-12mm long, in dense oblong clusters. Fields and waste places to 1500m. May-July. T, except Faeroes, IRL, IS; widely cultivated. **7a** *T. saxatile* is greyish-hairy, with small whitish or pinkish fls, 3-4mm long, few in *stalkless clusters*. Gravels and moraines, to 3100m. A, CH, eF, nI.

8 RED CLOVER *Trifolium pratense*. Variable low/tall erect hairy tufted per. Leaflets green, often-with a *white crescent zone,* oblong-lance-shaped or rounded; stipules triangular, bristle-tipped. Fls reddish-purple, sometimes pink or white, 12-15mm, in dense rounded clusters, sometimes paired. Meadows, fields and waste places, to 2700m. May-Oct. T; widely cultivated.

9 CREAM CLOVER *Trifolium noricum*. Low/short tufted hairy per. Lvs mostly basal; leaflets elliptical or oblong; stipules whitish, pointed. Fls green, 15mm long, in dense rounded heads. Meadows and pastures, on calcareous soils, 1600-2600m. July-Aug. A, I, nwYU; eastern Alps and Apennines.

10 ZIGZAG CLOVER *Trifolium medium*. Short/med slightly hairy per; stems usually *rather zigzagged*. Leaflets oval, oblong or elliptic, scarcely toothed; stipules triangular, hairless. Fls pale purple-red, 12-20mm long, in dense rounded or oval clusters. Poor grassland, woods and scrub, usually on calcareous or clayish soils, to 2100m. May-July. T, except Faeroes, IS. **10a** *T. alpestre* has small *unstalked* flheads and purple fls; stipules linear to narrow-lance-shaped, *hairy at top*. To 2300m. T, except Faeroes, GB, IRL, IS, N, NL, S, SF.

Pea Family (contd)

1 RED TREFOIL Trifolium rubens. Short hairless, erect, per. Leaflets oblong lance-shaped or elliptical, sharply toothed; stipules oval or lance-shaped. Fls purple, sometimes white, 15mm long, in dense oblong heads. Dry open woods, scrub and stony places, to 2050m. June-Aug. A, CH, CS, nE, c & sF, H, n & cl, PL, R, YU.

2 HUNGARIAN TREFOIL Trifolium pannonicum. Short/med erect, hairy, per. Leaflets oblong-lance-shaped or elliptical; stipules linear. Fls yellowish-white, 20-25mm long, in dense rounded or oblong, long-stalked, clusters. Meadows and open scrub, to 1200m. May-Aug.CS, eF, H, I, PL, R. **2a Sulphur Clover** T. ochroleucon has smaller fls, 15-20mm long, in short-stalked clusters. Shady and damp places, to 1800m. T, except DK, IRL, IS, N, NL, S, SF.

3 ALPINE BIRDSFOOT TREFOIL Lotus alpinus (= L. corniculatus var. alpinus). Low, rather tufted, hairless per. Lvs pinnate; leaflets 5, lance-shaped or rounded. Fls yellow marked red, 12-16mm long, in dense, grassy and stony places, 2000-3100m. May-Aug. A, sD, nE, sF, I, YU. **3a Birdsfoot Trefoil** Lotus corniculatus agg.* is a much larger sprawling plant, with 3-6-fld clusters. To 1600m. May-Sept. T (IS).

4 MOUNTAIN KIDNEY-VETCH Anthyllis montana. Short densely-tufted sub-shrub, hairy. Lvs pinnate,; leaflets narrow-elliptical to narrow-oblong, untoothed. Fls purple, in dense rounded, stalked, clusters; bracts shorter than fls. Meadows, rocky and stony places, usually on limestone, to 2400m. June-July. A, CH, E, s & eF, I, R, YU. **4a** A.m. subsp. jacquinii has pink fls and bracts longer than the fls. A, nel, nwYU; eastern Alps.

5 COMMON KIDNEY-VETCH Anthyllis vulneraria. Variable low/med, silkily-hairy, bien/per. Lvs pinnate, the lowest with 5-7 leaflets, the end leaflet larger than the others. Fls yellow or red, in rounded clusters; sepal tube red-tipped. Dry meadows, rocky and stony places, usually on limestone, to 3000m. May-Aug. B, D, DK, F, GB, IRL, N, NL, S, SF. The following subsp. are recognised: **5a** A.v. subsp. vulnerarioides like 5 but lowest lvs with 1-5 leaflets; fls yellow; calyx red-tipped, 7-9mm long. nE, s & eF, cl. **5b** A.v. subsp. forondae is like 5a but more robust, lowest lvs with 9-13 leaflets; calyx 11-13mm. nE, s & eF, nwl. **5c** A.v. susbp. carpatica is less hairy than 5a and all lvs with 1-7 leaflets. Fls pale or deep yellow or reddish; calyx white, 9-12mm. B, CH, CS, DK, F, GB, IRL, I, PL, YU. **5d** A.v. subsp. alpestris like 5c but calyx longer, 13-15mm, with greyish-black hairs. A, CH, CS, E, F, H, I, PL, R, YU. **5e** A.v. subsp. pyrenaica like 5c but calyx red-tipped; fls pink or red. nE, sF; Pyrenees and Cordillera Cantabrica. **5f** A. v. subsp. lapponica has lvs with 1-9 leaflets, silky stems and calyces and yellow fls. nGB, N, S, SF.

6 FALSE SENNA Coronilla emerus. Small loosely-branched deciduous shrub, 1-2m; twigs green. Lvs pinnate, greyish-green; leaflets 2-4 pairs, oval, broadest above the middle. Fls pale yellow, often red-tipped, 14-20mm long, in stalked-clusters of 2-4. Pod linear, pointed, 5-11cm long. Rocky places, woodland edges, to 1800m. Apr-May. T, except GB, IRL, IS, NL (DK).

7 SMALL SCORPION VETCH Coronilla vaginalis. Small deciduous shrub to 0.5 m. Lvs pinnate, green; leaflets 2-6 pairs, oblong to rounded, white-margined. Fls small, yellow, 6-10mm long, in 4-10-fld clusters. Pod linear-oblong, 1.5-3.5cm, constricted between seeds. Dry grassland, scrub and open woods, on limestone, to 2250m. June-Aug. A, CH, CS, sD, s & eF, H, I, R, YU. **8a** C. minima has unstalked leaflets and mambranous stipules. sCH, nE, s & eF, I. **8b** C. elegans has heads of up to 18 white or pink fls. Woods and scrub. A, CS, H, R, YU.

8 HORSESHOE VETCH Hippocrepis comosa. Short hairy per. Lvs pinnate; leaflets 3-8 pairs, linear to oblong. Fls yellow, 6–10mm long, in long-stalked clusters. Pod twisting, with horseshoe-shaped segments. Meadows and stony places, to 2800m. Apr-June. T, except DK, Faeroes, IRL, IS, N, S, SF.

3a

1

2

3

4

5

6

7

8

Pea Family (contd.)

1 ALPINE SAINFOIN *Hedysarum hedysaroides*. Low/short per, hairless or almost so. Lvs pinnate; leaflets 4-6 pairs, oval or elliptical. Fls reddish-violet, 13-25mm long, in long-stalked spikes. Pod oblong, *constricted between* the seeds into 2-5 segments. Pastures, stony places and screes, to 2800m. July-Aug. A, CH, CS, sD, s & eF, I, PL, R, nwYU. **1a** *H.h.* subsp. *exaltatum* is *taller* with 6-10 pairs of leaflets. sA, sCH, nl; southern Alps.

2 WHITE SAINFOIN *Hedysarum boutignyanum*. Med erect hairless per. Lvs pinnate; leaflets 4-8 pairs, elliptical to oval, broadest above the middle. Fls cream or white, sometimes bluish-veined, 15-25mm long, in long-stalked spikes. Pod oblong, constricted between the seeds into 2-5 segments. Pastures and stony places, to 2800m. July-Aug. eF; south-west Alps.

SAINFOINS *Onobrychis* have short fruits, not splitting or jointed, with *netted sides* and often toothed along the edges.

3 SILVERY SAINFOIN *Onobrychis argentea* subsp. *hispanica*. Short silkily-hairy per. Lvs pinnate; leaflets 5-8 pairs, elliptical to narrowly-oblong. Fls pink with darker veins, 10-14mm long, in long-stalked spikes. Pod rounded, 4-8mm, *hairy*. Meadows, rocky and stony places, to 2000m. June-Aug. n & eE, sF; Pyrenees and Spanish mountains. **3a** *O. pyrenaica* is *smaller* and less hairy; fls 8–10mm long. nE, sF; Pyrenees. **3b Rock Sainfoin** *O. saxatilis* is more tufted and *white-downy* with 6-15 pairs of leaflets; fls pale yellow veined with pink. Pod not tooth-edged. To 1800m. nE, s & eF, nl; eastern Pyrenees and south-west Alps.

4 MOUNTAIN SAINFOIN *Onobrychis montana*. Short/med *slightly hairy* per. Lvs pinnate; leaflets 5-8 pairs, elliptical to oval or oblong. Fls pink with purple veins, 10-14mm long, in long-stalked spikes. Pod rounded, 7-12mm, tooth-edged. Pastures and stony places, 1400-2500m. July. A, CH, CS, sD, eF, I, PL, R, YU.

5 SMALL SAINFOIN *Onobrychis arenaria*. Short/tall erect hairy or hairless per. Lvs pinnate; leaflets 3-12 pairs, linear-oblong to elliptical. Fls pink with purple veins, *smaller* than 4, 8–10mm long, in long-stalked spikes. Pod small, rounded, 4-6mm, tooth-edged. Pastures and stony places, to 2500m. June-Sept. A, CH, c & eF, I, PL, R, YU. **5a** *O.a.* subsp. *taurerica* has larger fls, 10-12mm, the standard petal *very pale pink on back*. seA, nel, nwYU; south-east Alps.

Wood-sorrel Family Oxalidaceae

Perennials with trifoliate lvs. Fls 5-parted, wide cup-shaped; stamens 10; opening in sunshine. Fr a capsule.

6 WOOD-SORREL *Oxalis acetosella*. Low creeping slightly hairy per. Lvs bright green; leaflets heart-shaped. Fls white, veined with lilac, sometimes tinged purple, *solitary*. Woods and shady places, to 2100m. Apr-July. T.

7 YELLOW OXALIS *Oxalis corniculata*. Low/short creeping per; stems rooting at lf junctions. Lvs green, often purplish tinted; leaflets heart-shaped. Fls yellow, 4-7mm, in *long-stalked umbels*. Dry open and bare places and cultivated ground. Occasional weed above 1000m. May-Oct. T, except Faeroes, IS (A, B, CS, D, GB, IRL, NL, PL, R, SF).

4

Geranium Family Geraniaceae

Hairy perennials, sometimes annuals, with opposite or alternate palmately *(Geranium)* or pinnately *(Erodium)* cut or lobed lvs. Fls cup-shaped, long-stalked with 5 petals and sepals and 10 stamens. Fr of 5-basal seeds with a long 'cranesbill' beak, which splits apart when ripe.

1 ROCK CRANESBILL *Geranium macrorrhizum.* Short/med per, *strongly aromatic* when crushed. Lvs deeply cut into 5-7 lobes. Fls pink to purplish-red, 20-25mm, in pairs or small clusters; petals rounded. Shaded limestone rocks and crevices, to 2500m. July-Aug.A, seF, I, R, YU (B, D, GB).

2 ASHY CRANESBILL *Geranium cinereum.* Low tufted per. Lvs all basal, cut almost to middle into 5-7 lobes. Fls in pairs, pale lilac with darker veins, 25-30mm, petals slightly notched. Grassy or rocky places, 1500-2400m. July-Aug. nE, sF; Pyrenees. **2a** *G.c.* subsp. *subcaulescens* has larger lvs and reddish-purple fls. c & sl. **2b** *G. argenteum* similar to 2 but lvs *silvery-grey* and the fls pale rose-pink. Limestone rocks and screes 1700-2200m. July-Aug. seF, n & cI, nwYU.

3 BLOODY CRANESBILL *Geranium sanguineum.* Low/short tufted per. Lvs mostly on the stems, cut almost to middle into 5-7 lobes. Fls bright reddish-purple, rarely pink or white, solitary or paired; petals slightly notched. Dry rocky or sandy places and open woods, to 1900m. June-Sept. T, except Faeroes, IS, NI.

4 MEADOW CRANESBILL *Geranium pratense.* Med/tall per. Lvs cut to the base into 5-7 lobes. Fls in pairs, bright violet-blue, 25-30mm; petals *rounded.* Fl stalks *bent down* after flowering, but erect when fr ripens. Meadows and grassy places, usually on limestone, to 1900m. June-Sept. T, except Faeroes, IS.

5 WOOD CRANESBILL *Geranium sylvaticum.* Low/med per. Lvs like 4. Fls in pairs, usually reddish-purple, 12-25mm; petals rounded. Fl stalks *always upright.* Meadows, woods and stony places, usually on acid soils, to 2400m. June-Aug. T. **5a** *G.s.* subsp. *rivulare* has *white fls* veined with red. eF, CH, nI; mainly western Alps. **5b** *G. s.* subsp. *caeruleatum* has more deeply dissected lvs and smaller *bright violet-blue* fls. R, nYU; southern Carpathians.

6 WESTERN CRANESBILL *Geranium endressii.* Med/tall per. Lvs cut almost to middle into 5 lobes. Fls solitary pink, 24-28mm, long-stalked; petals not or slightly notched. Wet meadows and stream banks, to 1200m. June-July. nE, swF; western Pyrenees (B, GB). **6a** *G. versicolor* has white or pale lilac fls with deep violet veins; petals deeply notched. c & sl, YU (F, GB, IRL).

7 KNOTTED CRANESBILL *Geranium nodosum.* Low/med per. Lvs cut *half-way* into 3-5 lobes. Fls bright pink or violet with *darker veins,* 20-30mm, in small clusters; petals notched. Open woods, to 1600m. May-Sept. CH, nE, c & sF, n & cI, wYU (B, F, GB, NL).

8 DUSKY CRANESBILL *Geranium phaeum.* Short/tall per. Lvs cut half-way into 5-7 lobes. Fls in pairs, *blackish-purple to brownish-purple,* rarely white, 15-20mm; petals slightly recurved, often pointed. Damp meadows and open woods, to 2400m. May-Aug. T, except Faeroes, IS and far north (B, DK, GB, IRL, NL, S).

9 MARSH CRANESBILL *Geranium palustre.* Short/med per. Lvs cut almost to middle into 5-7, wedge-shaped, lobes. Fls in pairs, *pale purple* or reddish-purple, 20-30mm; petals not or slightly notched. Fr stalk bent down. Damp meadows, to 1500m. June-Aug. T, except Faeroes, GB, IRL, IS, N, NL, nS. **9a** *G. asphodeloides* has pinkish-lilac fls with darker veins; petals often slightly ntched. cI, R.

10 SPREADING CRANESBILL *Geranium divaricatum.* Short/med branched ann. Lvs cut *almost to middle* into 3-5 lobes. Fls pink, 6-12mm, in small clusters; petals notched. Woods, hedgerows and stony places, to 2000m. May-Aug. CH, CS, D, E, F, H, I, PL, R, YU.

Geranium Family (contd.)

1 PYRENEAN CRANESBILL *Geranium pyrenaicum.* Short/med branched ann. Lvs cut *halfway* into 5-7 lobes. Fls in pairs, purplish-pink or lilac, 14-18mm; petals *deeply notched.* Meadows, open woods and waste places, to 1900m. May-Oct. T, except Faeroes, IS. **1a** *G. sibiricum* has lilac fls with darker veins, the petals *scarcely* notched; hairs on fruit spreading. R (A, CH, CS, D, F, H, PL).

2 DOVESFOOT CRANESBILL *Geranium molle.* Low/short, rather sprawling, grey-green ann/bien; stems *long-hairy.* Lower lvs cut less than half-way into 5-7 lobes; upper lvs alternate, more deeply cut. Fls in pairs, pinkish-purple, 5-12mm; petals deeply notched. Dry grassy and waste places, to 2000m. Apr-Sept. T, except Faeroes, IS (Faeroes). **2a** *G. pusillum** has stems with short hairs and pale lilac fls, 4-7mm. T, except Faeroes, IS (IRL). **2b** *G. rotundifolium** is like 2 but lvs rounded, *scarcely* cut; fls pink, 9-13mm, petal not or only slightly notched. To 1600m. T, DK, Faeroes, N, NL,S, SF.

3 HERB ROBERT *Geranium robertianum.* Short/med ann/bien, rather strong smelling, often reddish. Lvs cut to middle into 3-5 stalked lobes. Fls in pairs, bright pink, 15-22mm; petals blunt-ended, pollen orange. Shady places, rocks and banks, to 2000m. May-Sept. T, except Faeroes, IS. **3a** *G. purpureum* has *smaller* purplish-pink fls, 8-16mm, and yellow pollen. E, F, c & sGB, IRL, I, YU. **3b** *G. lucidum* has *shiny* lvs and keeled sepals. T, except Faeroes, IS, NL.

4 COMMON STORKSBILL *Erodium cicutarium.* Low/med ann/bien, often stickily-hairy. Lvs 2-pinnate. Fls purplish-pink, lilac or white, 7-18mm, in longstalked umbel-like heads; petals oval-elliptical, often unequal. Fields and waste places, to 2100m. Jurie-Sept. T, except Faeroes, IS.

5 ROCK STORKSBILL *Erodium petraeum.* Low/short tufted, *stem less,* per; strong-smelling. Lvs 2-pinnate, ferny, greyish or silvery. Fls pink, 15-25mm, in umbel-like heads of two to five, rarely solitary. Rocky and stony places on limestone, to 1700m. May-June. sF; central Pyrenees. **5a** *E.p.* subsp. *lucidum** has more or less hairless, shiny-green, lvs and white fls veined with pink. Generally on acid rocks. nE, sF; central and eastern Pyrenees. **5b** *E.p.* subsp. *glandulosum* has very hairy, sticky lvs and violet or purple fls, one or two upper petals larger and with a black blotch at base. nE, sF; Pyrenees and northern Spain. **5c** *E.p.* subsp. *crispum** like 5b but fls white, pale pink or lilac with red or purple veins, upper petals blotched; lvs not sticky. Limestone rocks. nE, sF; eastern Pyrenees and Corbieres.

6 LARGE PURPLE STORKSBILL *Erodium manescavi.* Low/short tufted, *stemless per.* Lvs large, 2-pinnate, hairy. Fls large, purple or carmine-red, 25-35mm, in umbel-like heads of five to twenty. Bracts rounded. Meadows and pastures, to 2300m. July-Aug. sF; central Pyrenees.

7 ALPINE STORKSBILL *Erodium alpinum.* Low, slightly hairy, per, with erect *stems.* Lvs 2-pinnate, green or greyish. Fls violet, 14-24mm, in umbel-like heads of two to nine; petals rounded or wedge-shaped. Bracts narrow-lance-shaped or triangular. Stony places to 2000m. July-Aug. cl; central Apennines.

2a   Basal leaves   **2b**

Spurge Family Euphorbiaceae

SPURGES *Euphorbia*. Stems with milky juice. Lvs alternate and usually stalkless and untoothed. Fls small in broad, branched, umbel-like clusters, each surrounded by two conspicuous usually green or yellowish-green, floral bracts; no sepals or petals, but a solitary 3-styled female fl surrounded by several 1-stamened male fls partly enclosed in a calyx-like cup with 4-5 glands along its perimeter. Fr a 3-parted capsule. **Poisonous.**

1 IRISH SPURGE *Euphorbia hyberna.* Med little-branched per. Lvs oblong, downy beneath, turning pinkish-red. Fls and floral bracts yellowish-green; glands kidney-shaped. Fr stalked, covered in long and short warts. Damp and shady places, to 2000m. Apr-July. E, F, GB, nl, s & wIRL. **1a** *E.h.* subsp. *canuti* has fr capsule *hardly stalked.* seF, nwl; Maritime Alps.

2 CARNIAN SPURGE *Euphorbia carniolica.* Short/med hairy or hairless per, forming tufts; stems *scaly* at base. Lvs oblong, large 40-70mm, narrowed to the base. Fl cups long-stalked; glands *brownish-yellow.* Fr covered with short warts. Woods and shrubby slopes, to 1900m. Apr-June. A, eCH, nI, R, YU.

3 PYRENEAN SPURGE *Euphorbia chamaebuxus.* Low hairless creeping per; stems erect, scaly at base. Lvs small, 10-30mm, elliptical to oblong, broadest above the middle. Umbels few fld, fls often solitary, glands 4, *reddish.* Fr covered with flap-like warts. Rocks and screes, to 2000m. nE, sF; western Pyrenees and Cordillera Cantabrica.

4 GLAUCOUS or BLUE SPURGE *Euphorbia myrsinites.* Low/short *bluish or greyish-green,* hairless, per; stems rather sprawling, thick, fleshy. Lvs crowded, oval to *almost rounded* with a pointed tip. Fls yellowish-green, glands with long club-shaped horns, often reddish-brown. Fr smooth. Rocky and grassy places, to 2260m. Mar-June. c & sI, R, YU.

5 ROCK SPURGE *Euphorbia saxatilis.* Low/short rather bluish-green, hairless, creeping per. Lvs small, 2-25mm, in *basal rosettes* and along stems; rosette lvs narrow-oblong, the others oblong to almost rounded. Fls greenish-yellow; glands with two horns. Fr smooth. Limestone rocks and screes, to 1200m. June-July. eA, nwYU; eastern Alps. **5a** *E. kerneri* is taller with broader lvs *not notched* at the end. seA, neI, nwYU; south eastern Alps.

6 VALLINO'S SPURGE *Euphorbia valliniana.* Rather like 5 but a more bluish-green per without basal lf rosettes. Lvs small, 3-19mm, rounded to oblong. Fls greenish-yellow, glands kidney-shaped, *not horned.* Fr almost smooth. Rocky calcareous slopes and screes, to 2000m. seF, nwl; south-west Alps.

7 CYPRESS SPURGE *Euphorbia cyparissias.* Short/med tufted, bright greenish-yellow, hairless per. Lvs *linear,* crowded, becoming red eventually. Fl heads golden-yellow; glands with short horns, brownish. Fr almost smooth. Grassy, rocky and waste places, to 2650m. Apr-June. T, except Faeroes, IRL, IS, and far north (DK, GB, N, S, SF).

8 ANNUAL MERCURY *Mercurialis annua.* Short/med slightly hairy or hairless ann; stems branched. Lvs *opposite,* oval to elliptical, toothed, short-stalked. Fls tiny, green, in stalked or unstalked tassels, male and female often on separate plants. Waste places, banks and cultivated ground, to 1800m. Apr-Nov. T, except Faeroes, IS (IRL, N, S, SF).

9 DOG'S MERCURY *Mercurialis perennis.* Low/short unbranched, downy, foetid per, often forming drifts. Lvs opposite, crowded towards stem tops, lance-shaped, toothed. Fls tiny greenish, male in long, stalked, tassels, female in small, almost stalkless, clusters and borne on separate plants. Woods and shady places, to 1800m. Feb-May. T, except Faeroes, IS and far north. **9a** *M. ovata* has broader more rounded lvs, not *crowded* at stem tops. A, CH, CS, sD, H, I, PL, R.

4

Flax Family Linaceae

Slender perennials or annuals with untoothed lvs; no stipules. Fls with 5 petals over-lapping spirally in bud and 5 sepals; opening in sunshine. Fr a capsule.

1 PERENNIAL FLAX *Linum perenne* agg. Short/med hairless, tufted, per. Lvs alternate, linear to narrow lance-shaped, 1-veined. Fls in branched clusters, pale to bright blue, 16-25mm, fl stalks *erect;* inner sepals often blunt. Dry grassy places, to 1700m. May-Aug. T, except B, Faeroes, DK, nGB, IRL, N, NL, S, SF. **1a** *L. austriacum* has *down-turned* fl stalks and some lvs generally 3-veined. A, CH, CS, sD, E, c & sF, H, I, PL, R, YU (DK). **1b Flax** *L. usitatissimum* is *ann;* all lvs 3-veined. Cultivated and widely naturalised in the region.

2 PYRENEAN FLAX *Linum suffruticosum* subsp. *salsoloides.* Low/short rather sprawling, hairless, per, stem branched, some none-flowering. Lvs alternate *linear,* greyish-green, margins rolled *under.* Fls white with a pink or violet centre, 20-30mm. Grassy and rocky places, to 1750m. May-July. n & cE, c, s & seF, nwI.

3 YELLOW FLAX *Linum flavum.* Variable med hairless, tufted per. Lvs alternate, spoon-shaped to lance-shaped, 3-veined. Fls in branched clusters, yellow, 25-30mm. Dry grassy places, to 1600m. May-Aug. A, CS, sD, H, I, PL, R, YU. **3a** *L. tauricum* is much-branched the stems with up to 20 (not 25 or more) fls. R, YU.

4 STICKY FLAX *Linum viscosum.* Med *hairy* per, forming tufts, upper lvs and bracts sticky. Lvs velvety, oval to lance-shaped, 3-5-veined. Fls in branched clusters, pink, 25-35mm. Meadows and grassy places, to 1900m. June-Aug. A, sD, nE, s & eF, nI, nYU. **4a** *L. hirsutum* is hairier and has *blue* fls. A, CS, H, PL, R, YU.

5 PURGING FLAX *Linum catharticum.* Low/short, slender, hairless ann. Lvs *opposite,* oblong to lance-shaped, 1-veined. Fls small, in loose branched clusters, white with a yellow centre, 4-6mm. Grassy places, especially on lime, to 2350m. May-Sept. T.

Milkwort Family Polygalaceae

Hairless perennials, with usually alternate, stalkless, untoothed lvs; no stipules. Fls with 5 sepals, the inner 2 large and petal-like (called wings) on either side of the 3 true petals (the keel), which are joined at the base; stamens 8, often fused into a tube. Fr flat, heart-shaped, often winged.

6 SHRUBBY MILKWORT *Polygala chamaebuxus.* Low more or less mat-forming, *evergreen subshrub.* Lvs oval to lance-shaped, shiny green, leathery. Fls with a yellow keel and white, pink or purple wings, 12-18mm long, in leafy spikes. Woods, pastures and rocky slopes, to 2500m. Apr-Sept. A, CH, sD, eF,, nI, R, YU.

7 PYRENEAN MILKWORT *P. vayredae.* Like 6 but lvs *linear* to *narrow* lance- shaped and fls pinkish-purple. Seldom above 800m. Apr-May. neE; eastern Pyrenees.

8 NICE MILKWORT *Polygala nicaeensis* agg. Variable low/short per, somewhat sprawling but with erect fl stems. Lvs lance-shaped to linear, the lower broadest above the middle. Fls blue or pink, 9-11mm long, in slender spikes; wings *3-5-veined.* Dry grassy and stony places, to 1700m. Apr-July. A, CH, sD, E, s & eF, H, I, YU.

9 TUFTED MILKWORT *Polygala comosa.* Rather like 8 in habit and If, but lower lvs *falling* before fls open. Fls lilac-pink, 4-6mm long, in long spikes; wings 1-3-veined. Dry grassy places and open woods, to 2200m. May-July. A, B, CH, CS, D, E, F, H, I, NL, PI, R, YU.

10 MOUNTAIN MILKWORT *Polygala alpestris.* Low/short slender tufted per. Lvs lance-shaped, *increasing* in size *upwards,* the uppermost crowded. Fls blue or white, 4-6mm long; wings 1-3-veined. Meadows, to 2200m. May-Aug. A, sD, E, s & eF, nI, YU.

11 THYME-LEAVED MILKWORT *Polygala serpyllifolia.* Low/short slender per. Lower lvs opposite, oblong to elliptical, the upper lvs narrow lance-shaped, usually alternate. Fls usually blue, 4.5-5.5mm, the upper petals *longer* than the wings. Acid meadows, to 1800m. May-Aug. T, except IS, S, SF. **11a** *P. caruleliana* has stem lvs blunt, *broadest* near apex; fls slightly larger with greenish, purple-tinged wings. nwI; Apuan Alps.

12 BITTER MILKWORT *Polygala amara.* Low/short per with numerous stem arising from a basal If rosette. Lvs *bitter tasting,* elliptical to oblong; stem lvs pointed, alternate. Fls blue, violet, pink or white, 4.5-8mm long, in long spikes. Damp meadows on lime, to 2600m. Apr-July. A, CS, sD, H, PL, R, YU. **12a** *P. amarella* has stem lvs *blunt* and broadest near the apex; fls 2-4.5mm long. T, except E, Faeroes, IRL, IS, YU.

13 ALPINE MILKWORT *Polygala alpina.* Low prostrate per with *leafy rosettes.* Lvs not bitter, oblong to linear; stem lvs much smaller, *alternate.* Fls bright blue, 4-4.5mm long, in short spikes. Pastures, usually on limestone, 1500-3000m. July-Aug. CH, nE, s & eF, nI. **13a** *P. supina* subsp. *hospita* is taller with oval lvs and larger fls, *only* 1-3 per raceme. Mountain rocks. swR, neYU.

Maple Family Aceraceae

A family of trees and shrubs with opposite palmate or pinnate lvs, sometimes with simple unlobed lvs. Fls small, often greenish or yellowish. Fr paired, winged (keys).

1 NORWAY MAPLE *Acer platanoides*. Large spreading tree to 30m; bark pale grey, smooth or shallowly ridged. Lvs large, with 5 *long-pointed lobes*, each further lobed, bright green but with bright yellow and red autumn colours. Fls yellowish-green, 8mm, in erect branched clusters, appearing before the lvs. Fr with widely diverging wings. Woods, but widely planted, to 1800m. April. T, except Faeroes, IRL, IS and far north (GB, NL). **1a** *A. lobelii* is a rather erect tree with dark grey bark. Lvs with lobes *not* further lobed, pale shiny green above. Fls smaller, 5mm, pale green. c & sl; central and southern Apennines.

2 FIELD MAPLE *Acer campestre*. Small tree or shrub to 25m; bark pale grey, fissured, *twigs downy*. Lvs small, divided into 5 blunt lobes, each lobe itself shallowly lobed, reddish when young, margined with hairs. Fls pale green, 6mm, in erect branched clusters with the lvs. Fr with horizontal wings, usually downy. Open woods and hedgerows, to 1500m. Apr-May. T, except Faeroes, IS and northern Scandinavia (IRL). **2a** *A. monspessulanum* has small *leathery* lvs not more than 8cm across, usually rather grey-green beneath. A, sD, E, sF, I, R, YU.

3 SYCAMORE *Acer pseudoplatanus*. Large spreading tree to 30m; bark smooth grey, flaking when old, twigs hairless. Lvs with 5 blunt, *toothed*, lobes, soon hairless beneath. Fls pale green, 6mm, in drooping clusters, with the young lvs. Fr with wings at right angles. Woods, hedges and streamsides, to 2000m. Apr-May. A, B, CH, CS, D, E, F, H, I, NL, PL, R, YU (DK, GB, IRL, sS). **3a Italian Maple** *A. opalus** is a smaller tree with rather leathery, less toothed, smaller lvs, usually *hairy beneath*; bark smooth. Fls pale yellow, with the young lvs. To 1900m. Apr. CH, wD, E, s & eF, c & sl. **3b** *A. obtusatum* is like *A. opalus* but *lf-lobes blunt*, not pointed and hairy beneath (hairs not confined to just the veins). c & sl, YU. **3c** *A. tataricum* is a shrub or small tree to 30m with generally *undivided* lvs, occasionally with three shallow lobes; fls greenish-white in ascending panicles; fr with almost parallel wings. A, CS, H, R, YU.

Spindle-Tree Family Celastraceae

Trees or shrubs with opposite lvs and 4-5 parted flowers. Fr a rather fleshy, brightly coloured, capsule; seeds with a conspicuously coloured pulpy aril.

4 SPINDLE TREE *Euonymus europaeus*. Deciduous shrub or small tree to 6m; twigs green, square, bark smooth, greyish. Lvs elliptical to oval, finely toothed, stalked, red tinged in the autumn. Fls greenish-white, 8-10mm, *4-petalled*, in lax clusters at base of lower lvs. Fr capsule bright coral pink, 4-lobed, seeds with a bright orange aril. Woods, scrub and hedges on calcareous soils, to 1600m. May-June. T, except Faeroes, IS, SF.

5 ALPINE SPINDLE-TREE *Euonymus latifolius*. Deciduous shrub or small tree, to 5m; twigs greyish-brown, *square*. Lvs larger than 5, oval, finely toothed, short stalked. Fls greenish-brown, 8-10mm, usually 5-petalled, in lax, long-stalked, clusters. Fr capsule pink, 5-lobed. Woods and scrub, to 1800m. May-June. A, CH, CS, sD, s & eF, I, R, YU . Poisonous. **5a** *E. verrucosus** is smaller with *round* stems and 4-petalled fls. A, CS, H, nl, PL, R, YU.

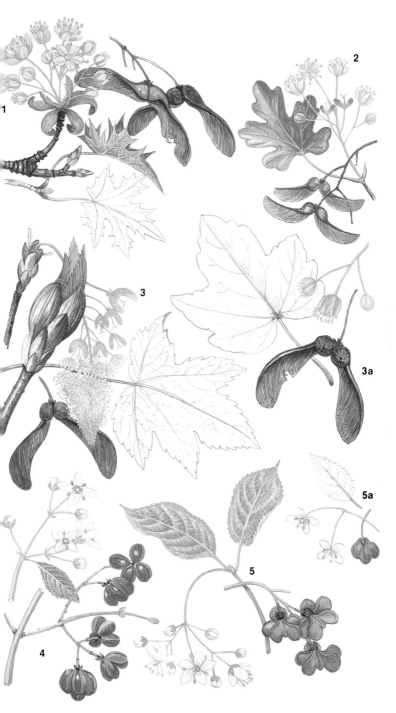

Holly Family Aquifoliaceae

A family of evergreen and deciduous trees and shrubs usually with alternate lvs and small 4-5-parted fls. Fr usually a berry.

1 HOLLY *Ilex aquifolium.* Small evergreen tree or shrub to 10m; bark smooth, grey. Lvs alternate, oval, spiny edged, deep shiny green. Fls white, 5-6mm, 4-petalled, in dense clusters at the base of the lvs; male and female on separate plants. Fr a scarlet berry. Woods, scrub and hedges, occasionally on cliffs, to 2000m. Apr-May. T, except CS, Faeroes, IS, PL and most of Scandinavia. **1a** *T. tomentosa* has young stems white with down and leaves also white-downy beneath. Tree to 30m with dull white fls in groups of 6-10. H, R, YU.

Lime Tree Family Tiliaceae

Deciduous trees with heart-shaped, alternate, toothed lvs. Fls in drooping clusters half-joined to a large oblong bract; 5-parted with many stamens. Fr a globular nut.

2 SMALL-LEAVED LIME *Tilia cordata.* Large spreading tree to 30m; bark smooth, dark brown, with large bosses, young twigs more or less hairless. Lvs heart- shaped, pointed, 3-8cm, greyish, hairless except for reddish hair tufts at vein angles beneath. Fls yellowish, *fragrant,* in small clusters of 4-10. Fr smooth. Woods, but widely planted, to 1500m. June-July. T, except IRI, IS and far north.

3 LARGE-LEAVED LIME *Tilia platyphyllos.* Large spreading tree to 30m, bark smooth, dark brown, *without* bosses, young twigs usually downy. Lvs larger than 1, 8-12cm, *greyish downy beneath.* Fls yellowish-white, fragrant, in small clusters of 2-5. Fr ribbed. Woods, but widely planted, to 1800m. June-July. T, except IRL, IS, N, n & cS, SF (GB). **3a** *T. tomentosa* has lvs white with star-shaped hairs beneath and dull white fls. H, R, YU. **3b** *T. x vulgaris** a hybrid with intermediate characters exists between 7 and 8 where they grow together.

Olive Family Oleaceae

A family of trees and shrubs with opposite lvs and 4-parted fls; fls with a tube and spreading lobes, not differentiated into sepals and petals.

4 ASH *Fraxinus excelsior.* Spreading deciduous tree to 40m; bark grey, smooth at first but becoming fissured; buds black. Lvs *opposite, pinnate;* leaflets toothed, un-stalked. Fls without sepals or petals, anthers dark purple, becoming greenish, in tufts, appearing before the Lvs. Fr a one-winged samara. Woods and hedges, to 1600m. Apr-May. T, except Faeroes, IS and far north. **4a** *F. angustifolia* has brown buds and twigs always hairless; leaves with narrow-oblong to linear-elliptical leaf-lets with as many teeth as lateral veins, not more. Deciduous woodland and river banks and meadows. A, CS, E, H, I, R, YU.

5 MANNA ASH *Fraxinus ornus.* Small spreading deciduous tree to 1 0- 20m; bark grey, smooth; buds greyish or brownish. Lvs opposite, pinnate; leaflets toothed, short-stalked. *Fls creamy-white,* in branched clusters, appearing with the lvs, petals linear. Mixed woods, thickets and rocky places, to 1500m. May-June. A, CH, CS, E, s & eF, H, I, R, YU. Forms with almost non-spiny lvs are occasionally seen in the wild but such plants usually have at least some lvs with marginal spines.

1

2

3b

3

4

5

Box Family Buxaceae

1 BOX *Buxus sempervirens.* Evergreen shrub or small tree to 5m. Lvs small, *opposite*, elliptical, shiny and leathery, untoothed. Fls tiny, whitish-green, 2mm, petaless, in dense clusters at base of upper lvs, lower fls in each cluster male, the upper female. Fr a small three-horned capsule. Dry hillslopes and open woods, to 1800m. Mar-Apr. Widely cultivated. A, B, CH, D, E, F, GB, I, YU (R).

Buckthorn Family Rhamnaceae

Deciduous shrubs or small trees, sometimes spiny, with opposite or alternate lvs; stipules present, soon falling. Fls usually 4 parted, calyx bell-shaped, petals small, sometimes absent; style divided. Fr a black berry, bitter tasting, with 2-4 seeds (nos. 2-4), *Rhamnus*, have 4-parted fls and buds with scales (nos. 5-6), *Frangula*, have 5-parted fls and naked buds.

2 BUCKTHORN *Rhamnus catharticus.* Deciduous shrub or small tree, to 6m, spiny; old branchlets *ending in* a single spine. Lvs opposite, broad oval-elliptic, 4-7cm. long, finely toothed, stalked; lateral veins 2-4 pairs. Fls 3-4 mm, greenish, in *dense* clusters arising from the old branches; male and female on separate plants. Berry red, then black. Woods, scrub and hedges, usually on calcareous soils, to 1500m. May-June. T, except Faeroes, IS and northern Scandinavia. **2a Rock Buckthorn** *R. saxatilis** is a much- branched very spiny shrub, often prostrate but sometimes to 2 m tall. *Lvs smaller,* 13cm long, elliptic to lance-shaped, with a very short stalk. Old branchlets with *several* spines. A, CH, CS, SD, E, s & eF, H, I, R, YU.

3 DWARF BUCKTHORN *Rhamnus pumilus.* Prostrate deciduous shrub much-branched with contorted old branches, *not spiny*. Lvs *alternate,* oval to elliptical, finely toothed, or untoothed with 4-9 pairs of veins. Fls yellowish-green, in clusters at base of young branches. Berry bluish-black. Rocky places, cliffs and screes, on limestone, 1100-3050m. May-Aug. A, CH, sD, E, s & eF, I, YU.

4 ALPINE BUCKTHORN *Rhamnus alpinus.* Erect deciduous shrub to 3.5m, branches seldom *contorted,* not spiny; twigs hairy. Lvs alternate, oval, blunt, often almost heart-shaped at the base, with 9-15 pairs of veins. Fls greenish, 3-4 mm, in clusters at base of young branches. Berry bluish-black. Open woods, rocky places and streamsides, to 2150m. May-June. A, CH, sD, E, s & eF, I. **4a** *R. a.* subsp. *fallax* has *hairless* twigs and lvs green above and below; an erect bush. A, YU. **4b** *R. a.* subsp. *glaucophyllus* is like 4a but lvs bluish- or greyish-green *above*. nwI; Apuan Alps.

5 ALDER BUCKTHORN *Frangula alnus.* Erect deciduous shrub or small tree to 5m, *not* spiny. Lvs alternate, oval, broadest above the middle, shiny green, *untoothed*. Fls greenish, 3mm, in small clusters on young stems. Berry red, but becoming black. Damp woods, heaths and hedges, to 1800m. May-June. T, except Faeroes, IS and far north.

6 ROCK FRANGULA *Frangula rupestris.* Small shrub to 80cm tall. Lvs elliptical to rounded, finely toothed or untoothed, hairy beneath, stalked. Fls small, greenish, 5-petalled, *in small clusters,* fl stalks hairy. Fr a red berry, becoming black. Rocky places, to 1200m. May-June. neI, YU.

1

2

2a

3

4

5

6

Mallow Family Malvaceae

Rather leafy, downy, or softly hairy, annuals or perennials. Fls in clusters at base of lvs, or solitary; petals five, notched; sepals in two rings; stamens numerous, bunched together on the end of a short stalk. Fr a flat disc, surrounded by sepals.

1 CUT-LEAVED MALLOW *Malva alcea.* Med/tall erect per; stems with branched hairs. Lvs rounded-heart-shaped, with five, toothed lobes; upper lvs more deeply cut and further lobed. Fls large, *solitary,* bright-pink 3.5-6cm; outer sepals *broad.* Grassy and scrubby places, woods, to 2000m. June-Sept. T, except GB, IRL, IS, northern Scandinavia (N, SF). **1a Musk Mallow** *M. moschata** has more deeply cut lvs with 5-7 narrow lobes; stems with *unbranched* hairs; outer sepals narrow. To 1500m. T, except nGB, IS (DK, H, N, S, SF).

2 COMMON MALLOW *Malva sylvestris.* Med/tall bien or per; stems with branched *or* unbranched hairs. Lvs rounded or kidney-shaped, with 3-7, toothed, lobes. Fls pink or purple with darker veins, 2-5cm, two or *more* together. Meadows and waste places, to 1800m. May-Sept. T, except Faeroes, IS.

3 DWARF MALLOW *Malva neglecta.* Rather sprawling or *prostrate* ann. Lvs rounded or kidney-shaped, with 5-7, toothed, lobes. Fls pale lilac to whitish, 1.5-2cm, in clusters of three to six. Fields and waste places, to 1900m. May-Sept. T, except Faeroes, IS.

Balsam Family Balsaminaceae

Succulent hairless annuals with alternate lvs and spurred fls. Fr exploding when ripe.

4 TOUCH-ME-NOT *Impatiens noli-tangere.* Short/tall ann. Lvs oval-elliptical to lance-shaped, stalked. Fls large yellow with brownish spots, 3-6 in *short-stalked* clusters; spur downcurved, 10-20mm. Damp shady places, to 1500m. July-Sept. T, except Faeroes, IRL, IS and far north. **4a Small Balsam** *I. parviflora* has small pale-yellow fls with *short* 3-5 mm spurs. (Naturalised throughout much of the region except the far north).

Oleaster Family Elaeagnaceae

5 SEA BUCKTHORN *Hippophae rhamnoides.* Deciduous shrub to 4m, branches brown, thorny. Lvs narrow-lance-shaped, untoothed, silvery-grey when young. Fls before lvs, tiny, greenish-yellow, no petals; male and female on different plants. Fr a bright orange berry, edible. River gravels and alluvium, to 2000m. Apr-May. T, except Faeroes, IS and far north (IRL).

Daphne Family Thymelaeaceae

Small shrubs, sometimes herbs, with alternate, untoothed lvs. Fls tubular with four spreading sepal-lobes, no petals. Fr a fleshy berry or a small nut.

6 ANNUAL THYMELAEA *Thymelaea passerina.* Low/med erect, usually hairless, ann. Lvs narrow-lance-shaped, pointed. Fls tiny, greenish, solitary or two to three together. Fr a hairy nut. Dry rocky and waste places, to 1200m. July-Sept. A, B, E, e & sF, H, I, Pl, R, YU.

7 TWISTED THYMELAEA *Thymelaea tinctoria* (= *Passerina tinctoria*). Dwarf shrub to 50cm, stems rough, twisted; young shoots hairy. Lvs narrow-oblong. Fls solitary, yellow 5-6mm long. Fr hairless. Rocky woods and scrub on limestone, to 1200m. Apr-June. neE, sF; Pyrenees. **7a** *T. dioica* has narrower lvs, *hairless* shoots and fls 5-9mm long; fr hairy. Limestone rocks, to 2000m. May-June. n & eE, s & seF, nwl; Pyrenees and south-west Alps. **7b** *T. calycina* like 7 but lf margin *rolled under* towards tip. Stony places, to 2500m. June-Sept. nE, sF; central and western Pyrenees, northern Spain. **7c Hairy Thymelaea** *Thymelaea pubescens.* Short, hairy per, base woody. Lvs narrow to broadly-elliptical. Fls yellow, 6mm long, in *clusters* of two or three. Fr hairless. Dry rocky places, to 1700m. June-July. ?sF, ne & eE; eastern Pyrenees.

Daphne Family *(contd.)*

1 MEZEREON *Daphne mezereum.* Deciduous shrub to 1 m. Lvs oblong-lance-shaped, pale green. Fls pinkish-purple, 7-9mm long, in clusters of two to four, fragrant. Fr a *bright-red* shiny berry. Woods and pastures, usually on limestone, to 2600m. Feb-July. T, except sE, Faeroes, w & nGB, IRL, sl, IS, northern Scandinavia (DK). Very poisonous.

2 SPURGE LAUREL *Daphne laureola.* Evergreen upright shrub to 1 m. Lvs leathery oblong-oval, broadest above middle, shiny dark green. Fls *yellowish-green,* 5-10mm long, in drooping clusters, slightly fragrant. Fr a *black* berry. Woods and clearings, to 1600m. Jan-Apr. T, except Faeroes, nGB, IRL, IS, N, NL, S, SF (DK). **2a** *D.l.* subsp. *philippi* is a lower, more spreading, shrub with smaller fls, 5-6mm long. nE, sF; Pyrenees.

3 ALPINE MEZEREON *Daphne alpina.* Dwarf deciduous shrub to 50cm, branches twisted. Lvs narrow-oblong, greyish-green, clustered at shoot tips. Fls white, 4-6mm, in small clusters. Limestone rocks, to 2000m. Apr-June. A, CH, nE, c, s & eF, n & cl, nwYU. **3a** *D. oleoides* is evergreen with leathery lvs and creamy-white fls with pointed lobes. Dry limestone rocks. c & sE, c & sl, YU; not Alps. **3b** *D. blagayana* has spreading sparse stems and fls with blunt lobes; bracts present. R, n & eYU; southern Carpathians.

4 GARLAND FLOWER *Daphne cneorum.* Evergreen *prostrate* bush, branches straight, young shoots *hairy.* Lvs oblong or narrow spoon-shaped, blunt. Fls pink with a 6-10mm tube, petal-lobes rounded, in clusters of six to ten, fragrant. Fr a brownish-yellow berry. Stony places and pastures, usually on limestone, to 2150m. Apr-Aug. A, CH, CS, sD, nE, s & eF, H, n & cl, PL, R, YU. Dwarf froms found in the Pyrenees are referable to var. *pygmaea.* **4a** *D. striata** is *completely* hairless, the lvs crowded at shoot tips; fls reddish-purple. 1500-2900m. May-Aug. A, CH, sD, eF, nl, nwYU; Alps.

5 ROCK MEZEREON *Daphne petraea.* Dwarf mat-forming evergreen shrub, branches twisted. Lvs lance or wedge-shaped, keeled below. Fls glistening, bright pink, rarely white, with a hairy, 9-15mm long tube, in clusters of three to five, fragrant. Limestone rock crevices, to 2000m. June-July. nl; Lake Garda area. Large-flowered forms are referable to var. *grandiflora.* **5a** *D. arbuscula* has linear lvs with *rolled* margins. Limestone rocks, 900-1300m. eCS.

Rockrose Family Cistaceae

Small thinly branched subshrubs with opposite, untoothed lvs. Fls 5 petalled, open cups in one-sided racemes; sepals unequal; stamens numerous. Fr an egg-shaped capsule.

6 COMMON ROCKROSE *Helianthemum nummularium.* Very variable, more or less prostrate, subshrub. Lvs oblong, lance-shaped or oval, downy-white beneath, one-veined. Fls yellow, orange or white, 14-22mm. Dry meadows and rocky places, usually on limestone, to 2800m. June-Sept. T, except Faeroes, IS, N. **6a** *H.n.* subsp. *glabrum*.* Lvs green above and below, hairless; fls yellow. A, CH, E, s & eF, I, YU. **6b** *H.n.* subsp. *semiglabrum** like 6a but fls pink. seF, nw & cl; Maritime Alps and northern Apennines. **6c** *H.n.* subsp. *grandiflorum** like 6a but lvs hairy. Distribution as 6a. **6d** *H.n.* subsp. *pyrenaicum*.* Lvs whitish-hairy beneath like 6 but fls *pink.* nE, sF. **6e** *H.n.subsp. berterianum** Like 6d but lvs greyish-hairy beneath. seF, I; Maritime Alps and Apennines. **6f** *H.n.* subsp. *obscurum** Like 6c but fls small. A, CH, CS, D, H, R, sS, YU.

7 APENNINE or WHITE ROCKROSE *Helianthemum apenninum.* Loose spreading subshrub, lvs linear to narrow-oblong, grey-white beneath, margin rolled *under.* Fls white, with a yellow *base* to each petal, 18-20mm. Grassy and stony places, on limestone, to 1800m. May-July. B, CH, sD, E, F, sGB, I.

8 ALPINE ROCKROSE *Helianthemum oelandicum* subsp. *alpestre* (= *alpestris*). Dwarf shrub to 20cm. Lvs oblong to narrow-lance-shaped, green, *usually hairless.* Fls yellow, 14-20mm. Dry meadows and stony places, often on limestone, 1600-2900m. May-Sept. A, CH, CS, E, F, I, PL, R, YU; subsp. *oelandicum* is confined to sS; Oland.

9 HOARY ROCKROSE *Helianthemum canum.* Erect or sprawling subshrub to 20cm. Lvs elliptical to narrow-lance-shaped, clustered at shoot tips, green or grey-hairy above, grey-white hairy below. Fls small, yellow, 9-15mm. Dry meadows and stony places on limestone, to 1650m. May-July. T, except B, Faeroes, NL and most of Scandinavia. **9a** *H.c.* subsp. *piloselloides* has *broader* lvs spaced all along the non-flowering shoots. nE, sF; Pyrenees mainly.

10 SHRUBBY ROCKROSE *Helianthemum lunulatum.* Dwarf subshrub to 20cm, stems twisted, prickly when old. Lvs elliptical-lance-shaped, green, slightly hairy. Fls yellow, petals with an orange-base, 14-16mm, solitary or two to three. Rocky places, to 1600m. June-Aug. nwl; Maritime Alps.

St. John's Wort Family Hypericaceae

Hairless, rarely hairy, perennials with opposite or whorled, untoothed, lvs which have transparent veins, often gland dotted, usually stalkless. Fls yellow, in branched clusters, sometimes solitary; petals and sepals 5, stamens numerous. Fr a capsule.

1 YELLOW CORIS *Hypericum coris.* Low/med subshrubby per; stems erect. Lvs *in whorls* of four, linear, the margins rolled under. Fls bright yellow, 20mm, in elongated clusters, rarely solitary. Sunny limestone rocks, to 2000m. May-July. CH, seF, n & cI.

2 WESTERN ST. JOHN'S WORT *Hypericum nummularium.* Short creeping per; stems erect. Lvs opposite, oval or rounded, bluish-green beneath, *with two black dots* near top. Fls yellow, sometimes red-veined, 20-30mm, in small clusters or solitary. Limestone rocks and crevices, to 2500m. June-Sept. nE, s & seF. **2a** H. hirsutum* is *downy* and with narrower lvs. Woods and riverbanks, to 1600m. T, except Faeroes, IS and far north.

3 MOUNTAIN ST. JOHN'S WORT *Hypericum montanum.* Short/tall erect per. Lvs opposite, oval to oblong-elliptical, margin beneath with *a row* of black dots. Fls pale yellow, 10-15mm, in flat-topped clusters, fragrant. Fields, woods and thickets, often on limestone, to 1900m. June-Sept. T, except Faeroes, IS and much of northern Scandinavia.

4 ALPINE ST. JOHN'S WORT *Hypericum richeri.* Low/med erect per, patch-forming. Lvs opposite, oval to elliptical or almost triangular, without black dots on the surface. Fls bright yellow, 20-25mm, in flat-topped clusters; petals *covered* by tiny black dots. Meadows, screes and rocks, usually on limestone, to 2500m. June-Sept. CH, E, s & eF, I, R, YU. **4a** *H.r.* subsp. *burseri* (= H. burseri) has lvs *clasping* stem at their base and *larger fls*, 30-45mm. nE, sF; Pyrenees and Cordillera Cantabrica. **4b** H. umbellatum has *lvs* black-dotted and fr without black glands. Mountain woods. R, YU.

5 IMPERFORATE ST. JOHN'S WORT *Hypericum maculatum.* Short/med per; stems four-sided, erect. Lvs opposite oval or oblong, without translucent dots usually. Fls golden yellow, 20mm in branched clusters; petals with tiny black dots and streaks in centre. Damp meadows, wood margins and stream banks, to 2650m. June-Sept. T, except IS and far north.

6 PERFORATE ST. JOHN'S WORT *Hypericum perforatum* agg. Short/tall per; stems erect with *two raised lines* running down them. Lvs oval to linear with numerous *translucent* dots. Fls golden-yellow, 20mm; petals with tiny dots in the centre and along margin. Dry fields, woods and scrub, to 2000m. May-Sept. T, except Fareroes and IS. **6a** H. elegans has small black-glandular teeth along sepal margins. A, CS, D, H, R, YU.

7 TRAILING ST. JOHN'S WORT *Hypericum humifusum.* Slender, *usually prostrate*, per. Lvs opposite oblong or lance-shaped, with translucent dots. Fls small, yellow, 8-10mm. Open woods and scrub on acid rocks, to 1800m. July-Oct. T, except Faeroes, sl, IS, N, nS.

Tamarix Family Tamaricaceae

8 MYRICARIA *Myricaria germanica.* Hairless evergreen shrub, to 2m. Lvs tiny, *scale-like*, overlapping along the slender stems, bluish-green. Fls pink, 5-6mm long, in dense, *catkin-like*, spikes. Seeds with fluffy tufts of hairs. Rocky places and gravels along rivers and streams, to 2400m. May-Aug. T, except B, Faeroes, GB, IRL, sl, IS, NL.

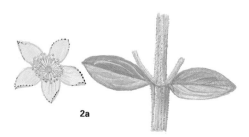

2a

Violet Family Violaceae

VIOLETS and PANSIES *Viola.* Tuft-forming perennials, sometimes annuals, with or without stolons. Lvs alternate, often in basal clusters, toothed, with *stipules* at base. Fls solitary with 5 petals, the lower-most largest, lip-like and spurred behind. Fr a small 3-valved capsule, splitting. Hybrids frequently occur.

1 SWEET VIOLET *Viola odorata.* Low creeping hairy per, with *long, rooting, runners.* Lvs round-heart-shaped, long-stalked; stipules oval. Fls dark violet or white, 13-15mm, *fragrant;* sepals blunt. Woods scrub and hedgerows, to 1400m. Mar-May and sometimes Aug-Sept. T, except Faeroes, IS, SF. **1a** *V. suavis* has short thick runners; fls larger, violet with a white *throat.* A, CH, CS, E, F, I, PL, R, YU (D).

2 WHITE VIOLET *Viola alba* subsp. *scotophylla.* Variable low creeping, slightly hairy per, with long *non-rooting* runners. Lvs dark green, oval or triangular-heart-shaped, long-stalked; stipules narrow lance-shaped, *hairy along edge.* Fls white, sometimes violet, 15-20mm, fragrant. Woods and hedgerows, to 1200m. Mar-June. A, CH, CS, I, R, YU.

3 HAIRY VIOLET *Viola hirta.* Low downy per, *no runners.* Lvs pale green, heart-shaped; stipules broad lance-shaped, hairy edged. Fls violet, 15mm, not fragrant; spur dark violet. Pastures and open woods, usually on calcareous soils, to 2000m. Mar-June. T, except Faerores, Is and far north. **3a Hill Violet** *V. collina* has narrow stipules and pale blue fragrant fls, spur *whitish.* Mar-Apr. T, except DK, Fareoes, GB, IRL, IS, NL and far north.

4 AUSTRIAN VIOLET *Viola ambigua.* Low slight hairy per, no runners. Lvs *oblong-oval,* long-stalked; stipules *dark green,* broad lance-shaped, short toothed. Fls dark violet, 10-15mm, fragrant. Meadows, heaths and rocky places on acid soils, to 2300m. Apr-Aug. A, CS, H, R, YU. **4a** *V. thomasiana* has lvs slightly heart-shaped at base and narrow lance-shaped stipules; fls lilac or almost white, to 2300m. A, CH, eF, nI; mainly central and southern Alps.

5 PYRENEAN VIOLET *Viola pyrenaica.* Low slightly hairy per. Lvs *shiny-green,* heart-shaped; stipules lance-shaped, short toothed. Fls pale violet with a *white throat,* 15mm, fragrant. Meadows, open woods and rocky places, to 2250m. Mar-July. A, CH, nE, s & eF, n & cl, YU.

6 TEESDALE VIOLET *Viola rupestris* (= *V. arenaria*) Low tufted, hairy, per. Lvs heart-shaped, long-stalked; stipules oval-lance.shaped, toothed or not. Fls reddish-violet, pale blue or white, 10-15mm; spur short, pale violet. Dry meadows, gravels and heaths on limestone, to 3100m. Mar-July. T, except Faeroes, IRL, IS. **6a** *V. mirabilis* is larger with pale violet, *fragrant* fls, 20mm; spur *long* whitish. Woods, to 1800m. T, except Faeroes, GB, IRL, IS, NL. **6b** *V. jooi* has stipule fused to the petioles, not free; fls reddish or violet-purple, fragrant. Calcareous rocks. cR.

7 COMMON DOG VIOLET *Viola riviniana.* Variable low/short, almost hairless, tufted per. Lvs heart-shaped, long-stalked; stipules lance-shaped, toothed. Fls bluish-violet, 14-25mm, *unscented,* petals broad; spur short, whitish or pale purple. Dry grassy places and woods, to 1800m. Apr-June. T. **7a Early Dog Violet** *V. reichenbachiana* * has narrow lvs and stipules; fls violet, darker in centre, 12-18mm, petals narrow, spur *deep violet.* T, except Faeroes, IS, SF and northern Scandinavia. **7b** *V. sieheana* has *larger* fls than 7, pale blue or white and a stout whitish spur. Woodland and shaded rocks. R.

8 HEATH DOG VIOLET *Viola canina* agg. Variable low/short hairless or slightly downy per with spreading to ascending stems. Lvs *not in a tuft,* oval to lance-shaped, heart-shaped at base; stipules usually toothed. Fls blue, 15-25mm; spur white or greenish-yellow; sepals *pointed.* Open woods and heaths on acid soils, to 2500m. Apr-July. T. **8a** *V. c.* subsp. *montana* has *erect* stems, less markedly heart-shaped lvs and blue or white fls. T.

9 BOG VIOLET *Violet palustris.* Low, usually hairless, slightly tufted per. Lvs *kidney-shaped;* stipules oval-lance-shaped, toothed or not. Fls pale lilac, 10-15mm, unscented. Bogs and marshes, 1200-2600m. Apr-July. T, except the far south sand south-east.

10 YELLOW WOOD VIOLET *Viola biflora.* Low fragile, *creeping,* slightly hairy per. Lvs tufted, pale green, kidney or heart-shaped; stipules small oval, slightly toothed. Fls *bright yellow,* 15mm, solitary or paired. Damp or shady places, to 3000m. May-Aug. T, except B, DK, Faeroes, GB, IRL, IS, NL.

Violet Family (contd.)

1 FINGER-LEAVED VIOLET *Viola pinnata.* Low slightly hairy tufted per. Lvs *fan-shaped* with finger-like lobes; stipules whitish, lance-shaped. Fls pale violet, 10-20mm, fragrant. Meadows, rocky places and screes, to 2500m. June-Aug. A, CH, eF, nI, nwYU; Alps.

2 DIVERSE-LEAVED VIOLET *Viola diversifolia.* Low stiff-hairy tufted per. Lower lvs rounded to broadly-oval, *untoothed,* stalked, the upper narrow-oblong or oval; stipules oblong, toothed. Fls violet, 15-20mm, fragrant. Meadows and rocky places to 2600m. June-July. nE, sF; east and central Pyrenees.

3 MT. CENIS PANSY *Viola cenisia.* Low hairy or hairless per. Lvs *small,* oval or oblong, untoothed, long-stalked; stipules *like lvs,* but smaller. Fls bright violet, 20-25mm; spur slender, 5-8mm long. Limestone rocks and screes, to 2900m. June-Sept. CH, eF, nwI; south-west and central Alps. **3a** *V. comollia* has bright violet fls with an *orange or deep* yellow spot; spur short, 3-5mm. nI; Orobie Alps.

4 MARITIME ALPS PANSY *Viola valderia.* Rather like 3 but lvs larger and stipules *deeply toothed* at base. Fls bright violet, 20mm; spur slender, 7-10mm. Acid rocks and screes, to 2900m. June-Sept. seF, nwI; Maritime Alps. **4a** *V. magellensis* has stipules slightly toothed at base and lvs with *short stout* stalks; fls violet or pink, the upper two petals often dark reddish-violet. Limestone pastures and screes, to 2900m. cl; central Apennines.

5 ALPINE PANSY *Viola alpina.* Low tufted, *stemless,* hairless per. Lvs shiny-green, oval-heart-shaped, blunt-toothed, long-stalked. Fls violet, 20-30mm; spur short, 3-4mm. Meadows and screes, on limestone, 1600-2200m. June-July. A, CS, PL, R; eastern Alps and Carpathians. **5a** *V. nummariifolia* has short stems and smaller *bright blue* fls, 10-12mm across. Meadows and acid rocks. seF, nwI; Maritime Alps.

6 LONG-SPURRED PANSY *Viola calcarata.* Low tufted hairy or hairless per. Lvs rounded, oval or lance-shaped, blunt-toothed, stalked; stipules oblong, slightly toothed. Fls 1-2 together, violet, 20-30mm; *spur long,* 8-15mm. Meadows and screes, 1300-2400m. Apr-Oct. A, Ch, sD, eF, nI, nwYU. **6a** *V.c.* subsp. *zoysii** has *yellow* fls. Limestone rocks. seA; Karawanken Alps. **6b** *V.c.* subsp. *villarsiana* has *deeply toothed* stipules and fls in groups of 1-4, yellow, blue or white. wCH, eF, nwI; south-western Alps.

7 HORNED PANSY *Viola cornuta* rather like 6 but *stipules* oval-triangular, deeply tooth-cut; fls *fragrant,* violet or lilac, occasionally white, 20-35mm, narrow-petalled; spur long and pointed, 10-15mm. nE, sF; Pyrenees (A, CH, CS, GB, I, R, YU).

8 BERTOLONI'S PANSY *Viola bertolonii* (= *V. heterophylla*). Low/short usually hairless per. Lvs variable, rounded, oval or lance-shaped, blunt-toothed, long-stalked; *stipules* pinnately-lobed. Fls violet or yellows 20-30mm; spur long, 9-12mm. Meadows, to 2150m. July-Aug. seF, n & neI; Maritime Alps and northern Apennines.

9 DUBY'S PANSY *Viola dubyana.* Low hairy or hairless per. Lvs rounded, blunt-toothed, stalked, the upper linear to lance-shaped; stipules pinnately-lobed. Fls violet with a yellow *central spot,* 20-25mm; spur slender short, 5-6mm. Dry meadows and rocky places, on limestone screes, to 2100m. May-July. nI; Italian Alps. **9a** *V. declinata* has *leafy runners* and deep violet fls; spur 3-4mm. 800-2000m. CS, R.

10 HEARTSEASE *Viola tricolor.* Variable low/short, hairless or downy ann/bien. Lvs heart-shaped to oval or lance-shaped, blunt toothed; stipules pinnately-lobed, with a *long end-lobe.* Fls violet or yellow or bicoloured, 10-25mm, petals narrow; spur short, 3-6.5mm. Grassy and waste places, to 2700m. Apr-Oct. T. **10a** *V.t.* subsp. *subalpina* is usually *per* with yellow fls, the upper petals sometimes violet. A, CH, CS, nE, s & eF, nI, R, YU. **10b** *V. eugeniae* has larger violet or yellow fls with *broad* petals; lvs rounded, long-stalked. I; Apennines.

11 MOUNTAIN PANSY *Viola lutea.* Low/short hairy or hairless per, with *slender creeping* stems. Lvs oval, oblong or lance-shaped, toothed, long-stalked; stipules pinnately-lobed, the end lobe not larger than the others. Fls yellow, violet or bicoloured, 15-30mm; spur short, 3-6mm. Grassy and rocky places, on acid rocks, to 2000m. May-July. A, B, CH, CS, D, nE, F, GB, IRL, NL, PL. **11a** *V. bubanii* has violet fls with a *long,* 10mm, spur. nE, sF; Pyrenees and northern Spanish Mountains.

Willowherb Family Onagraceae

Generally hairy perennials with opposite or alternate lvs. Fls in racemes with 4 sepals and 4 notched-petals (2 only in *Circaea)* and 8 stamens. The fr of willowherbs are long narrow pods, splitting into four when ripe to release the seeds which are covered in silky plumes. Hybrids are frequent.

1 ALPINE ENCHANTER'S NIGHTSHADE *Circaea alpina.* Short/med slightly hairy per. Lvs opposite, *heart-shaped,* toothed, stalked. Fls tiny, white, with 2 deeply notched petals. Fr oblong, covered *in* short hooked bristles. Damp woods, stony places and stream banks, usually on acid soils, to 2200m. June-Aug. T, except Faeroes, IRL, IS.

2 ROSEBAY WILLOWHERB *Epilobium* (= *Chamerion*) *angustifolium.* Robust tall, almost hairless, patch-forming per. Lvs *alternate,* lance-shaped, slightly toothed. Fls large, bright pink-purple, 20-30mm, petals *scarcely notched.* Fr pinkish-purple. Open woods, banks and waste places, to 2500m. June-Sept. T, rarer in the south.

3 ALPINE WILLOWHERB *Epilobium* (= *Chamerion*) *fleischeri.* Short/med, patch-forming, hairless per. Lvs alternate, narrow lance-shaped, slightly toothed. Fls bright pink, 20-25mm, petals oblong-elliptic, *not notched.* Gravels, moraines and riverbanks, usually on acid soils, to 2700m. July-Sept. A, CH, sD, nI, nwYU; Alps. **3a** *E. dodonaei* is taller with narrower, *slightly hairy* lvs. To 1500m. A, Ch, sD, c & eF, H, I, PL, R, YU. **3b** *E. latifolium* is like 3 but racemes few-flowered (not more than 7) and petals elliptical, *not notched.* IS.

4 WESTERN WILLOWHERB *Epilobium duriaei.* Short/med slightly hairy per. Lvs opposite, oval, slightly toothed, upper lvs alternate. Fls pink, petals notched 6-10mm long. Stigma *4-lobed.* Acid rocks and banks, to 2500m. June-Sept. wCH, nE, s & eF. **4a Greater Willowherb** *E. hirsutum** is much taller and very hairy with *lvs clasping* stem at base; fls larger, purple pink; petals 10-16mm long. Damp and waste places. T, except Faeroes, IS. **4b** *E. parviflorum* like 4a but lvs narrower, *not clasping;* petals 4-9mm long. T, Faeroes, IS.

5 MOUNTAIN WILLOWHERB *Epilobium montanum.* Short/med slightly hairy per; stems *round.* Lvs opposite oval, toothed, upper lvs alternate. Fls purplish-pink, petals notched 6-10mm long. Stigma *4-lobed.* Shady and waste places, to 2600m. May-Aug. T, except IS. **5a** *E. collinum* is *smaller* with pale purplish-pink fls, petals 3-6mm long. T, except DK, Faeroes, GB, IRL, IS, NL. **5b** *E. lanceolatum* is like 5 but stems slightly 4-angled and lvs *mostly* alternate, longer stalked. *Fls white,* becoming pink. T, except DK, Faeroes, IRL, IS, N, S, SF.

6 WHORLED-LEAVED WILLOWHERB *Epilobium alpestre* (= *E. trigonum*). Short/med hairy per. Lvs usually *in whorls* of 3-4. Fls pink-violet, petals 5-12mm long. Stigma *club-shaped.* Rocky *and* waste places, open woods, to 2400m. June-Aug. A, CH, CS, sD, nE, s & eF, I, PL, YU. **6a** *E. tetragonum* has *opposite stalkless* lvs and purplish-pink fls; petals 3-7mm long. T, except Faeroes, IRL, IS (N).

7 NODDING WILLOWHERB *Epilobium nutans.* Low/short per. Lvs *all opposite,* oval or elliptic, scarcely toothed, *stalkless.* Fls pale violet, petals 3-6mm long. Stigma club-shaped. Moors and waysides, to 2500m. June-Aug. A, CH, CS, nE, s & eF, I, PL, R. **7a** *E. palustre* has *untoothed lvs* and pale pink or white fls. Wet places, to 2300m. T. **7b** *E. roseum* has distinctly *stalked* lvs and white fls, becoming pink streaked. T, except Faeroes, IS.

8 PIMPERNEL-LEAVED WILLOWHERB *Epilobium anagallidifolium* (= *E. alpinum*). Low creeping, almost hairless per. Lvs opposite, oval or elliptic, scarcely toothed, upper lvs alternate. Fls *small,* pale purplish, petals 3-4.5mm long. Stigma club-shaped. Wet places on acid soils, to 3000m. June-Sept. T, except B, DK, IRL, NL.

9 CHICKWEED WILLOWHERB *Epilobium alsinifolium.* Low/short creeping, slightly hairy per, rather like 8 but larger. Lvs toothed. Fls purplish-pink, *petals* 7-11mm long. Wet places, to 2900m. June-Aug. T, except B, DK, NL.

4a

Dogwood Family Cornaceae

Deciduous perennials, shrubs or small trees with opposite, untoothed, stalked lvs. Fls in clusters, 4-petalled. Fr a berry.

1 COMMON DOGWOOD *Cornus sanguinea* (= *Thelycrania sanguinea*). Well-branched shrub to 3-4m with straight *reddish twigs*. Lvs broadly-elliptical or oval, pointed, pale green, but reddening in the autumn. Fls white 7-12mm, in dense clusters. Fr a black berry. Banks and hedgerows on calcareous soils, to 1550m. May-July. T, except Faeroes, IS.

2 CORNELIAN CHERRY *Cornus mas*. Much-branched shrub or small tree to 7-8m with greenish-yellow twigs. Lvs oval or elliptical. Fls yellow, 3-4mm, in small clusters, *appearing before* the lvs. Fr a large shiny red berry, edible. Woods, shrub and banks, to 1500m. Feb-Mar. A, B, CH, CS, sD, eF, H, I, R, YU; widely planted elsewhere.

3 DWARF CORNEL *Chamaepericlymenum suecicum* (= *Cornus suecica*). Short creeping per, often carpeting the ground. Lvs rounded to elliptical, unstalked. Fls tiny, purplish-black in a cluster surrounded by 4 conspicuous *white petal-like bracts*. Fr a small red berry. Heather and bilberry moors and heaths, to 1200m. June-Aug. D, DK, Faeroes, nGB, IS, N, NL, PL, S, SF

Ivy Family Araliaceae

4 IVY *Hedera helix*. Variable, often very vigorous, evergreen creeper or climber. Lvs shiny deep green, usually triangular in outline with 3-5 shallow lobes, but those of fl shoots unlobed. Fls usually 5-petalled, pale green with yellow anthers, in *dense umbels*. Fr a small berry, black when ripe. To 1800m. Sept-Nov. T, except Faeroes, IS, SF.

Carrot Family Umbelliferae

A large and readily recognised family with fls usually in flat-topped umbrella-like clusters (umbels) with all the fl stalks (rays) converging on one point, the primary rays often carrying smaller secondary umbels. Lvs alternate, without stipules. Fls small 5-petalled, the petals often of differing sizes; stamens 5. Bracts often present at base of primary rays. Fr dry, often ridged in various ways and flattened, splitting into 2 seeds, very important in identification (see p. 194).

5 SANICLE *Sanicula europaea*. Short/med hairless per; stems often reddish. Basal lvs rounded in outline, palmately 3-5-lobed, shiny, long-stalked. Fls whitish or pale pink, in clusters of small tight umbels. Fr rounded with hooked spines. Woods, often on calcareous soils, to 1600m. May-July. T, except Faeroes, IS.

6 HACQUETIA *Hacquetia epipactis*. Low/short hairless creeping per. Basal lvs rounded in outline, palmately *3-lobed, the* lobes wedge-shaped, toothed, shiny green. Fls yellow, in small umbels surrounded by a *ruff* of large shiny-green, toothed, bracts. Woods and shrub, to 1500m. Apr-May. A, CS, nel, PL, YU.

MASTERWORTS *Astrantia*. Readily recognised by their small pin-cushion-like umbels surrounded by many narrow pointed, papery, petal-like bracts. Lvs 3-9-palmately lobed, toothed, the lower long-stalked.

7 GREAT MASTERWORT or MOUNTAIN SANICLE *Astrantia major*. Med/tall per, usually unbranched. Basal lvs 3-5-lobed, lobes broadly oval, coarsely toothed. Umbels 20-30mm with greenish-white or pinkish fls; bracts green and pink or purplish above, whitish beneath and equalling the umbel. Meadows and woods, generally on calcareous soils, to 2000m. June-Sept. T, except B, Faeroes, IRL, IS, N, NL, S, SF (DK, GB, SF). **7a** *A. m.* subsp. *carithiaca* has bracts twice as wide as the umbel. sA, sCH, nE, s & seF, nl.

8 LESSER MASTERWORT *Astrantia minor. A* shorter, more delicate plant than 7. Basal lvs 5-9-lobed, the lobes lance-shaped or elliptical, *separated* to lf centre. Umbels 10-15mm with pinkish fls; bracts thin, greenish flushed pink above, whitish beneath, exceeding the umbel. Meadows, woods and stony places, often on acid soils, to 2700m. July-Aug. wCH, nE, s & eF, nwl; Pyrenees and south-western Alps.

9 BAVARIAN MASTERWORT *Astrantia bavarica*. Short/med slender per. Basal lvs 5-lobed, *only* the middle lobe separated to lf centre. Umbels 10-20mm, with white fls; bracts whitish, exceeding the umbel, *without* cross veins. Meadows, shrub and woods on calcareous soils, to 2300m. June-Aug. A, sD, nl, nwYU. **9a** *A. carniolica* has no leaf-lobe separated to the lf centre and bracts *shorter* than the umbel. sA, nel, nwYU; south-eastern Alps.

2

3

4

7

5

8

9

6

Carrot Family (contd.)

1 ALPINE ERYNGO or QUEEN OF THE ALPS *Eryngium alpinum.* Med/tall erect bluish-green per, hairless. Basal lvs oval to heart-shaped, *spine-toothed,* long-stalked. Fls small steely-blue in dense egg-shaped clusters surrounded by a ruff of narrow, spiny-toothed, *violet-blue bracts.* Meadows and grassy places, usually on limestone, to 2500m. July-Sept. A, CH, ?CS, eF, nl, YU.

2 SILVER ERYNGO *Eryngium spinalba.* Short stout hairless per. Basal lvs rounded to heart-shaped, irregularly lobed and with large spiny-teeth, long-stalked. Fls bluish-white in egg-shaped heads surrounded by a ruff of narrow, spiny, *greenish-white bracts.* Dry rocky places and screes, usually on limestone, 1400-1700m. June-July. seF, nwl; south-western Alps.

3 PYRENEAN ERYNGO *Eryngium bourgatii.* Short/med, erect, hairless per, stems usually flushed with steely-blue. Basal lvs deeply cut and lobed, spine-toothed, green with white-patterning along veins. Fls bluish in dense globular heads, surrounded by a ruff of steely-blue, scarcely toothed, spiny bracts. Dry rocky and stony places, to 2000m. July-Aug. E, sF; Spanish mountains and Pyrenees.

4 HAIRY CHERVIL *Chaerophyllum hirsutum.* Med/tall deep-green, softly-hairy, per. Lvs 2-3-pinnate, segments wedge-shaped, pointed. Fls white to pinkish, in loose umbels; petals *edged* with tiny hairs. Fr narrow-oblong, 8-12mm, tapering to the top. Damp meadows, woods and shady places, to 2500m. July-Aug. A, CH, CS, sD, E, F, H, I, PL, R, YU (B, DK). **4a** *C. elegans* has *narrower,* long-pointed, lf segments. A, CH, nl. **4b** *C. villarsii* is like 4a but with fewer, *stiff,* hairs and larger frs, 8-20mm. A, CH, sD, eF, nl, YU.

5 SWEET CICELY *Myrrhis odorata.* Tall, stout, very hairy per, *aromatic.* Lvs 2-3-pinnate, segments oblong-lance-shaped, toothed. Fls white with *unequal petals* in umbels, 1-5cm across; bracts absent. Fr narrow-oblong, beaked, 15-25mm, dark shiny-brown when ripe. Grassy and stony places, woods, to 2000m. June-Aug. A, CH, sD, E, F, I, YU; widely naturalised throughout the region except far north.

6 MOLOPOSPERMUM *Molopospermum peloponnesiacum.* Tall, robust, hairless per; *unpleasant smelling.* Lower lvs large, 2-4-pinnate, segments lance-shaped, sharply-toothed. Fls white, in loose umbels; *bracts present.* Fr oval, ridged, with narrow wings, 12mm. Stony places and scrub, usually on calcareous soils, to 2000m. May-Aug. CH, sD, nE, seF, nl, nwYU.

7 BUNIUM *Bunium alpinum* subsp. *petraeum.* Med tuberous rooted hairless per. Basal lvs 2-3-pinnate, segments narrow-elliptical, blunt. Fls white, petals oval, *notched;* umbels 3-5-rayed; bracts linear. Fr oblong, 3.5-5.5mm, ridged. Rocky and grassy places to 2500m. July-Aug. cl; central Apennines.

8 CONOPODIUM *Conopodium pyrenaicum.* Short/med erect, tuberous- rooted per, hairless. Basal lvs 2-3-pinnate, with *sheathing lf stalks,* segments oval, blunt. Fls white, petals oval, notched, *brown-veined* on back; umbels 6–16-rayed. Fr oblong, 3-4mm, narrowly ridged. Grassy and rocky places, to 1500m. June-July. nE, sF; west Pyrenees and mountains of northern Spain.

1, basal leaf

3, basal leaf

Carrot Family *(contd.)*

1 GREATER BURNET SAXIFRAGE *Pimpinella major.* Med/tall hairless per; stems deeply grooved, hollow, branched in the upper half. Lower lvs very large, usually 1-pinnate with 3-9 segments; stem lvs smaller with *sheath-like* bases. Fls white to deep pink, in dense umbels; no bracts; rays 10-15. Fr egg-shaped, slightly flattened, 2-3.5mm, whitish with prominent ridges. Grassy, stony places and banks, to 2300m. May-Sept. T, except Faeroes, IS and far north. **1a** *P. siifolia* is shorter with narrower lf segments and narrowly-winged frs, 5-6mm. Mountain pastures. nE, swF: western Pyrenees and Picos de Europa. **1b Burnet Saxifrage** *P. saxifraga* * is like 1 but stems solid and only slightly grooved, usually softly hairy. T, except IS, SF.

2 DETHAWIA *Dethawia tenuifolia.* Short/med, slender stemmed, hairless per. Lvs mostly basal, 3-pinnate with crowded lobes. Fls white with elliptical petals; rays 4-10; bracts 1-3 unequal. Fr egg-shaped, 4-6mm, with prominent ridges. Rocks and screes, to 2000m. July-Aug. nE, sF; Pyrenees and Cordillera Cantabrica.

3 PYRENEAN SESELI *Sesili nanum.* Low *cushion-forming,* hairless per. Lvs 2-pinnate with elliptical-oblong lobes. Fls white or pink in dense rounded umbels; rays 5-8; bracts absent usually. Fr oblong, flattened, *bristly.* Rock crevices and screes, to 2400m. July-Sept. nE, sF; Pyrenees. **3a** *S. montanum* is *not* caespitose, to 70cm tall and with lax umbels. CH, nE, s & eF, c & sI, YU; rare in Alps. **3b** *S. cantabricum* is like 3a but petals pale yellow or purplish. nE; eastern Cordillera Cantabrica.

4 ATHAMANTA *Athamanta cretensis.* Med hairy per; stems erect. Lvs 3-5pinnate with linear to narrow-oblong lobes. Fls white, the *petals notched;* rays 5-15; bracts present or absent, sometimes pinnately-cut. Fr oblong, 6–8mm, finely hairy. Rocky places and screes, to 2700m. June-Aug. A, CH, E, eF, I, YU. **4a** *A. cortiana* is low and *much-branched;* umbels dense with 1520 rays. nI; Apuan Alps.

5 GRAFIA *Grafia golaka* (= *Hladnikia golaka*). Med/tall hairless, *bluish-green,* per. Lvs 3-4-pinnate, the lobes oval or diamond-shaped. Fls white with notched petals; rays 12-22; bracts numerous, oval, pointed. Fr oblong, 8–13mm, with prominent ridges. Limestone rocks, to 1800m. July-Aug. ne & cI, wYu; central Apennines, south-eastern Alps.

6 XATARDIA *Xatardia scabra.* Short thick hairless, usually unbranched per. Lvs 2-3-pinnate, the lobes narrow-triangular, toothed; lf stalk broadly sheathing the stem at base. *Fls greenish-yellow;* the petals lance-shaped; rays very unequal in length, bristly. Fr egg-shaped, 6-7 mm, prominently ridged. Screes of limestone and schist, 1600-2300m. July-Sept. neE, sF; eastern Pyrenees.

7 TROCHISCANTHES *Trochiscanthes nodiflora.* Tall hairless per; stems with *opposite or whorled* branches. Lvs 3-4-pinnate, the lobes oval-toothed. Fls greenish-white in small but numerous loose umbels; rays 4-8; bracts 1 or absent. Fr egg-shaped, 6mm, with prominent, slender, ridges. Mountain woods, to 1600m. May-July. swCH, seF, nI.

8 BALDMONEY or SPIGNEL *Meum athamanticum.* Short/med, *strongly aromatic,* hairless per. Lvs 3-4-pinnate with numerous *thread-like* lobes, mostly basal. Fls white or purplish. the petals oval; rays 3-15; bracts 0-2. Fr oblong-egg-shaped, 4-10mm, with prominent stout ridges. Rocks and screes, usually on limestone, to 2700m. June-Aug. A, B, CH, CS, sD, nE, F, GB, I, PL, YU (N).

9 PLEUROSPERMUM *Pleurospermum austriacum.* Tall slightly hairy bien/per; *stems ridged,* hollow. Lvs 2-3-pinnate, *triangular,* the lobes oval, pirinately-lobed. Fls white with rounded petals; rays 12-20; bracts numerous, downturned. Fr egg-shaped, ridged. Damp grassy and stony places, open woods, to 2000m. June-Sept. A, CH, CS, sD, eF, H, I, PL, R, S, YU.

1b, basal leaf

Carrot Family (contd.)

HARE'S-EARS *Bupleurum*. Hairless annuals or perennials with undivided lvs. Fls small, yellow or purplish, in small umbels; secondary umbels surrounded by a ruff of oval or rounded 'leaf-like' bracts (except in 5). Fr egg-shaped.

1 LONG-LEAVED HARE'S-EAR *Bupleurum longifolium*. Med/tall yellowish or pur-ple-tinged per. Lower lvs *elliptical-spoon.shaped* or lance-shaped, long-stalked, the upper lvs oval or rounded, clasping the stem. Fls yellowish, the umbels with 5-12 rays. Meadows, open woods and stony places, to 2000m. July-Aug. A, CH, CS, sD, c & eF, H, PL, R, YU.

2 PYRENEAN HARE'S-EAR *Bupleurum angulosum*. Short/med per. Basal lvs linear to lance-shaped, stalked, the upper lvs 3-5, heart-shaped, clasping the stem. Fls yel-lowish, the umbels with 3-6 rays. Limestone rocks, 1500-2300m. July-Aug. n & neE, sF; Pyrenees mainly. **2a** *B. stellatum** has a *single*, narrower, stem lf. Meadows, scrub and rocky places, on acid soils, to 2650m. A, CH, eF, nI; Alps.

3 ROCK HARE'S-EAR *Bupleurum petraeum*. Short/med per. Basal lvs *linear,* grassy, the stem lvs usually *absent*. Fls yellowish, the umbels with 5-15 rays. Limestone rocks and screes, 1300-2300m. July-Aug. A, seF, nI, nwYU; mainly south and eastern Alps.

4 THREE-VEINED HARE'S-EAR *Bupleurum ranunculoides*. Short/med per. Lower lvs linear to narrow lance- or spoon-shaped, *3-veined,* flat-stalked; upper lvs oval, pointed, partly clasping the stem. Fls yellowish, the umbels with 3-10 rays. Mead-ows and rocky places, often on limestone, to 2600m. July-Aug. A, CH, CS, nE, s & eF, n & cI, PL, R, YU. **4a** *B.r.* subsp. *gramineum* has lower lvs with *inrolled edges,* upper lvs linear-lance-shaped. sA, sCH, nI, YU.

5 SICKLE HARE'S-EAR *Bupleurum falcatum*. Med/tall per. Basal lvs oblong-elliptical, *often curved,* stalked, the stem lvs lance-shaped to linear, partly clasping the stem. Fls yellowish, the umbels with 3-15 thread-like rays; bracts of secondary *umbels lin-ear-lance-shaped,* unequal in size. Grassy and waste places, to 1600m. July-Oct. T, except DK, Faeroes, nGB, IRI, IS, N, NL, S, SF. **5a** *B.f.* subsp. *cernuum* has *linear* stalk-less lvs. sA, sCH, sCS, nE, s & seF, I, sR, YU.

6 ENDRESSIA *Endressia pyrenaica*. Low/short, usually unbranched, hairless per with *lfless* stems. Lvs all basal 2-pinnate, lobes narrow oblong-lance-shaped. Fls white, the umbels with 9-25 rays, *no bracts.* Fr oval. Meadows and fields, to 2200m. Aug-Sept. neE, sF; eastern Pyrenees. **6a** *E. castellanum* has *hairy* stems. nE; not Pyrenees.

7 CARAWAY *Carum carvi*. Med/tall hairless per, with *leafy branched* stems. Lvs 2-3-pinnate; lobes linear-lance-shaped. Fls white, the umbels with 5-16 rays, usually without bracts. Fr oblong, ridged, *aromatic* of caraway when crushed. Meadows and waste places, to 2200m. May-July. T (Faeroes, GB, IRL, IS). **7a** *C. rigidulum* has broad, rather than narrow, lower lf segments; fls often yellowish-white. nI; Apuan Alps.

8 PYRENEAN ANGELICA *Selinum pyrenaeum* (= *Angelica pyrenaea*). Short/med, often slightly branched, hairless per; stem with 1-2 lvs or leafless. Lvs 2-3-pinnate, lobes linear to lance-shaped. Fls *yellowish-white,* petals heart-shaped, the umbels with 3-9 rays; bracts and sepals *absent,* secondary bracts linear. Meadows and pas-tures, to 2300m. June-Aug. n & nwE, c, e & sF. **8a** *S. carvifolia* has strongly ribbed leafy stems. T, except Faeroes, IRL, IS.

2a

Carrot Family (contd.)

1 UNBRANCHED LOVAGE *Ligusticum mutellinoides.* Low/short almost hairless per; stems *unbranched.* Lvs all basal, 2-3-pinnate, oval in outline, with narrow oblong pointed lobes. Fls white or pink, the petals notched; *rays* 8-20; lower bracts *numerous,* linear. Fr elliptical, 3-5mm, ridged, usually smooth. Grassy and stony places, often exposed, 1900-3350m.July-Aug. A, CH, CS, sD, eF, nl, PL, R, YU. **1a** *L. feru-laceum* has branched stems, narrower leaflets and *pinnately cut bracts.* e & seF, nwl; Jura and south-western Alps.

2 ALPINE LOVAGE *Ligusticum mutellina.* Short/med almost hairless per; stems with 1-2 *alternate branches.* Lvs mostly basal, 2-3-pinnate triangular in outline, with narrow lance-shaped lobes. Fls red or purple usually, with notched petals; rays 7-10; *lower bracts* 1-2, lance-shaped or absent. Fr oblong, 4-6mm, ridged. Damp meadows and open woods, to 3000m. July-Aug. A, CH, sD, eF, I, PL, R, YU. **2a** *L. lucidum* is much taller, the stems with *opposite or whorled branches;* umbels large with 20-50 rays. CH, E, s & eF, I, YU.

3 WILD ANGELICA *Angelica sylvestris.* Tall robust, almost hairless per; stems often purplish. Lvs 2-3-pinnate, with broad toothed lobes; upper lvs much smaller with *inflated sheathing* stalks. Fls white or pinkish in large umbels; petals lance-shaped; lower bracts often absent, upper thread-like. Fr oval flattened, 4-5mm, with *broad membranous wings.* Damp and shady places, to 1800m. July-Sept. T. **3a Angelica** *A. archangelica* has *green stems* usually and cream or greenish-white fls; fr with *corky wings.* T; widely grown as a confection and naturalised especially in the north. **3b** *A. razulii* is like 3 but fr larger, 8mm, with narrow wings. n & nwE, sF.

4 LOVAGE *Levisticum officinale.* Tall strong-smelling branched per. Lvs 2-3-pinnate, *glossy* with broad toothed lobes. Fls greenish-yellow; rays 12-20, grooved; bracts numerous, upper ones joined at base. Fr oblong-egg-shaped, 5-7mm, yellow or brown. Widely cultivated and naturalised in grassy places, to 1200m. June-Aug. (T, except Faeroes, IRL, IS).

5 SOUTHERN MASTERWORT *Peucedanum venetum.* Med/tall hairless, *purplish,* per; stems much branched. Lvs 2-4-pinnate, the lobes usually pinnately lobed; upper lvs much smaller with broad *sheathing stalks.* Fls white in *broad umbels,* petals oval; rays 10-25; bracts narrow lance-shaped. Fr oblong, 5.5-6mm, winged. Grassy and stony places, to 1500m. June-Aug. sCH, neE, s & seF, I, nwYU.

6 MASTERWORT *Peucedanum ostruthium.* Med/tall almost hairless per, stems with *alternate* branches. Lvs 2-trefoil, the lobes oval, toothed; upper lvs small with *inflated sheathing* stalks. Fls white or pinkish, no lower bracts; rays 30 or more. Fr almost rounded, 4-5mm, broadly winged. Meadows, woods, rocky places and stream banks, 1400-2800m. June-Aug. A, Ch, CS, sD, E, s & eF, I, PL, YU (B, DK, GB, N, S). **6a** *P. verticillare* is taller with *opposite or whorled* branches; fr 7-9mm, broadly winged. A, eCH, H, n & cl, nwYU.

7 AUSTRIAN HOGWEED *Heracleum austriacum.* Short/med hairy per, stems slender, branched. Lvs *pinnate,* the lobes oval toothed, hairy. Fls white, petals *deeply notched,* or pink in flattish umbels, unequal; rays 6-13; bracts usually present. Fr broad oval, 7-11mm, broadly winged. Fields and scrub, to 2100m. July-Sept.A, cCH, seD, nel, nwYU; eastern Alps mainly. **7a Hogweed** *H. sphondylium* is a much larger plant with thick, often bristly stems, umbels with 15-45 rays. T, except Faeroes, IS. **7b** *H. minimum* is like 7 but smaller with small *hairless* lf lobes; umbel rays 3-6. Limestone screes, to 2500m. July-Aug. seF.

8 BROAD-LEAVED SERMOUNTAIN *Laserpitium latifolium.* Med/tall almost hairless per. Lvs large 2-pinnate; lobes oval-heart-shaped, *toothed.* Fls white with notched petals; rays 25-40, bracts numerous. Fr oval 5-10mm, narrowly-winged. Open woods and stony places to 2000m. July-Aug. T, except Faeroes, GB, IRL, IS, NL and northern Scandinavia. **8a** *L. siler* has narrower, *untoothed* leaflets, and 20-50 rays. A, sD, E, s & eF, I, YU. **8b** *L. nestleri* like 8 but umbels with few bracts and these soon *falling.* Limestone rocks.E, sF. **8c** *L. krapfii* like 8b but fls *greenish-yellow* or pinkish; fr wings of different sizes. A, CH, I, PL, R, YU. **8d** *L. peucedanoides* like 8a but umbels only 2-15 rayed, lower lvs 2-3-trifoliate. A, nel, nwYU; south-eastern Alps. **8e** *L. nitidum* like 8 but bracts with *hairy margins.* nl; Italian Alps. **8f** *L. halleri* like 8 but smaller, lf lobes *cut into 5-7 linear lobes;* fls white or pink. A, CH, eF, nl; local in the Alps.

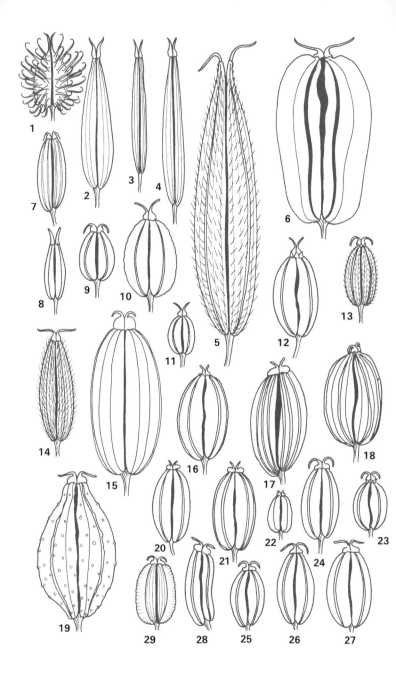

Umbellifer fruits; scale x 4

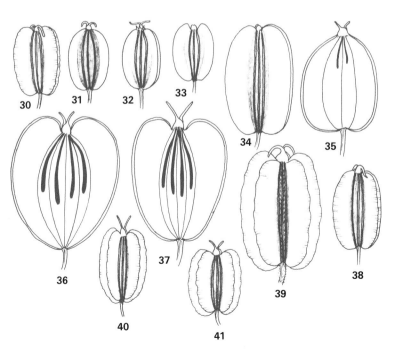

Wintergreen Family Pyrolaceae

Attractive evergreen creeping, hairless, perennials with basal or whorled, stalked lvs. Fls 5-petalled drooping, closed or open cups in spike-like racemes or umbels. Fr a dry capsule.

1 LESSER WINTERGREEN *Pyrola minor.* Low per. Lvs in basal rosettes, broadly elliptical, finely toothed, pale green; stalk *shorter* than lf blade. Fls white or lilac-pink, 7mm, globular-cups in stalked spikes; style *not* protruding. Woods, moors and heaths, to 2700m. June-Aug. T.

2 INTERMEDIATE WINTERGREEN *Pyrola media.* Low/short per. Lvs in basal rosettes, rounded to oval, finely toothed, dark green; stalk as long or shorter than lf blade. Fls white or pale pink, 7-10mm, globular-cups in stalked spikes; style straight, *protruding.* Woods, moors and heaths, to 2200m. June-Aug. T, except B, Faeroes, sl, S, NL. **2a** *P. grandiflora* has *larger* fls, 15-20mm and a curved style. Tundra. IS.

3 ROUND-LEAVED WINTERGREEN *Pyrola rotundifolia.* Like 2 but lf stalk *longer* than lf blade. Fls pure white, 8-12mm, globular-cups; *style S-shaped,* protruding, expanded below into a disc. Woods, heaths and marshes, usually over limestone, to 2300m. June-Sept. T, except Faeroes, GB, sl, IRL, IS, NL and far north. **3a** *P. norvegica* is shorter, with more rounded lvs, the veins *forming a network* around the edge; style curved, not expanded below into a disc. To 1450m. July-Aug. N, S, SF. **3b** *P. carpatica* is like 3a but bracts longer than fl stalks, not shorter. CS, R; Carpathians.

4 PALE-GREEN WINTERGREEN *Pyrola chlorantha.* Low per. Lvs oblong to rounded, finely toothed, pale green above, darker beneath; stalk *longer* than lf blade. Fls pale *yellowish-green,* 8-12mm, in stalked spikes; style S-shaped, protruding. Coniferous woods and grassy places, to 2200m. June-Aug. T, except GB, IRL, IS, NL and far north; rare in the west.

5 NODDING WINTERGREEN *Orthilia secunda* (= *Pyrola secunda*). Low per. Lvs in basal rosettes, oval, elliptical or rounded, toothed, pale green; stalk shorter than lf blade. Fls greenish-white, 5-6mm, oval-cups in *one-sided spikes;* style straight, protruding. Woods, moors and rocky places, to 2200m. July-Aug. T (B).

6 ONE-FLOWERED WINTERGREEN *Moneses uniflora.* Low per. Lvs *opposite,* rounded or oval, toothed, tapered into the stalk, pale green. Fls *solitary,* white, 13-20mm, wide open cups; style straight, protruding. Woods, especially coniferous, to 2100m. May-Aug. T, except Faeroes, IRL, IS (B).

7 UMBELLATE WINTERGREEN *Chimaphila umbellata* (= *Pyrola umbellata*). Low per. Lvs in *whorls* or opposite, narrowly-oval, broadest above middle, toothed, narrowed into the stalk. Fls pale pink, 7-12mm, globular-cups in *umbel-like* clusters; style not protruding. Woods, especially coniferous and rocky places, to 500m, not reaching alpine levels in south. June-July. T, except B, E, GB, I, IRL, IS, NL.

Birdsnest Family Monotropaceae

8 DUTCHMAN'S PIPE or YELLOW BIRDSNEST *Monotropa hypopitys.* Low greenless saprophytic per, with erect yellowish stems, unbranched. *Lvs scale-like,* oval-elliptic, yellowish, turning brown eventually. Fls pale yellowish or ivory-white, long bells with 4-5 petals, in drooping clusters; becoming erect in fr. Damp woods, especially beech and pine, to 1800m. June-Sept. T, except Faeroes, IS.

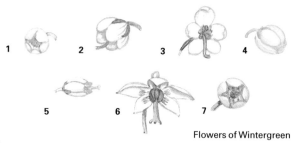

Flowers of Wintergreen

1
2
3
4
5
6
7
8

Diapensia Family Diapensiaceae

1 DIAPENSIA *Diapensia lapponica.* Low evergreen, *cushion-forming* subshrub, hairless. Lvs narrow-spoon-shaped, shiny, leathery, untoothed. Fls white, 10mm, 5-petalled, solitary on short stalks; stamens 5, stigma 3-lobed. Bare mountain ridges, to 1600m. May-July. nwGB, IS, N, S, SF; very rare in GB.

Crowberry Family Empetraceae

2 CROWBERRY *Empetrum nigrum.* Low, heath-like, evergreen shrub, usually mat-forming; young twigs reddish. Lvs *alternate,* narrow-oblong, deep shiny green, margins *rolled under.* Fls tiny, pink or purplish, 1-2mm, at base of lvs, 6-petalled; male and female on separate plants. Fr a rounded *black* berry, green at first. Moors and bogs, to 3050m. T, except sl and most of the Alps. **2a** *E.n.* subsp. *hermaphroditum* is a more upright plant with broader lvs; fls with both sexes, the stamens often *persisting* round the fr. A, B, CH, D, DK, n & cl, N, S, SF; rare in the south.

Heather Family Ericaceae

Small evergreen or deciduous shrubs or subshrubs with usually untoothed, deep green, lvs. Fls generally 4-5-parted, bell-, cup- or funnel-shaped, clusters or solitary. Fr a dry capsule or a fleshy berry, edible in *Vaccinium* and *Arctostaphylos.*

3 MATTED CASSIOPE *Cassiope* (= *Harrimanella*) *hypnoides.* Prostrate mat-forming subshrub. Lvs *alternate,* scale-like, narrow-oblong, pointed, *overlapping* up stem. Fls white with crimson sepals, rounded-bells, 4-5mm, solitary, drooping on long stalks. Damp, mossy tundra, by streams and snow patches, to 1900m. July-Aug. IS, N, S, SF; Arctic Europe and higher mountains of Scandinavia.

4 CASSIOPE *Cassiope tetragona.* More upright than 3 with *opposite* lvs, forming four ranks. Fls creamy-white with yellowish sepals, drooping bells, 6-8mm. Dry stony heaths, usually on limestone, to 1650m. June-Aug. N, S, SF; Arctic Europe.

5 LAPLAND RHODODENDRON *Rhododendron lapponicum.* Low, *mat-forming,* evergreen subshrub. Lvs oblong, leathery, dark green above, rusty with scales beneath; margins *rolled under.* Fls violet-purple open bells, 8mm long, in clusters of 3-6. Dry heaths and stony places, in calcareous soils, to 1350m. May-June. N, S, SF.

6 CRANBERRY *Vaccinium oxycoccus.* Low creeping evergreen subshrub. Lvs oval, dark green above, bluish-white beneath; margin rolled under. Fls pink, with 4 *spreading or reflexed* petals and prominent stamens, solitary or up to four in a cluster; fl stalks long and downy. Fr a rounded or pear-shaped berry, red or brownish, often speckled. Peat bogs, to 2000m. May-Aug. T, except E, Faeroes, sF, c & sl; rare in the south. **6a** *V. microcarpum* has more triangular lvs and smaller fls with *hairless* stalks. A, CH, CS, D, GB, nl, IS, N, NL, PL, R, S, SF, YU.

7 COWBERRY *Vaccinium vitis-idaea.* More or less prostrate, creeping, *evergreen* subshrub. Lvs elliptical to oblong, dark green above, paler with dark dots beneath, margins rolled under. Fls white tinged pink, open bells, 5-6mm long, in drooping clusters of 3-6. Fr a rounded *red berry.* Moors, heaths, coniferous woods and sub-alpine pastures, to 3050m. May-Aug. T, except E, c & sl.

8 BOG WHORTLEBERRY *Vaccinium uliginosum.* Upright *deciduous* shrub to 0.75m. Lvs oval, bluish-green, with netted veins. Fls pale pink bells, 4-6mm, in clusters of 1-3. Fr a rounded, *bluish-black* berry. Moors, heaths, coniferous woods and sub-alpine pastures, to 3000m. May-June. T, except IRL, c & sl. **8a** *V.u.* subsp. *microphyllum* is lower and smaller, *often mat-forming.* N, S, SF; Arctic and subarctic Europe.

9 BILBERRY or WHORTLEBERRY *Vaccinium myrtillus.* Rather like 8 but lvs bright green and toothed. Fls pale green tinged pink, 4-6mm, usually solitary. Fr a bluish-black berry. Heaths, moors and open woods, to 2800m. Apr-July. T.

Heather Family (contd.)

1 ALPENROSE *Rhododendron ferrugineum.* Evergreen shrub to 1 m, often forming dense thickets. Lvs elliptic-oblong, shiny, deep-green above, *reddish-scaly* beneath, margins *rolled under.* Fls pale to deep pinkish-red, bell-shaped, in small clusters. Fr a dry capsule. Mountain slopes, open woods or scrubland, to 3200m. May-Aug. A, CH, nE, s & eF, nl, nw & wYU; Pyrenees, Alps, Jura mainly. **1a Hairy Alpenrose** *R. hirsutum* * has bright green, hairy-*edged* lvs and bright pink fls, smaller than 1. Open woods, scrub and screes, on limestone, to 2600m. May-July. A, CH, sD, F, nl, nw & wYU (CS, R).

2 MARSH ANDROMEDA or BOG ROSEMARY *Andromeda polifolia.* Creeping hairless undershrub. Lvs narrow-elliptical, shiny greyish-green above, whitish beneath. Fls bright pink, turning white, drooping rounded-bells, in small clusters. Sphagnum bogs and wet heaths, to l150m. June-Aug. T, except E, Faeroes, sF, IS; very local in the southern Alps and eastern Carpathians.

3 BEARBERRY *Arctostaphylos uva-ursi.* Prostrate *mat-forming,* evergreen shrub. Lvs oval, broadest above middle, dark green, *untoothed.* Fls greenish-white to pink, drooping bells, in small clusters. Fr a shiny red berry, edible. Heaths, open woods and rocky places, to 2800m. June-Sept. T, except B, E, Faeroes; scarcer in the south. **3a Alpine Bearberry** *A. alpinus* (= *Arctous alpinus*) * is deciduous with bright-green, *toothed* lvs; fr a black berry. To 2700m. May-July. T, except B, Faeroes, sGB, IRL, IS, NL.

4 SPRING HEATH *Erica herbacea* (= *E. carnea*) has Lvs in *fours;* fls bright or flesh-pink, urn-shaped, with projecting dark-purple anthers. Coniferous woods and stony places, to 2700m. Mar-June. A, CH, CS, sD, eF, n & cl, YU. **4a Bell Heathe**r *E. cinerea.* Thickly-branched dwarf hairless undershrub. Lvs in *threes,* linear, deep green, often bronzed. Fls bright red-purple bells, in branched clusters. Heaths, woods, dry moors and rocky places, to 1500m. May-Sept. B, wD, E, F, Faeroes, GB, nl, IRL, sN, NL. **4b Cornish Heath** *E. vagans* * has lvs in fours or fives; fls lilac-pink or white, with projecting purple-brown anthers, in long *dense leafy spikes.* Heaths and woodland over acid rocks, to 1800m. May-Aug. E, wF, swGB (CH).

5 CROSS-LEAVED HEATH *Erica tetralix.* Short greyish downy undershrub. Lvs in *fours,* linear, pointed. Fls pale pink, drooping rounded-bells, in compact heads; anthers not protruding. Bogs, wet heaths and pine woods on acid soils, to 2200m. June-Oct. T, except A, Faeroes, I, IS, R, YU (CH, CS). **5a Eastern Heath** *Bruckenthalia spiculifolia* has lvs irregularly arranged in whorls of 4-5, often hair-tipped, and flowers 4-parted in terminal racemes, reddish-pink, bell-shaped, 3mm; sepals *fused together* not free. Acids pastures and open woodland. R, n & eYU.

6 HEATHER or LING *Calluna vulgaris.* Short/med carpeting subshrub. Lvs tiny, opposite and in rows, *scale-like.* Fls pinkish-lilac or pale purple, sepals and petals coloured, *not joined,* in slender leafy spikes. Moors, heaths and open woods on acid soils, to 2700m. July-Oct. T.

7 DWARF ALPENROSE *Rhodothamnus chamaecistus.* Dwarf hairy shrub. Lvs elliptical-oblong, bright green, *hairy-margined.* Fls pale pink, large saucer-shaped, with *separate petals,* solitary or two to three together. Dry rocky slopes and screes on limestone, 1000- 2400m. May-July. A, seD, nel, nwYU; eastern Alps.

8 CREEPING AZALEA *Loiseleuria procumbens.* Prostrate *mat-forming,* evergreen undershrub, hairless. Lvs oblong, shiny, deep-green; margins rolled under. Fls *tiny,* pale pink, in clusters of two to five. Dry stony or peaty places, often exposed, on acid soils, 1500-3000m. May-July. T, except B, CS, DK, sGB, c & sl, IRL, NL, PL.

9 MOUNTAIN HEATH *Phyllodoce caerulea.* Low short undershrub, heath-like. Lvs alternate, narrow-oblong, rough-edged. Fls lilac to pinkish-purple, drooping bells, *larger* than 4-6, in clusters of 2-6 at top of shoots. Heaths and rocky moors, 2000-2600m. sF, nGB, IS, N, S, SF; rare in Scotland and the Pyrenees.

1

Primrose Family Primulaceae

Perennials, sometimes annuals, with undivided lvs. Fls with 5 petals (except Chickweed Wintergreen, p. 212) often joined into a short/long tube, sepal 5. Fr a small capsule.

PRIMULAS *Primula* have basal rosettes of lvs and open-throated fls in long-stalked umbel-like clusters, or directly from the leaf rosettes; petals lobes notched, joined into a narrow tube with the stamen attached either in the middle or near the top; sepal-tube with short teeth.

1 PRIMROSE *Primula vulgaris.* Low hairy per. Lvs oblong, *crinkled, tapering* to stalk. Fls pale yellow with orange central marks, 20-30mm, *solitary* on long hairy stalks, fragrant. Woods, scrubland and grassy banks, to 1500m. Mar-June. T, except IS, PL, S, SF. *Hybridises* with 2 and 3.

2 OXLIP *Primula elatior.* Low hairy per. Lvs like 1 but *more abruptly* narrowed to stalk. Fls pale yellow with orange central marks, 15-25mm, 1-20 in a nod*ding, one-sided cluster; not* fragrant. Meadows and woods, to 2700m. MarAug. T, except IRL, IS and far north. **2a** *P.e.* subsp. *intricata* has *less* abruptly narrowed lvs and markedly ta*pered* fr capsules. Moist grassland A, CH, E, s & eF, I, YU. **2b** *P. e.* subsp. *leucophylla* has lvs grey-hairy beneath and *short* calyces, 6-8mm long. R; eastern Carpathians.

3 COWSLIP *Primula veris.* Low/short hairy per. Lvs very *abruptly* narrowed at base into stalk, crinkled, hairless or almost so beneath. Fls deeper yellow than 1-2 with orange spots in centre, 10-15mm, up to 30 in a nodding, one-sided cluster, *fragrant.* Meadows and pastures, to 2200m. Apr-June. T, except IS and far north. **3a** *P. v.* subsp. *columnae* has lvs hairy beneath and with a *heart-shaped* base. A, CH, E, s & eF, nI, YU.

4 BIRDSEYE PRIMROSE *Primula farinosa.* Low per, *mealy white* on stems and underneath lvs. Lvs spoon-shaped or elliptical, toothed. Fls lilac-pink, purple, rarely white, with *yellow eye,* 8-16mm, 2 to many in an umbel. Marshes and damp pastures, usually on acid soils, to 3000m. May-Aug. T, except B, IRL, IS and far north. **4a** *P. nutans* has no farina (white meal) and bracts with small 'ears' at the base. Meadows, often coastal. N, S, nSF. **4b** *P. egaliksensis* has small flowers only 5-8mm, white or lilac; leaves without farina. Meadows, often coastal. nIS.

5 LONG-FLOWERED PRIMROSE *Primula halleri* (= *P. longiflora*). Low/short per. Lvs pale green, oblong or spoon-shaped, slightly toothed, *mealy* yellow beneath, Fls lilac or violet with a yellow eye, 15-20mm, each with along *thin tube,* 2-12 in an umbel. Meadows and rock crevices, to 2900m. June-July. A, CH, CS, eF, nI, PI, R, YU.

6 STICKY PRIMROSE *Primula glutinosa.* Low *sticky* per. Lvs deep green, narrow-spoon-shaped, blunt-toothed. Fls deep violet, 12-18mm, 2-8 in an umbel; petal lobes *deeply notched,* fragrant. Meadows and granitic rocks, 1800-3300m. June-Aug. A, eCH, nI, wYU; eastern Alps.

7 SPECTACULAR PRIMROSE *Primula spectabilis.* Low/short, somewhat sticky, per. Lvs bright *glossy* green, oblong to rhombic, tending to curl backwards, with a *horny-white edge.* Fls pinkish-red or violet, 20-30mm, 2-5 in an umbel; petal lobes *rather* wavy, deeply notched. Rocky and stony slopes on limestone, to 2500m. May-Aug. nI; southern Alps. **7a Glaucous Primrose** *P. glaucescens* has glossy, *bluish-green* lvs which tend to curl inwards, without darkish dots above. To 2400m. nI; southern Alps.

8 WULFEN'S PRIMROSE *Primula wulfeniana.* Like a smaller version of 7. Lvs *glossy blue-green* with a membranous edge, glandular-hairy. Fls pinkish-red or lilac with a *white eye,* 2530mm, 1-2 in an umbel. Limestone rocks and meadows to 2200m. May-Aug. A, neI, R, YU; Carnic, Karawanken and Julian Alps, S Carpathians. **8a** *P. clusiana* has green lvs with a *horny and hairy* edge but hairless above; fls pinkish-red or violet, with a white eye, 1-4 in an umbel. May-July. nA, sD; neAlps. Not overlapping in distribution with 8. **8b** *P. kitaibeliana* is like 8a but lvs hairy *above.* Calcareous rocks. wcYU.

9 LEAST PRIMROSE *Primula minima.* Very low per with tiny leafy rosettes. Lvs glossy deep green, wedge-shaped, the apex *deeply* toothed. Fls bright pink with a white eye, 15-30mm, 1-2 in a *short-s talked* umbel; petal lobes deeply notched. Grassy places and rocky ledges on limestone and granite, often by snow patches, 2000-3000m. June-July. A, CS, sD, I, PL, R, wYU.

Primrose Family (contd.)

1 ENTIRE-LEAVED PRIMROSE *Primula integrifolia.* Low, slightly sticky per. Lvs bright green, lance-shaped or oval, with *hairy, untoothed* edges. Fls rosy-purple or pinkish-lilac, 15-25mm, 1-3 in an umbel, stalks often reddish. Stony and grassy places, often by snow patches, on acid rocks, 1900-2700m. May-Aug. A, CH, nE, s & eF,nl; eastern Pyrenees and central Alps. **1a** *P. tyrolensis** has more rounded, finely toothed lvs and lilac-pink fls with a white centre, *solitary* or sometimes 2 on a *short stalk*. Dolomitic rocks, to 2300m. May-June. nel; Dolomites.

2 ALLIONI'S PRIMROSE *Primula allionii.* Low, *very sticky* per with small leaf rosettes. Lvs greyish-green, oblong or rounded, narrowed at base, toothed or untoothed, *gland dotted*. Fls rose-pink to purplish, rarely white, 5-20mm, solitary or up to 5, *scarcely stalked*. Shady limestone cliffs, to 1900m. Mar-May. seF, nwl; Maritime Alps.

3 VISCID PRIMROSE *Primula latifolia* (= *P. viscosa*). Low/short sticky, rather fleshy, per. Lvs pale green, broad-oblong, narrowed at base into stalk, sometimes toothed at top; Fls purplish or dark violet with *a mealy-white* throat, 14-16mm, 2-20 in a one-sided umbel, stalk long, *sticky.* Acid rock crevices, 1800-3050m. June-July. CH, nE, s & eF, nl; Pyrenees, south-west and central Alps.

4 MARGINATE PRIMROSE *Primula marginata. Low/short, mealy-white* per. Lvs lance-shaped, deeply toothed. Fls bluish- or pinkish-lilac with a mealy throat, 18–28mm, 3-15 in a mealy-stalked umbel. Rock crevices and screes, to 2600m. June-July. seF, nwl; south-western Alps.

5 AURICULA or BEAR'S-EAR *Primula auricula* Low/short per. Lvs smooth or mealy-white, lance-shaped or rounded, toothed or not. Fls *yellow* with a mealy-white throat, 15-25mm, 2-30 in a long-stalked umbel. Damp grassy places and rock crevices, to 2900m. May-July. A, CH, CS, sD, eF, H, I, PL, R, YU. **5a** *P. palinuri* has *fragrant,* sticky lvs and narrower more bell-shaped fls. Coastal cliffs. swl; near Naples.

6 PIEDMONT PRIMROSE *Primula pedemontana. Low/short per. Lvs smooth shiny-green,* oblong or lance-shaped, tapered into the stalk, toothed or untoothed and *with tiny red dots.* Fls purple or deep pink with a white eye, 20-25mm, 2-15 in an umbel. Acid rocks and stony pastures, 1400-3000m.June-July.nE, s & seF, nwl; south-western Alps and Cordillera Cantabrica. **6a** *P. apennina* is smaller the lvs *covered* with yellowish-brown dots; fls pale to rose pink. Sandstone cliff ledges. May-Aug. nl; northern Apennines. **6b** *P. daonensis* like 6 but lvs narrower, *long-stalked,* very sticky, *covered* with red dots; fls paler. Acid rocks and stony pastures, 1600-2800m. June-July. A, eCH, nl; Rhaetian Alps to the Dolomites.

7 VILLOUS PRIMROSE *Primula villosa.* Low/short, very sticky, fleshy per. Lvs oval, usually toothed, tapered to a thin stalk, covered with tiny red dots. Fls rose-pink to lilac with a white eye, 20-30mm, 2-5 on a sticky stalk *much longer* than lvs. Acid rocks and stony pastures, to 2200m. Apr-June. A, seF, nl, nwYU. **7a** *P. hirsuta** is smaller with more rounded, *coarse-toothed* lvs. Fls lilac to deep purplish-red, 1-15 on stalks *as long* as lvs. To 3600m. Apr-July. A, CH, s & eF, nE, nl; central Pyrenees and Alps.

8 SCOTTISH PRIMROSE *Primula scotica.* Like a small Birdseye Primrose. Low ann/bien with *mealy-white* stems and lvs. Lvs elliptical, untoothed. Fls dark purple with a pale yellow eye, 5-8mm, in *short-stalked* clusters. Short coastal turf, at low altitudes. May-June. nGB; northern Scotland. **8a Northern Primrose** *P. scandinavica* has lvs mealy only beneath, and *long-stalked* fl clusters. Damp meadows on calcareous soils to 1500m. N, nwS. **8b** *P. stricta* is a small version of 8a with narrower, stalked lvs, with *scarcely any meal.* Fls pale lilac or violet. Meadows and cliffs to 750m. June-July. IS, N, S, SF.

9 VITALIANA *Vitaliana primuliflora* (= *Androsace vitaliana, Gregoria vitaliana*). Variable low mat or tuft-forming per. Lvs in tiny rosettes, linear-lanceolate to linear, *untoothed,* green or grey-green. Fls *yellow,* 9-11mm, with oblong petal lobes, 1-5 together, *almost stalkless.* Screes, rocky and stony places or short turf, often on acid rocks, 1700-3100m. May-July. eA, nel, nwYu; south-eastern Alps. **9a** *V. p.* subsp. *canescens* has hairy lvs and calyces. nE, s & eF, nwl. **9b** *V. p.* subsp. *cinerea* has lvs with dense *star-shaped* (stellate) hairs above. Ch, nE, s & eF, nw I. **9c** *V. p.* subsp. *praetutiana* has *oblong* lvs with a rounded woolly apex. cl; central Apennines.

Primrose Family *(contd.)*

ROCK-JASMINES *Androsace* (see p. 209 for leaf identification). A genus of primarily cushion-forming perennials, occasionally annuals, with leaves mostly in basal rosettes; rosettes often small and crammed closely together. Leaves simple, with a toothed or untoothed margin, sometimes edged with bristles, variously adorned with simple or branched hairs. The fls are solitary or borne in lax to tight, umbel-like clusters; calyx with 5 equal lobes; corolla with a short tube and 5 spreading, often rounded lobes, constricted at the mouth. Fr a 5-parted capsule containing few to numerous seeds.

1 MILKWHITE ROCK-JASMINE Androsace *lactea*. Low, slightly hairy per, forming loose mats of small rosettes. *Lvs linear,* pointed, *untoothed.* Fls milk-white with a yellow eye, 8-12mm, solitary or up to six in a long-stemmed umbel; petal lobes *notched.* Rocks and screes and turf, to 2400m. May-Aug. A, CH, CS, sD, eF, nl, PL, R, w & cYU.

2 BLUNT-LEAVED ROCK-JASMINE *Androsace obtusifolia.* Low, slightly hairy per, forming loose tufts. Lvs spoon-shaped, *blunt-ended,* with a few star-shaped hairs along edge. Fls white or pale pink, 59mm, solitary or up to seven in long-stemmed umbels; petals not notched. Acid rocks and screes, 1500-3500m. June-Aug. A, CH, CS, sD, eF, n & cl, PL, R, YU.

3 PINK ROCK-JASMINE *Androsace carnea.* Low, tufted, slightly hairy per, with closely-packed, bright green, lf rosettes. Lvs linear, pointed, 10-15mm long, *hairy,* with a margin bristly. Fls pink or white with a yellow eye (both illustrated), 5-8 mm, two to eight in short or long-stemmed umbels; petals rounded. Acid rocks and screes or short turf, 1400-3100m. July-Aug. s & eF, VCH, nE, nl. **3a** *A. c.* subsp. *laggeri** has smaller lf-rosettes with lvs 4-6mm long, hairless. nE, sF; central Pyrenees. **3b** *A. c.* subsp. *rosea** has larger lf-rosettes than 3 with the lvs 10-25mm long, hairless. e & scF, neE; Massif Central to eastern Pyrenees. **3c** *A.c.* subsp. *brigantiaca** has slightly toothed lvs up to 30mm long and white fls in longer stemmed clusters than 3. swCH, seF, nwl; south-western Alps.

4 CILIATE ROCK-JASMINE *Androsace chamaejasme.* Low, lax, per forming flattish cushions or tufts. Lvs oblong, 5-16mm, with *an edge* of long silky-white hairs. Fls white or pale pink with a yellow eye, 5-7mm, two to seven in short or long-stemmed umbels. Rocks and short turf, on limestone or acid rocks, to 3000m. June-July. A, CH, CS, D, s & eF, nl, PL, R, YU. **4a** *A. villosa** is very variable but with more rounded lf rosettes. Lvs covered *all over* by long silky hairs, especially towards the top. Limestone rocks and screes, short turf, 1200-3000m. A, CH, nE, s & eF, I, R, YU.

5 PYRENEAN ROCK-JASMINE *Androsace pyrenaica.* Low per forming dense, deep-green, rounded-cushions. Lvs narrow-oblong, 3-7mm, overlapping, covered in straight *hairs.* Fls white with a yellow eye, 4-5mm, solitary. Granitic rocks and screes, 2000-3000m. June-Oct. nE, sF; central and eastern Pyrenees.

6 SWISS ROCK-JASMINE *Androsace helvetica.* Low per forming dense, grey, rounded-cushions. Lvs oblong to spoon-shaped, 2-6mm, covered in short straight hairs. Fls white with a yellow eye, 4-6mm, solitary. Limestone screes and rocks, 2000-3500m. May-Aug. A, CH, sD, eF, nl. **6a** *A. vandelii** (= *A. imbricata)* has downy, *starry-haired,* Lvs and fls on *short stalks.* 2000-3000m. A, CH, E, s & eF, nl; especially in the Pennine Alps.

7 CYLINDRIC ROCK-JASMINE *Androsace cylindrica* (= *A. hirtella*). Low per forming dense grey-green, rounded cushions. Lvs oblong, 5-8mm, *downy* with straight or starry-hairs. Fls white with a yellow eye, or sometimes pink, 7-9mm, solitary, on short *slender stalks.* Limestone rocks and cliffs, 2000-3500m. JulyAug. nE, sF; central Pyrenees, rare.

8 MATHILDA'S ROCK-JASMINE *Androsace mathildae.* Low cushion-forming per; lf rosettes large. Lvs linear, 10-15mm, *shiny-green,* hairless. Fls white or pink, 5mm, solitary, on short slender stalks. Rock crevices, 2000-2800m. July-Aug. cl-Abruzzi Apennines.

9-10, see p.208

9 HAIRY ROCK-JASMINE *Androsace pubescens.* Low per, forming grey-green cushions; lf rosettes rather loose. Lvs oblong or spoon-shaped, 4-10mm, covered in short, straight or *branched, hairs.* Fls white or pink with a yellow eye,4-6mm, solitary, short-stalked. Rock cliffs and screes, limestone or granite, 2000-3800m. June-July. CH, nE, s & eF, nI. **9a** *A. ciliata** is larger with bristle-edged lvs and fls 5-8mm, pink or violet with an orange or yellow eye. 2800-3400m. nE, sF; central Pyrenees, rare. **9b** *A. hausmannii** has narrow lance-shaped fleshy lvs, slightly recurved ,starry-haired; fls white or pink with a yellow eye. Limestone crevices, 1900-3100m. July-Aug. A, sD, nI, wYU; eastern Alps.

10 ALPINE ROCK-JASMINE *Androsace alpina.* Low per, rather flat, mat-like, cushions. Lvs oblong-lance-shaped, 5-10mm, covered in *short starry hairs.* Fls white or pink with a yellow eye, 7-9mm, solitary, short-stalked. Granite screes and rocks, 2000-4000m. July-Aug. A, CH, eF, nI. **10a** *A. wulfeniana** denser cushions, lvs 3-5mm and fls larger, deep-pink, 10-12mm, petals straight-ended. Sandstone and shaly cliffs and rocks, 2000-2600mm. June-July. A, neI; mainly Tauern and Carnic Alps. **10b** *A. brevis* is similar to 10 but lvs smaller, 3-5mm, and spoon-shaped, bearing branched hairs only. sCH, nI; region of Lake Como.

Hybrids. These may be occasionally found in the wild where two or more species grow in close proximity to one another. The principal hybrids found in the region are as follows:

A. x *aretioides* (*A. alpina* x *A. obtusifolia*): lax mats of elliptical lvs with star-shaped hairs. Stalks 10-20mm long bear solitary fls or 2-3-flowered umbels of pink fls with a yellow 'eye'.

A. x *escheri* (*A. chamaejasme* x *A. obtusifolia*): very similar to *A. chamaejasme* but lvs with a mixture of straight silky hairs and star-shaped hairs.

A. x *heeri* (*A. alpina* x *A. helvetica*): intermediate, with laxer leaf-rosettes than *A.helvetica*, the lvs with forked hairs. Fls pale pink.

A. x *hybrida* (*A. helvetica* x *A. pubescens*): plants with open leaf-rosettes similar to those of *A. pubescens*; lvs smaller with straight hairs. Fls white.

A. x *pedemontana* (*A. carnea* x *A. obtusifolia*): small tufted plants similar to *A. obtusifolia* but with tighter umbels of white fls with a yellow 'eye'.

Androsace leaves, scale 1-7 x 2½; 8-20 x 4

The shape and size of the leaves can be important in correct diagnoses. Even more important are the types and distribution of hairs; whereas some species have only straight simple hairs others bear branched or star-shaped (stellate) hairs or a mixture. In addition, several species have hairs confined to the leaf margin, rather than the surface.

1 *A. maxima*
2 *A. septentrionale*
3 *A. chaixii*
4 *A. elongata*
5 *A. lactea*, p. 206
6 *A. obtusifolia*, p. 206
7 *A. carnea*, p. 206
7a *A. c.* subsp. *laggeri*, p. 206
7b *A. c.* subsp. *rosea*, p. 206
7c *A. c.* subsp. *brigantiaca*, p. 206
8 *A. chamaejasme*, p. 206
9 *A. pyrenaica*, p. 206

10 *A. villosa*, p. 206
11 *A. helvetica*, p. 206
12 *A. vandelii*, p. 206
13 *A. cylindrica*, p. 206
14 *A. mathildae*, p. 206
15 *A. pubescens*, p. 208
16 *A. ciliata*, p. 208
17 *A. alpina*, p. 208
18 *A. hausmannii*, p. 208
19 *A. wulfeniana*, p. 208
20 *A. brevis*, p. 208

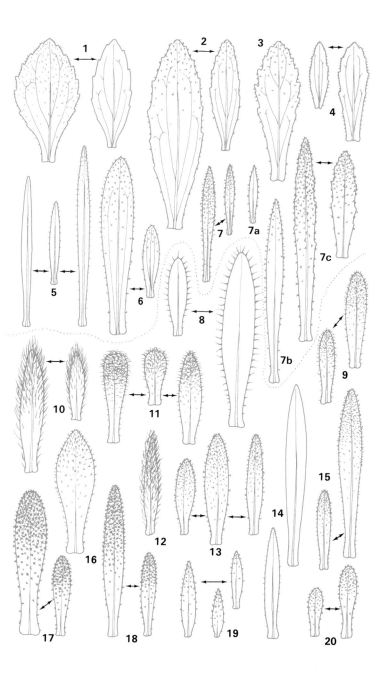

Primrose Family (contd.)

1 ANNUAL ANDROSACE *Androsace maxima*. Low hairy ann. Lvs round or oblong, toothed, all in a basal rosette. Fls tiny, white or pale pink *surrounded* by larger green sepals, in an umbel. Dry fields and waste places, to 1600m. Apr-May. A, CH, CS, D, E, F, H, I, R, YU.

2 NORTHERN ANDROSACE *Androsace septentrionalis*. Low downy ann/bien. Lvs oblong to elliptical, toothed, all in a basal rosette. Fls white or pale pink 4-5mm across, *long-stalked,* in 5-30 fld umbels. Dry meadows and sandy places, to 2200m. Apr-July. A, CH, CS, DK, eF, I, N, PL, R, S, SF. **2a** *A. chaixii* is similar but with *laxer* 5-8 fld umbels and *larger* fls. Open woodland, short turf and rocky ground, to 1800m. Apr-July. seF; French Maritime Alps.

3 ELONGATED ANDROSACE *Androsace elongata*. Similar to 2 but *almost hairless* and the lvs often toothless. Fls tiny white, with a yellow throat, 3mm across, concealed amongst the sepal teeth. Dry, grassy places, to 2200m. May-July. A, CH, CS, c & sD, nE, s & eF, H, PL, R, YU.

4 ALPINE BELLS *Cortusa matthiola*. Short hairy per. Lvs *rounded,* lobed and toothed, deep green, in basal tufts. Fls rosy-purple nodding bells, 9-11mm, in clusters at top of long leafless stems. Woods and damp places, over limestone, to 2200m. June-July. A, CH, CS, sD, eF, I, PL, R, YU.

5 DWARF SNOWBELL *Soldanella pusilla*. Low hairless per forming small mats of deep green, rounded or kidney-shaped, lvs. Fls rosy violet, *narrow nodding-bells* with a *shallow* fringe, solitary. Wet alpine soils and turf on acid rocks, often by snow patches, to 3100m. May-Aug. A, eCH, sD, n & cI; eastern Alps.

6 LEAST SNOWBELL *Soldanella minima*. Similar to 5 but lvs smaller and stems and lfstalks *covered* in short glandular hairs. Fls pale violet or white, *conical bells* with a *shallow* fringe, solitary. Damp soils and turf over limestone, to 2500m. May-July.A, seD, nI, wYU; eastern Alps. **6a** *S.m.* subsp. *samnitica* has *narrow bell* fls. cI; Apennines. **6b Austrian Snowbell** *S. austriaca** similar to 6 but lvs more rounded, slightly *heart-shaped* at base. Fls whitish. A.

7 ALPINE SNOWBELL *Soldanella alpina*. Low hairless, mat-forming per. Lvs deep green, round-heart-shaped or kidney-shaped, stalked; stalks with sessile glands. Fls violet or violet-blue, wide nodding bells, *deeply-fringed,* in clusters of 2-4. Wet pastures and stony places, particularly on limestone, to 3000m. Apr-Aug. A, CH, sD, E, c, s & eF, nI, nwYU. **7a Hungarian Snowbell** *S. hungarica* has lf stalks and stems *covered* in short glandular hairs; lvs often violet beneath. Coniferous woodland and wet moors, to 1700m. May-July. CS, PL, R. **7b** *S. h.* subsp. *major* has *up to* 8 flowers to a cluster and lvs up to 50mm wide. A, CS, I, PI, R, YU. **7c Mountain Snowbell** *S. montana* similar to 7a but more hairy and fls in clusters of six to eight. A, CS, sD, nI, PL, R (SF). **7d** *S. carpatica*. Like 7 but lvs *often* violet beneath. CS, PL; western Carpathians.

8 PYRENEAN SNOWBELL *Soldanella villosa* is more robust than 7a and 7b, the leafstalks and stems *very* hairy. Lvs *green below*. Fls violet, deeply fringed bells in clusters of 3-4. Damp shady places on limestone, to 1700m. May-July. nwE, swF; western Pyrenees.

9 WATER VIOLET *Hottonia palustris*. Pale green aquatic hairless per with *submerged* pinnate Lvs. Fls pale lilac with yellow eye, in whorled racemes above the water. Still fresh water, ditches and ponds, to 1500m. May-July. T, except IRL, IS, N, SF; local.

10 SOWBREAD *Cyclamen purpurascens* (= C. *europaeum)*. Low tuberous rooted per, almost hairless. Lvs *rounded-heart-shaped,* stalked, shiny deep green, often mottled (variegated), purplish beneath. Fls carmine-pink, deeper at mouth, rarely pure white, with *reflexed* petals, throat rounded, fragrant. Fl stalk, *coiling* in fruit. Stony woods and scrub, particularly on limestone, to 1800m. June-Oct. A, CH, CS, sD, seF, H, nI, YU, PL. **10a** C. *hederifolium* (= C. *neapolitanum)** has lobed, *ivy-like,* lvs; fls pale pink or white with an angular, *5-sided* throat, often appearing before lvs. Scrubland and stony places, to 1200m. Aug-Nov. sCH, s & seF, I, YU; sA-Italian and Julian Alps.

Primrose Family (contd.)

1 YELLOW PIMPERNEL *Lysimachia nemorum.* Evergreen creeping hairless per. Lvs pale green, rounded or lance-shaped, pointed, opposite. Fls bright yellow, saucer-like, 6-8.5mm, with *narrow* sepal-teeth. Damp or shaded places, to 1800m. May-July. T-except IS and far north.

2 CREEPING JENNY *Lysimachia nummularia.* Similar to 1 but lvs rounded-heart-shaped, blunt. Fls yellow, *cup-shaped,* 8-16mm, with broad sepal-teeth. Ditches, damp grassland and other moist places, to 1800m. May-July. T, except IS and far north (SF).

3 BROOKWEED *Samolus valerandi.* Low/short hairless per, stems branched or un-branched. Lvs oval or spoon-shaped, pale green, in a basal rosette and alternate up the stem. Fls *white,* cup-shaped, 2-3mm, in lax racemes. Damp or shady places often on limestone, to 1200m. June-Aug. T, except Faeroes, IS, N.

4 CHICKWEED WINTERGREEN *Trientalis europaea.* Low hairless per with a creeping rootstock. Lvs lance-shaped, shiny green, mostly in a *single whorl* near the top of the stem. Fls white starry with 5-9 petals, usually solitary. Damp grassy places, coniferous woods and other acid places, to 2000m. June-July. T, except IRL; very local.

5 CHAFFWEED *Anagallis minima.* Tiny hairless erect ann. Lvs oval, alternate. Fls white or pink hidden at base of lvs, the petals *shorter* than the sepal teeth. Damp open woods, heaths and sandy places, to 1150m. June-Aug. T, except Faeroes, IS.

6 BOG PIMPERNEL *Anagallis tenella.* Slender *mat-forming* hairless per. Lvs oval or rounded, short-stalked, opposite. Fls pink, rarely white, open cups 6-10mm. Damp turf, bogs and marshy places, to 1200m. May-Sept. A, B, CH, D, F, GB, IRL, NL, nl.

Thrift Family Plumbaginaceae

Alpine species with basal tufts of lvs. Fls 5-parted in rounded clusters with papery bracts, borne on slender leafless stalks.

7 PLANTAIN-LEAVED THRIFT *Armeria alliacea* (= *A. plantaginea*). Short/med per. Lvs spear-shaped, pointed, *several veined,* grey-green. Flheads purple to white, 10-20mm. Dry grassland, stony meadows and screes, to 3000m. May.Sept. CH, s & eF, sD, E, I. **7a** *A. ruscinonensis* is similar to 7 but with *blunt-tipped* lvs, shorter stems and pink or white flheads. Acid cliffs near coast, to 1300m. neE, sF.

8 HALLER'S THRIFT *Armeria maritima* subsp. *halleri* (= *A. halleri*). Low/short downy per. Lvs grassy, hairy.margined, *l-veined.* Flheads bright pink or reddish, 10-15mm. Stony meadows particularly on serpentine rocks, 1800-2900m. June.Aug. sD, nE, F, NL, Pl. **8a Mountain Thrift** *A. m.* subsp. *alpina* (= *Statice montana*) has *hairless* lvs and flheads 18-30mm. Screes and damp meadows, 1400-3100m. July-Aug. A, CH, CS, sD, nE, s & eF, nl, R, YU. **8b** *A. m.* subsp. *sibirica.* Like 8a but lvs *less* than 2mm wide. Northern Scandinavia.

Phlox Family Polemoniaceae

9 JACOB'S LADDER *Polemonium caeruleum.* The only European alpine member of the family Polemoniaceae. Med/tall tufted hairless per. Lvs *pinnate,* alternate up the stem. Fls blue or white open-cups, 18-25mm, 5 petals joined halfway. Rocks, damp meadows and woodland, to 2300m. May-Aug. T, except IRL; rather uncommon.

Bindweed Family Convolvulaceae

Twining annuals or perennials, sometimes parasitic. Lvs alternate, no stipules. Fls 5-parted funnel or bell-shaped. Fr a capsule.

10 FIELD BINDWEED *Convolvulus arvensis.* Per with twining or creeping stems, slightly downy when young. Lvs arrow-shaped, stalked. Fls pink and/or white, trumpet-shaped. 15-30mm. Cultivated fields, meadows and waste places, to 1850m. June-Sept. T, except Faeroes, IS and far north.

11 COMMON DODDER *Cuscuta epithymum.* Slender climbing ann, stems *thread-like,* reddish. Lvs tiny scale-like. Fls tiny, pale pink, cup-shaped, in tight clusters, petals and sepals pointed. Parasitic on gorse, heather and many other plants. Grassy places and heaths, to 2200m. June-Oct. T, except Faeroes, IS. **11a Greater Dodder** *C. europaea* has larger, blunt-petalled fls; often *with* yellowish green stems. On nettles and other herbaceous plants. T, except Faeroes, IRL. IS.

Bogbean Family Menyanthaceae

Aquatic perennials with five-parted fls and alternate lvs. Petals joined at base into a short tube. Fr a capsule. Closely related to the Gentian Family.

1 BOGBEAN *Menyanthes trifoliata.* Creeping hairless per, with short erect shoots. Lvs trifoliate, lflets oblong or rhombic, slightly toothed, held above water. Fls pink and white, 15mm, *fringed* with long white hairs, in loose racemes. Marshes, bogs, ponds and ditches, to 1800m. May-July. T.

2 FRINGED WATERLILY *Nymphoides peltata.* Creeping hairless per with floating lvs and stems. Lvs *rounded-heart-shaped,* green, sometimes purple spotted. Fls yellow, 30-40mm, with serrated edge to petals. Lakes, ponds and slow-flowing rivers, to 1200m. June-Sept. T, except IRL, IS, N, S, SF (CH, DK, S); often local.

Gentian Family Gentianaceae

Hairless annuals or perennials with opposite untoothed lvs. Fls solitary or in whorled or branched clusters, generally 4-5parted, but sometimes with as many as 12 petals or lobes; petals joined at base or with a long tube or trumpet-shaped, with smaller intermediate lobes (plicae) between main petal lobes. Fr a many-seeded dry capsule, splitting into two.

3 GREAT YELLOW GENTIAN *Gentiana lutea.* Med/tall per. Lvs large oval, pointed, *ribbed,* bluish-green, the upper clasping the stem. Fls yellow, 5-9 petalled, starry, in whorled clusters at base of upper lvs; petals 30-45mm long. Anthers not joined. Meadows, marshes and rocky slopes, to 2500m. June-Aug. A, CH, sD, E, s & eF, I, R, YU (CS). **3a** *G.l.* subsp. *symphyandra* has its anthers *joined* together. sA, nel, wYU ; south-east Alps.

4 SPOTTED GENTIAN *Gentiana punctata.* Short/med per. Lvs elliptical or lance-shaped, grey-green, ribbed; the lower stalked. Fls pale greenish-yellow, purple-spotted, upright bells, 15-35mm long in clusters at base of upper lvs. Sepal tube with 5-8 teeth. Meadows, open woods and rocky places, to 3050m. July-Sept. A, CH, CS, D, s & eF, I, PL, R, YU. **4a** *G. burseri* has yellow, brown-spotted fls; sepal tube papery, *split down one side.* To 2700m. July-Aug.s & eF, nwl; south-west Alps.

5 PURPLE GENTIAN Gentiana *purpurea.* Short/med per. Lvs lance-shaped or oval, strongly ribbed,the lower stalked. Fls *reddish-purple* with dark-purple spots, upright bells, 15-25mm long, in clusters at base of upper Lvs. Sepal tube papery, split *down* one *side.* Meadows and open woods, 1600-2750m. July-Oct. A, CH, sD, eF, nl, sN. **5a Brown Gentian** *G. pannonica,* has purple fls with red-black spots; sepal tube *with 5-8 teeth.* To 2500m. July-Sept. A, CH, swCS, D, nl, nwYU.

6 WILLOW-LEAVED GENTIAN *Gentiana asclepiadea.* Short/med per with slender erect or arching stems. Lvs lance-shaped, long-pointed, stalkless. Fls blue trumpets with paler bands, 35-50mm long, at base of lvs. Woods, damp meadows and rocks, often on limestone, to 2200m. Aug-Oct. A, CH, CS, sD, eF, H, I, PL, R, YU.

7 MARSH GENTIAN *Gentiana pneumonanthe.* Low/short per with slender, more or less erect, stems. Lvs narrow-oblong or lance-shaped, *1-veined,* stalkless. Fls bright blue trumpets, green-striped outside, 25-50mm long, solitary or several. Marshy places and heaths on acid soils, to 1500m. July-Oct. T, IRL, IS and far north

Gentian Family (contd.)

1 STYRIAN GENTIAN *Gentiana frigida.* Low tufted per. Lvs strap-shaped, pale green. Fls *yellowish-white,* blue-flushed and striped outside, long-bell-shaped, 20-35mm, solitary or two to three. Meadows and stony places, on limestone, 2000-2500m. July-Sept. cA, CS, PL, R; Styrian Alps and Carpathians.

2 KARAWANKEN GENTIAN *Gentiana froelichii.* Low tufted per. Lvs linear-lance-shaped or oblong, pointed. Fls clear blue, *unspotted,* erect tubular-trumpets, 30-40mm, solitary or two on short stems. Screes and turf, on limestone, 1400-2400m. July-Sept. eA, nel, nwYU; south-east Alps.

3 CROSS GENTIAN *Gentiana cruciata.* Med leafy per. Lvs oval-lance-shaped, shiny green. Fls dull blue, greenish outside, 20-25mm, erect, petal tube with *four* lobes, in tight clusters at base of lvs. Meadows, woods and rocky places, to 2000m. July-Oct. A, B, CH, CS, D, E, s & eF, H, NL, I, PL, R, YU. **3a** *G. c.* subsp. *phlogifolia* has linear (not broad-triangular) calyx teeth and corolla only *twice* as long (not three times) as the calyx. R.

4 PROSTRATE GENTIAN *Gentiana prostrata.* Low *annual* with thin prostrate or erect stems. Lvs small, narrow-oblong or spoon-shaped, greyish-green. Fls steel-blue, greenish at base, 10-20mm long, solitary, petal tube with *four* lobes. Short turf and stony places, 2000-2800m. July-Aug. A, eCH, nl; eastern Alps.

5 PYRENEAN GENTIAN *Gentiana pyrenaica.* Low tufted per. Lvs small, narrow-lance-shaped, pointed, overlapping. Fls violet-blue, wide erect trumpets, 20-30mm long, appearing ten-lobed, solitary. Damp meadows and boggy areas, to 2800m. June-Sept. neE, sF, R; eastern Pyrenees and Carpathians.

6 CLUSIUS'S GENTIAN *Gentiana clusii.* Low tufted per. Lvs leathery, elliptical to oblong-lance-shaped. Fls large trumpets, mid to dark blue, 40-60mm, not or scarcely green spotted inside, solitary; sepal teeth *triangular,* widest at base. Mountain pastures and stony places, generally on limestone, to 2800m. Apr-Aug. A, CH, CS, s & swD, sF, nl, PL, R, n & wYU.

7 PYRENEAN TRUMPET GENTIAN *Gentiana occidentalis.* Similar to 6 but sepal-teeth *narrowed* at base, and petal-lobes acute. Turf and stony places, on limestone, to 3000m. May-Aug. sF, nE; western Pyrenees and Cordillera Cantabrica. **7a** *G. ligustica* has fls with green spotting inside and petal-lobes drawn out into a *long fine point.* To 2800m. May-Aug. seF, ne & cl; Maritime Alps and central Apennines. **7b** *G. dinarica.* Like 7 but *lvs* broadly elliptical and petal-lobes more finely pointed. cl; Abruzzi.

8 TRUMPET GENTIAN *Gentiana acaulis* (= *G. kochiana*). Low tufted per. Lvs elliptical or lance-shaped, blunt, greyish-green. Fls large trumpets, deep blue with *green spotting* inside, sometimes purplish or pinkish, rarely white, 40-70mm, petal-lobes pointed, solitary, stalked. Sepal-teeth narrow-lance-shaped, broadest above base. Turf and stony places and bogs, on acid rocks, 1400-3000m. May-Aug. A, CH, CS, sD, neE, n & cl, R, nwYU. **8a** *G. angustifolia* has *narrow* strap or spoon-shaped lvs. Turf and stony places, on limestone, to 2500m. May-Aug. Ch, s & eF, nwl; Pyrenees, south-western Alps and Jura.

9 SOUTHERN GENTIAN *Gentiana alpina.* Low tufted per like a dwarf form of 8. Lvs *round-oval,* greyish-green. Fls medium trumpets, deep blue or sky blue, green-spotted inside, 40mm, solitary, scarcely stalked; petal-lobes rounded. Turf and stony places, on acid rocks, 2000-2600m. June-Aug. w & sCH, nE, s & eF, nl; south-west and south-central Alps, central Pyrenees.

8

Gentian Family (contd.)

1 SPRING GENTIAN *Gentiana verna.* Low tufted per. Lvs lance-shaped or elliptical, *bright green,* mostly in a basal rosette. Fls solitary, pale to deep blue or purplish, rarely white, 15-25mm, petal-tube with 5 oval lobes; stigma white, in centre of fl. Calyx *narrowly winged.* Meadows, heaths and marshy places on acid and alkaline rocks, to 3000m. Mar-Aug. A, CH, CS, sD, c, s & eF, nGB, wlRL, I, PL, R, YU. **1a** *G.v.* subsp. *tergestina* (= *G. tergestina*) has narrower, longer, lvs and *broader wings* on calyx. Dry turf on limestone, to 2000m. Apr-June. I (southern Alps and Apennines), YU.

2 SHORT-LEAVED GENTIAN *Gentiana brachyphylla.* Low tufted per. Lvs rounded to diamond-shaped, bluish-green, leathery, mostly in a basal rosette. Fls solitary, bright pale to mid blue, 15-25mm, with narrow oval lobes. Calyx very slender, *not winged.* Turf, stony places and alluvium on acid rocks, 1800-4200m. July-Aug. A, CH, sD, nE, s & eF, nl, YU. **2a** *G.b.* subsp. *favratii* has narrowly winged calyces and deep blue fls with *rounded* petal lobes. Turf and stony places on limestone, 2000-2800m. July-Sept. A, CH, nl, R, nwYu; Alps and Carpathians. **2b** *G. pumila** like 2 but *with* narrow-lance-shaped lvs and sapphire-blue fls with triangular-pointed, petal-lobes. Damp meadows on limestone, 1600-2800m. June-Aug. A, eCH, nl, nwYu; eastern Alps. **2c** *G.p.* subsp. *delphinensis* like 2b but with blunt petal lobes. swCH, s & eF, nwl; Pyrenees and south-west Alps.

3 BAVARIAN GENTIAN *Gentiana bavarica.* Low mat-forming per. Lvs small, yellowish-green, oblong to spoon-shaped, blunt, overlapping along stem. Fls solitary, dark blue, sometimes violet or white, 16-20mm, petal tube with 5 pointed lobes. Damp meadows and marshy places, 1800-3600m. July-Sept. A, CH, sD, eF, nl, nwYu. **3a** *G. rostanii* has bright-green narrow-lance-shaped, pointed lvs and sky blue fls. 2400-2900m. eF, nwl; south-west and south-central Alps. **3b Triglav Gentian** *G. terglouensis** is like a small version of 3 but with sky blue fls, petal lobes *pointed;* lvs oval-lance-shaped, more or less erect. Meadows and stony places on limestone, 1900-2700m. A, eCH, nl, nwYU; south and east Alps. **3c** *G.t.* subsp. *schleicheri* has *spreading* lvs, the basal forming a lax rosette. wCH, seF.

4 SNOW GENTIAN *Gentiana nivalis.* Low, tiny, slender ann, erect; stems branched. Lvs opposite, oval or elliptical. Fls bright, deep blue, 8mm, petal tube with 5 pointed lobes. Meadows, marshes, heaths and stony places, 1600-3000m. June-Aug. T, except B, DK, sGB, IRL, NL.

5 BLADDER GENTIAN *Gentiana utriculosa.* Low/short, slender, erect ann; stems branched. Lvs opposite, basal ones in a rosette, lance-shaped or elliptical, pale green. Fls intense blue, 12-18mm, petal tube with 5 pointed lobes. Calyx slightly inflated, with broad wings. Damp meadows, bogs and stony places, to 2500m. May-Aug. A, CH, sD, s & eF, I, R, YU.

GENTIANELLAS *Gentianella.* Like *Gentiana* but fls with a fringed whitish throat; corolla lobes 4-5, plicae absent.

6 FRINGED GENTIAN *Gentianella ciliata.* Low to short bien. Lvs lanceolate to linear-lanceolate, the basal spoon-shaped. Fls solitary, blue, 25-50mm, *long-fringed* along the margins of the oval petals but not in the centre of the fl. Meadows and woodland margins. T, except GB, IRL, IS, N, S, SF. **6a** *G. detonsa* has *unequal* calyx-lobes and a short fringe along the petal margins. Damp grassy places and low scrub, often coastal. IS, nN. **6b** *G. aurea* has small pale yellow, occasionally blue, fls, *only* 7-10mm long. IS, N, S, SF; Arctic Europe.

7 SLENDER GENTIAN *Gentianella tenella.* Low unbranched ann. Lvs spoon-shaped or elliptical, mostly in a basal rosette. Fls all from base, sky-blue, violet, rarely white, 4-6mm long, long-stalked, with 4-petal lobes. Damp pastures and stony places, usually on acid rocks, 1500-3100m long.July-Sept. A, CH, CS, sD, E, s & eF, nl, IS, N, PL,R, S, SF. **7a** *G. nana* is small with 5-parted fls. Rocky places and moraines on limestone, 2200-2800m. JulySept. A, nel; eastern Alps.

8 APENNEAN GENTIANELLA *Gentianella columnae.* Low branched per. Lvs lance-shaped. Fls purple or whitish, 10-15mm long, with 4 petal lobes. Calyx with 2 broad outer lobes not *enclosing* the 3 narrow, inner ones. Meadows and stony places, to 1800m. July-Sept. cl; central Apennines.

9 FIELD GENTIAN *Gentianella campestris.* Short branched ann/bien. Lvs oval, pointed on stem. Fls bluish-lilac or white, 15-25mm long, with 4 petal lobes. Calyx with 2 broad outer lobes enclosing the 3 narrow, inner ones. Grassland and heath, to 2750m. July-Oct. T. **9a** *G. hypericifolia* is like 8 but sepal lobes broadest *above,* not below, the middle. nE, sF; west and central Pyrenees.

Gentian Family *(contd.)*

1 FELWORT *Gentianella amarella.* Low/short ann/bien, stems branched above base. Lvs oval to narrow-lance-shaped. Fls reddish-violet, sometimes white or yellowish, 16-22mm long, with 5 petal lobes. Calyx with 5 *equal* lobes. Meadows and sandy places, to 1800m. June-Oct. T, except E, nGB, IS, NL. **1a** *G. a.* subsp. *septentrionalis* has somewhat smaller, often 4-parted, fls. nGB (northern Scotland), IS.

2 GERMAN GENTIAN *Gentianella germanica.* Like 1 but plant long-branched *from the base.* Fls always with 5 petal lobes, lavendar, blue or violet, 10-40mm long, sometimes white; corolla more than twice as long as calyx. Meadows, marshes and waste places, usually over limestone, to 2700m. A, B, CH, CS, sD, F, GB, I, NL, R, YU. A complex group in which the following can be recognised: **2a** *G. bulgarica* has fls 10-20mm long; calyx-tube much shorter than lobes. R, eYU. **2b** *G. ramosa.* Like 2a but fl-stalks (pedicels) *very* short. CH, nI. **2c** *G. engadienensis* has off-violet or white fls, less than 20mm long, and calyx-lobes with a minutely *fringed* margin. CH, nI. **2d** *G. anisodonta* is like 2c but *fls* violet-blue, 21-30mm long. A, CH, CS, sD, nwYU. **2e** *G. aspera.* Like 2c but calyx-lobes more or less equal, hairy *along* the midrib. A, CH, CS, sD, nwYU. **2f** *G. austriaca.* Like 2c but fls 24-45mm long, purplish or violet; calyx *glabrous.* A, CS, D, H, PL, R, YU. **2g** *G. lutsecens.* Like 2f but fls *often yellowish*, 18-25mm long. A, CS, D, PL, R, YU.

3 COMMON CENTAURY *Centaurium erythraea.* Variable short/med bien, stems branched. Lvs elliptical to spoon-shaped, in a basal rosette, smaller up stems. Fls pink or purplish, rarely white, 10-l4mm, in rather flat-topped clusters; petal tube with 5 lobes. Dry grassland, scrub and stony places, to 1400m. June-Sept. T, except Faeroes, IS, N, SF. **3a** *G. suffruticosum* like 3 but rosette lvs *broad* rather than narrowed at the base. June-Sept. E, sF.

4 LESSER CENTAURY *Centaurium pulchellum.* Low/short branched or unbranched ann, *without* a basal lf-rosette. Lvs oval to lance-shaped. Fls pinkish-purple, rarely white, 5-9mm, in loose clusters; petal tube with 5, rarely 4, lobes. Open places and damp meadows, to 1200m. June-Sept. T, except Faeroes, IS.

5 YELLOW-WORT *Blackstonia perfoliata.* Med erect greyish ann. Lvs oval or triangular, joined *round* stem; basal Lvs oblong in a rosette. Fls yellow, 10-15mm, with 6-12 oblong petals. Grassy, shaded and rocky areas, to 1300m. May-Sept. T, except DK, IS, N, S, SF.

6 LOMATOGONIUM *Lomatogonium carinthiacum.* Short rather thin stemmed ann. Lvs mostly basal, oval to oblong, pale green. Fls pale blue, saucer-shaped, 10-25mm, solitary on long leafless stems; petals 4 or 5. Meadows and grassy stream banks, 1400-2700m. Aug-Oct. A, CH, sD, I, R. **6a** *L. rotatum* has linear-lanceolate *calyx-lobes,* equalling or longer than the corolla. Wet habitats. IS.

7 MARSH FELWORT *Swertia perennis.* Med erect, unbranched per. Lvs oval to elliptic, yellowish-green, the upper clasping the stem. Fls blue or violet-red, rarely yellowish-green or white, *starry,* 20-30mm, in branched clusters; petals 4 or 5, pointed. Marshes and wet meadows, to 2500m. July-Oct. A, CH, CS, sD, nE, F, I, PL, R, YU.

Periwinkle Family Apocynaceae

8 LESSER PERIWINKLE *Vinca minor.* Trailing evergreen *per,* almost hairless; stems thin, rooting down at nodes. Lvs opposite, lance-shaped or elliptical, deep shiny-green. Fls solitary, blue-violet, 25-30mm, *propeller-shaped,* with 5 joined petals. Fr linear, forked at base. Woodlands and shaded banks and rocks, to 1320m. Feb-May. T, except IS. **8a** *V. herbacea* is herbaceous, dying down in the winter with narrower lvs with very faint veins; fls blue 25-35mm. A, CS, H, R, YU.

Milkweed Family Asclepiadaceae

A mainly tropical family with one alpine species.

1 SWALLOW-WORT *Vincetoxicum hirundinaria*. Med erect, clump forming, per. Lvs *opposite*, oval to lance-shaped, untoothed. Fls whitish, purplish in bud, 5-10mm, 5-parted, in clusters at base of lvs. Fr a double-pod usually. Woods, scrub land and stony places, to 1800m. May-Aug. T, except GB, IRL, IS and northern Scandinavia. 1a. V. h. subsp. intermedium has yellow fls. neE, sF. **Poisonous.**

Borage Family Boraginaceae

Annuals or perennials, often rough or bristly, with uncut alternate lvs and fls borne in spiralled clusters. Fls 5-parted; petals joined into a short or long tube. Fr, consisting of 4-nutlets, hidden at base of persisting sepal tube. A difficult family with many species which look rather alike.

2 GROMWELL *Lithospermum officinale*. Med/tall bristly per, tufted. Lvs broad to narrowly lance-shaped, pointed. Fls yellowish or greenish-white, 4-6mm, in dense spirals. Nutlets *shiny* white. Hedges, scrub and woodland margins, to 1600m. May-Aug. T, except Faeroes, IS and far north.

3 BLUE GROMWELL *Buglossoides* (= *Lithospermum*) *purpurocaerulea*. Med hairy tufted, per. Lvs lance-shaped to narrowly elliptical, pointed. Fls at first reddish-purple *but soon turning* bright blue, 14-19mm, in small cluster at ends of stems. Nutlets shiny white. Scrub and woodland margins, to 1200m. Apr-June. T, except IRL, IS and Scandinavia. **3a** *B. gastonii* has lvs *clasping* the stem and smaller fls, 12-14mm; nutlets yellowish. Woods and rocky slopes, to 2000m. swF; western Pyrenees.

4 CORN GROMWELL *Buglossoides* (= *Lithospermum*) *arvensis*. Short/med, rough-hairy ann. Lvs oblong to spoon-shaped, pointed. Fls small, dull white, purplish or blue, 4-9mm, in small clusters. Nutlets brownish. Wood margins, waste and rocky places, to 2300m. Apr-Sept. T, except Faeroes, IS.

5 SHRUBBY GROMWELL *Lithodora* (= *Lithospermum*) *oleifolia*. Laxly branched undershrub to 0.5m, stiff-hairy. Lvs oblong to spoon-shaped, blunt, dull green above, *whitish beneath*. Fls pale pink becoming blue, 6-7mm, in small clusters; petal lobes rounded. Rocky places, to 1100m. May-July. neE; eastern Pyrenees, rare (sF).

GOLDEN DROPS *Onosma*. Tufted bristly pers with drooping tubular yellow fls.

6 PYRENEAN GOLDEN DROP *Onosma bubanii*. Short grey-green per. Lvs narrow-oblong covered in *straight* bristles. Fls pale-yellow, 16-20mm long, smooth; flstems *unbranched*. Dry stony places, mainly on limestone, to 1700m. May-June. nE; Spanish Pyrenees. **6a** *O. vaudensis* is more robust, the lower lvs broadest above the middle and the *fl stems branched*. wCH; Rhone Valley.

7 GOLDEN DROP *Onosma arenaria*. Per or bien with a single stem and basal rosettes of oblong-spoon-shaped lvs. Lvs covered with *straight and star-shaped hairs*. Fls pale yellow, 12-l9mm long, in branched clusters. Rocky and stony places to 1700m. May-July. A, CS, sD, H, R, YU. **7a** *O. austriaca* has several branched fl stems and larger fls, 18-22mm. eA; Austrian Alps. **7b Swiss Golden Drop** *Onosma helvetica** is a tufted per with lvs like 7. Fls pale-yellow, 20-24mm, finely hairy. Stony and sandy places, to 2500m. May-June. wCH, seF, nwl; southwestern Alps.

8 BORAGE *Borago officinalis*. Med ann, roughly hairy. Lvs oval, pointed, wavy-margined, the lower stalked. Fls bright blue, 20-25mm, starry with pointed rather reflexed petal lobes and a *protruding* column of stamens. Dry, often waste places to 1800m. May-Sept. T, except IRL, IS and Scandinavia, but widely naturalised.

1, fruit & seeds

8

Borage Family *(contd.)*

1 LESSER HONEYWORT *Cerinthe minor.* Low/med hairless ann/bien/per. Lvs oblong to oval, greyish-green rough and often *white-spotted;* upper lvs stalkless. Fls pale yellow, sometimes with 5 violet spots in the throat, 10-12mm, bell-shaped with pointed lobes. Meadows, fields and waste places, over limestone, to 2200m. May-Sept. A, CH, CS, sD, e & seF, H, I, PL, R, YU. 1a *C. m.* subsp. *auriculata* is per with more swollen fls and fl stalks with *short bristles.* A, CH, I, YU.

2 SMOOTH HONEYWORT *Cerinthe glabra.* Short/med hairless bien/per. Lvs oblong to oval, smooth, *unspotted;* upper lvs heart-shaped at base, unstalked. Fls yellow with 5 dark reddish-purple spots in the throat, 8-13mm, tubular-bells with *rounded* lobes. Meadows and damp woods, on limestone, to 2600m. May-July. A, CH, CS, sD, ?nE, s & eF, I, PL, R, YU.

3 MOLTKIA *Moltkia suffruticosa.* Dwarf cushion-forming densely-lfy subshrub. Lvs linear, pointed, rough-hairy, green above and *whitish* beneath. Fls blue, 13-16mm, narrow upturned bells with rounded lobes, in dense clusters. Stony places, on limestone, to 1200m. May-July. nl; Apuan and south-eastern Alps, northern Apennines.

4 VIPER'S BUGLOSS *Echium vulgare.* Med/tall erect bristly bien. Lvs elliptical to lance-shaped, the upper narrower. Fls blue, pink in bud, 10-19mm, funnel-shaped with rounded lobes, in large branched clusters; stamens *protruding.* Meadows and dry rocky places, to 1800m. July-Sept. T, except Faeroes, IS and far north.

5 COMMON LUNGWORT *Pulmonaria officinalis.* Short tufted hairy per. Lvs *heart-shaped,* green, spotted white. Fls pink turning blue or bluish-violet, 13-18mm, funnel-shaped, in small clusters. Damp open woods, mainly on limestone, to 1900m. Mar-May. T, except IRL, IS, N, nS, SF (GB). **5a** *P. obscura* has *unspotted* or faintly green- spotted lvs. Similar distribution. **5b** *P. rubra* has oval, rough-hairy lvs which are rarely spotted and *red* fls. R, c & eYU. **5c** *P. filarszkyana* is like 5b but lvs narrower and softly hairy, never spotted. R; Carpathians.

6 STYRIAN LUNGWORT *Pulmonaria stiriaca.* Short tufted hairy per. Lvs oblong, pointed, narrowed at the base, green, spotted white. Fls bright blue, 14-18mm, funnel-shaped. Open woods and damp places, to 1300m. Apr-June. A, nwYU; eastern Alps. **6a** *P. saccharata* has reddish-violet or bluish-violet fls. seF, n & cI (B).

7 MOUNTAIN LUNGWORT *Pulmonaria montana.* Short/med tufted per with sticky *stems.* Lvs long-lance-shaped, shining above with soft hairs, unspotted or occasionally green-spotted; upper lvs heart-shaped at base. Fls pink turning bright blue, 15-20mm, funnel-shaped. Meadows and damp woods, to 1900m. Apr-May. B, CH, D, F, NL. **7a** *P. mollis* (= *P. montana* subsp. *mollis*) has softly hairy lvs and *sticky* inflorescences; fls violet-blue or violet. A, CH, CS, D, H, PL, R, YU.

8 NARROW-LEAVED LUNGWORT *Pulmonaria angustifolia* (= *P. azurea*). Short/med rough,tufted, per. Lvs *narrow lance-shaped,* tapered into a short stalk, unspotted. Fls red or purplish turning bright blue, 12-20mm, funnel-shaped. Sepal tube narrow in fr. Woods and meadows, on acid soils, to 2600m. Apr-July. A, CS, D, DK, F, H, I, PL, sS. **8a** *P. visianii* has shorter lvs and a broad sepal tube in fr. To 2600m. Apr-July. A, CH, nI, nwYU. **8b** *P. kerneri* like 8a but with white spotted lvs. Apr-July. A; north-east Alps.

9 LONG-LEAVED LUNGWORT *Pulmonaria longifolia.* Rather like 8 but with white-spotted lvs, sometimes green spotted. Fls red turning violet or blue-violet, 8-12mm, funnel-shaped, in dense clusters. Woods and shady places, to 2000m. Apr-July. F, sGB, H.

Borage Family (contd.)

1 COMMON COMFREY *Symphytum officinale.* Med/tall rough-hairy per, stems *winged.* Lvs broad lance-shaped, lowest very large, stalked. Fls creamy-white, pinkish or purple-violet, tubular-bells, 12-18mm, in *forked, spiralled clusters.* Damp meadows and ditches, to 1600m. May-June. T, except IS (DK, IRL, N, S, SF). **1a Tuberous Comfrey** *S. tuberosum* is a smaller plant, with pale yellowish-white fls, the basal lvs withered at flowering time. Woods and damp places, to 1600m. A, CH, CS, D, E, F, sGB, H, I, PL, R, YU.

2 ALKANET *Anchusa officinalis.* Short/tall, rough-hairy per/bien, well-branched. Lvs long lance-shaped, the lower ones stalked. Fls violet or reddish, sometimes white, 7-15mm, fl tube 5-7mm long, in spiralled clusters. Meadows, banks and rocky places, often over limestone, to 1800m. May-Sept. T, except E, GB, IRL, IS, SF and far north (GB). **2a Bugloss** *A. arvensis* (= *Lycopsis arvensis*) is annual with small blue fls, 4-6mm. T, except IS and far north. **2b** *A. barrelieri* is similar to 2, but fls blue or bluish-violet, 7-10mm, fl-tube *only* 1.5mm long. Woods and fields, to 2300m. May-July. H, I, R, YU.

3 MADWORT *Asperugo procumbens.* Low sprawling ann, bristly. Lvs opposite usually, lance-shaped. Fls purplish, 2-3mm, 1-3 on short drooping stalks at base of lvs. Fr surrounded by enlarged calyx. Cultivated and waste ground, to 2600m. May-Nov. T, except B, GB, IRL, IS (NL).

FORGET-ME-NOTS *Myosotis.* Annuals or perennials, usually softly-hairy, with oblong or lance-shaped Lvs, generally stalkless. Fls small, blue, often pinkish in bud, in forked, loose spira lled clusters. Seeds shiny, brown or black.

4 FIELD FORGET-ME-NOT *Myosotis arvensis.* Low/med bien. Basal lvs broadest above the middle, in a rosette. Fls bright blue, 3-4mm; sepal tube with many hooked hairs. Dry and waste places, shady areas, to 2000m. Apr-Oct. T. **4a** *M. ramosissima* is smaller, ann, often only a few cm tall; sepal teeth spreading in fr. T, except Faeroes and IS.

5 CHANGING FORGET-ME-NOT *Myosotis discolor.* Slender low/short ann. Lvs oval-lance-shaped. Fls pale cream at first but turning blue, 3-4mm; sepal teeth incurved in fr. Bare and waste places, to 2000m. May-June. T. **5a** *M. stricta* has lvs with hooked hairs and tiny pale or deep blue fls, 1-2mm. T, except GB, IRL, Faeroes. **5b** *M. speluncicola* is similar to 5a but fls *white.* Mountain caves. seF, cl.

6 WOOD FORGET-ME-NOT *Myosotis sylvatica* agg. Short per, well branched. Lvs oval or elliptic. Fls sky-blue, 6-8mm, flat; sepal tube with short spreading hooked hairs. Woods and grassy places, to 2000m. Apr-July. T, except IRL, IS and far north. **6a** *M. decumbens* has fl tubes *longer* than the calyx. T, except Faeroes, IRL, IS, NL.

7 ALPINE WOOD FORGET-ME-NOT *Myosotis alpestris.* Low/short per, often tufted. Leaves oval to spoon-shaped, hairy beneath, the basal sometimes stalked. Fls bright or deep blue, sometimes whitish, 6-9mm, flat; sepal tube with *hooked hairs*, teeth incurved in fr; seeds black. Damp woods and meadows, 1500-2800m. Apr-Sept. A, CH, CS, D, E, F, GB, I, PL, R, YU.

8 ALPINE FORGET-ME-NOT *Myosotis alpina* (= *M. pyrenaica*) like 7 but lvs hairless beneath and *fl stalks* as well as sepal tube with hooked hairs. Rocks, screes and mountain pastures, 1500-2800m. Apr-Sept. nE, sF; Pyrenees. **8a** *M. stenophylla* is like 7 and 8 but with *no* hooked hairs on calyx. A, CS, H, PL, R.

9 TUFTED FORGET-ME-NOT *Myosotis laxa* (incl. *M. caespitosa*). Short/med ann or bien, branched from base. Fls bright blue, 2-4mm; sepal tube long-stalked, with only straight hairs. Fr seeds dark brown. Wet stony and grassy places, to 1600m. May-Sept. T, except IS.

10 WATER FORGET-ME-NOT *Myosotis scorpioides* agg. Low/med *creeping* per; hairs closely pressed to stems, lvs and sepal tube; no hooked hairs. Fls sky-blue, sometimes pink or whitish, 4-8mm, petals slightly notched. Wet places, ditches, river margins, to 2000m. June-Sept. T, except E.

11 LAMOTTE'S FORGET-ME-NOT *Myosotis lamottiana.* Like 10 but the stems *rough-hairy*, shining, and the fls rather smaller. Wet meadows, 1500-2000m. June-Sept. nE, sc & sF.

Borage Family *(contd.)*

1 KING OF THE ALPS *Eritrichium nanum.* Low dense, *cushion-forming*, silky-hairy per; like a dwarf forget-me-not. Lvs in rosettes, narrow-oblong to spoon-shaped, up to 3mm wide. Fls pale to brilliant blue, rarely whitish, 7-9mm, in short-stalked clusters of 3-7. Acid rocks and screes, sometimes dolomite, 2500-3600m. July-Aug. A, eCH, nI, R, YU. **1a** *E. n.* subsp. *jankae* is densely white-hairy with *lvs* 3mm wide or more. R; east and southern Carpathians.

2 BUR FORGET-ME-NOT *Lappula squarrosa* (= *L. myosotis*). Med branched hairy ann/bien. Lvs greyish, oblong to lance-shaped, unstalked. Fls pale blue, 2-4mm, in loose *leafy clusters.* Fr erect, egg-shaped with two rows of hooked bristles forming a mitre-like erection. Dry slopes and waste places, to 2500m. June-Aug. T, except GB, IRL, IS, and far north (D, DK, NL, PL, SF). **2a** *L. deflexa* (= *Hackelia deflexa*) has larger fls, 3-6mm; fr *drooping.* A, CH, CS, D, E, F, I, N, R, SF.

3 BLUE-EYED MARY *Omphalodes verna.* Low/short creeping per, slightly hairy. Lvs mostly clustered at base, oval to *heart-shaped,* pointed, long-stalked. Fls sky blue, 8-l0mm, in loose racemes; petals rounded. Damp mountain woods, to 1200m. Mar-May. A, I, R, YU (B, CH, CS, D, F, GB, H, NL, PL). **3a** *O. scorpioides* is bien with lance- or spoon- shaped lvs; fls *small,* blue, 3-4mm. eA, CS, D, H, PL, R.

4 HOUND'S TONGUE *Cynoglossum officinale.* Med greyish, softly hairy bien. Lvs oblong to lance-shaped, the upper clasping the stem. Fls dull *maroon-purple,* funnel-shaped, 5-6mm long. Fr flattened, covered with hooked *spines.* Dry and stony places, to 2400m. May-Aug. T, except IS, and far north. **4a** *C. magellense* (= *C. apenninum*) is a lower *per* with narrow-lance-shaped lvs and reddish fls, 8mm long. Meadows, to 2000m. June-Aug. c & sl; central and southern Apennines. **4b** *C. nebrodense* is smaller than 4 with reddish-violet fls and *rounded fr.* Woods to 2150m. E, c & sl.

5 SOLENANTHUS *Solenanthus apenninus.* Tall bien. Basal lvs large, elliptical or broad lance-shaped, the upper smaller, *clasping* stem. Fls purple, funnel-shaped, 7-9mm long, in *dense* branched spirals. Woods and pastures, to 1800m. c & sl; central and southern Apennines, Sicily.

Verbena Family Verbenaceae

6 VERVAIN *Verbena officinalis.* Med roughly-hairy per, stems stiff, *square.* Lvs opposite, diamond-shaped, the lower pinnately-lobed, stalked. Fls lilac-blue, 2-5mm, in slender lfless spikes; petal tube 5-lobed, more or less *2-lipped.* Waste places and rocks, to 1500m. June-Sept. T, except Faeroes, IS, N, S, SF.

Mint Family Labiatae

Aromatic *square-stemmed* annuals or perennials, sometimes subshrubs. Lvs usually undivided *opposite.* Fls clustered or whorled, rarely solitary; calyx tubular, 5-toothed, often 2-lipped; corolla 2-lipped and open-mouthed. Stamens 4 or 2. Fr 4 nutlets hidden inside calyx.

7 ALPINE SKULLCAP *Scutellaria alpina.* Short slightly hairy per. Lvs oval, toothed, the lower stalked. Fls purplish, lower lip often *whitish,* 20-25mm long, in *quadrangular* clusters. Bracts often purplish. Limestone rocks and screes, grassy slopes, to 2500m. June-Aug. CH, D, E, s & eF, I, R, YU. **7a** *S. orientalis* has grey lvs and *yellow* fls. R, YU.

8 MOUNTAIN GERMANDER *Teucrium montanum.* Low/short mat-forming subshrub. Lvs leathery, elliptical, untoothed, whitish beneath, margins rolled *under.* Fls in flattish clusters, yellowish-white, 12-15mm long. Rocks, screes and dry pastures, usually on limestone, to 2400m. May-Aug. T, except DK, GB, IRL, IS, N, S, SF.

9 PYRENEAN GERMANDER *Teucrium pyrenaicum.* Low, slender, creeping, hairy per. Lvs rounded to oval, *toothed.* Fls in rounded clusters, white or purple with a white lower lip, 14-16mm long. Rocks, screes and dry pastures, usually on limestone, to 2000m. June-Aug. nE, sF; Pyrenees.

10 WALL GERMANDER *Teucrium chamaedrys.* Short tufted per, slightly hairy. Lvs oblong or broadly-oval, toothed, *dark green,* shiny. Fls pale to deep purple, 9-16mm long, in *leafy spikes.* Dry places, banks and open woodland, to 1800m. May-Sept. T, except IRL, IS and Scandinavia (GB). **10a** *T. lucidum* is larger and more or less *hairless.* June-Aug. seF, nwI; south-west Alps.

Labiate Family (contd.)

BUGLES *Ajuga.* Tufted perennials, sometimes annuals. Upper lip of corolla very short, the lower 3-lobed. Calyx with 5 equal teeth.

1 PYRAMIDAL BUGLE *Ajuga pyramidalis.* Low/short creeping per, stems hairy all *round.* Lvs oval, slightly toothed or untoothed, the lower stalked. Fls pale violet-blue or deep violet, rarely pink or white, 10-18mm long, in dense leafy pyramidal spikes. Meadows, stony places and scrub, often on acid soils, 1300-2800m. Apr-Aug. T, except sE, c & sl. **1a** A. *genevensis* has more distinctly toothed, often shallowly lobed, lvs and bright blue, rarely pink, fls. Meadows and woodland clearings, on calcareous soils. T, except GB, IRL, IS, N. **1b** A. *laxmannii* has solitary fls and *clasping* stem lvs. H, R, YU.

2 COMMON BUGLE *Ajuga reptans.* Low short, creeping per with rooting *runners;* stems hairy on two sides. Fls blue, rarely pink or white, 14-17mm long, in leafy spike, the lf-like bracts often purplish. Damp grassy places and woods to 2000m. Apr-July. T, except IS and far north.

3 GROUND PINE *Ajuga chamaepitys.* Low greyish-hairy ann, smelling faintly of pine when crushed. Lvs with *3-narrow* lobes, the lobes often further lobed or toothed. Fls yellow, red spotted, 10-15mm long, partly hidden amongst lvs. Stony and grassy places, often on calcareous soils, to 1600m. May-Sept. T, except IRL, IS and Scandinavia.

4 TENORE'S BUGLE *Ajuga tenorii.* Low, often stemless slightly hairy or hairless per. Lvs oblong to spoon-shaped,toothed. Fls bright blue, 16-25mm long; upper bracts *shorter* than the fls. Siliceous soils, to 1400m. May-June.c & sl; Apennines.

5 SIDERITIS *Sideritis hyssopifolia.* Short/med hairy or hairless sub-shrubby per. Lvs linear to oval or spoon-shaped, slightly toothed or untoothed, scarcely stalked. Fls pale yellow, sometimes purple tinged, 10mm long, in dense oblong clusters; stamens not protruding. Pastures, woods and rocky places, often on limestone, to 1800m. July-Aug. E, s & eF, wCH, nI (D). **5a** S. *endressii* is similar, the fls in loose clusters, yellow outside *but* brown or purple tinged inside, 9-20mm. To 1800m.eE, sF. **5b** S. *montana* has black or brown *fls* with a yellow lower lip. A, CS, E, seF, H, I.

HEMP-NETTLES *Galeopsis.* Annuals with fls in terminal or branched clusters or whorls. Fls with the upper lip hooded and the lower 3-lobed. Calyx bell-shaped, 5-toothed.

6 LARGE PINK HEMP-NETTLE *Galeopsis ladanum* (= G. intermedia). Short/med ann, stems square hairy almost to the base. Lvs oval to lance-shaped, narrowed at base, toothed. Fls deep pink with yellow blotches on the lip, 15-28mm long; calyx green. Fields and stony places, often on acid soils, to 2400m. July-Oct. T, except GB, IRL, IS and far south. **6a Red Hemp-nettle** G. *angustifolia*** has *narrower,* linear or linear-lance-shaped lvs and white-hairy calyces. To 2000m. T, except IS, N. **6b** G. *reuteri* is taller than 6 with wiry *rounded* stems, hairless in the lower half. Rocks and screes, to 1600m. seF, nwl; Maritime Alps.

7 PYRENEAN HEMP-NETTLE *Galeopsis pyrenaica.* Short/med hairy ann, stems square. Lvs oval to triangular, toothed, short-stalked, velvety-hairy. Fls pinkish purple with darker blotches, 17-25mm long. Acid sands and gravels by streams, to 2200m. Aug-Sept. neE, sF; eastern Pyrenees. **7a Downy Hemp-nettle** G. *segetum* has larger *pale yellow* fls, the lower lip sometimes purple blotched. July-Sept. B, CH, D, DK, E, F, GB, I, NL (A, CS, H, R, YU).

8 LARGE-FLOWERED HEMP-NETTLE *Galeopsis speciosa.* Med/tall branched, hairy ann. Lvs oval to lance-shaped, pointed, toothed, short-stalked. Fls *yellow* with a large purple blotch on the lower lip, 27-34mm long. Cultivated land and waste places, to 1740m. July-Sept. T, except E, IS and far south (IRL).

6a

Labiate Family *(contd.)*

1 HAIRY HEMP-NETTLE *Galeopsis pubescens.* Med white-hairy ann. Lvs oval, pointed, square or heart-shaped at the base, toothed, stalked. Fls bright pinkish- red with *yellow blotches* on the lower lip, 20-25mm long. Open woods, fields, banks and hedgerows, to 1600m. July-Sept. A, CH, CS, D, c & sF, H, I, PL, R, YU (B, NL).

2 COMMON HEMP-NETTLE *Galeopsis tetrahit.* Short/med rough-hairy ann. branched. Lvs lance-shaped to broadly oval, pointed, *narrowed* at the base, toothed, stalked. Fls pale pinkish-purple with darker markings, rarely yellowish or whitish, 15-20mm long. Open woods, heaths, paths and waste places, to 2400m. July-Oct. T. **2a** *G.t.* subsp. *glaucocerata* has glaucous *stems.* eF; French Alps. **2b** *G. bifida* has smaller fls than 2, rarely exceeding 15mm long, the middle lobe of the lower lip *distinctly* 2-lobed. T, except Faeroes, IS and far north.

SALVIAS *Salvia.* Perennials with fls in whorls forming long spikes; upper lip of corolla straight or curved, the lower 3-lobed. Calyx 2-lipped. Stamens 2; style protruding.

3 JUPITER'S DISTAFF, STICKY SAGE *Salvia glutinosa.* Med/tall branched, sticky-hairy, per. Lvs oval to heart-shaped, toothed, stalked. Fls *yellow* with reddish-brown markings, 30-40mm long, 2-6 per whorl. Woods, copses and clearings, generally on limestone, to 1800m. June-Sept. T, except B, nF, GB, IRL, IS, NL and Scandinavia. **3a** *S. austriaca* has lvs *hairless* above, and yellowish white fls, 12-17mm long, 4-9 per whorl. A, CS, H, R, YU.

4 MEADOW CLARY *Salvia pratensis.* Med/tall hairy, slightly aromatic, per. Lvs oval or oblong, blunt-toothed, stalked, the upper lvs smaller, unstalked. Fls violet-blue, 20-30mm long, 3-6 per whorls. Dry grassland; usually on limestone, 1920m. May-Aug. T, except DK, nGB, IRL, IS, N. **4a** *S. dumetorum* has narrower on long or oval lvs and with *most fls* 10-20mm long. R. **4b** *S. transsylvanica* has lvs dense with white hairs beneath and violet or blue fls 16-21mm long. n & cR.

5 WHORLED CLARY *Salvia verticillata.* Med/tall hairy, rather unpleasant smelling, often purple tinged, per. Lvs oval-heart-shaped, with one or *two* lobes at base, toothed, stalked. Fls lilac-blue, violet-blue or purplish, 8-15mm long, 15-30 in *tight whorls.* Dry grassland, paths and stony places, to 2400m. May-Aug. A, CH, E, F, H, I, PL, R, YU (B, D, DK, GB, N, NL, S).

6 WIND SALVIA *Salvia nemorosa.* Med hairy per lvs oblong-heart-shaped, blunt toothed, stalked, the upper lvs smaller, unstalked. Fls small, violet-blue, 8-12mm long, 2-6 per whorl. Meadows and grassy places, to 1450m. May-Aug. A, CH, CS, D, H, I, PL, R, YU (F, GB, N, S).

Labiate Family (contd.)

DEADNETTLES *Lamium*. Annuals or perennials with upright stems and whorls of fls at the lf-bases. Calyx tubular with 5-teeth. Corolla with the upper lip 'hood-like' and the lower generally heart-shaped.

1 BALM-LEAVED ARCHANGEL *Lamium orvala*. Med/tall hairless or slightly hairy per. Lvs triangular-oval, stalked and with coarse, irregular teeth, Fls pink to dark purple, or whitish, *25*-45mm long, the upper and lower lips with *serrated* edges, Woods, shady places and banks, to 1800m. May–July. wA, sH, nl, wYU. **1a** *L. garganicum* subsp. *laevigatum* has somewhat smaller fls, with the upper corolla lip shallowly toothed, 10-15 (not 15-20)mm long; anthers *hairy*, not glabrous. Mountain rocks. eF, I, R, YU.

2 WHITE DEADNETTLE *Lamium album*. Short/med hairy creeping per, stems erect; faintly aromatic. Lvs heart-shaped, toothed, stalked. Fls white, 20-25mm long, hairy. Banks, hedgerows, paths and waste places, to 2300m. Apr–Nov. T (IRL, IS). **2a Spotted Deadnettle** *L. maculatum** is more *strongly* aromatic and with pinkish-purple fls. To 2000m. Apr–Oct. T, except DK, N, IRL, IS (GB, S).

3 RED DEADNETTLE *Lamium purpureum*. Low/short hairy, often purplish, ann. Lvs oval or heart-shaped, blunt-toothed, stalked. Fls pinkish-purple, 10-18mm long. Cultivated and waste ground, to 2500m. Mar–Dec. T (IS). **3a** *L. hybridum* has more sharply toothed lvs and rather smaller fls. T, except IS.

4 HEN BIT DEADNETTLE *Lamium amplexicaule*. Low/short hairy ann. Lvs rounded or oval, blunt-toothed, the lower stalked but the upper stalkless and half-clasping the stem. Fls pinkish-purple, 14-20mm long. Cultivated and waste ground, to 2550m. Apr–Dec. T, (IS).

5 YELLOW ARCHANGEL *Lamiastrum galeobdolon*. Short/med hairy creeping per, stems erect. Lvs narrow to broadly oval, dark green (sometimes varigated), blunt-toothed, stalked. Fls *yellow* streaked with green, 17-25mm long, 8-16 in dense whorls; lower lip 3-lobed. Woods and shady places, to 2000m. Apr–July. T, except IS and far north (N, SF). **5a** *L.g.* subsp. *montanum* has more sharply toothed lvs and *whorls* of 20-30 fls. T, except IS and far north; rarer in the north. **5b** *L.g.* subsp. *flavidum* like 5a but plants *not* creeping and with smaller fls. A, CH, sD, I, nwYU.

6 SHRUBBY HOREHOUND *Ballota frutescens*. Much branched, slightly pungent, shrub to 60cm. Lvs small, oval to oblong, untoothed or finely toothed, stalked. Fls white or lilac, 12-l5mm long, in small whorls of 8-12. Rocky places, to 1200m. seF, nwI; south-western Alps.

7 BLACK HOREHOUND *Ballota nigra*. Med/tall, rather straggly, hairy per; strongly aromatic. Lvs oval or oblong, toothed, stalked. Fls pink or lilac, 12-14mm long, in dense whorls at lf-bases; calyx with 5 finely-pointed teeth, curved back in fr. Banks, woodland margins and waste places, to 1530m. June–Sept. T, except Faeroes, IS, N, nS, SF.

CATMINTS *Nepeta*. Med/tall hairy pers with dense whorls of fls up leafy stems. Lower lip of corolla 3-lobed, the upper 2-lobed. Calyx with 5 almost equal teeth, 1-veined.

8 BROAD-LEAVED CATMINT *Nepeta latifolia*. Med/tall densely hairy, rather bluish-green, per. Lvs oval-oblong, heart-shaped at base, toothed, *almost stalkless*. Fls blue, 8-11mm long, in whorls forming a long spike. Meadows and pinewood clearings, to 1700m. July–Sept. E, sF.

9 COMMON CATMINT *Nepeta cataria*. Med/tall branched grey-woolly per with a *minty scent*. Lvs 0val-heart~shaped, toothed, stalked. Fls white with purple spots, 7-10mm long, in a spike with the lower whorls separated. Banks, hedgerows and rocky places, to 1500m. June–Sept. T; widely naturalised in the region.

2a

Labiate Family (contd.)

1 LESSER CATMINT *Nepeta nepetella*. Med/tall greyish-green branched per. Lvs lance-shaped to oblong, grey-hairy beneath, toothed, stalked. Fls white, pink or bluish-violet, 10-12mm long, in loose, often branched spikes. Dry rocky and stony places and river gravels, to 1700m. July-Aug. E, s & eF, I.

BETONYS or WOUNDWORTS *Stachys*. Hairy perennials, sometimes annuals with erect stems. Fls in whorls forming dense or loose leafy spikes. Lower lip of corolla 3-lobed, the upper 1-2-lobed. Calyx with 5 equal teeth, 5-10-veined.

2 ALPINE BETONY *Stachys monieri* (= *S. densiflora*). Short/med bristly-hairy per with basal leafy rosettes. Lvs oblong, heart-shaped at the base, toothed, the upper short-stalked. Fls pink or purplish, 20-24mm long, in dense short, blunt spikes. Dry meadows, generally on limestone, to 2400m. July-Aug. A, CH, E, F, I, H, R.

3 BETONY *Stachys officinalis* (= *Betonica officinalis*). Variable short/tall softly hairy or almost hairless per with basal leafy rosettes. Lvs oblong to oval, heart-shaped at the base, toothed, the lower stalked. Fls reddish-purple, 12-18mm long, in dense blunt spikes. Light woodland, grassy places and heaths, to 1800m. June-Oct. T, except IS and far north (N, SF).

4 DOWNY WOUNDWORT *Stachys germanica*. Med/tall *downy* greyish-white per. Lvs oblong to heart-shaped, finely toothed, the lower long-stalked but the upper stalkless, green above, greyish-white beneath. Fls pale pinkish-purple, 15-20mm, in whorled spikes. Woodland edges and clearings, rocky ground and screes, often on limestone, to 1750m. June-Sept. T, except DK, IRL, IS, NL. **4a Alpine Woundwort** *S. alpina* has glandular-hairy stems and dull purple fls, 15-22mm. Shady and damp stony places, on limestone, to 2000m. T, except DK, nGB, IRL, IS, N, S, SF.

5 HEDGE WOUNDWORT *Stachys sylvatica*. Med/tall, rough-hairy, green per, pungent. Lvs oval-heart-shaped, toothed, *all* stalked. Fls dull reddish-purple with white markings on the lower lip, 13-18mm long, in loose spikes. Hedges, banks and shady places, to 1700m. June-Oct. T, except Faeroes, IS and far north.

6 MARSH WOUNDWORT *Stachys palustris*. Short/med hairy per. Lvs oblong to lance-shaped, heart.shaped at the base, toothed, only the *lower* stalked. Fls pale purple, 12-15mm long, in whorled spikes. Damp places, often by fresh water, to 1600m. June-Oct. T. Often hybridises with 5.

7 YELLOW WOUNDWORT *Stachys recta*. Variable short/tall sparsely hairy aromatic per. Lvs oblong or oval, green, finely toothed, the lower stalked, the upper narrower and stalkless. Fls pale yellow with purplish streaks, 15-20mm long, in narrow whorled, branched spikes. Dry rocky and waste places, to 2250m. June-Sept. A, B, CH, CS, D, F, H, I, PL, R, YU. **7a** *S. annua* is shorter and annual with all the lvs stalked. Fls white or pale yellow. Cultivated fields and waste places, generally on limestone. T, except GB, IRL, IS (DK, N, S). **7b Yellow Betony** *Stachys alopecuros* has persistent basal lf-rosettes and more triangular-shaped lvs and pale yellow fls; stamens protruding. Meadows, scrub and screes, on limestone, to 2000m. June-Aug. A, CH, D, E, c & sF, I, YU.

8 BASTARD BALM *Melittis melissophyllum*. Short/med hairy, strong smelling, per, with erect stems. Lvs oblong or oval, heart-shaped at the base, toothed, stalked. Fls white with pink markings, pink or purple, 25-40mm long, *few* to each whorl at base of lvs. Woods, hedges, banks and other shady places, to 1400m. May-July. T, except DK, nGB, IRL, IS, N, S, SF.

8, colour forms

236

Labiate Family *(contd.)*

1 GROUND IVY *Glechoma hederacea.* Low creeping, softly-hairy per with long rooting runner. Lvs kidney-shaped, blunt toothed, long stalked. Fls pale violet or pinkish, 15-22mm long, in loose whorls at lf-bases. Woods, grassy and waste places, to 1800m. Mar-June. T, except Faeroes ans IS. **1a** *G. hirsuta* has fls 20-30mm long, pale blue with white spots; plant more densely hairy. Similar habitats. A, CS, H, I, PL, R, YU.

2 NORTHERN DRAGONHEAD *Dracocephalum ruyschiana.* Med per with erect stems. Lvs narrow-lance-shaped, hairless, untoothed, the *margins rolled under.* Fls blue-violet, rarely pink or white, 20-28mm long, in terminal clusters of 2-6. Dry grassy places and open woods, to 2200m. June-Sept. A, CH, D, s & eF, nH, I, N, PL, R, S. **2a** *D. austriacum** has larger fls and lvs *divided* into 3-5 narrow-lance-shaped segments. May-June. A, CH, CS, eF, H, I, R. **2b** *D. thymiflolium* has *small* lilac blue fls, 7-9mm long and oval lvs with a heart-shaped base. R (DK, PL, S, SF).

3 SELF-HEAL *Prunella vulgaris.* Low creeping, slightly hairy per. Lvs oval to diamond-shaped, blunt-toothed or untoothed, the lower stalked. Fls deep violet-blue, 13-15mm long, in *dense oblong clusters* with lvs at the base. Woods and dry meadows, particularly over limestone, to 2400m. June-Oct. T. **3a Large Self-heal** *Prunella grandiflora* is larger, the fls 20-25mm, violet-blue with a whitish tube and lower lip, *without* lvs at the base of the fl head. T, except GB, IRL, IS, N, NL, SF.

4 CUT-LEAVED SELF-HEAL *Prunella laciniata.* Low creeping, hairy per. Lvs oblong, *pinnately lobed,* the lower stalked. Fls creamy-white, rarely rose or purplish, 15-17mm long, in oblong heads. Dry grassy and waste places, to 1320m. June-Oct. T, except IRL, IS, N, NL, S, SF (GB).

5 ALPINE CALAMINT *Acinos alpinus* (= *Calamintha alpina*). Short/med hairy per with slender stems. *Lvs elliptical to oval,* untoothed or with a few small teeth near the tip. Fls violet with white marks on the lower lip, 10-20mm long, in small clusters at lf bases. Meadows, rocky places and screes, usually on limestone, to 2500m. June-Sept. A, CH, CS, sD, s & eE, F, I, PL, R, YU. **5a Basil-thyme** *A. arvensis* (= *Calamintha acinos*)* is similar but annual usually, the fls only 7-l0mm long. To 2000m. T, except Faeroes and IS. **5b** *A. suaveolens.* Like 5 but lvs *narrower,* 2-3 times as long as broad, pointed. c & sI, R, c & eYU. **5c** *A. rotundifolius* is like 5a but lvs *rounded,* strongly veined beneath. C & sE, cI, R, YU.

6 LARGE-FLOWERED CALAMINT *Calamintha grandiflora.* Short/med slightly hairy per. Lvs oval to, oblong, pointed, toothed, stalked. Fls *large,* pink, 25-40mm long, in loose leafy heads. Loamy woodland, to 2100m. July-Sept. A, E, s & eF, I, R, YU.

7 WOOD CALAMINT *Calamintha sylvatica.* Med/tall hairy, *mint-scented,* per. Lvs oval to almost rounded, toothed, stalked, dark green. Fls pink or lilac, 10-22mm long, in loose leafy spikes. Open woodland and thickets and stony places, to 1600m. June-Oct. T, except DK, IS, N, S, SF.

8 LESSER CALAMINT *Calamintha nepeta.* Med/tall hairy per. Lvs greyish, broadly oval, blunt, with small teeth. Fls pale lilac or white, 10-15mm, in loose leafy spikes; sepal tube with *protruding* hairs in fr. Dry stony and scrubby places, to 1300m. July-Oct. A, CH, E, s & eF, sGB, H, I, YU (D).

9 MICROMERIA *Micromeria marginata* (= *M. piperella,* *Thymus margin*atus). Dwarf spreading thyme-like subshrub with short erect branches. Lvs oval, blunt, untoothed. Fls purplish or violet, 12-l6mm long, borne in loose heads. Rocks and stony places, to 1500m. June-Aug. seF, nwI; Maritime Alps. **9a** *M. thymifolia* is a larger plant with elliptical lvs and *smaller* white or violet fls, 5-9mm long; calyx teeth equal, not unequal. Rocky habitats. H, n & cI, YU.

5a

Labiate Family *(contd.)*

1 MARJORAM *Origanum vulgare.* Low spreading downy per, pleasantly aromatic. Lvs oval, untoothed or slightly so, stalked. Fls purplish or whitish, 4-7mm, in branched clusters, with *dark purple bracts* and protruding stamens. Dry grassland, screes and rocky places, to 2000m. July-Sept. T, except Faeroes, IS and far north.

THYMES *Thymus.* Aromatic creeping or subshrubby pers. Lvs small, thick, blunt, untoothed, bristly on the edge towards the base. Fls in small heads or spikes, with protruding stamens.

2 WILD THYME *Thymus serpyllum.* Low matted per with *non-flowering* creeping branches, stems hairy all round. Lvs linear to elliptical with a *hairy margin,* un-stalked. Fls pale pink to rosy-purple, 3-6mm long, in rounded heads. Dry grassy and stony places and scrub, to 3000m. Apr-Sept. T, except A, CH, CS, c & sF, IRL, IS, I, R, YU.

3 GLABRESCENT THYME *Thymus glabrescens.* Low subshrubby per with creeping branches ending in a fl cluster; stems hairy all round. Lvs elliptical-lance. shaped to narrow-oval, those of the fl stems at least 3mm broad. Fls pale pink to purplish, 3-6mm, in rounded heads, often with a separate cluster below. Dry grassy and stony places, to 1500m. May-Aug. A, CH, CS, F, H, I, PL, R, YU; absent from much of the southern Alps. **3a** *T.g.* subsp. *decipiens* has fl stem lvs *less than* 3mm broad. 900-1400m. sA, sCH, nI, swYU.

4 HAIRY THYME *Thymus praecox* subsp. *polytrichus.* Low creeping subshrub; stems hairy on two sides only. Lvs oval to spoon-shaped, short-stalked. Fls rosy-purple, 3-6mm, in rounded heads. Meadows and rocky places, to 3000m. MaySept. A, CH, I, E, s & eF, nwYU. **4a** *T. nervosus* is similar but with very *narrow lvs,* not more than 1.5mm broad, spoon.shaped. nE, s & seF; Pyrenees and Mt Ventoux. **4b** *T. pulcherrimus* has lvs with a strong *marginal vein* on each side. nc & eCS, PL, R.

5 LARGER WILD THYME *Thymus pulegioides.* Low/med tufted subshrubby per, *without* rooting runners. Stems hairy all round. Lvs oval to oblong, hairless above, stalked. Fls pinkish purple, 6mm long, in whorled spikes. Grassy and waste places, to 2000m. July-Sept. T, except IS and far north. **5a** *T. alpestris* has creeping, *non-flowering* branches as well. A, CS, PL, R.

6 HYSSOP *Hyssopus officinalis.* Med aromatic subshrubby per. Lvs narrow- lance-shaped, hairy or hairless, untoothed. Fls violet or blue, rarely white, 7-12mm long, in *leafy* whorled spikes. Dry hills and rocky places, to 2000m. July-Sept. A, CH, CS, E, F, H, I, YU (B, D, NL, PL). **6a** *H.o.* subsp. *aristatus* has a 1-2mm *whitish tip* to the upper lvs. E, sF.

MINTS *Mentha.* Aromatic pers with creeping stolons. Fls small, 4-lobed, lilac or pale purple, in dense spikes or spiked-whorls; stamens protruding. The species cross readily producing many hybrids.

7 CORN MINT *Mentha arvensis.* Low/med hairy per with a sickly scent. Lvs lance.shaped to broadly oval, toothed. Fls lilac or white, in dense whorls, the stem tip leafy. Damp places and ditches, to 1800m. July-Oct. T, except Faeroes, IS, and far north.

8 WATER MINT *Mentha aquatica.* Short/med hairy, often purplish per, pleasantly aromatic. Lvs oval, toothed, stalked. Fls lilac in *dense oblong-heads,* sometimes branched below. Swamps, ditches and damp places, to 1700m. July-Oct. T (IS).

9 HORSE MINT *Mentha longifolia.* Med/tall downy per with a musty scent; stems *white or greyish.* Lvs oblong-elliptical, pointed, toothed, usually unstalked, whitish-downy. Fls lilac or white, in *narrow whorled spikes,* branched below. Fields, hedges and damp places, to 1900m. July-Oct. T, except GB, IRL, IS, N, NL, nS, SF. **9a Spearmint** *Mentha spicata* is strongly aromatic with *green,* almost hairless, lvs. T, except IS and far north; naturalised in much of the area and commonly used as a culinary herb.

10 PENNYROYAL *Mentha pulegium.* Short/med downy per, strongly aromatic; stems prostrate or erect. Lvs oval, scarcely toothed, short-stalked. Fls lilac, 4.5-6mm long, in dense whorled spikes but without a terminal head. Wet places and damp meadows, to 1800m. July-Oct. T, except DK, Faeroes, IS, N, S, SF.

Labiate Family (contd.)

1 LAVENDER Lavandula angustifolia. Much branched aromatic shrub to 50cm. Lvs lance-shaped to linear, grey-green. Fls lavender-blue or purplish, in dense oblong clusters. Warm rocky slopes, usually on limestone, to 1800m. June-July. E, s & eF, I, YU. **1a** L.a. subsp. pyrenaica has bracts longer than the calyces. neE, sF; mainly eastern Pyrenees.

2 DRAGONMOUTH Horminum pyrenaicum. Low/med tufted, slightly hairy per. Lvs in basal clusters, oval to rounded, blunt-toothed, long stalked, deep green. Fls dark violet-blue, 17-21mm long, in small clusters forming one-sided spikes. Meadows, rocky places, open woods, on limestone, to 2500m. June-Aug. A, CH, sD, E, c, s & eF, I, YU.

Figwort Family Scrophulariaceae

Annuals, biennials or perennials with rounded or ridged (not square usually) stems and alternate or paired lvs. Fls flat, cup-shaped or tubular with 4-5 lobes, sometimes 2-lipped; stamens 2 or 4. Fr a capsule containing many small seeds.

3 CREEPING SNAPDRAGON Asarina procumbens (= Antirrhinum asarina). Low stickily-hairy per with thin sprawling stems. Lvs all opposite, oval-heart-shaped, toothed, stalked. Fls solitary, pale whitish-yellow, a yellow patch on the lower lip, 30-35mm long. Shaded rocky and stony places, to 1800m. Apr-Sept.sF, neE; eastern Pyrenees; dwarf forms are found at the higher elevations.

4 CHAENORHINUM Chaenorhinum origanifolium (= Linaria origanifolia). Low/short slightly hairy, usually rather sprawling, per. Lvs green, lance-shaped or oval, untoothed, the lower opposite. Fls snapdragon-like, purple with an orange patch on the lower lip, open-mouthed, 9-20mm long, in loose leafy racemes; spur short, 2-5mm. Rocky and stony places and screes, to 1500m. Apr-July. sF, neE; eastern Pyrenees.

5 SOFT SNAPDRAGON Antirrhinum molle. Dwarf shrubby per, softly downy, with thin rather sprawling stems. Lvs oval to elliptical, the lower opposite. Fls white or pale pink with a yellow mouth, 25-35mm long, spurless, in lax leafy spikes. Calcareous rocks and walls, stony places, to 1800m. May-Aug. neE; east and central Spanish Pyrenees and Andorra. **5a Rock Snapdragon** A. sempervirens* is a more slender brittle plant with leathery deep green oblong or elliptical lvs covered in short hairs. Fls smaller 15-25mm long, white with yellow or violet mouth coloration. Rocky places, to 2000m. nE, sF; central French and Spanish Pyreneess. **5b Common Snapdragon** A. majus* is a tall erect per with large 33-45mm yellow, pink or purple fls. To 1600m. May-Oct. E, c & sF (A, B, CH, CS, D, GB, IRL, NL, R, YU).

6 COMMON TOADFLAX Linaria vulgaris. Variable med/tall erect hairless per. Lvs linear, alternate. Fls pale to mid-yellow, 25-33mm long, in dense spikes; spur long, 10-l3mm. Fields, rocky and waste places, to 1600m. May-Sept. T, except Faeroes, IS and far north. **6a** L. angustissima has smaller pale yellow fls with a 7-l0mm long spur. A, CH, CS, E, s & eF, H, I, R, YU. **6b Pyrenean Toadflax** L. supina (= L. pyrenaica) * is a low/short grey-green ann/per, often stickily hairy above, at least the lower lvs in whorls. Fls pale yellow, often violet tinged, 13-20mm long, in short spikes; spur long, 10-15mm. To 2000m. E, s & eF, I. **6c** L. tonzigii is like 6b but lvs broader oblong-elliptical and fls larger, in rounded clusters. Dolomitic screes, 2000-2500m. nI; Bergamasque Alps.

7 ALPINE TOADFLAX Linaria alpina. Low hairless ann/per with sprawling stems. Lvs linear to oblong-lance~shaped, whorled, grey-green. Fls violet with a yellow patch on the lower lip, or white, 13-22mm, in rounded clusters; spur long 8-10mm. Screes, rocks and river gravels, 1500-3800m. May-Aug. A, CH, CS, D, E, s & eF, I, R, YU.

8 STRIPED TOADFLAX Linaria repens. Short/med hairless, greyish per with erect stems. Lvs linear to elliptical, pointed, in whorls, the upper alternate. Fls white or pale lilac, deeper veined, 8-15mm long, in loose spikes; spur short, 3-5mm. Dry places and rocks, to 2300m. June-Sept. Hybridises with 6. sD, nE, c & sF (A, CH, CS, D, F, GB, IRL, N, NL, P, SF).

9 IVY-LEAVED TOADFLAX Cymbalaria muralis. Trailing, thin stemmed, hairless per. Lvs palmately-lobed, mostly alternate. Fls lilac or violet with a yellow patch on the lower lip, 9-15mm long, spur short, 1.5-3mm, solitary on long stalks at If bases. Shady rocks and woods, to 2000m. Apr-Oct. T, except IS. **9a** C. pallida has pale lilac-blue fls with a spur 6-9mm long. Rocks and screes. cI (CS, GB).

10 FAIRY FOXGLOVE Erinus alpinus. Low tufted hairy per. Lvs oval, broadest at the tip, toothed, clustered towards the base. Fls bright purple, rarely white, 6-9mm across, with 5, notched, petal lobes, unspurred. Rocks, screes and stony grassland, to 2400m. May-Oct. wA, sCH, E, c & sF, n & cI.

Figwort Family *(contd.)*

FIGWORTS *Scrophularia.* Perennials with square stems. Lvs usually opposite, toothed and stalked. Fls small, in slender branched terminal clusters, usually two-lipped, with five blunt-lobes.

1 YELLOW FIGWORT *Scrophularia vernalis.* Med/tall softly-hairy bien/per. Lvs oval to heart-shaped, stalked; bracts like Lvs. Fls *yellowish-green, not* two-lipped, 6-8mm. Woods, scrub and damp waste places, to 1800m. Apr-June. A, CS, sD, sF, H, I, PL, R, YU (B, DK, GB, NL, S).

2 PYRENEAN FIGWORT *Scrophularia pyrenaica.* Short/tall, hairy per. Lvs *rounded,* often heart-shaped at base; bracts mostly like the lvs. Fls yellowish with a reddish-brown upper lip, 8-11mm. Rocky places, usually shaded, to 1900m. June-July. nE, sF; Pyrenees, local.

3 ITALIAN FIGWORT *Scrophularia scopolii.* Med/tall, more or less hairy per. Lvs oval to lance-shaped, often heart-shaped at the base; bracts narrow lance-shaped, *mostly not like* the lvs. Fls greenish with a purple-brown upper lip, 7-12mm. Woods and damp places, to 2300m. June-Aug. A, CS, H, I, PL, R, YU. **3a S.** *alpestris* has larger lvs, to 15cm long, simple-toothed (not double-toothed). nE, sF; Pyrenees and mountains of northern Spain. **3b** *S. heterophylla* has deeply toothed or pinnately dissected *lvs;* fls reddish-purple to greenish, 6-9mm. Rocky habitats. R, eYU.

4 COMMON FIGWORT *Scrophularia nodosa.* Med/tall *hairless* per; stems narrowly winged. Lvs oval to lance-shaped, sometimes heart-shaped at the base; bracts narrow lance-shaped, sometimes heart-shaped at the base. Fls green with a purple-brown upper lip, 7-10mm. Damp and shady places, to 1850m. June-Sept. T, except Faeroes, IS and far north. **4a Water Figwort** *S. auriculata* often has *two lobes* at the base of the lf; sepal teeth white-edged. Damp places, particularly riversides. B, CH, sD, E, F, GB, I, IRL, NL. **4b Green Figwort** *S. umbrosa* like 4a but stems with broader wings; fls *olive-brown.* T, except Faeroes, IS and far north.

5 ALPINE FIGWORT *Scrophularia canina.* Short/med per. Lvs often purple tinged, *2-pinnately-lobed,* only the lowest opposite, lobes linear, pointed; bracts linear. Fls dark *purple-violet* with white markings, the upper lip only one third the length of the fl tube; flstalks glandular, not hairy. Stony places, screes and waste ground, often on limestone, to 2200m. June-Aug. A, CH, sD, E, c & sF, I, YU . **5a** *S.c.* subsp. *hoppii* (= *S. hoppii*) has *glandular-hairy* fl stalks; fls with the upper lip at least as long as the fl tube. se & eF, sCH, I; Jura, southern Alps and Apennines.

6 MUDWORT *Limosella aquatica.* Low hairless ann with *creeping runners.* Lvs in basal tufts, spoon-shaped, untoothed, long-stalked. Fls tiny, white, often tinged with pinkish-purple, 4-5 petalled, solitary on slender stalks, downturned in fr. Wet muddy places, to 1800m. June-Sept. T, except Faeroes.

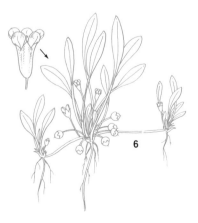

6

1

fr

2

3

fl

fl

4

5

Figwort Family *(contd.)*

MULLEINS *Verbascum*. Tall robust biennials forming a large leafy rosette in the first year. Lvs alternate up the stems. Fls flattish, 5-petalled, in long tapered, sometimes branched, spikes; stamens 5.

1 ORANGE MULLEIN *Verbascum phlomoides*. Greyish-white or yellowish mealy bien. Basal lvs oblong-elliptical, toothed or untoothed; upper lvs oval to lance-shaped, sharply pointed. Fls yellow or orange-yellow, 20-55mm; stamens with white or yellowish hairs; fl-spikes unbranched. Dry stony places and scrub, to 1400m. July-Sept. A, CH, CS, D, E, F, H, I, PL, R, YU (B, GB). **1a** V. *densiflorum* is similar but the stem lvs held closely against the stem; *bracts* 15mm long or more (not 9-15mm). A, B, CH, CS, D, DK, E, F, H, I, NL, PL, R, YU.

2 AARON'S ROD *Verbascum thapsus*. Greyish or whitish mealy bien. Basal lvs elliptical to oblong, broadest towards the tip; upper lvs held close to the *winged* stem. Fls yellow, 12-35mm, petal-lobes oval; stamens with white hairs; fl-spikes, unbranched. Dry stony or gravelly places and scrub, to 1850m. July-Sept. T, except IS and far north. **2a** V.t. subsp. *crassifolium* is similar but the *lower lvs* are stalked and the petal-lobes oblong. A, CH, E, c & eF, I, YU. **2b** V. *argenteum* has branched fl-spikes, the stamens with *violet* coloured hairs. sl; southern Apennines.

3 HOARY MULLEIN *Verbascum pulverulentum*. Densely white mealy bien. Basal lvs oval to oblong, broadest towards the tip; stem lvs held away from the *rounded stems*. Fls yellow, 18-25mm; stamens with white hairs; fl-spikes branched. Stony and waste places, to 1200m. July-Aug. B, CH, D, E, F, c & sGB, H, I, R, YU (A). **3a** V. *lychnitis* has angled *stems* and lvs almost hairless above, dark green. Fls yellow or white. T, except nGB, IRL, IS and far north (N, S, SF).

4 DARK MULLEIN *Verbascum nigrum*. Green, not mealy, hairy per with ridged stems. Basal lvs oval to oblong, heart-shaped at base, blunt-toothed, stalked. Bracts and calyces *hairy*. Fls yellow or cream with purple spots; stamens with violet *hairs;* fl-spikes unbranched or with a few short branches. Dry open places, banks and rocks, to 1800m. July-Sept. T, except nGB, c & sl, IRL and far north. **4a** V. *chaixii* has *un-ridged* stems and grey-green lvs. Fls yellow with a *purple* throat, borne in branched spikes. June-Sept. A, CH, CS, neE, H, I, PL, R, YU.

5 LANATE MULLEIN *Verbascum lanatum*. Greenish per with ridged stems, to 1.2m tall. Lvs oval or oblong, heart-shaped at base, blunt toothed, stalked, green above, greyish hairy beneath. Bracts and calyces *hairless*. Fls yellow, 18-28mm; stamens with violet- hairs; fl-spikes dense, unbranched. Rather similar to 4, but with almost *hairless bracts*. Mountain woods, to 2000m. June-Sept. A, nI, R, YU. **5a** V. *glabratum* is similar but has *branched* fl-spikes. R, n & eYU; mainly eastern Carpathians and Balkan Mountains.

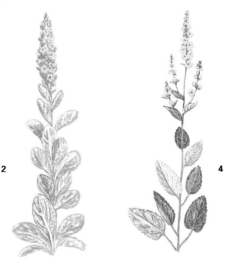

2   4

Figwort Family *(contd.)*

1 LARGE YELLOW FOXGLOVE *Digitalis ambigua* (= *D. grandiflora*). Med/tall bien/per. Lvs oval- lance-shaped or almost triangular, finely toothed, stalkless, shiny green above, greyish-hairy beneath. Fls *pale yellow* outside, cream netted maroon inside, 40-50mm long, tubular-bells, in long loose one-sided spikes. Woods and stony places, to 2000m. June-Aug. A, B, CH, CS, sD, c e& eF, H, I, PL, R, YU; not in the Pyrenees. Poisonous. **1a Small Yellow Foxglove** *D. lutea* has dense spikes of *small*, 9-25mm, pale yellow or whitish fls. A, B, CH, sD, E, F, I I (CS, PL) . **1b** *D. ferruginea* has small fls, 15-35mm long, yellowish brown or reddish brown with a network of *darker veins*. H, c& sl, R, YU. **1c** *D. lanata* is like 1b, but axis of inflorescence *glandular-pubescent* not glabrous and flowers whitish or yellowish with violet or brown veins. Woods and bushy places. H, R, eYU (A). **1d Foxglove** *D. purpurea* with large *purple* fls, 40-55mm long is occasionally found up to 1700m in the central and western Pyrenees. nwE, swF.

2 WULFENIA *Wulfenia carinthiaca*. Short/med, almost hairless, per. Lvs in basal rosettes, rounded to oval, broadest above the middle, blunt toothed, stalked, deep green. Fls dark violet-blue, 12-15mm long, tubular-bells, in dense spikes. Moist, humus rich, grassland over acid rocks, 1500-2000m. July-Aug. eA, nel, nwYU; south-eastern Alps.

SPEEDWELLS *Veronica*. Annuals or perennials with opposite lvs. Fls solitary or in spike-like racemes with 4 joined-petals and 4 sepals, the lowermost petal often smaller; stamens 2. Fr a small flattened, heart-shaped, capsule.

3 VIOLET SPEEDWELL *Veronica bellidioides*. Low/short, tufted, hairy per. Lvs oblong or spoon-shaped, usually finely toothed, short-stalked, the basal ones rosetted. Fls deep violet-blue, 9-l0mm, in small clusters. Dry pastures, often on acid soils, 1400-3000m. July-Aug. A, CH, CS, sD, E, c & sF, I, PL, R, YU. **3a** *V.b.* subsp. *lilacina* has lilac fls with a *white* centre. swCH, nE, s & seF, nwl; Pyrenees and south-western Alps.

4 THYME-LEAVED SPEEDWELL *Veronica serpyllifolia*. Low/short creeping *and rooting*, hairy per with erect fl stems. Lvs oval, untoothed or finely toothed, short-stalked, pale green. Fls white or pale blue with darker lines, 6-10mm, short stalked, in loose spikes of 20-40. Grassy shady places, to 2500m. May-Aug. T, but primarily at lower levels. **4a** *V.s.* subsp. *humifusa* has spikes of 8-15, long-stalked fls. T, but mainly in the mountains.

5 ALPINE SPEEDWELL *Veronica alpina*. Low hairy or hairless per. Lvs bluish-green, oval to elliptical, untoothed or finely toothed, stalkless. Fls deep blue, 7mm, in small clusters. Meadows and stony places, to 2000m. July-Aug. T, except B, DK, NL, IRL.

6 ROCK SPEEDWELL *Veronica fruticans*. Low/short sprawling, hairy per. Lvs narrow-oblong to oval, usually broadest above the middle, untoothed or finely toothed, short-stalked. Fls deep blue with a *reddish centre*, 11-15mm, in *small clusters*. Stony grassland and rocky places, to 3000m. July-Sept. T, except B, DK, IRL, NL. **6a** *V. fruticulosa* * has *smaller* fls, 9-12mm, marked with red. Limestone rocks and screes, to 2800m. A, CHG, sD, E, c& sF, nl, nwYU.

7 PYRENEAN SPEEDWELL *Veronica nummularia*. Low *matted* hairy per with short upright stems, woody at base. Lvs broadly-elliptical to oval or rounded, untoothed, short-stalked. Fls blue or pink, 6mm, in small clusters. Damp rocks and screes, often on schists, above 1800m. June-Aug. nE, sF; Pyrenees and Cordillera Cantabrica.

8 SPIKED PYRENEAN SPEEDWELL *Veronica ponae*. Short/med, creeping, hairy per; fl stems erect. Lvs oblong-lance-shaped to oval, toothed, almost stalkless. Fls bluish-lilac, 10mm, in loose *spikes*. Damp rocks, woods and shady places, 1200-2500m. June.Aug. E, sF; Pyrenees and Spanish Mountains.

9 SPANISH SPEEDWELL *Veronica aragonensis*. Low/short rather weak, sprawling hairy per. Lvs oblong to elliptical, untoothed or blunt-toothed. Fls pale blue, 8-l0mm, in loose spikes. Limestone rocks and screes, to 2100m. June-July. nE; central Spanish Pyrenees.

10 LARGE SPEEDWELL *Veronica austriaca*. Variable short/med erect or somewhat sprawling per. Lvs broadly-oval to narrow lance-shaped or pinnately-lobed, toothed, short-stalked. Fls bright blue, 10-13mm, in *paired spikes;* calyx hairy. Grassy places, to 1800m. June-Aug. A, CS, nI, PL, R, YU. **10a** *V.a.* subsp. *teucrium* (= *V. teucrium*) is taller with untoothed or sharply toothed lvs. T, except DK, GB, IRL, IS, N, S, SF. **10b** *V. prostrata* * is more sprawling and *matted* with smaller fls, 6-11mm, calyx always hairless. A, B, CH, CS, sD, F, H, I, NL, PL, R, YU.

Figwort Family (contd.)

1 NETTLE-LEAVED SPEEDWELL *Veronica urticifolia.* Short/med erect, slightly hairy per. Lvs triangular-oval, sharply toothed, unstalked. Fls lilac, 7mm, in *opposite stalked spikes* at the upper lvs. Woods and shady places, usually on calcareous soils, to 2000m. May-July. A, CH, sD, c & sF, n & cI, PI, R, YU.

2 COMMON or HEATH SPEEDWELL *Veronica officinalis.* Low creeping hairy per. Lvs oval to elliptical, toothed, short-stalked. Fls dull lilac-blue, 8mm, in opposite stalked spikes. Woods and heaths, to 2150m. May-Aug. T. **2a** V. *allionii* is more or less hairless; fls *deep blue* in solitary spikes usually. Dry alpine meadows, 1800-2700m. July-Aug. seF, nwl; south-western Alps.

3 WOOD SPEEDWELL *Veronica montana.* Low/short, rather sprawling per, stems *hairy all round.* Lvs broad-oval, toothed, stalked, pale green. Fls pale lilac-blue, 8-10mm, in *alternate spikes.* Woods, to 1400m. Apr-July. T, except Faeroes, IS, N, nS, SF. **3a Marsh Speedwell** V. *scutellata* * is usually *hairless,* more slender with narrow-oblong, slightly toothed lvs, stalkless; fls smaller, 5-6mm. Marshes and wet places, to 1800m. June-Aug. T, except Faeroes.

4 WATER SPEEDWELL *Veronica anagallis-aquatica.* Short/med fleshy hairless per; rootstock *creeping and rooting.* Lvs pale green, oval or lance-shaped, toothed, the upper half-clasping the stem. Fls blue with violet veins, 5-10mm, in opposite stalked spikes. Stream banks and other wet places, to 1450m. June-Aug. T, except Faeroes. **4a** V. *catenata* * has dark green, narrow lance-shaped lvs and smaller *pinker* fls, 3-5mm. T, except Faeroes, IS, N, nS, SF.

5 WALL SPEEDWELL *Veronica arvensis.* Low/short erect or somewhat sprawling, hairy ann. Lvs triangular-oval, toothed, the lower short-stalked. Fls tiny, blue, 2-3mm, in dense leafy spikes *at shoot tips.* Dry places, walls and cultivated ground, to 2100m, Mar-Oct. T, except Faeroes (IS). **5a Spring Speedwell** V. *verna* * is shorter, the upper lvs *pinnately-lobed.* T, except Faeroes, IRL, IS and far north.

6 FIELD SPEEDWELL *Veronica agrestis.* Low sprawling hairy ann. Lvs *mostly alternate,* except the lowest, oval, toothed, short-stalked. Fls whitish with a pink or blue upper petal, 3-8mm, *solitary,* long-stalked. Fr 2-lobed. Cultivated land, often on acid soils, to 1800m. Mar-Nov. T, except Faeroes, IS. **6a** V. *polita* * has *blue fls* and more rounded lvs, sepal teeth oval, overlapping at base. To 2100m. T, except Faeroes, IS. **6b** V. *opaca* * like 6a but sepal teeth oblong lance-shaped, *not* overlapping. T, except nE, sF, Faeroes GB, IRL, IS.

7 IVY-LEAVED SPEEDWELL *Veronica hederifolia.* Low sprawling downy ann. Lvs mostly alternate, rounded in outlines, but *with 3-7 lobes.* Fls blue or lilac, 4-9mm, *solitary,* long-stalked. Fr 4lobed. Cultivated areas mainly, to 1800m. Apr-Aug. T, except Faeroes, IS.

8 LONG-LEAVED SPEEDWELL *Veronica longifolia.* Variable med/tall erect per, hairy or hairless. Lvs *opposite or in whorls* of 3-4, lance-shaped to almost linear, pointed, toothed, short-stalked. Fls pale blue or lilac, 6-8mm, in dense spikes, often with short branches. Woods, riverbanks and other damp places, to 1250m. June-July. T, except E, sF, Faeroes, GB, IRL, IS. **8a** V. *paniculata* has *more branched* stems, and blue fls 7-14mm. borne on pedicels 3-5mm long. Rocky and grassy habitats. A, CS, H, PL, R, YU. **8b** V. *bachofenii* is like 8 but lvs *more triangular* with a heart-shaped base. Woodland rocks. n & R, eYU.

1

2

3

3a

4a

4

5

5a

6

6a

6b

7

8

Figwort Family *(contd.)*

1 LEAFLESS-STEMMED SPEEDWELL *Veronica aphylla.* Low *stemless* or short-stemmed, matted, hairy per. Lvs in rosettes, elliptical to spoon-shaped, sometimes toothed, short-stalked. Fls deep blue or lilac, 6-8mm, in clusters of 2-6, on *leafless stalks.* Rocks and stony pastures, usually on limestone, 1200-3000m. July-Sept. A, CH, CS, sD, E, s & eF, PL, R, YU. **1a** *V. baumgartenii* has ascending leafy stems and *hairless* lvs. Similar habitats. R, eYU.

2 GERMANDER SPEEDWELL *Veronica chamaedrys.* Low/short sprawling hairy per. Lvs oblong to oval, toothed or lobed, short-stalked or unstalked. Fls bright blue with a white eye, l0mm, in opposite spikes towards tops of stems. Grassy places, hedges, stony and waste places, to 2250m. Mar-July. T, except Faeroes (IS).

3 BROOKLIME *Veronica beccabunga.* Short/med creeping and rooting, rather fleshy, hairless per. Lvs thick, rounded to oblong, toothed, short-stalked. Fls pale to dark blue, 5-7mm, in opposite spikes. Streams, pools and wet places, to 2500m. May-Sept. T. **3a** *V. scardica* has *thin* lvs, often with reddish veins. Similar habitats. A, CS, H, R, YU.

4 SPIKED SPEEDWELL *Veronica spicata.* Very variable low/med hairy creeping per, with erect stems 5-45cm tall. Lvs linear to lance-shaped or oval, blunt-toothed, short-stalked. Fls blue, 4-8mm, in dense *terminal spikes.* Grassland, wood margins, dry and rocky places, to 2050m. July-Nov. T, except B, IRL, IS, (NL); rare in GB.

PAEDEROTAS. Like speedwells (*Veronica*) but the fls 2-lipped and with a short tube.

5 BLUISH PAEDEROTA *Paederota bonarota* (= *Veronica paederota*). Low/short hairy, greenish or bluish per. Lvs oval to rounded, toothed, short-stalked, the upper lvs narrower. Fls violet, blue or pinkish, 10-l3mm long, in short terminal spikes. Limestone rock crevices, to 2500m. June-Aug. A, nl, nwYU; eastern Alps.

6 YELLOW VERONICA *Paederota lutea* (= *Veronica lutea*). Low/short, dark green, hairy per. Lvs oval to lance-shaped, toothed, unstalked or short-stalked. Fls pale yellow, 10-13mm long, in short terminal racemes. Limestone rock crevices, to 2100m. June-Aug. A, nl, w YU; eastern Alps and mountains of western Yugoslavia.

COW-WHEATS *Melampyrum.* Variable semi-parasitic annuals with opposite, usually toothed, lvs. Floral lvs (bracts) toothed or not. Fls 2-lipped with a short tube, the upper lip rounded, the lower 3-lobed. Calyx 4-toothed; stamens 4.

7 CRESTED COW-WHEAT *Melampyrum cristatum.* Short/med, slightly downy per. Lvs narrow lance-shaped, unstalked; bracts purple, serrately-toothed. Fls yellow and purple, 12-15mm, mouth almost closed, in short squarish spikes. Dry grassy and rocky places, woodland margins, to 1500m. June-Sept. T, except Fareoes, IRL, IS, nN, NL, nS. **7a** *M. velebiticum* has *yellow fls,* 20mm long, open-mouthed; only the uppermost bracts toothed, if at all. CH, s & eF, nl, nwYU. **7b** *M. subalpinum* is like 7a but bracts *deeply* toothed. A. **7c** *M. vaudense* like 7 but *fls yellow* 16-20mm long; bracts *deeply* toothed. wCH, eF; south-western Alps and Jura. **7d** *M. italicum* like 7c but bracts only *shallowly* toothed. Fls 14-l8mm. I; mainly in the Apennines. **7e** *M. bihariense* has calyces with hairs on veins and larger fls 18-24mm long. H, R, cYU.

8 FIELD COW-WHEAT *Melampyrum arvense.* Short/med per. Lvs lance-shaped, toothed or untoothed; bracts green, whitish or reddish-pink, deeply toothed. Fls purplish-pink marked with yellow, 20-25mm, mouth closed, in loose spikes. Dry grassy and rocky places to 1500m. June-Sep't. T, except c & sE, c & nGB, sl, IRL, IS, N, c & nS, nSF.

9 COMMON COW-WHEAT *Melampyrum pratense.* Very variable low/med hairless or bristly ann. Lvs linear to oval, untoothed; bracts *green,* untoothed or toothed. Fls whitish to bright yellow, sometimes purple tinged, 10-l8mm, mouth usually closed, in loose leafy one-sided *spikes.* Open woods, clearings and peaty ground, to 2250m. June-Sept. T, except Faeroes, IS. **9a Wood Cow-wheat** *M. sylvaticum* is shorter *with smaller fls,* 8-10mm, often purple-spotted, open-mouthed, to 2500m. July-Sept. T, except c & sE, Faeroes, sl. **9b** *M. nemorosum* has stalked lvs and at least the *uppermost bracts purple.* To 1500m. A, CH, CS, D, DK, H, I, PL, R, sS, SF, YU.

10 TOZZIA *Tozzia alpina.* Short/med hairy, semi-parasitic, per; stems 4-angled. Lvs opposite, oval, toothed, unstalked. Fls golden-yellow, purple-spotted inside, 4-l0mm long, funnel-shaped, with 5-lobes. Damp meadows and streamsides, often amongst coarse herbs, on limestone, to 2250m. June-July. A, CH, sD, nE, s & eF, n & cl, wYU. **10a** *T. a.* subsp. *carpathica* has *pale yellow* fls 4-7mm long. CS, PL, R, eYU.

Figwort Family (contd.)

EYEBRIGHTS *Euphrasia*. Small annuals with small opposite, toothed and unstalked lvs. Fls in small clusters or spikes, open mouthed, the upper lip 2-lobed, the lower larger and 3-lobed. A large and complicated genus with many species in the mountains of the area.

1 COMMON EYEBRIGHT *Euphrasia rostkoviana*. Short hairy, often red-tinted, ann. Lvs oval or oblong, toothed. Fls white, yellow-throated, the upper lip often lilac, 8-12mm long. Meadows, open woods and stony places, to 3000m. July-Oct. T-except Faeroes, IRL, IS. **1a** *E. hirtella* is shorter with fls only 4-7mm long. Meadows, to 2300m. A, CH, D, E, F, I, R, YU. **1b** *E. drosocalyx* is like 1a but the lvs are *narrowed* at the base and only slightly hairy. A, CH, sD, eF, nwYU; Alps mainly.

2 EASTERN EYEBRIGHT *Euphrasia picta*. Short ann. Lvs rounded to triangular or oblong, toothed. Fls white or lilac, with violet veins, yellow-throated, 7-10mm long. Meadows and pastures, 1500-2500m. July-Sept. A, CH, CS, sD, H, I, PL, R, YU; Alps to Carpathians. **2a Arctic Eyebright** *E. arctica* has lvs with *glandular hairs* and fruit capsules at least twice as long as broad. CS, DK, Faeroes, GB, IRL, N, PL, R, S, SF.

3 WIND EYEBRIGHT *Euphrasia nemorosa*. Low/short hairy ann to 35cm. Lvs elliptical to oblong or triangular, toothed, *usually densely hairy*. Fls small, white to lilac, 57mm. Meadows, to 2300m. June-Sept. T, except Faeroes, H, I, IS, R, YU. **3a** *E. coerulea* is *never* more than 15cm tall with purple or white fls, with a lilac upper lip. CS, PL, R.

4 GLOSSY EYEBRIGHT *Euphrasia stricta*. Short erect, branched ann, usually strongly tinged with purple. Lvs *glossy green,* hairless, oval or lance-shaped, toothed. Fls lilac or white veined blue, yellow-throated, 7-l0mm long. Meadows, dry grassy places and scrub, to 2600m. June-Sept. T, except Faeroes, IRL, IS and the far north (GB). **4a** *E. pectinata* is *rarely* purple tinged and has slightly smaller white or sometimes lilac fls. A, CH, CS, E, F, H, I, R, YU.

5 ALPINE EYEBRIGHT *Euphrasia alpina*. Low/short, purple tinged ann, few branched. Lvs oval or lance-shaped, toothed, hairy or hairless. Fls usually deep lilac, 8-14mm. Meadows and pastures on acid rocks, 1500-2500m. May-Sept. CH, nE, s & eF, n & cI; Pyrenees, western Alps and northern and central Apennines. **5a** *E. christii* has pale *yellow* fls. CH, nI. **5b Dwarf Eyebrighf** *E. minima* is smaller than 5 and not purple tinged. Fls 4-6mm long, whitish or pale yellow with a lilac upper lip. To 3250m. A, CH, CS, sD, nE, c, s & eF, I, PI, R, YU. **5c** *E. micrantha* like 5 but the lvs *always hairless* and narrower and the fls lilac or purple, 4-7mm. Heaths, often with *Calluna*. T, except the far south.

6 IRISH EYEBRIGHT *Euphrasia salisburgensis* agg. Variable low/short purple or bronze tinged ann. Lvs narrow oblong or oval, few toothed, narrowed at the base, hairless. Fls white, sometimes purplish, yellow-throated, 5-7.5mm long. Meadows, scrub and screes, on limestone, to 2600m. July-Sept. T, except B, DK, Faeroes, c, n & eIRL, IS, NL. **6a** *E. portae* has *green lvs* usually; fls 7.5-9mm with a white lower and a lilac upper lip. To 2300m. nI; southern Alps.

ODONTITES. Semi-parasitic annuals with opposite stalkless lvs. Fls small, in one sided terminal spikes, 2-lipped, the lower lip glandular-hairy-lobed; stamens protruding.

7 STICKY ODONTITES *Odontites viscosa*. Short/med glandular-hairy branched ann. Lvs linear to oblong untoothed or almost so. Fls yellow, 5-8mm long. Woods and dry slopes, to 1600m. July-Sept. swCH, E, sF, nwI.

8 YELLOW ODONTITES *Odontites lutea*. Short/med almost hairless, well branched, ann. Lvs linear, toothed or not. Fls bright yellow, 5-8mm long, in loose spikes. Dry meadows and scrubland, on limestone, to 1800m. July-Sept. A, CH, CS, sD, E, F, H, I, PL, R, YU.

9 RED BARTSIA *Odontites verna*. Short often *purplish-hairy,* well branched ann. Lvs lance-shaped, toothed. Fls pink, 8-10mm long, in dense leafy spikes; corolla hairy. Meadows, cultivated fields, waste places and pathways, to 1800m. Aug-Oct. , except Faeroes, IS. **9a** *O. granatensis* has hairless corollas, dull purple, 6-7mm long. nE; Cordillera Cantabrica.

10 ALPINE BARTSIA *Bartsia alpina*. Low/short semi-parasitic downy per, unbranched. Lvs opposite oval, toothed, stalkless. Fls dark purple, 15-20mm long, 2-lipped, open mouthed, in short purple-bracted spikes. Damp meadows and snowbeds, to 2700m. June-Aug. A, CH, CS, D, E, F, Faeroes, GB, I, IS, N, PL, R, S, YU. **10a** *B. spicata* often has slightly branched stems, the *upper bracts* narrower and untoothed. nE, sF; Pyrenees and Cordillera Cantabrica.

Figwort Family (contd.)

LOUSEWORTS *Pedicularis*. Semi-parasitic pers with pinnately-lobed lvs, the lobes toothed or further lobed; stem lvs alternate or in groups. Fls 2-lipped, open-mouthed and deadnettle-like, the upper lip curved and hood-like, often beaked, the lower 3-lobed; calyx lobed; stamens 4. For Key, see p000.

1 STEMLESS LOUSEWORT *Pedicularis acaulis*. Low stemless per. Lvs in tufts, pinnately-lobed. Fls rose-pink, 18-35mm long, clustered at lf-bases. Damp or shady meadows, to 1500m. July-Aug. nI, nwYU.

2 LEAFY LOUSEWORT *Pedicularis foliosa*. Short/med hairy per; stems leafy mainly in the *upper half*. Lvs 2-3-pinnately-lobed. Fls pale yellow, 15-25mm long, in dense short spikes, the upper lip not beaked. Bracts like lvs, longer than the fls. Meadows, streamsides and scrub, often on limestone, to 2500m. July-Aug. A, CH, sD, E, c, s & eF, I. **2a** *P. hacquetii* is taller, the calyces *densely woolly*. To 1700m. A, CS, I, PL, R, YU; south-east Alps and Carpathians.

3 BEAKLESS RED LOUSEWORT *Pedicularis recutita*. Short/med almost hairless per. Lvs pinnately-lobed. Fls greenish-yellow *tinged* with dull crimson, 12-15mm long, in dense spikes; upper lip not beaked. Bracts shorter than fls. Meadows and damp or shady places, 1500-2500m. July-Aug. A, CH, sD, eF, I, YU.

4 VERTICILLATE LOUSEWORT *Pedicularis verticillata*. Low/short hairy or hairless per. *Lvs in whorls* of 3-4, pinnately-lobed; bracts often purplish. Fls purplish-red, 12-18mm long, in dense blunt spikes, the upper lip not beaked. Damp mountain pastures, 1500-3100m. June-Aug. A, CH, CS, D, E, F, I, PL, R, YU. **4a Pink Lousewort** *Pedicularis rosea*. Low/short hairy per, often purple tinged above. Lvs pinnately-lobed, mostly *basal,* not whorled. Fls pink to lilac, 12-18mm long, in tight rounded clusters, the upper lip darker, not beaked. Bracts *longer* than fls. Screes and stony grassland to 2700m. July-Aug. A, nI, nwYU. **4b** *P.r.* subsp. *allionii* has the *upper bracts* 2-lobed. s & seF, nwI. **4c** *P. hirsuta* like 4a but with *woolly* upper stems and calyces. To 1400m. June. N, S, SF.

5 CRIMSON-TIPPED LOUSEWORT *Pedicularis oederi*. Low/short hairy per; stems few lvd or lfless. Lvs pinnately-lobed. Fls yellow with a *crimson* tip to the upper lip, 12-20mm long, in dense clusters; calyx hairy. Bracts shorter than fls. Damp meadows and rocky places, generally on limestone, to 1950m. July-Aug. A, CH, CS, D, F, I, N, PL, R, S, YU. **5a** *P. flammea* is shorter; fls 10-12mm long; calyx hairless. To 1300m. IS, N, S.

6 RED RATTLE or MARSH LOUSEWORT *Pedicularis palustris*. Low/med hairy or hairless ann/bien, branched from the base, often purplish. Lvs 1-2-pinnately-lobed. Fls reddish-pink or pale pink, 15-25mm long, in loose spikes, the upper lip with two tiny lobes, not beaked; calyx 2-lipped, inflating in fr; inflorescence with lateral flowering branches. Bracts as long as fls. Damp meadows and marshes on acid soils, to 1800m. May-Sept. T, except c & sE, c & sI, IS. **6a Common Lousewort** *P. sylvatica* is generally per, the upper lip of the fls *without* lobes; calyx not 2-lipped. T, except Faeroes, IS, nN, nS, SF. **6b** *P. asparagoides* like 6a but stems unbranched; fls purpl-red. neE, sF; primarily eastern Pyrenees. **6c** *P. sudetica* is perennial without lateral flowering branches; fls pink to reddish purple. CS, PL; Sudeten Mountains.

7 CRESTED LOUSEWORT *Pedicularis comosa*. Short/tall hairy per with leafy stems. Lvs 2-pinnately-lobed. Fls pale yellow, 15-25mm long, in dense blunt spikes, the upper lip with a *short* beak. Bracts shorter or longer than the fls. Meadows and stony slopes, 1400-2250m. June-Aug. CS, nE, c & sF, I, R, YU.

8 LONG BEAKED YELLOW LOUSEWORT *Pedicularis tuberosa*. Short hairy per with leafy stems. Lvs 2-pinnately-lobed. Fls pale yellow, 15-20mm long, in dense heads, the upper lip long-beaked; calyx hairy all over. Bracts shorter than the fls. Meadows, open woods and screes on acid rocks, 1200-2900m. June-Aug. A, CH, nE, s & eF, n & cI. **8a** *P. elongata* is taller with *two lines* of hairs down the stems and smaller fls, to 16mm long; calyx hairy only along teeth margins. Dry meadows and screes, on limestone, to 2300m. eA, neI, nwYU; south-eastern Alps. **8b** *P. julica* like 8a, but calyx hairy all over. eA, neI, nwYU; south-eastern Alps. **8c Lapland Lousewort** *P. lapponica* has less deeply lobed lvs than 8 and smaller fl clusters; fls held almost horizontally; calyx bell-shaped. To 1700m. N, S, SF. See drawings p. 258.

Figwort Family (contd.)

1 BEAKED LOUSEWORT *Pedicularis rostratocapitata*. Low/short per; stems with two *opposite lines* of hairs. Lvs hairless, green tinged purple, 2-pinnate, with oblong, toothed or untoothed, segments; bracts pinnate. Fls pink or purplish-red, 15-25mm long, long-beaked, in terminal clusters; sepal tube usually hairless. Pastures and screes, usually on limestone, to 2800m. June-Aug. A, CH, sD, nI, nwYU; mainly eastern Alps. **1a** *P. kerneri* stems often spreading and a *hairless* lower lip to the fl. Usually on acid pastures and screes. A, CH, nE, s & eF, nI; Pyrenees and Alps.

2 ASCENDING LOUSEWORT *Pedicularis ascendens*. Short more or less hairless per. Lvs pinnate with lobed segments, bracts pinnate. Fls dull yellow, 12-16mm, beaked, in dense spikes; sepal tube hairless. Meadows on limestone, to 2000m. CH, eF, nI. **2a** *P. baumgartenii* has bract segments hairy and toothed; fls 14-20mm long. Dry meadows. R; southern Carpathians.

3 FLESH-PINK LOUSEWORT *Pedicularis rostratospicata* (= *P. incarnata*). Short/med hairy-stemmed per. Lvs 2-pinnate, hairless; bracts untoothed. Fls pink to purplish-red, 10-13mm long, long-beaked, in loose spikes; sepal tube hairy. Damp calcareous meadows, 1500-2700m. July-Aug. A, CH, sD, s & eF, nI, nwYU; Alps; rare in Pyrenees where it is confined to Mt Canigou.

4 PYRENEAN LOUSEWORT *Pedicularis pyrenaica*. Short per; stems with two opposite lines of hairs. Lvs 2-pinnate, hairless; bracts as lvs but shorter. Fls pink, 15-20mm long, long-beaked, in rounded clusters; sepal tube hairless. Meadows and screes, 1500-2800m. June-Aug. nE, sF; Pyrenees. **4a** *P. mixta* has *hairless* and more densely leafy stems; fls pink with a deep crimson beak. nE, sF; Pyrenees and Cordillera Cantabrica. **4b Mt. Cenis Lousewort** *P. cenisia** like 4 but the stems, bracts and calyces white-hairy; fls as 4a. Meadows 1500-2600m. July-Aug. seF, nI; south-western Alps, Apuan Alps and northern Apennines.

5 TUFTED LOUSEWORT *Pedicularis gyroflexa*. Short downy per. Lvs 2-pinnate; bracts as lvs but shorter. Fls rose-red, 18-25mm long, short-beaked, in dense clusters; sepal tube downy. Meadows and screes on limestone, 1600-2800m. July-Aug. s & swCH, s & eF, nwI; Pyrenees and southern Alps. **5a** *P.g.* subsp. *praetutiana* has hairless lvs. I; Apennines. **5b** *P. elegans* like 5a but with smaller, stalked fls; sepal tube only slightly hairy. c & sI; central and southern Apennines.

6 TAUERN LOUSEWORT *Pedicularis portenschlagii*. Low per; stems with *two opposite* lines of hairs. Lvs hairless, pinnate, with oval, toothed, segments; bracts as lvs but shorter. Fls rose-pink or purplish, 20-25mm, solitary or 2-3-clustered; sepal tube hairless or almost so. Meadows and screes on acid rocks, 1700-2600m. June-Aug. A; north-eastern Alps.

7 FERN-LEAVED LOUSEWORT *Pedicularis asplenifolia*. Low per; stems *red-hairy in* the *upper half*. Lvs hairless, narrow pinnate; bracts as lvs but shorter, red-woolly. Fls rose-red, 15-17mm, short-beaked, in clusters of 2-5; sepal tube red-woolly. Meadows and screes, on acid rocks, 1900-2800m. July-Aug. eCH, A, nI; mainly eastern Alps.

4b

Figwort Family *(contd.)*

RATTLES *Rhinanthus*. Erect, semi-parasitic annuals. Fls yellow in terminal spikes, mixed with leafy bracts, 2-lipped, the upper lip hooded or beak-like; calyx larger, rounded, rather inflated. A very difficult group with variable species.

1 YELLOW RATTLE *Rhinanthus minor.* Variable short/med almost hairless ann, stems often spotted. Lvs oval-oblong to narrow lance-shaped, toothed, dark green; bracts triangular, finely toothed, hairless. Fls bright yellow with a violet tip, 13-15mm long, straight, open-mouthed. Grassy meadows, to 2000m. May-Sept. T. **1a** *R. groenlandicus* has deeply and sharly toothed lvs and bracts. Faeroes, IS, N, S, SF.

2 APENNINE RATTLE *Rhinanthus wettsteinii.* Short ann. Lvs lance-shaped with a few teeth towards the tip; bracts longer than calyx, triangular, *hairy.* Fls yellow, 18mm long, *mouth* closed. Grassy meadows, to 1 500m. June-Sept. c,sAp. **2a** *R. antiquus* has broader Lvs and hairless bracts. c & sl; central and southern Apennines.

3 ARISTATE YELLOW RATTLE *Rhinanthus aristatus. Low/med ann, stems black streaked.* Lvs narrow lance-shaped, toothed, bracts narrow triangular, hairless, the lower teeth long and *slender.* Fls yellow, tipped with violet, 15-18mm long, curved, open-mouthed. Meadows and thickets, to 2500m. June-Sept. A, CH, CS, sD, seF, nI, wYU. **3a** *R. alpinus* has bracts without long slender teeth at the base and fls yellow *tinged* purple. eA, CS, PL, R. **3b** *R. carinthiacus* like 3a but bracts and calyces *hairy.* seA; Kärnten.

4 BURNAT'S YELLOW RATTLE *Rhinanthus burnatii.* Med ann, stems unstreaked. Lvs oblong, toothed; bracts longer than calyx, both *hairy along edges.* Fls plain yellow, 20mm long, mouth closed. Meadows, to 2000m. June-Sept. seF, nI, wYU; mainly southern Alps. **4a** *R. songeonii* has hairless bracts and calyces. seF, nI; southern Alps. **4b** *R.rumelicus* has teeth of bracts crowded towards base (not evenly spaced). CS, H, R, YU.

5 SOUTHERN YELLOW RATTLE *Rhinanthus ovifugus.* Med ann, stems black streaked. Lvs narrow lance-shaped or oval, toothed; bracts slightly longer than ca-lyx, hairless, the lower teeth long and slender. Fls yellow, 20mm long, slightly curved, *mouth* closed. Meadows and thickets to 2000m. June-Sept. sCH, seF, nI, wYU. **5a** *R. borbasii* has bracts *much longer* than calyces. A, CS, H, R, YU.

6 NARROW-LEAVED RATTLE *Rhinanthus angustifolius.* Very variable med ann; stems black streaked. Lvs linear to lance-shaped, toothed; bracts longer than calyx, hairless, with small teeth. Fls pale yellow 16-20mm long, slightly curved, mouth closed. Meadows to 2500m. June-Sept. T, except E, Faeroes, I, IRL, IS.

7 GREATER YELLOW RATTLE *Rhinanthus alectorolophus.* Med/tall ann, stems un-streaked. Lvs lance-shaped to oval, toothed, pale *green;* bracts broad- triangular, hair-less, evenly toothed. Fls yellow, 20mm long, slightly curved, mouth closed. Meadows and grassy places, to 2300m. May-Sept. A, B, CH, CS, F, nI, NL, PL, n & nwYU.

8 TOOTHWORT *Lathraea squamaria.* Low/med, slightly downy parasitic per; stems white, pale pink or yellowish, scaly. Scale lvs alternate, oval-heart-shaped, un-toothed. Fls white tinged with pale purple, 14-17mm long, tubular bells, in dense one-sided spikes, drooping at first. On trees and shrubs, particularly Hazel, Beech and Alder, to 1600m. Mar-May. T, except Faeroes, IS and far north.

Gloxinia Family Gesneriaceae

9 RAMONDA *Ramonda myconi* (= *R. pyrenaica, Verbascum myconi*). Low hairy per. Lvs deep green, forming *flat rosettes*, oval, toothed, corrugated, rusty-hairy be-neath. Fls blue to violet, 20-30mm, 5-lobed, solitary or in small clusters on long stems; anthers yellow. Shady rock crevices, to 1800m. June-Aug. nE, sF; west and central Pyrenees.

Rattle middle bracts

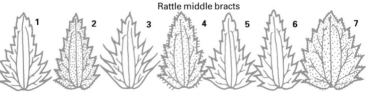

Nightshade Family Solanaceae

Herbs with alternate Lvs, no stipules, often poisonous. Fls 5-parted, petals joined into a short or long tube; stamens joined to petal tube. Fr a fleshy berry or a capsule.

1 DEADLY NIGHTSHADE *Atropa belladonna.* Med/tall hairy or hairless per, well branched. Lvs large, oval, pointed, untoothed, short-stalked. Fls brownish-violet or greenish, *bell-shaped,* 25-30mm, solitary usually. Fr a large *shiny-black* berry. Damp and shady places on lime, to 1700m. June-Sept. T, except Faeroes, IS, N, SF (DK, IRL, S). Very poisonous.

2 SCOPOLIA *Scopolia carniolica.* Short/med hairless per, usually slightly branched. Lvs elliptical or oval, pointed, untoothed, stalked, the *lower scale-like.* Fls dark brownish-violet outside, yellowish-green inside, drooping, funnel-shaped, 15-25mm, solitary. Fr a rounded capsule. Waste & rocky places, banks, to 1200m. May-Aug. A, CS, H, I, PL, R, YU (D, DK).

3 HENBANE *Hyposcyamus niger.* Med/tall stickily-hairy, unpleasant smelling, ann/bien. Lvs oval to oblong, untoothed, sometimes slightly lobed, the lower stalked, the upper clasping the stem. Fls pale yellow with a *network of purple veins,* broad bells, 20-30mm, in dense leafy, one-sided spikes. Fr a capsule. Bare and disturbed ground, frequently as a weed, to 1900m. May-Sept. T, except Faeroes, IS. Poisonous. **3a** *H. albus* has stem lvs *clearly stalked*; fls yellowish white with a green or purplish throat. E, sF, I, R, YU. Poisonous.

4 BITTERSWEET *Solanum dulcamara.* Scrambling hairless to downy per, to 2m. Lvs oval, pointed, often *heart-shaped or two lobed* at the base, untoothed, stalked. Fls dark purple, rarely white, 10-15mm, petals turned-back, with prominent yellow anthers ins column; in loose branched clusters. Fr a shiny red berry. Damp woods and hedgerows, to 1700m. May-Sept. T, except Faeroes, IS. Poisonous.

5 BLACK NIGHTSHADE *Solanum nigrum.* Variable low/med, branched, hairless or downy ann. Lvs oval-rhombic to lance-shaped, blunt-toothed or not, stalked. Fls white, 10-14mm, petals turned back, anthers yellow in a column; in small loose clusters opposite lvs or in between. Fr a *dull black or green* berry. Bare and waste places, cultivated ground, to 1750m. July-Oct. T, except Faeroes, IS. Poisonous. **5a** *S. luteum* is similar but the fls are in clusters of 3-5 (not 5-10) and the *ripe berries* are yellow, orange or red. Waste, disturbed and cultivated ground. T, except IRL, IS and much of the north (B, DK, NL, sS).

6 BOX THORN *Lycium barbarum.* A shrub to 2.5m with arched stems armed with a few slender spines usually. Lvs *narrow-elliptical,* up to 10cm long. The funnel-shaped fls, 8-9mm long are purple at first but become brownish on ageing; they are solitary or in small clusters at the leaf nodes and have the stamens protruding prominently. The fruit is a berry, red when ripe. Hedgerows and scrub; widely naturalised from cultivation. A native of China (A, B, CH, CS, D, DK, GB, IRL, H, I, N, NL, PL, R, sS, YU). **6a** *L. chinense* is similar but the lvs are widest below the middle, lance-shaped, the lower much larger than the upper. Fls 10-15mm long. Hedgerows; locally naturalised. Native of China. (CH, CS, D, F, GB, H, I, IRL, NL, R, sS).

Besides these, the **Potato,** *Solanum tuberosum,* **Tomato,** *Solanum lycopersicum* and **Tobacco,** *Nicotiana rustica,* are common crop plants, the latter two grown mainly in the south of the area.

1

2

3

4

5

6

Globularia Family Globulariaceae

Perennials or dwarf subshrubs, often mat forming. Lvs usually untoothed, alternate or in rosettes, shiny. Fls small in dense globular heads; corolla 2-lipped, the upper lip 2-lobed, the lower 3-lobed; stamens 4.

1 APENNINE GLOBULARIA *Globularia incanescens.* Low deciduous creeping per. Lvs *grey-green*, rather mealy, rounded to lance-shaped, narrowing abruptly into the stalk, untoothed. Flheads pale blue, 15mm, on leafy stalks 3-6cm long. Rocky and stony slopes, to 2000m. May-Aug. nI; Apuan Alps and northern Apennines.

2 COMMON GLOBULARIA *Globularia punctata* (= *G. aphyllanthes, G. willkommii*) Short/med tufted evergreen per, stems erect. Basal lvs oval to spoon-shaped, sometimes 3-toothed or notched at tip, long-stalked, green; stem lvs pointed, stalkless. Flheads blue, 10-15mm. Meadows, rocks and open woods, often on limestone, to 1650m. May-June. A, B, CH, CS, sD, F, H, I, R, YU.

3 MATTED GLOBULARIA *Globularia cordifolia.* Low *creeping* evergreen sub-shrub, forming dense mats. Lvs all basal, deep green, spoon-shaped, notched or slightly 3-lobed at tip. Flheads lilac-blue or grey-blue, 10-20mm, on erect stalks with 1-2 scales sometimes. Rocks and screes, to 2600m. May-July. A, CH, CS, E, sD, s & eF, H, I, YU. **3a** *G. repens** is smaller with lance-shaped or elliptical pointed lvs, 10-20mm long. E, s & seF, nwI. **3b** *G. meridionalis**. Like 3 but more *robust*; lvs 20-90mm long. e & seA, I, YU.

4 LEAFLESS-STEMMED GLOBULARIA *Globularia nudicaulis.* Short/med tufted evergreen per; stems erectlfless but with several small scales. Lvs dark green, oval to spoon-shaped, rounded or notched at tip, stalked. Flheads blue, 15-30mm. Rocky places, dry meadows and open woods, to 2700m. June-Aug. A, CH, sD, nE, s & eF, nI, nwYU. **4a** *G. gracilis* is smaller and with short *runners;* flheads not more than l5mm. nE, sF; Pyrenees.

Butterwort Family Lentibulariaceae

Insectivorous perennials of bogs and wet places. Lvs in sticky rosettes in the butterworts – margins inrolled; finely divided with tiny bladders and submerged below water in bladderworts. Fls 2-lipped, spurred; lower lip 3-lobed. The sticky leaves trap small insects and spiders.

5 ALPINE BUTTERWORT *Pinguicula alpina.* Low per. Lvs elliptical-oblong or lance-shaped, pale yellowish-green. Fls white with 1-2 yellow spots in throat, 8-10mm long; spur short, blunt. Bogs, stream banks and damp rocks, to 2600m. June-Aug. T, except B, DK, Faeroes, IRL, IS, NL; extinct in Britain.

6 SOUTHERN BUTTERWORT *Pinguicula leptoceras.* Low per. Lvs oblong to oval, yellowish-green. Fls blue with a white-hairy throat patch, 16-25mm long; spur short, 4-6mm long. Marshes and wet meadows, to 2500m. May-July. A, CH, eF, nI; Alps, Apuan Alps and northern Apennines. **6a** *P. villosa* is smaller with brownish lvs; fls very small, 7-8mm, pale violet with 2 yellow spots in throat. Sphagnum bogs usually, to 1100m. July. N, S, SF.

7 LONG-LEAVED BUTTERWORT *Pinguicula longifolia.* Low per. Lvs narrow-elliptical to narrow-lance-shaped. Fls large, lilac to pale blue with a large white-hairy patch in throat, 30-46mm long; petal lobes rounded; spur long, curved, 10-18mm. Wet rocks, to 1600m. July. nE, sF; Pyrenees. **7a** *P.l.* subsp. *reichenbachiana* has very *narrow* sepals and smaller lvs. seF, nw & cI: mainly Apuan Alps and central Apennines. **7b** *P. l.* subsp. *caussensis* has smaller fls, only 22-35mm long. scF; Causse.

8 LARGE-FLOWERED BUTTERWORT *Pinguicula grandiflora.* Low/short per. Lvs oblong to oval, pale green. Fls violet to pale lilac, white-throated, 25-35mm; petal lobes oblong; spur 10-12mm long. Bogs and wet rocks, to 2500m. Apr-July. wCH, nE, s & eF, swIRL (wGB).

9 COMMON BUTTERWORT *Pinguicula vulgaris.* Low per. Lvs oblong to oblong-oval, yellowish-green. Fls violet 15-22mm long with a white-throat patch; *spur* short 6-8mm. Bogs, wet heaths and rocks, to 2300m. May-July. T.

10 LESSER BLADDERWORT *Utricularia minor.* Slender aquatic per. Lvs submerged, cut into thread-like lobes, bearing tiny translucent bladders. Stems slender, erect, carrying 2-6 fls above the water. Fls pale-yellow, 6-8mm long, with a short spur. Ponds, ditches and bogs, to 1850m. June-Sept. Probably T.

Plantain Family Plantaginaceae

PLANTAINS *Plantago.* Perennials with strongly veined or ribbed lvs in basal rosettes, sometimes flat on the ground. Fls tiny, usually 4-parted, in dense, long-stalked spikes, often elongating in fruit; stamens conspicuous, long-stalked. Fr a small capsule.

1 ALPINE PLANTAIN *Plantago alpina.* Low hairless or slightly hairy tufted *per,* with several or many rosettes. Lvs *linear,* soft, 3-veined, the innermost triangular-shaped. Fls whitish-green in narrow spikes, 10-30mm; bracts oval, shorter than the fls. Meadows, sometimes screes, to 3000m. July-Aug. A, CH, sD, c, E, s & eF, I.

2 DARK PLANTAIN *Plantago atrata* (= *P. fuscescens, P. montana*). Variable low tufted per with several or many rosettes, usually slightly hairy. Lvs *green,* narrow lance-shaped, long-pointed. Fls brownish-green, in oblong spikes, 15-30mm; anthers yellowish or violet; bracts *rounded* with membranous edges. Meadows and stony places, usually on calcareous soils, 1500-2500m. May-Aug. A, CH, CS, sD, E, c, s & eF, I, PL, R, YU. **2a** *P. monosperma* has shorter *silvery-hairy* lvs and shorter spikes; anthers white. 1500-2800m. July-Aug. nE, sF; central and eastern Pyrenees.

3 FLESHY PLANTAIN *Plantago maritima* subsp. *serpentina* (= *P. serpentina*). Low/short tufted, *usually hairless* per, with several or many rosettes. Lvs linear, thick and slightly fleshy, 2mm or more wide, sometimes with a few teeth. Fls whitish-green in *long spikes,* 30-70mm, anthers yellowish; bracts oval, long- pointed. Meadows, rocky places, screes and gravels, often on poor calcareous soils, to 2400m. June-Aug. A, CH, nE, sF, I, YU. **3a** *P. maritima* subsp. *maritima* is a maritime plant of saline and base-rich habitats throughout most of Europe. **3b** *P. holosteum* (= *P. carinnata, P. recurvata*) has *very narrow* rigid lvs, less than 2mm wide and shorter spikes. Usually on acid soils, to 2600m. May-Sept. sA, sCH, nE, s & seF, I.

4 RIBWORT PLANTAIN *Plantago lanceolata.* Low/med tufted, hairy or almost hairless per, with several rosettes. Lvs *lance-shaped,* slightly toothed or untoothed, 3-veined. Fls brown, in blackish oblong spikes, 5-50mm long, on 5-ridged stalks; anthers pale yellow. Meadows, grassy, rocky and waste places, to 2300m. Apr-Oct. T, except far north. **4a** *P. argentea** has a single or a few lf-rosettes; lvs untoothed, often *silvery-hairy* beneath; spikes 5-20mm long, the stalks with 6 or more ridges, anthers *white.* Dry places on calcareous soils. neE, s & eF, H, I, R, YU.

5 GREATER PLANTAIN *Plantago major.* Low/short downy or hairless per, often with a solitary rosette only. Lvs *broad-oval to elliptical,* stalked, toothed or not, 3-9-veined. Fls pale greenish-yellow, in long pointed spikes equal in length to their *unridged* stalks; anthers pale purplish, then yellowish-brown. Grassy and waste places, paths, banks, to 2800m. June-Oct. T (IS). Plants from central and north-eastern Europe with 3-5-veined lvs, yellowish-green rather than deep green, are referable to subsp. *winteri.*

6 HOARY PLANTAIN *Plantago media.* Low/short *downy-greyish* per with a solitary or few rosettes. Lvs elliptical or oval-elliptical, stalked, toothed or not, 7-9-veined. Fls whitish, fragrant, in blunt spikes, 20-60mm long, shorter than the long *ridged stalks;* anthers lilac, sometimes whitish, with lilac filaments. Grassy, stony and waste places, on calcareous soils, to 2450m. May-Aug. T. Dwarf plants and those with narrower lvs than normal are found scattered in the mountains of central and southern Europe; they are generally considered to be ecological variants of the species. **6a** *P. gentianoides* has hairless or only slightly hairy lvs with 3-5 main veins; filaments of stamens *white,* not lilac. Lf rosette nearly always solitary. Damp habitats amongst rocks and stony pastures. R, nYU; mainly south and eastern Carpathians.

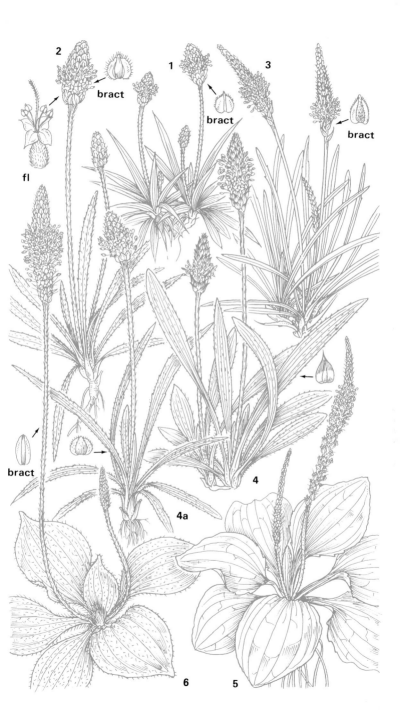

2 bract

fl

1 bract

3

bract

4

bract

4a

6

5

Broomrape Family Orobanchaceae

Hairy unbranched perennials, sometimes annuals, parasitic on the roots of other plants and without green pigment. Stems erect with scale-like lvs and dense spikes of tubular 2-lipped fls; upper lip slightly 2-lobed, lower lip 3-lobed. Fr an egg-shaped, many-seeded capsule. Often very local. Identification of the host plant often helps in identification of these difficult species.

1 SAND BROOMRAPE *Orobanche arenaria.* Short/med glandular-hairy, bluish or violet tinted per. Scale-lvs lance-shaped. Fls bluish-violet, 25-35mm long, with *hairy anthers* and a white stigma. Bracts 3 to each fl. Parasitic on Wormwoods, Dog Daisies and other herbs. Alluvial river flats, to 1800m. June-July. A, CH, CS, D, E, F, H, I, PL, R, YU. **1a** *O. purpurea* has smaller bluish-violet fls veined *with deep* violet and hairless anthers. Parasitic on Sneezeworts, Wormwoods and other Composites. Waste places, to 1800m. T, except Faeroes, nGB, IRL, IS, N, nS, SF.

2 THYME BROOMRAPE *Orobanche alba.* Short, glandular-hairy, purplish-red tinted, *fragrant,* per. Scale lvs lance-shaped. Fls purplish-red, yellow or whitish, 15-25mm long, middle lobe of lower lip larger than adjacent lobes, stamen-stalks *hairy* at base. Bracts short, one to each fl. Parasitic on Thymes and other Labiates. Woods and grassy places, to 1800m.Apr-Aug. T, except Faeroes, IS, N, NL, nS, SF. **2a Thistle Broomrape** *O. reticulata* is taller, brownish-violet or yellowish-purple tinged fls; stamens hairless usually; lower lip with 3-equal lobes. On Thistles. Fields and stony places, to 2500m. T, except B, Faeroes, IRL, IS, N, nS, SF.

3 AMETHYST BROOMRAPE *Orobanche amethystea.* Short/med slightly glandular-hairy, brownish, pink or bluish tinted ann/per. Scale lvs narrow-lance-shaped to oval, pointed. Fls *cream or white* tinged with violet, pink or brown, 15-25mm long, stamen stalks hairy at base; upper lip deeply two-lobed. Bracts one to each fl. Parasitic on Eryngos, Carrot, Woundworts and various Composites. Fields and stony places, to 2200m. June-Aug. CH, sD, E, F, GB, I, YU. **3a Mugwort Broomrape** *O. loricata* has white or pale yellow fls tinged and veined violet, upper lip only *slightly* two-lobed. On Wormwoods and other Composites, or occasionally on Umbellifers. May-July. A, B, CH, CS, DK, E, F, H, I, NL, PL, R, YU. **3b Common Broomrape** *O. minor* is smaller than 3; *bracts* to 15mm long, not 10-22mm. Parasitic mainly on Clovers. T, except B, Faeroes, IRL, IS. (DK, IRL, PL, sS).

4 CLOVE-SCENTED BROOMRAPE *Orobanche caryophyllacea.* Short/med yellowish or purplish ann. Scale lvs triangular-lance-shaped, pointed. Fls *fragrant,* pink or pale yellow tinged dull purple, 20-32mm long, stamen stalks hairy at base, stigma purple. Bract short, one to each fl. Parasitic on Bedstraws. To 1500m. T, except DK, Fareoes, IRL, IS, N, S, SF. **4a** Germander Broomrape *O. teucrii* is smaller and parasitic on Germanders. A, B, sD, E, F, H, I, R, YU. **4b** *O. lutea* like 4 but with yellowish or reddish-brown fls and a yellow or white stigma. On Clovers, Medicks and other Legumes. A, CH, CS, sD, E, F, NL, H, I, PL, R, YU.

5 KNAPWEED BROOMRAPE *Orobanche elatior.* Short/med reddish or honey-brown per. Fls yellow, often tinged pink, 18-25mm long, stamens stalks hairy at base, stigma yellow. Bract one, as *long as fls.* On Knapweeds, Globe Thistles and other Composites. To 1600m. June-July. T, except Faeroes, B, DK, c & sl, IRL, IS, N, NL, nS. **5a Alsace Broomrape** *O. alsatica* has its stem *swollen* at the base and with smaller fls and bracts; fls often tinged purple or brown. On Umbellifers. A, CH, CS, sD, H, PL, R, YU.

6 SERMOUNTAIN BROOMRAPE *Orobanche laserpitii-sileris.* Rather like 5 but more robust and stem swollen at the base. Fls brownish-violet, yellowish at base, 22-30mm long with one bract to each. Parasitic on Sermountain. To 1500m. June-Aug. A, CH, eF, nwYU; very local in the Alps.

7 YELLOW BROOMRAPE *Orobanche flava.* Short/med yellowish or brownish per, stem scarcely swollen at the base. Fls yellow, slightly red tinged, 15-22mm long, stamen stalks hairy at base, stigma pale yellow. Parasitic on Butterburs, Coltsfoot and Adenostyles. Stony places, to 1700m. June-July. A, CH, CS, F, H, I, PL, R, YU. **7a Sage Broomrape** *O. salviae* is shorter with a hairy style and yellow stigma turning orange-brown. On Salvias, to 1200m. A, CH, sD, eF, nl, R, YU. **7b** *O. lucorum* like 7a but the stigma *turning* reddish or purplish with age. On Barberry. A, CH, sD, nl.

8 SLENDER BROOMRAPE *Orobanche gracilis.* Short/med yellow or reddish per. Scale lvs oval to lance-shaped. Fls yellow tinged red outside, *shining dark red inside,* 15-25mm long, stigma yellow. Bract short, one to each fl. On various Legumes, to 1350m. June-Aug. A, CH, CS, sD, E, F, H, I, PL, R, YU.

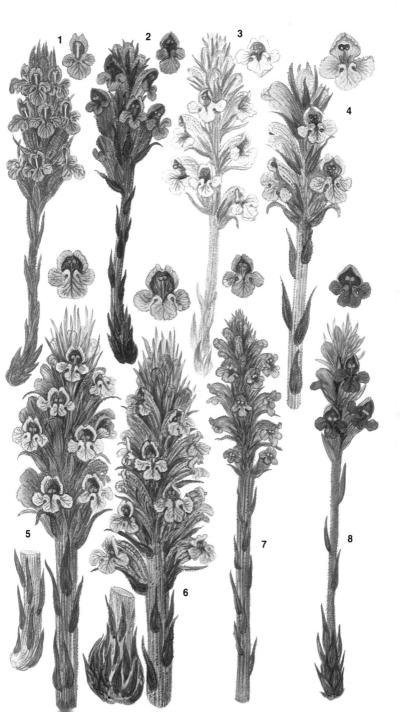

Bedstraw Family Rubiaceae

Perennials, rarely annuals, with weak square stems. Lvs in whorls. Fls small, funnel-shaped, 4-lobed; sepals absent. Fr a 2-lobed nutlet.

BEDSTRAWS *Galium.* Annuals or perennials, often with rather weak square stems and lvs in whorls, sometimes prickly. Fls usually white or yellow, in branched terminal or lateral clusters, 3-4 parted. Fr 2-parted, each with one seed, sometimes covered with hooked bristles. A difficult group with many closely related species.

1 NORTHERN BEDSTRAW *Galium boreale.* Variable short/med rather stiff erect per, sometimes slightly hairy; stems square. Lvs lance-shaped, *usually in fours,* dark green, 3-veined, rough on edges. Fls white, 3-4mm, in dense terminal clusters. Fr with hooked bristles. Grassy, shrubby and rocky places, to 2200m. June-Aug. T, except Faeroes.

2 WOODRUFF *Galium odoratum* (= *Asperula odorata*). Short *carpeting per;* stem erect, square, leafless, except at the nodes. Lvs elliptical, in whorls of 6-9, rough edged. Fls white, 4-7mm, in loose heads, fragrant. Fr with hooked bristles. Open deciduous woods, to 1600m. Apr-June. T, except Faeroes, IS.

3 CONIFEROUS BEDSTRAW *Galium triflorum.* Short/med per, stems rather weak, square, *slightly hairy.* Lvs narrow-elliptical, in whorls of 6-8. Fls tiny, white, 1.5-3.5mm, in loose terminal or lateral clusters. Fr with hooked bristles. Rocky coniferous woods, to 1200m. June-Aug. CH, N, S, SF; Scandinavia and central Alps where it is rare.

4 MARSH BEDSTRAW *Galium palustre.* Variable, rather straggling per, stems square, rough-edged. Lvs elliptical, broadest above the middle, in whorls of 4-6. Fls white, 2-3mm, 4-parted, in loose, stalked, clusters, anthers red. Fr *black, smooth.* Wet places, to 2100m.June-Aug. T. **4a Fen Bedstraw** *G. uliginosum* has narrow lance-shaped lvs ending in *a sharp point,* in whorls of 6-8; anthers yellow. Marshes and wet places. T, except Faeroes and northern Scandinavia. **4b** *G. trifidum* has lvs in whorls of 4 and *3-parted* fls. eA, sF, N, PL, S, SF.

5 HEDGE BEDSTRAW *Galium mollugo.* Variable med/tall, often sprawling per, sometimes hairy; stems square, smooth. Lvs oblong, *1-veined,* in whorls of 6-8. Fls white, 2-3mm, in loose, branched, clusters. Fr black. Grassy places and hedgebanks, to 2100m. June-Sept. T, except DK, Faeroes, IS, N. **5a** G. *album* has larger fls, 3-4mm. JuneSept. T, except Faeroes (IRL, IS, N, S, SF).

6 *Galium lucidum* agg. Short/med per, stems smooth, usually hairless. Lvs narrow lance-shaped. Fls *pale yellow to greenish,* 3-5mm, in branched clusters. Calcareous rocks and screes, to 1800m. May-Aug. A, CH, CS, sD, E, s & eF, H, n & cl, R, YU.

7 WOOD BEDSTRAW *Galium sylvaticum.* Tall hairless per, stems *rounded.* Lvs elliptical to lance-shaped, bluish-green, rough edged. Fls white, 2-3mm, often nodding before flowering, in lax clusters. Fr blue-green, smooth. Woods and scrub, to 1600m. June-Sept. A, B, CH, CS, F, H, NL, nl, PL, YU; extinct in D. **7a** *G. aristatum* is shorter and usually hairless but *with square stems* and bright green lvs. Open woods. A, sD, s & eF, nl. **7b** *G. laevigatum* has stems *rooting* at the lower nodes. A, CH, eF, I, YU; Alps and Apennines.

8 CUSHION BEDSTRAW *Galium saxosum**. Low/short *cushion-forming* per, stems square, hairless. Lvs lance-shaped to linear, 5-6 in a whorl, with an apical point. Fls white, 1.5-2mm, in rounded clusters. Fr smooth. Calcareous screes, to 2500m. eF, nl; western and south-central Alps. **8a** *G. cometerhizon** has lvs *broadest* above the middle and few lateral fls. Siliceous screes. nE, sF; central and eastern Pyrenees. **8b** *G. palaeoitalicum** has lvs *not more* than 1mm wide. Rocky and grassy places. I; Apuan Alps and southern Apennines. **8c** *G. pyrenaicum** has *very narrow,* closely overlapping lvs. E, sF. **8d** *G. austriacum** like 8 but fls smaller and whiter and lvs *shiny* metallic green when dry. Grassy places and coniferous woods. A, CS, H, wYU; eastern Alps and western Carpathians.

9 REDDISH BEDSTRAW *Galium rubrum**. Short/med per, stems rather weak, rounded, hairy at the base. Lvs elliptical, broadest above the middle, in whorls of 7-9. Fls *dark purple,* 1.6-2mm, in large oblong clusters. Woods, to 2000m. JuneAug. sCH, nl; southern Alps and northern Apennines. **9a** *G. obliquum** has yellow or greenish fls usually and narrower lvs. Dry places. cl; central Apennines.

10 *Galium anisophyllon**. Low/short cushion-forming per, almost hairless. Lvs elliptical, broadest above the middle, in whorls of 7-9, rough. Fls *yellowish-white,* 2-4mm, in rounded clusters. Grassy and rocky places, to 2900m. June-Aug. A, CH, CS, sD, c & eF, I, PL, R, YU.

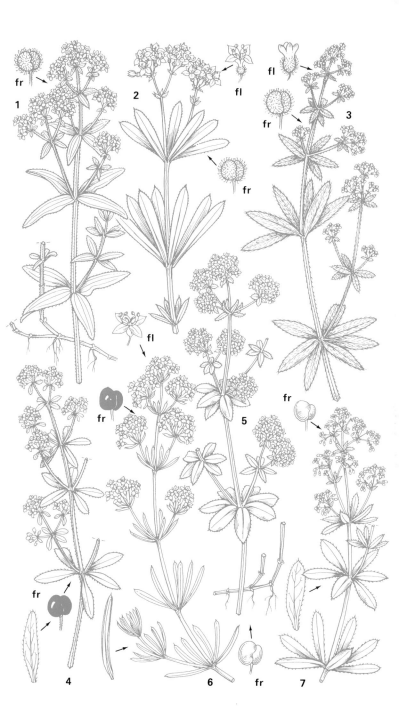

fr

1

2

fl

fl

fr

3

fr

fl

fr

4

fr

fl

5

fr

6

fr

7

Bedstraw Family (contd.)

1 LADY'S BEDSTRAW *Galium verum.* Short/tall slightly hairy per; stem slender. Lvs linear, deep shiny green above. Fls golden-yellow, 2-3mm, short-tubed, fragrant. Meadows and hedgebanks to 2000m. June-Sept. T, except Faeroes.

2 SWISS BEDSTRAW *Galium megalospermum* (= *G. helveticum*). Low, sprawling, almost hairless per. Lvs oval, in whorls of 4-8, the margins with hooked prickles. Fls yellowish-white, 2mm. Meadows and screes, to 3200m. June-Aug. A, CH, sD, eF, nl; Alps.

3 SIX-LEAVED WOODRUFF *Asperula hexaphylla.* Low/short sprawling hairless per. Lvs lance-shaped, generally in *whorls of 6.* Fls rose pink, 5-8mm long, borne in terminal clusters. Limestone rocks, to 2000m. June-July. seF; nwl; south-western Alps. **3a** *G. hirta** a has smaller hairy-margined lvs. July-Aug. nE, sF; west and central Pyrenees.

4 PYRENEAN WOODRUFF *Asperula pyrenaica.* Variable loose cushion- forming per; stems weak, finely hairy below. Lvs green or greyish, linear to elliptical, in *groups of 2-4,* the lower broader. Fls pale pink or purplish, 2.8-4mm long, finely hairy outside. Rocky and grassy places, on limestone, to 2000m. June-Aug. nE, sF; Pyrenees. **4a** *A. neilreichii* has the upper lvs *paired* and the flowers hairless outside. A, CS, R; north-east Alps and Carpathians. **4b** *A. rupicola* is like 4 but stems *hairless* and flowers 4-5mm. seF, nwl; south-west Alps. **4c** *A. cynanchica* is taller, the stems generally *more than* 15cm; lvs lax, always in fours, all narrow lance-shaped. Fls white or pale purple, 2.5-3.5mm. T, except DK, Faeroes, IS, N, S, SF.

5 SOUTHERN WOODRUFF *Asperula taurina.* Short/med hairy per, creeping underground. Lvs lance-shaped or oval, in whorls of 4, 3-veined. Fls white or pale yellowish, 7-11mm long, in dense clusters surrounded by a ruff of Lvs. Deciduous woods, scrub and shady rocks, to 1300m. A, CH, E, s & eF, H, I, R, YU (D, DK, GB).

6 BLUE WOODRUFF *Asperula arvensis.* Short/med slender hairless ann. Lvs lance-shaped, blunt, in whorls of 6-8. Fls *bluish-violet,* 3-6mm long, in dense branched clusters. Fields and waste places, to 1500m. Apr-July. T, except B, Faeroes, GB, IRL, IS (CS, DK, N, S).

Honeysuckle Family Caprifoliaceae

Shrubs or subshrubs with opposite lvs. Fls 5-lobed, with a short or long tube, sometimes 2-lipped; ovary below fl; calyx consisting of 5 tiny teeth. Fr a fleshy berry.

7 TWIN FLOWER *Linnaea borealis.* Evergreen creeping subshrub. Lvs oval, toothed. Fls pinkish-white, bell-shaped, 5-9mm, drooping, *in pairs* on long stalks, fragrant. Coniferous woods and heaths, 1200-2200m. June-Aug. T, except B, E, Faeroes, IS; GB rare and confined to Scotland.

8 BLUE.BERRIED HONEYSUCKLE *Lonicera caerulea.* Deciduous shrub to 2m, slightly hairy. Lvs elliptical to oblong, hairless. Fls yellowish-white bell-shaped with *5-equal* lobes, 12-18mm, hairy outside, in pairs. Berry blue-black. Woods and scrub on acid soils, 1300-2600m. May-July. A, CH, CS, D, nE, F, I, R, S, SF YU (N). **8a** *L. c.* subsp. *pallasii* has *hairy* lvs and narrower fls. neA, CS, R.

9 PYRENEAN HONEYSUCKLE *Lonicera pyrenaica.* Deciduous shrub to 1m, *hairless.* Lvs bluish-green, oval, broadest above the middle, pointed. Fls white, often red tinged, bell-shaped with 5 equal lobes, 12-20mm, in pairs. Berry *bright red.* Woods and rocks, mainly limestone, to 1500m. May-July. nE, sF; Pyrenees and NE Spain.

10 ALPINE HONEYSUCKLE *Lonicera alpigena.* Deciduous shrub to 3m, slightly hairy. Lvs oblong to elliptical, pointed, *hairy on edges* when young. Fls yellowish or greenish-yellow, tinged reddish-brown, 2-lipped, 12-20mm long, in pairs. Berry scarlet. Woods, scrub and rocks to 2300m. May-July. A, CH, CS, sD, E, s & eF, I, R, YU.

11 BLACK-BERRIED HONEYSUCKLE *Lonicera nigra.* Deciduous shrub to 2m, hairy or hairless. Lvs narrow elliptical to oblong, *bluish-green* beneath. Fls pale pink, 2-lipped. 6-10mm, hairy outside, in pairs, faintly fragrant. Berry black. Woods, scrub. stony places, to 1800m. May-July. A, CH, CS, sD, nE, s & eF, H, I, PL, R, YU.

12 FLY HONEYSUCKLE *Lonicera xylosteum.* Deciduous shrub to 3m, hairy. Lvs almost rounded or oval, stalked, grey-green, *hairy* above and beneath. Fls yellowish-white. 2-lipped, 6-12mm long, hairy outside, in pairs. Berry bright red. Woods and scrub, generally on limestone, to 1800m. May-June. T, except Faeroes, IRL, IS and far north; GB rare.

13 COMMON HONEYSUCKLE *Lonicera periclymenum.* Deciduous twining *woody* climber. Lvs oblong to elliptical, dark green above, bluish-green beneath. Fls creamy-white, often red tinged, 2-lipped, 35-50mm, in terminal clusters, *highly fragrant.* Berry red. Woods, scrub and hedgerows, to 1800m. June-Oct. T, except Faeroes, IS, R, SF and far north (CS).

Honeysuckle Family *(contd.)*

1 WAYFARING TREE *Viburnum lantana.* Downy deciduous shrub to 6m. Lvs oval, finely toothed, stalked, green and wrinkled above, whitish beneath. Fls creamy-white, cup-shaped, 5-9mm, in dense *flat-topped clusters*, fragrant. Fr a black berry, at first red. Open woods and scrub, on limestone, to 1600m. Apr-June. T, except DK, Faeroes, nGB, IS, NL, PL, SF and far north (N, S). **1a Guelder Rose** *V. opulus* has 3-5-lobed lvs; outer fls of clusters *much* larger than the inner one and sterile. Berry red when ripe. T, except Faeroes, IS and far north.

2 ALPINE or RED-BERRIED ELDER *Sambucus racemosa.* Deciduous shrub to 4m; bark grey. Lvs *pinnate;* leaflets oval or elliptical, toothed. Fls creamy-white, cup-shaped, in dense branched *pyramidal clusters.* Fr a shiny red berry. Woods and shady rocky places, to 2050m. Apr-June. T, except Faeroes, IS and far north (DK, GB, N, S, SF). **2a Common Elder** *S. nigra* has flat-topped fl clusters and black berries. To 1500m. T, except Faeroes, IS and far north. **2b Dwarf Elder** *S. ebulus* is a *spreading per* to 2m with leafy stipules. Fls white with *purple anthers;* berry black. T, except Faeroes, IS, N, SF (DK, GB, IRL, S).

Moschatel Family Adoxaceae

3 MOSCHATEL *Adoxa moschatellina.* Low *carpeting* hairless, pale green per. Lvs 2-trifoliate, long stalked; lflets lobed. Fls pale green, tiny, 5-lobed, in a tight box-like cluster. Fr a green berry, drooping. Damp woods, hedgerows and shady rocks, to 2400m. Mar-June. T, except E, Faeroes, IS; rare in IRL.

Valerian Family Valerianaceae

Perennials with opposite lvs, whorled at base of stems; no stipules. Fls small with 5 petals joined into a tube, often spurred or pouched at the base, in clusters; stamens 3 (1 in *Centranthus*). Fr small, one-seeded, with a rather feathery persisting calyx.

4 COMMON VALERIAN *Valeriana officinalis.* Variable short/tall per with *furrowed hairless stems.* Lvs pinnate, the lower stalked. Fls pink or white, 2-5.5mm long, the tube pouched at the base, borne in rounded branched clusters. Damp or dry meadows and stony places, to 2400m. May-Aug. T, except B, DK, Faeroes, GB, IRL, N, NL, S, SF. **4a** *V.o.* subsp. *collina* has stems *densely hairy* below and smaller fls, 2-2.5mm long. A, CH, sD, E, F, GB, IRL; local in north-eastern Europe. **4b** *V. o.* subsp. *sambucifolia* is stoloniferous. B, D, DK, N, NL, S, SF; local in central and southern Europe.

5 PYRENEAN VALERIAN *Valeriana pyrenaica.* Tall dark green per with solitary furrowed stem, *hairy at the nodes.* Basal lvs oval, heart-shaped at base, toothed, long stalked; stem lvs with 1-2 pairs of small leaflets at base, stalkless. Fls pink, 2.5-3mm long, in dense clustered heads. Damp meadows and woods, to 2400m. June-Aug. nE, sF; Pyrenees and Cordillera Cantabrica (GB, IRL).

6 GLOBULARIA-LEAVED VALERIAN *Valeriana globulariifolia.* Low/short creeping per, with erect hairless stems. Basal lvs oblong or spoon-shaped, untoothed, stalked; stem lvs with 3-5 narrow leaflets, stalked. Fls pink, 4-5mm long, in small dense clusters. Limestone rocks, to 2200m. June-Aug. nE, sF; Pyrenees and Cordillera Cantabrica. **6a Marsh Valerian** *V. dioica* is taller, the stems slightly *hairy* at the *nodes* and the fls 1.5-2.5mm long. Marshes and wet places, to 1800m. May-June. T, except Faeroes, IRL, IS, nN, nS, SF.

7 THREE-LEAVED VALERIAN *Valeriana tripteris.* Short/med per, stems hairy at the nodes. Basal lvs oval, heart-shaped at the base, toothed, long stalked; stem lvs *trifoliate*, usually short-stalked. Fls pink or white, 2-4mm long, in stalked clusters. Woods, scrub and rocky places. usually on limestone, to 2600m. June-Aug. A, CH, CS, sD, nE, F, H, I, PL, R, YU. **7a** *V. montana* has untoothed lower lvs and oval toothed upper lvs, not *divided.* Apr-July. A, CH, CS, sD, E, c & sF, I, R, YU.

8 ENTIRE-LEAVED VALERIAN *Valeriana saliunca.* Low/short tufted per, stems *hairless.* Basal lvs lance to spoon-shaped. untoothed, short-stalked; stem lvs one pair only, lance-shaped, sometimes 3-lobed, stalkless. Fls deep pink, 3.5-4.5mm long, borne in small terminal clusters. Rocks, screes and stony slopes, usually on limestone, 1800-2700m. July-Aug. A, CH, eF, n & cl; Alps and central Apennines.

9 CELTIC SPIKENARD *Valeriana celtica.* Low/short hairless per. All lvs oval or oblong, untoothed, stalked, the upper narrower. Fls yellowish or brownish, 1-2mm long, in small *whorled spikes;* male and female on separate plants. Acid alpine pastures, 1800-2800m. July-Aug. A, CH, eF, nI; Alps.

Valerian Family (contd.)

1 ROCK VALERIAN *Valeriana saxatilis.* Low/short per, stems hairless. Basal lvs elliptical-oblong or lance-shaped, long-stalked, toothed or not; *stem lvs absent or* one pair. Fls white, 1-2mm, in loose branched clusters. Limestone rocks, to 2500m. June-Aug. A, CH, sD, nI, nwYU; mainly east and central Alps and N Apennines.

2 ELONGATED VALERIAN *Valeriana elongata.* Low/short per with hairless stems. Basal lvs oval or oblong, scarcely toothed, long-stalked; stem lvs 1-2 pairs, oval or triangular, short-stalked. Fls *brownish or greenish,* 1-2mm, in long loose clusters. Limestone rocks and screes, 1400-2200m. June-Aug.nA, nI, nwYU; eastern Alps.

3 DWARF VALERIAN *Valeriana supina.* Low per with *hairy stems.* Basal lvs spoon-shaped or rounded, blunt toothed or untoothed, stalked; stem lvs 1-2 pairs, narrower, unstalked. Fls deep pink, 3-4mm, in dense clusters; male and female on separate plants. Limestone rocks and screes, often by snow patches, 1800-2900m. July-Aug.A, CH, sD, nI, nwYU; central and eastern Alps.

4 NARROW-LEAVED VALERIAN *Centranthus* (= *Valeriana*) *angustifolius.* Med/tall branched, hairless, *blue-green* per. Lvs linear, blunt, untoothed with clusters of smaller lvs at the nodes. Fls pink, 7-9mm long, with a spur at the base of each, in loose, branched, clusters. Rocky slopes and screes, usually on limestone, to 2000m. May-Aug. nwCH, s & eF, n & cl. **4a** *C. lecoqii* is shorter, the stems scarcely branched and the lvs lance-shaped, pointed, *without* clusters of smaller lvs at each node. n & eE, sF; mainly Pyrenees and mountains of north and north-eastern Spain.

Bellflower Family Campanulaceae

Perennials or annuals with alternate undivided lvs, often with a milky latex when cut; no stipules. Fls 5-parted, solitary or clustered in heads or spikes; corolla bell-shaped or starry, the petals joined into a short or long tube. Fr a many seeded capsule.

5 MOUNTAIN SHEEPSBIT *Jasione montana.* Low/med, hairy ann/bien, stems leafless in the upper half. Lvs narrow-oblong to narrow lance-shaped, usually untoothed but often wavy-edged; bracts oval or triangular, shorter than fls. Fls blue, rarely pink or white, in *globular heads;* calyx teeth hairy. Dry grassy places and heaths on acid soils, to 1700m. May-Sept. T, except Faeroes, IS, nN, nSF.

6 DWARF SHEEPSBIT *Jasione crispa* (= *J. humilis*). Variable *low* densely tufted, hairy per, often with short non-flowering shoots. Lvs oblong or lance-shaped, 1mm wide, toothed or not; bracts oval, toothed, green or purplish. Fls blue in globular heads; calyx teeth *hairless.* Meadows and screes on acid soils, to 2500m. July-Aug. sF, neE; eastern Pyrenees. **6a** *J. laevis* (= *J. perennis*) is taller (generally 20cm or more) with numerous, rather creeping, non-flowering shoots and *deeply toothed* bracts. Dry meadows. B, sD, E, F, I, R, YU (SF).

RAMPIONS *Phyteuma* and *Physoplexis.* Fls in dense globular heads or spikes; corolla with 5 long strap-shaped lobes joined near the base; stigma long, protruding.

7 DEVIL'S CLAW *Physoplexis comosa* (= *Phyteuma comosum*). Low tufted hairless per. Lvs kidney-shaped to oblong, coarsely toothed, stalked, bright shiny- green. Fls pinkish lilac, tipped with blackish-violet, 16-20mm long, the lobes *not separating* at top, borne in globular heads. Limestone and dolomitic rock crevices, to 2000m. July-Aug. s & seA, neI, nwYU; southern and south-eastern Alps and Dolomites.

8 SPIKED RAMPION *Phyteuma spicatum.* Med/tall hairless per. Lvs oval-heart-shaped, toothed; upper lvs linear; bracts linear, short. Fls yellowish or *greenish-white,* in cylindric spikes up to 6cm long. Meadows and woods, to 2100m. May-July. T, except Faeroes, IRL, IS, nN (S, SF). **8a** *P. pyrenaicum* has its basal lvs *withered* by flowering time; lvs slaty blue. n & cE, sF. **8b Dark Rampion** *P. ovatum* (= *P. halleri*) is like 8 but bracts oval and fls *blackish-violet.* To 2400m. July-Aug. A, CH, sD, s & eF, nI, nwYU.

9 BETONY-LEAVED RAMPION *Phyteuma betonicifolium.* Short/med per, stems often slightly hairy at the base. Lvs oval-lance-shaped, truncated at base, toothed. Fls reddish-blue to reddish-violet in cylindric spikes up to 4cm long. Meadows and woods, to 2850m. May-Aug. A, CH, sD. eF, nI; Alps and mountains of northern Italy.

10 SCORZONERA-LEAVED RAMPION *Phyteuma scorzonerifolium.* Med/tall almost hairless per. Lvs narrow-lance-shaped, toothed, the upper smaller; bracts linear, inconspicuous. Fls pale bluish-lilac in cylindric spikes to 5cm long. Meadows and open woods, to 2200m. June-July. CH, eF, nI; central and south-western Alps, northern and central Apennines. **10a** *P. michellii* is shorter with narrower lvs which are *hairy-margined* at the base. July-Aug. seF, nI; south-western and southern Alps. **10b** *P. zahlbruckneri* is like 10 but lvs rounded or heart-shaped *at the base.* Fls deep blue or blue-black. A, nwYU; eastern Alps.

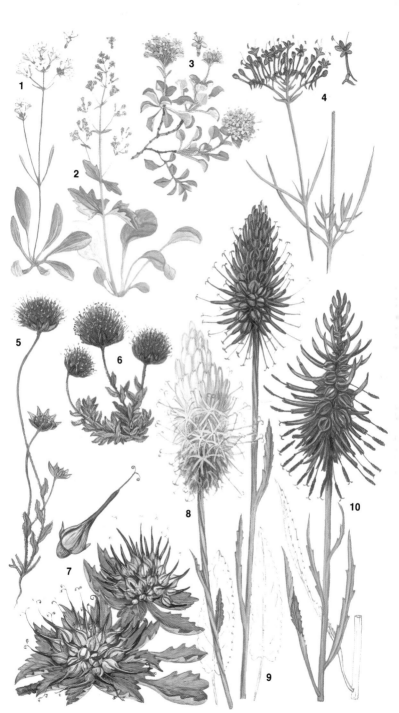

Bellflower Family (contd.)

1 BLACK RAMPION *Phyteuma nigrum.* Short/med hairless per. Lvs oblong-elliptical, heart-shaped at base, blunt-toothed, stalked, the uppermost much narrower; bracts linear, *longer than fls.* Fls blackish-violet, rarely blue or white, in oval or cylindric heads. Meadows and woods, to 1200m. July-Sept. A, B, CS, D, c & eF.

2 MARITIME RAMPION *Phyteuma cordatum* (= *P. balbisii*). Short slender hairy or hairless per. Lvs rounded or kidney-shaped, toothed, long-stalked, the upper lvs heart-shaped, short-stalked; bracts *small.* Fls bluish-white in globular or oblong heads. Limestone rocks, to 2000m. July-Aug. seF, nwl; Maritime Alps.

3 ROUND-HEADED RAMPION *Phyteuma orbiculare.* Short/med sometimes slightly hairy per. Lvs narrow lance-shaped to heart-shaped, toothed, stalked; uppermost narrower, scarcely stalked; bracts oval, toothed or not, variable in size. Fls dark blue or violet-blue, rarely white, in globular heads. Dry meadows and rocky ground, often on limestone, to 2600m. May-Oct. A, B, CH, CS, sD, E, F, sGB, H, I, PL, R, YU. **3a** *P. sieberi* has *broader,* oval-lance-shaped, stalkless, upper lvs and broader bracts. Limestone rocks, 1600-2600m. July-Sept. A, nl, nwYU; south-eastern Alps.

4 HORNED RAMPION *Phyteuma scheuchzeri.* Short/med hairless per. Lvs lance-shaped to heart-shaped, thick, bluish-green, toothed, long-stalked, the upper narrow lance-shaped, toothed; bracts linear, *much longer* than fls. Fls deep blue in globular heads. Rocky slopes, to 2600m. June-July. sCH, seF, nl, nwYU; southern Alps and northern Apennines. **4a** *P. charmelii* has thinner bright *green lvs,* the basal ones usually withered at flowering time. To 1900m. July-Aug. E, s & F, sl.

5 RHAETIAN RAMPION *Phyteuma hedraianthifolium.* Low/short, more or less erect, hairless per. *All lvs linear,* broadest in the middle, finely toothed; bracts linear, longer than fls. Fls dark blue-violet, straight in bud, in globular heads. Rocky and stony places, 1800-3100m, July-Aug. CH, nl; central and southern Alps.

6 GLOBE-HEADED RAMPION *Phyteuma hemisphaericum.* Low/short hairless per. Lvs lance-shaped to linear, *usually untoothed,* the upper linear; bracts oval, sometimes toothed at the base. Fls dark violet-blue, curved in bud, in globular heads. Meadows, stony slopes and screes, on acid rocks, to 2900m. July-Aug. A, CH, sD, E, s & eF, l.

7 DWARF RAMPION *Phyteuma humile.* Low/short hairless per. Lvs linear, broadest above the middle, scarcely toothed, crowded towards the base; bracts oval, toothed, *as long as* fls. Fls dark blue-violet, in globular heads. Stony meadows, acid rocks, screes and moraines, 1800-3250m. July-Aug. CH, eF, nwl; western and south-western Alps.

8 ROSETTE-LEAVED RAMPION *Phyteuma globulariifolium.* Low almost hairless per, stems almost leafless. Lvs in a *basal* rosette, oblong or spoon-shaped, blunt-toothed, stalked; bracts oval, generally shorter than fls, with a *hairy margin.* Fls deep violet-blue, curved in bud, in globular heads. Acid rocks and screes, 2000-3000m. July-Sept. eA, nl; eastern Alps. **8a** *P.g.* subsp. *pedemontanum* (= *P. pedemontanum*) is taller with *pointed* lvs and lance-shaped bracts, 1300-2600m. wA, CH, nE, s & eF; Pyrenees and western Alps. **8b** *P. rupicola* like 8 but the basal lvs *rounded* and the heads only 4-6 fld. sF; eastern Pyrenees. **8c** *P. confusum* (= *P. nanum*) like 8 but taller with broader lvs, the bracts *without* a hairy margin. A, R, YU.

9 EDRAIANTHUS *Edraianthus graminifolius* (= *Wahlenbergia graminifolia*). Low/short tufted per, stems hairy. Lvs narrow lance-shaped or linear, untoothed, the upper lvs smaller; bracts oval, pointed, generally shorter than the fls. Fls blue or bluish-violet, 12-20mm long, *upright bells* in close clusters of 3-6. Fr pods opening at top. Rocky and stony places, 1500-1800m. May-Aug. c & sl, wR, YU. **9a** *E. dinaricus* has lvs with inrolled margins, grey-hairy above, not more than 2.5mm wide. w & cYU. **9b** *E. serpyllifolius* has hairless, flat, spatular shaped lvs and dark violet fls. wYU.

Bellflower Family (contd.)

BELLFLOWERS *Campanula*. Perennials, sometimes biennial or annual, with solitary, clustered or racemed, nodding or upright bell-flowers, blue or purple, sometimes white (yellow in C. *thyrsoides*).

1 MT. CENIS BELLFLOWER *Campanula cenisia*. Low, rather sprawling hairy per with numerous non-flowering runners forming leafy-rosettes. Lvs blue-green, oval, broadest above the middle, untoothed, stalkless. Fls blue, 10-15mm, *starry open* bells, erect, solitary. Moraines, screes and rocky ledges, seldom on limestone, 2000-3100m. July-Sept. A, CH, eF, nl; Alps. **1a** C. *arvatica* has *toothed* lvs and larger fls of pale blue or violet. Limestone rocks. nwE.

2 CRIMPED BELLFLOWER *Campanula zoysii*. Low delicate, tufted, hairless per. Lvs oval to oblong, untoothed. Fls pale blue, 15-20mm long, solitary or up to five, narrow bells crimped in at the end. Limestone rock crevices and screes, to 2300m. July-Aug. sA, neI, nwYU; Julian and Karawanken Alps.

3 SPREADING BELLFLOWER *Campanula patula*. Med hairy or hairless rather *rough* per; stems slender, erect. Lvs oval, broadest above the middle, toothed, the upper narrower and unstalked. Fls violet-blue, sometimes white, 20-25mm long, erect wide bells in *spreading clusters;* sepal teeth linear. Grassy places, woods and scrub, to 1600m. June-July. T, except Faeroes, IRL, IS (DK, N, S). **3a** C.p. subsp. *costae* is more robust with long, toothed, sepal teeth. sF; Pyrenees, Val d'Aran. **3b Rampion Bellflower** C. *rapunculus* has smaller pale blue or white fls, 10-12mm, often in branched clusters. To 1800m. T, except Faeroes, IRL, IS (DK, GB, S).

4 CREEPING BELLFLOWER *Campanula rapunculoides*. Med/tall slender, hairy or almost hairless, per. Lvs oval, heart-shaped, the lower long-stalked, the upper narrower and stalkless. Fls deep purple or violet, 20-30mm, *drooping,* in long spikes; sepal teeth curved backwards. Fields and woods, to 2000m. July-Aug. T, except Faeroes, IS and Arctic Europe (GB, IRL).

5 PEACH-LEAVED BELLFLOWER *Campanula persicifolia*. Med/tall hairless per. Lvs lance-shaped or oval, peach-like, pointed, finely toothed, unstalked. Fls violet-blue, 30-40mm *long, half-nodding* broad bells in loose racemes. Meadows, woods and scrub, to 2000m. May-Aug. T, except Faeroes, IRL, IS and far north (GB).

6 BEARDED BELLFLOWER *Campanula barbata*. Short hairy per, unbranched. Lvs mainly in basal rosettes, lance-shaped or oblong, bristly, wavy-edged, untoothed. Fls pale blue, 20-30mm long, *white-hairy inside,* nodding in loose one-sided racemes. Meadows, open woods and stony places, to 3000m. June-Aug. A, CH, CS, sD, eF, sN(rare), PL, nwYU; mainly Alps and eastern Sudeten Mountains.

7 ALPINE BELLFLOWER *Campanula alpina*. Low/short, hairy, erect per. Lvs mostly in basal rosettes, narrow-lance-shaped, *finely toothed*. Fls lilac to lavendar-blue, 15-20mm long, half-nodding bells in loose clusters. Rocky and stony places, 1250-2400m. July-Aug. A, CS, sD, nl, PL, R, YU; eastern Alps and Carpathians.

8 PYRENEAN BELLFLOWER *Campanula speciosa* (= C. *corbariensis*, C. *oliveri*). Short/med erect, unbranched, rather bristly, bien/per. Lvs narrow-lance-shaped, 5-10cm, lightly toothed, crowded towards base of the stem. Fls blue-violet, 28-32mm long, almost erect bells in *pyramidal clusters;* epicalyx segments short, broad, bent backwards. Limestone rocks and screes, to 1500m. July-Aug. nE, s & seF; Corbieres, Cevennes, central and eastern Pyrenees. **8a** *Campanula affinis* subsp. *bolosii*. Short/med bristly, unbranched, bien; lvs narrow-lance-shaped, 10-15cm, stalkless; fls violet 20-40mm long, rather inflated bells, petal lobes hairy-edged. neE; eastern Pyrenees.

9 LARGE-FLOWERED BELLFLOWER *Campanula alpestris* (= C. *allionii*). Low creeping, rather sprawling, hairy per. Basal lvs in rosettes, narrow-lance-shaped, unstalked, scarcely toothed; upper lvs linear. Fls pale to deep blue, 30-45mm long, *usually solitary,* slightly nodding bells. Limestone rocks and screes, 1400-2800m. July-Aug. seF, nwl; south-western Alps.

Bellflower Family (contd.)

1 ROCK BELLFLOWER *Campanula petraea.* Short/med hairy per. Lvs oval-lance-shaped, toothed, stalked, white-hairy beneath. Fls pale yellow, l2mm long, borne in *tight heads*. Limestone rocks, to 1300m. seF, nI; south-western and southern Alps, very local.

2 CLUSTERED BELLFLOWER *Campanula glomerata.* Very variable short/med *rough-hairy*, tufted per. Lower lvs lance-shaped to oblong or elliptical, heart-shaped or rounded at base, toothed, long-stalked; upper lvs narrower, unstalked. Fls deep violet or blue-purple, 15-25mm long, in *tight heads;* sepal teeth lance-shaped. Meadows, woodland margins and scrub, to 1700m. June-Aug. T, except Faeroes, IRL, sI, IS. **2a** *C. foliosa* is larger with *slightly winged* lf stalks; sepal teeth very narrow. To 1800m. c & sI, cYU. **2b** *C. transsilvanica* has lower lvs narrowed at the base and with *winged stalks*; upper lvs heart-shaped and unstalked. Meadows and pastures. R.

3 SPIKED BELLFLOWER *Campanula spicata.* Med/tall hairy per. Basal lvs tufted, narrow-lance-shaped, untoothed; stem lvs narrower, pointed. Fls lilac-purple or blue, 17-22mm long, in *long leafy spikes*. Meadows, rocky and stony places, 1500-2400m. July-Aug. A, CH, eF, n & cI, nwYU; Alps, northern and central Apennines.

4 YELLOW BELLFLOWER *Campanula thyrsoides.* Short/med bristly-hairy bien to 40cm, forming a leafy rosette in the first year. Lvs oblong-lance-shaped with wavy untoothed margins; upper lvs narrower, clasping. Fls pale yellow, 17-22mm long, in *dense blunt spikes*. Meadows and stony places, on limestone and schist, 1500-2700m. July-Sept. A, CH, sD, eF, nI, nwYU; Alps and Jura. **4a** *C. t.* subsp. *carniolica* has laxer spikes, to 60cm, with bracts *longer than* fls. Woodland margins. eA, YU.

5 RAINER'S BELLFLOWER *Campanula raineri.* Low tufted hairy per. Lvs greyish-green, oval or oblong, lightly toothed, almost stalkless. Fls usually solitary, pale blue, 30-40mm long, broad erect bells. Limestone crevices, 1300-2200m. Aug-Sept. neI; Bergamasque Alps. **5a** *C. morettiana* has more rounded, deeper-toothed, lvs and *smaller narrower* deep blue fls. 1500-2300m. Aug-Sept. neI; Dolomites. **5b** *C. carpatica* has broad *oval or rounded* basal lvs and pale blue, occasionally white, fls. CS, PL, R (H); Carpathians.

6 GIANT BELLFLOWER *Campanula latifolia.* Med/tall hairy per; stems slightly angled. Lvs oval, heart-shaped at base, toothed, long-stalked, the uppermost stalkless. Fls large, blue, 40-55mm, in *loose racemes*; sepal teeth erect. Meadows, woods and riverbanks, to 1600m. July-Sept. T, except Faeroes, IS and far north (B, NL). **6a Nettle-leaved Bellflower** *C. trachelium* has more angular, *bristly stems* and rough-hairy lvs; fls violet-blue or pale blue, 30-40mm long. T, except Faeroes, IS and far north. **6b** *C. bononiensis* like 6b but lvs *white-hairy* beneath and fls smaller, 10-20mm, in one-sided racemes. To 1500m. A, CH, CS, sD, seF, nI, H, PL, R, YU.

7 HAREBELL *Campanula rotundifolia* agg. Very variable short/med hairless per; *stems slender*, erect from a leafy mat. Lvs rounded to kidney-shaped, blunt-toothed, stalked, mostly crowded at base of stems; upper lvs narrow-lance-shaped, stalkless. Fls pale to mid-blue, 12-20mm long, *nodding* bells, solitary or in loosely branched clusters, erect in bud. Meadows, open woods, shrub and banks, to 2200m. May-Nov. T. **7a Flax-leaved Bellflower** *C. carnica*, has fls *drooping* in bud; fls larger, 22-26mm. Limestone crevices, to 2000m. s & eA, nI, nwYU. **7b** *C. scheuchzeri* like 7 but *all lvs* narrow lance-shaped or linear, unstalked. To 3400m. A, CH, sD, nE, s & eF, nI, PL, YU. **7c** *C. rhomboidalis* like 7 but with *oval* stem lvs. CH, e & seF, nI (A, B, CS, D, NL). **7d Arctic Bellflower** *C. uniflora* * is shorter than 7 with small *solitary* fls, 5-10mm; basal lvs oval, untoothed. Heaths and grassy places, to 1600m. July. IS, N, S, SF.

5

Bellflower Family (contd.)

1 SPANISH BELLFLOWER *Campanula hispanica*. Med/tall per; stems erect, hairy in the lower half. Basal lvs heart-shaped, toothed, stalked; stem lvs lance-shaped, crowded in the lower half of stem. Fls blue, 10-14mm long, in loose few-flowered clusters, erect in bud; sepal teeth linear, *pressed* against petal tube. Fr drooping. Rocky, stony or sandy places, to 2500m. June-Aug. sF, E. **1a** *C. h.* subsp. *catalanica* is taller to 75cm, with *laxer* racemes. neE; eastern Pyrenees. **1b** *C. fritschii* has stems leafless in the upper half and larger fls, 18-22mm. seF; Provence Alps. **1c** *C. apennina* like 1 but with *hairless stems* which are densely leafy up to the fls; *fr erect*. cI; central Apennines. **1d** *C. bertolae* is like 1c but fls larger, 12-20mm, borne on hairy stems; fr drooping. nwI. **1e** *C. pseudostenocodon* is like 1c but shorter with stems *often hairy* in the lower part. sI; southern Apennines. **1f** *C. moravica* has stems leafless in the *upper part* and denser flowered inflorescences. nA, CS, H, R, nYU.

2 FRENCH BELLFLOWER *Campanula recta*. Short/med hairy per. Basal lvs oval-lance-shaped, *untoothed*, stalked; stems with numerous narrow lvs, stalkless. Fls blue, 15-25mm, in few-flowered close clusters, *drooping in bud*; sepal teeth spreading. Fr drooping. Grassy and rocky places, to 1800m. June-Aug. c & sF, nE; Pyrenees and mountains of southern and central France. **2a** *C. precatoria* has slightly toothed lvs; stem lvs half-clasping, but absent just below the fls. Meadows and pastures. neE; eastern Pyrenees.

3 PANICULATE BELLFLOWER *Campanula witasekiana*. Short slightly hairy per; stems angular, leafy up to the fls. Basal lvs rounded or kidney-shaped, blunt-toothed, stalked; upper lvs lance-shaped to linear, untoothed, stalkless. Fls blue, 12-16mm long, in *branched clusters*, drooping in bud; sepal teeth narrow-triangular, spreading. Meadows and rocky places to 1800m. July-Aug. A, nI, YU; mainly eastern Alps.

4 FAIRY'S THIMBLE *Campanula cochlearifolia* (= *C. pusilla*). Variable low, slender, creeping, hairy or hairless per. Basal lvs heart-shaped to rounded, toothed, stalked, present at flowering time; stem lvs lance-shaped, toothed. Fls blue or violet, rarely white, l2-l6mm long, *solitary or few* in a cluster; drooping in bud; sepal teeth linear, spreading. Rocky and stony places, screes, often on limestone, to 3400m. June-Aug. A, CH, CS, sD, nE, s & eF, I, PL, R, YU. **4a** *C. cespitosa* is taller with oval or diamond-shaped basal lvs *narrowed* at the top. Limestone rocks and screes, to 2100m. Aug-Sept.A, neI, nwYU; eastern Alps.

5 JAUBERT'S BELLFLOWER *Campanula jaubertiana*. Very low creeping per; stems *densely hairy*. Basal lvs rounded to elliptical, heart-shaped at base, blunt-toothed, stalked; stem lvs oval to elliptical, toothed. Fls blue, 8-l2mm long, solitary or 2-4 clustered, narrow bells drooping in bud. Limestone rocks, to 2000m. July-Aug. nE, sF; central and eastern Pyrenees.

6 COTTIAN BELLFLOWER *Campanula stenocodon*. Short per, hairy in the lower part. Basal lvs rounded or heart-shaped, sharp-toothed, stalked, absent at flowering time; stem lvs linear-lance-shaped, sometimes untoothed. Fls blue-purple, 12-18mm long, *narrow pendulous bells* in few-flowered clusters, drooping in bud. Rocky and stony places to 1800m. July -Aug. seF, nwI; south-western Alps. **6a** *C. beckiana* is taller with *many fls* in branched clusters. Meadows and open woods. July-Sept. eA, nwYU; mainly north-estern Alps.

7 SOLITARY HAREBELL *Campanula pulla*. Low/short slender per; stems hairy on the angles or hairless. Basal lvs oval or rounded, blunt-toothed, stalked; stem lvs oval to elliptical. Fls deep blue-purple, 18-24mm, *solitary,* pendulous bells, drooping in bud. Grassy and rocky places and screes, often on limestone, 1500-2200m. July-Aug. nA; north-eastern Alps.

8 PERFORATE BELLFLOWER *Campanula excisa*. Low creeping per; stems hairy. Basal lvs heart-shaped to rounded, sharp-toothed, stalked; stem lvs narrow lance-shaped, untoothed. Fls blue or lilac-blue, 10-16mm long, narrow, rather pleated bells, the lobes narrowed at the mouth and *apparently perforated*. Acid rocks and screes, 1400-2350m. June-Sept. CH, nwI; south-western and central Alps.

Scabious Family Dipsacaceae

Annuals or perennials with opposite lvs, the basal ones often rosetted. Fls in dense composite-like heads, each floret with 4-5 petal lobes joined into a tube, a calyx and 4 projecting stamens; outer florets often with 2-3 enlarged petal lobes. Fr small, one seeded.

1 ALPINE SCABIOUS *Cephalaria alpina*. Tall robust hairy per. Basal lvs pinnate or lyre-shaped with 3-8 pairs of lance-shaped leaflets; stem lvs smaller with few leaflets or undivided. *Flheads yellow*, 20-30mm, flattish, on longer slender stalks. Meadows, woods, scrub and screes, to 1800m. July-Aug. A, CH, eF, nwYU; Alps and Jura. **1a** *C. radiata* has the upper lvs *linear* and larger flheads. R. **1b** *C. laevigata* is like 1a but with hairless lvs. R, nYU.

2 SHINING SCABIOUS *Scabiosa lucida*. Short hairless per, stems unbranched, leafless in the upper half. Lvs glossy-green, oval-lance-shaped with shallow rounded-teeth, stalked; upper lvs pinnately-lobed with a large end lobe. Flheads reddish-purple, 10-20mm, flattish. Dry meadows and stony places. June-Sept.A, CS, CH, sD, s & eF, H, I, PL, R, YU . **2a** *S. l.* subsp. *stricta* has stems leafy for much of the way and mostly with undivided lvs. eA, nwYU. **2b** *S. columbaria* usually has *branched* stems and bristly leaves, as well as bluish-lilac flower heads. Meadows, open woodland and waysides to 1500m. A, B, CH, CS, D, DK, E, F, GB, H, I, NL, PL, R, sS, YU. In the central and eastern Carpathians the typical plant is replaced by subsp. *pseudobanatica* which has longer and hairier flbracts. **2c** *S. ochroleuca* is like 2b but the with smaller *pale yellow or cream* flheads, 15-25mm across. A, CS, D, H, n & cl, PL, R, YU (F).

3 TYROLEAN SCABIOUS *Scabiosa vestina*. Short/med hairy per. Basal lvs narrow spoon-shaped, untoothed, stalked; stem lvs pinnately-lobed, the leaflets linear or lance-shaped. Fl heads purple, 20-30mm, flattish, the outer florets twice the size of the inner. Limestone rocks, to 1900m. June-Sept. nI; southern Alps and northern Apennines. **3a** *S. graminifolia* is a denser more tufted plant with *silvery-grey* stems and lvs, all the lvs *undivided*; flheads blue-violet. To 1800m. CH, E, s & eF, I, YU. **3b** *S. silenifolia* is a shorter plant *not more* than 12cm tall and with smaller flheads than 3, lilac-blue. Rocky pastures. CI, YU; not in the Alps.

4 PYRENEAN SCABIOUS *Scabiosa cinerea* (= *S. pyrenaica*). Short/med whitish-hairy per, stems leafless in the upper half. Basal lvs lance-shaped, toothed, stalked; stem lvs with a large end leaflet and 1-2 pairs of smaller, linear, leaflets. Flheads bluish-purple, 10-20mm, flattish. Dry meadows and stony places, to 2000m. June-Sept. nE, sF; Pyrenees. **4a** *S.c.* subsp. *hladnikiana* has greyish lvs and stems *leafy* most of the way up. neI, nwYU; mainly eastern Alps.

5 DEVILS-BIT SCABIOUS *Succisa pratensis* (= *Scabiosa succisa*). Med/tall hairy per. Basal lvs in a rosette, elliptical, untoothed, stalked, often purple-blotched; upper lvs narrower, sometimes toothed. Flheads rounded, mauve to dark purple, 15-25mm; florets all more or less equal in size, sometimes only female. Damp meadows and woods, to 2400m. July-Oct. T. **5a** *S. pinnatifida* has basal lvs toothed and middle stem lvs lobed. nwE.

6 WOOD SCABIOUS *Knautia dipsacifolia* (= *Scabiosa sylvatica*). Variable med/tall hairy per. Lvs bright green, variable on same plant, oblong-oval, constricted or tapered to the base, toothed. Flheads lilac or purplish, 25-40mm, the outermost florets rather larger than the inner ones. Shady places, woods and scrub, to 2000m. June-Sept. A, eB, CH, CS, D, c & eF, H, I, PL, R, YU. **6a** *K. ressmannii* has lower stem internodes *hairless* (not hairy) and shiny thick lvs. Coniferous woodland and grassy places. neI, nwYU; south-eastern Alps. **6b** *K. salvadoris* has lower lvs *hairless* and often untoothed; flheads pink. sF, neE; eastern Pyrenees. **6c** *K. longifolia* has rather *shiny* lvs, hairless except for the margins and larger pinkish-purple flheads, 3.5-5cm. A, CH, nI, R, YU. **6d** *K. velutina* has lvs shiny with short silky hairs, the upper lobed; flheads purple, 2-3cm. Limestone rocks. nI; southern Alps. **6e** *K. subcanescens* is like 6 but lvs *greyish-white* with hairs beneath; flheads violet-purple. Meadows. seF, nwI; south-western Alps. **6f** *K. baldensis* is like 6e but lvs *narrow-lance-shaped* (not oval to broad lance-shaped) densely hairy above. nI; Lake Garda region only. **6g** *K. kitaibelii* has lobed stem lvs and *yellow* flheads, 3-4cm. A, CS, D, H, PL.

Daisy Family Compositae

The Daisies or Composites form a very large and versatile family. Fls small, closely packed in compound heads surrounded by several to many sepal-like bracts; the flbracts. Petals joined in a tube ending in either 5 small teeth (forming the disc) or in a strap-shaped petal (the rays); flheads consisting either of all disc florets (thistles), or of ray florets (dandelions) or a central disc surrounded by rays (the daisies). Fr tiny, usually surrounded by a feathery or hairy pappus which floats in the wind.

1 GOLDEN ROD *Solidago virgaurea.* Variable short/med hairy, or almost hairless, tufted per. Lvs lance-shaped or oblong, broadest above the middle, toothed, stalked, the upper narrower, stalkless. Flheads bright yellow, 15-20mm, *short* rayed, in branched racemes. Woods, clearings, stony places and heaths, to 2800m. July-Oct. T, except Faeroes, IS.

2 DAISY *Bellis perennis.* Low hairy per. Lvs in rosettes, spoon-shaped, slightly toothed. Flheads solitary, long-stalked, white with a yellow disc, 15-25mm. Grassy and waste places, to 2500m. Flowering for most of the year. T (Faeroes, IS, N, S, SF).

ASTERS *Aster.* Flheads large with one row of long, blue, purple, lilac or white, spreading rays, surrounding a yellow disc.

3 ALPINE ASTER *Aster alpinus.* Low/short tufted hairy per. Lvs elliptical to spoon-shaped, untoothed, the upper narrower, stalkless. Flheads solitary, violet-blue, mauve or rarely white, 35-45mm. Dry meadows, rocky and stony places, to 3200m. July-Sept. A, CS, CH, sD, E, c & sF, I, PL, R, YU. **3a False Aster** *A. bellidiastrum* (= *Bellidiastrum michelii*) has broader often toothed lvs; flheads pink or white, 20-40mm, on *leafless stalks.* To 2800m. A, CS, CH, sD, seF, I, Pl, YU (H).

4 EUROPEAN MICHELMAS DAISY *Aster amellus.* Short/med tufted hairy per. Lvs lance-shaped to oval, slightly toothed or untoothed. Flheads blue or purplish, 20-30mm, in branched flat-topped clusters, rarely solitary; outer flbracts shorter than inner. Meadows, open woods and rocky places, to 1400m. Aug-Sept. A, CS, CH, D, F, H, I, Pl, R, YU.

5 PYRENEAN ASTER *Aster pyrenaeus.* Med/tall hairy per. Lvs oblong-lance-shaped, slightly toothed, half-clasping the stem. Flheads lilac-blue, 20-35mm, long-stalked, solitary or 2-5 in a cluster; flbracts *all the same length.* Damp meadows and stony places, to 2000m. July-Sept. sF; west and central French Pyrenees.

6 THREE-VEINED ASTER *Aster sedifolius* subsp. *trinervis.* Med/tall slightly hairy per, sometimes ann. Lvs linear to lance-shaped or elliptical, the *lower 3-veined.* Flheads blue or lilac, few rayed, 15-20mm, in dense branched clusters. Fields, dry and waste places, to 1800m. June-Sept. A, CS, sF, E, H, I, R, YU.

FLEABANES *Erigeron.* Like Aster but flheads small with several rows of narrow short rays and a pale yellow disc. A variable and difficult group.

7 GREEK FLEABANE *Erigeron atticus.* Short/med per; stems glandular-hairy. Lvs oval, broadest above the middle, the lower stalked. Flheads 25-35mm, in clusters, with erect violet or purplish rays. Meadows and rocky places, to 2200m. July-Sept. A, CH, CS, sD, s & eF, I, PL, R, YU. **7a** *E. gaudinii* (= *E. glandulosus*) is shorter with stems branched at or below the middle. A, CH, sF, eF, nI; Alps and Black Forest. **7b Blue Fleabane** *E. acer* is a greyish ann/bien; stems hairy *not* glandular, often purplish; flheads, 10-l5mm, rays dull purple, very short. T, except Faeroes, IS.

8 VARIABLE FLEABANE *Erigeron glabratus* (= *E. polymorphus*). Variable low/short slightly hairy per, stems slender. Lvs narrow-spoon-shaped or oblong, stalked. Flheads 15-20mm, with spreading lilac or white rays, the disc yellow or reddish-brown, solitary or in small clusters; *flbracts green* with a brown centre, slightly hairy. Short grassy and rocky places, to 3000m. July-Sept. A, CH, CS, sD, E, s & eF, I, PL, R, YU.

9 ALPINE FLEABANE *Erigeron alpinus.* Variable short per; stems unbranched, downy. Lvs narrow-elliptical to spoon-shaped, pointed, the lower stalked. Flheads solitary or few clustered, 20-30mm, with spreading lilac rays and a pale yellow disc; flbracts *lilac-tipped,* hairy. Meadows, rocky and stony places, 1500-3050m. JulySept. A, CH, CS, sD, E, F, I, PL, R, YU. **9a** *E. epiroticus* is *shorter,* rarely exceeding l0cm tall; flheads solitary, rays purplish, flbracts woolly. cl; central Apennines.

Daisy Family (contd.)

1 ONE-FLOWERED FLEABANE *Erigeron uniflorus*. Rather like a shorter version of theVariable Fleabane. Flheads small, solitary, 10-15mm, the ray florets white or pale lilac, the disc yellow; flbracts *white-woolly*, lilac-tipped. Damp meadows, stony places and moraines, often around snow patches, 1200-3000m. July-Sept. T, except B, DK, Faeroes, GB, IRL, IS, NL. **1a** *E. humilis* has *black or dark violet* flbracts. To 1400m. IS, N, S, SF.

2 NEGLECTED FLEABANE *Erigeron neglectus*. Low/short hairy per. Lvs spoon-shaped or lance-shaped, *hairy along edge only*, the upper stalkless. Flheads solitary, 12-18mm, ray florets lilac, the disc yellow; flbracts hairy, lilac-tipped. Limestone rocks, 1800-2500m. July-Sept. A, CH, sD,eF, nl; Alps. **2a** *E. borealis* has flexuous stems and hairy young lvs. Meadows and stony places. nGB, IS, N, S, SF.

3 CATSFOOT *Antennaria dioica* (= *Gnaphalium dioicum*, *Omalotheca dioica*). Low/short, mat-forming, downy per, with *rooting runners*. Lvs oval-spoon- shaped, blunt, untoothed, grey-green above, white-woolly beneath. Flheads in small clusters, rayless, white, pink or reddish; male 6mm, female larger, on separate plants. Meadows, heaths and dry places, on acid soils, to 3000m. May- July. T, except Faeroes, IS. **3a Alpine Catsfoot** *A. alpina* is shorter with lvs almost hairless and smaller flheads. To 2200m. July-Aug. N, S, SF. **3b** *A. nordhageniana* is like 3 but not grey-downy; stems and lower surface of lvs *purplish*. nN; rare.

4 CARPATHIAN CATSFOOT *Antennaria carpatica* (= *Gnaphalium carpaticum*). Low/short tufted, white-downy per; similar to 3 but *no runners*. Lvs oblong to linear, pointed. Flheads in small clusters, brown or blackish. Damp meadows, rocky and stony places, 1500-3100m. July-Aug. A, CH, CS, nE, s & eF, nl, PL, R, YU.

5 EDELWEISS *Leontopodium alpinum*. Low/short, white or greyish-woolly, tufted per. Lvs oblong, broadest above the middle, untoothed, greenish above, greyish beneath; upper lvs narrower. Flheads small, yellowish-white, closely clustered, but *surrounded by* conspicuous large oblong, woolly-white, bracts. Grassy and rocky slopes, usually on limestone, 1700-3400m. July-Sept. A, CS, CH, s & eF, nl, PL, R, YU. **5a** *L. nivale* has densely white woolly lvs and bracts; lvs short, spoon-shaped. cAp; Abruzzi Mountains.

6 DWARF CUDWEED *Omalotheca supina* (= *Gnaphalium supinum*). Low tufted, greyish-woolly, per. Lvs narrow lance-shaped, untoothed, 1-veined. Flheads small, rounded, rayless, reddish, hidden by brown bracts, in *clusters* amongst uppermost Lvs. Damp meadows, stony places, moraines and by snow patches, usually on acid soils, 1400-3400m. July-Sept. T, except B, H, IRL, NL. **6a** *O. hoppeana* is *not* tuft forming; taller and more slender, to 2850m. A, CS, CH, sD, eF, nl, PL, YU; Jura, Alps and western Carpathians.

7 WOOD CUDWEED *Omalotheca sylvatica* (= *Gnaphalium sylvaticum*). Short/med tufted, grey-woolly, per. Lvs lance-shaped to linear, untoothed, *usually 1-veined*, green above, white-felted beneath. Flheads reddish or yellowish, hidden by brown sepal-like bracts, solitary or in long leafy spikes. Open woods and clearings, to 2500m. July-Sept. T, except Faeroes. **7a Highland Cudweed** *O. norvegica* (= *Gnaphalium norvegicum*) is shorter with broader, lance-shaped, *3-veined*, lvs, white-felted *on both sides*. Meadows, open woods and stony places, usually on acid soils, *1200*-2800m. T, except B, Faeroes, sGB, IRL, NL.

8 MOUNTAIN DOG-DAISY *Anthemis cretica* (= *A. montana*). Variable low/short downy to slightly hairy per. Lvs pinnately-lobed, stalked, whitish-hairy or green- hairless. Flheads solitary, white with a yellow disc, 25-40mm, rays sometimes absent; flbracts woolly. Rocky places and screes, on acid rocks, to 2000m. July-Sept. wCS, sF, I, R, YU. **8a** *A.c.* subsp. *alpina* (= *Santolina alpina*) is usually taller, the lvs densely *yellowish-hairy*; rays generally absent. Limestone rocks. cl; Abruzzi Mountains. **8b Carpathian Dog-daisy** *A. carpatica**. Similar to 8 but lvs pale *green,* 1-2 pinnately-lobed. Flheads 30-50mm; flbracts hairless or almost so. Grassy and stony places. A, CH, nE, I, PL, R, YU; Southern Pyrenees, eastern Alps and Carpathians. **8c** *A.c.* subsp. *petraea* similar to 8b but *hairless* with smaller flheads, 20-30mm. cl; central Apennines; possibly in the eastern Pyrenees.

9 SOUTHERN DOG-DAISY *Anthemis triumfetti* (= *Cota triumfetti*). Med/tall slightly hairy, erect per; stems solitary, branched above *the middle*. Lvs pinnately-lobed, the lobes toothed. Flheads solitary to each branch, white with a yellow disc, 30-50mm. Woods and rocky places, to 1800m. May-Aug. CH, E, s & eF, lm R, YU. **9a Corn Chamomile** *A. arvensis* is a *branched annual* with 1-3 pinnately-lobed greyish lvs. Cultivated areas and waste ground, to 1950m. T, except Faeroes.

Daisy Family *(contd.)*

MOON DAISIES *Leucanthemum.* Perennials with toothed, or pinnately-lobed lvs. Flheads flat, daisy-like, with white rays and a yellow disc.

1 MOON or OX-EYE DAISY *Leucanthemum vulgare* agg (= *Chrysanthemum leucanthemum*) agg. Variable short/tall grey or dark green, hairy or hairless per. Lower lvs oblong-spoon-shaped or oblong, pinnately-lobed, toothed or untoothed, long-stalked; upper lvs stalkless, toothed only in the upper part, *clasping the stem.* Flheads usually solitary, 25-50mm; flbracts with a brown margin. Fields, meadows, open woods and pathways, to 2700m. June-Aug. T (Faeroes, IS).

2 SAW-LEAVED MOON DAISY *Leucanthemum (= Chrysanthemum) atratum* agg. Variable short/med mat-forming per, hairy or hairless. Basal lvs spoon-shaped, blunt-toothed or lobed, long-stalked; stem lvs similar, stalkless, *regularly toothed.* Fl heads solitary, 20-50mm; flbracts with a dark brown margin and a *small scale-like appendage* at the top. Rocky and stony places, screes and gravels, usually on limestone, to 2850m. July-Sept. A, CH, sD, eF, I, YU; mainly Alps and Apennines.

3 ALPINE MOON DAISY *Leucanthemopsis (= Chrysanthemum or Pyrethrum) alpina.* Low tufted hairy per, stems rather weak, almost lfless. Lvs oval to spoon-shaped, toothed or pinnately-lobed, greenish or grey. Flheads solitary, 20-40mm, rays white but often *turning pink.* Short grass, rocky places, screes and moraines, 1800-2800m. July-Aug. A, CH, CS, sD, nE, s & eF, n & cI, PL, R, YU.

4 LAVENDER COTTON *Santolina chamaecyparissus.* Dwarf evergreen, *silvery-white-downy*, subshrub to 50cm, *aromatic.* Lvs linear, pinnately-lobed or toothed. Flheads *globular,* deep yellow, 10-15mm, rayless; flbracts white-downy. Dry rocky ground and banks, to 1200m. July-Sept. nE, s & seF, nwI (CH). **4a** *S.c. subsp. tomentosa* is taller with hairless lvs and whitish or pale yellow flheads. nE, s & seF, cI.

MILFOILS, SNEEZEWORTS *Achillea.* Rather aromatic perennials with alternate, 1-3-pinnately-lobed lvs. Fls small, short-rayed, usually in flat-topped clusters, often branched.

5 ALPINE SNEEZEWORT *Achillea oxyloba.* Low/short hairy, creeping, per. Lvs mostly basal, pinnately-lobed. Flheads *solitary or 2-3-clustered*, white with a pale yellow disc, 20-30mm. Stony meadows and rocky places, on limestone, 1600-2800m. July-Sept. eA, neI; south-eastern Alps. **5a** *A.o.* subsp. *mucronulata* has 2-pinnately-lobed lvs, mostly on *the stems* and not basal. I; Apennines. **5b** *A. o. subsp. schurii* is like 5a but lf lobes *lance-shaped*, not linear. CS, R; Carpathians. **5c** *A. barrelieri* like 5 but lvs and stems *silvery-hairy.* c & sI; central and southern Apennines.

6 DARK-STEMMED SNEEZEWORT *Achillea atrata.* Short only slightly aromatic per; stems *brown-hairy,* at least in the upper half. Lvs deep green, 2-pinnately-lobed, lobes narrow lance-shaped, almost hairless. Flheads white with a whitish disc, 12-18mm, in clusters of 2-10. Stony pastures, rocky places and screes, usually on limestone, 1700-3000m. July-Sept. A, CH, sD, eF, nI, nwYU; Alps.

7 MUSK MILFOIL *Achillea moschata.* Variable low/short almost hairless per, strongly aromatic, lax or tufted. Lvs bright green, pinnately-lobed; lobes lance-shaped. Fl heads white with a *whitish disc*, 10-l5mm, in loose clusters of 5-15. Stony pastures, rocks and screes, usually on acid rocks, 1450-3500m. July-Sept. A, CH, I; central Alps and Apennines. Sometimes included in *A. erba-rotta.*

8 DWARF MILFOIL *Achillea nana.* Low/short *greyish-downy* tufted per. Lvs 1-2-pinnately-lobed; lobes crowded, lance-shaped; lower lvs long-stalked. Flheads off-white, 9-11mm, in tight clusters of 5-8. Acid rocks and screes, 1700-3800m. Ju ly-Sept. A-except CH, eF, n & cI.

3

Daisy Family *(contd.)*

1 SILVERY MILFOIL *Achillea clavennae.* Short creeping, silvery-hairy per. Lvs pinnately-lobed, the lobes lance-shaped, sometimes toothed; basal lvs long-stalked. Flheads white with an off-white disc, 10-20mm, in *loose clusters* of 5-25. Rocks and screes, often on limestone, 1500-2500m. July-Sept. A, CH, sD, , nl, nw & wYU.

2 SIMPLE-LEAVED MILFOIL *Achillea erba-rotta.* Short almost hairless per. Lvs *not* pinnately-lobed, spoon-shaped to lance-shaped, toothed, teeth at base often larger. Flheads white, 14-18mm, in loose clusters of 10-30. Grassy meadows and rocky places, on acid soils usually, 2000-3200m. July-Aug. swCH, seF, nwI; south-western Alps. **2a** *A.e.* subsp. *rupestris* is a more densely tufted plant with mostly *untoothed* lvs. Limestone rocks. I; Apennines.

3 LARGE-LEAVED SNEEZEWORT *Achillea macrophylla.* Med/tall more or less hairless per. Lvs large, pinnately-lobed; lobes 6-12, lance-shaped, toothed, pointed. Flheads white, 13-15mm, in loose clusters of 5-40. Damp or shady places, on humus rich soils, to 2500m. July-Sept. A, CH, sD, nl (CS); Alps and northern Apennines. **3a** *A. lingulata* is similar but with toothed, not lobed lvs, gland-dotted.; flheads somewhat smaller. Rocks and meadows. R, c & eYU.

4 TANSY MILFOIL *Achillea distans.* Med/tall slightly downy per. Lvs pinnately-lobed, lobes broad, toothed; lower leaflets of upper lvs clasping the stem. Flheads white, rarely pink, 5-6mm across, rays 1-2.5mm long, many in *broad,* branched clusters. Pastures, wood margins and scrub, to 2500m. July-Sept. A, CH, eF, H, I, PL, R, YU. **4a** A.d. subsp. *tanacetifolia* flheads *pink,* rays 2.5-4mm long. sA, nl; southern Alps.

5 YARROW *Achillea millefolium* agg. Short/med downy per, aromatic. Lvs 2-3-pinnate, feathery, dark green, hairy above. Flheads white or pink with a creamish disc, 4-6mm, in *large flat-topped* clusters. Grassy and waste places, to 2800m. July-Sept. T. **5a** *A. collina* has lvs hairless above; fls white. A, CH, CS, sD, nl, R, YU. **5b** *A. pannonica* is like 5 but *grey- or silvery-hairy,* fls white. Dry stony places. A, CS, H, R, YU.

6 ANDORRAN MILFOIL *Achillea chamaemelifolia.* Short/med tufted, slightly hairy per; stems branched at base. Lvs pinnately-lobed, hairless; lobes linear, untoothed. Flheads white, 7-9mm, in loose clusters. Rocky places, to 1700m. June-Aug. neE, sF; eastern Pyrenees.

7 CREAM-FLOWERED SNEEZEWORT *Achillea odorata.* Short hairy aromatic per; stems unbranched below flhead. Lvs 1-2-pinnately-lobed; segments ovate, toothed. Flheads white to pale yellow, 3-4mm, in large *dense clusters.* Dry stony places, to 1450m. May-July. E, s & seF, nwl.

8 SNEEZEWORT *Achillea ptarmica.* Med/tall hairy per, *not aromatic.* Lvs not divided, lance-shaped, finely-toothed, stalkless, the upper half-clasping the stem, hairless. Flheads white with a creamish disc, 14-l8mm, in loose branched clusters. Damp grassy places on acid soils, to 1700m. July-Sept. T, except c & sl, eR, YU (IS).

9 PYRENEAN SNEEZEWORT *Achillea pyrenaica.* Short/med slightly hairy per. Lvs deep green, not divided, lance-shaped, toothed, stalkless, *covered in* short glandular-hairs. Flheads white with a cream disc, 18-20mm, in loose branched clusters. Damp grassy places, to 1800m. July-Sept. nE, c & sF; Pyrenees and mountains of central southern France.

8, middle leaves

Daisy Family (contd.)

ARTEMISIAS *Artemisia* – usually aromatic perennials with alternate, pinnately-divided lvs. Flheads small, rayless, in branched spikes.

1 WESTERN WORMWOOD *Artemisia vallesiaca.* (= *A. maritima* subsp. *vallesiaca*) Short/med stout *white-downy per with many basal leafy rosettes; strongly aromatic.* Lvs 1-3-pinnately-lobed; uppermost lvs not lobed. Flheads egg-shaped, yellow or orange-yellow, 3-4mm long. Grassy and stony places, on limestone, to 1300m. Aug-Oct. swCH, seF, nwI; south-western Alps.

2 DIGITATE-LEAVED WORMWOOD *Artemisia eriantha (= A. petrosa).* Low/short tufted, silvery-white-downy per with basal leafy rosettes. Lvs *2-trifoliate or digitate,* stalked, the upper stalkless. Flheads yellow, 3-4.5mm, nodding in slightly branched spikes; florets hairy; flbracts oval membranous with a brown edge, hairy. Rocks and screes, 2000-3150m. July-Sept. CS, nE, s & eF, n & cI, PL, R, YU. **2a Genipi** *A. genipi* (A. nivalis) is less hairy with *hairless* florets. 2000-3800m. A, CH, eF, nI; Alps.

3 *Artemisia insipida.* Short/med tufted per, *not aromatic.* Lvs 1-2-pinnately-lobed, lobes linear, green above, *silvery-hairy beneath.* Flheads nodding, yellow, 3mm, in branched spikes, florets hairy; flbracts with a membranous margin, hairy. Grassy banks and rocky places, to l400m. July-Sept. seF; Gap region; possibly extinct.

4 *Artemisia chamaemelifolia.* Med *hairless* per, aromatic. Lvs 2-3-pinnately-lobed, the upper stalkless, *half-clasping* the stem. Flheads yellow, 2-3mm, in crowded branched spikes; flbracts linear or oblong, usually hairless. Rocky places, to 2400m. July-Aug. nE, s & seF, nwI; Pyrenees and Cordillera Cantabrica, south-western Alps.

5 NARROW-LEAVED WORMWOOD *Artemisia nitida.* Short/med tufted per, *silvery* with silky hairs. Lower lvs digitate, upper pinnately-lobed, lobes all stalked, linear. Flheads yellowish, 4-5mm, nodding, in *one-sided* spikes, 20 or more per flhead. Calcareous rocks, 1300-2000m. July-Sept. seA, neI, nwYU; south-eastern Alps. **5a** *A. pedemontana* is similar but plants white-woolly; flheads 4-6mm. Limestone rocks to 1500m. n & cE, c & sI, R; local.

6 YELLOW GENIPI *Artemisia mutellina* (= *A. umbelliformis*). Low/short *cushion-forming,* silvery-hairy per. Lvs digitately-lobed; lobes linear. Flheads yellow, 3.5-4.5mm, erect, in slender spikes, florets downy up to 15 per flhead; flbracts silvery-hairy. Rocks, screes and moraines, usually on acid rocks, 1300-3700m. July-Sept. A, CH, sD, seF, nI; Alps and northern Apennines. **6a Glacier Wormwood** *A. glacialis* has fls in small *rounded clusters;* florets hairless, 1900-3200m. swCH, seF, nwI; south-western Alps.

7 DARK ALPINE WORMWOOD *Artemisia atrata.* Short/med slightly hairy per, not aromatic. Lvs *green,* 2-3-pinnately-lobed, fern-like, *dotted with glands.* Flheads greenish-yellow, 3-4mm, in slender branched or unbranched spikes, florets hairy at the top. Dry grassy and stony places, on acid soils, 1800-2400m. July-Aug. wF, nI, nwYU; always very local. **7a Norwegian Wormwood** *A. norvegica* has *fewer than* 10 flheads to a spike, each long-stalked and slightly nodding, 8-10mm. To 1900m. nwGB, cN.

8 PYRENEAN WORMWOOD *Artemisia herba-alba* (= *A. aragonensis*). Short/ med, grey-downy aromatic per, stem *branched from the base.* Lvs *small,* pinnately-lobed, short stalked or stalkless. Flheads yellowish, 2.5-3mm, in branched spikes, florets hairless. Rocky places, to 2000m. July-Aug. sF, n & cE; local.

9 FIELD WORMWOOD *Artemisia campestris.* Variable short/tall, slightly aromatic, tufted per; stems *hairless, brownish-red.* Lvs 2-3-pinnately-lobed, silvery-hairy when young, but becoming hairless, the lowest stalked. Flheads yellowish or reddish, 1.5-4mm, in wide-branched spikes. Waste places, often sandy, to 2000m. Aug-Sept. T, except Faeroes, IRL, IS. **9a** *A.c.* subsp. *alpina* is shorter with *narrow* fl clusters, 1000-2000m. A, CH, sD, eF, nI, nwYU; local. **9b Arctic Wormwood** *A.c.* subsp. *borealis* (= *A. borealis*) is shorter than 9a, seldom reaching 25cm tall and with larger flheads, 5-8mm. Dry rocky ridges and screes, 1500-2800m. A, CH, sD, eF, nI, nwYU.

Daisy Family *(contd.)*

1 COLTSFOOT *Tussilago farfara.* Low/short creeping, downy per. Lvs all basal, round-heart.shaped with pointed teeth, stalked, *white-downy beneath,* green above. Flheads bright yellow, *short-rayed,* solitary on stems covered with *purplish scales,* often before the lvs. Fr a white 'clock'. Bare and waste ground, fields and banks, to 2800m. Feb-Aug. T.

2 ALPINE COLTSFOOT *Homogyne alpina.* Low/short creeping per with erect stems. Lvs mostly basal, kidney-shaped, blunt-toothed, long-stalked, *dark-shiny-green above,* pale or purplish and hairy beneath; stem lvs bract-like. Flheads reddish-purple or violet, *rayless,* goblet-shaped, 10-15mm, solitary. Damp meadows, open woods, streamsides, to 3000m. May-Aug. A, CH, CS, D, nE, c, s & eF, n & cI, PL, R, YU (GB). **2a** *H. discolor* has lvs white-woolly *beneath.* A, seD, neI, nwYU. **2b** *H. sylvestris* has *shallowly lobed* lvs. eA, neI, nwYU; south-eastern Alps.

3 WHITE BUTTERBUR *Petasites albus* (= *Tussilago alba*). Low/short, patch-forming, downy per; stems scaly. Basal lvs round-heart-shaped, regularly lobed and toothed, *white-downy* beneath, long-stalked. Flheads yellowish-white, rayless, brush-like, in dense rounded clusters; flbracts pale green. Damp meadows, woods, streamsides and gullies, to 2200m. T, except B, IRL, IS, nN, NL, nS, SF (Faeroes, GB). **3a Alpine Butterbur** *P. paradoxus* (= *P. niveus, Tussilago nivea*) has triangular, heart-shaped lvs; flheads purplish-lilac with *reddish flbracts.* Damp places on limestone, to 2500m. A, nE, s & eF, nI, R, nw & wYU. **3b Butterbur** *P. hybridus* like 3 but flheads pale lilac-pink or yellowish, not *fragrant.* To 1800m. T, except Faeroes, IS (DK, N, S, SF). **3c** *P. frigidus* like 3 but with smaller lvs, irregularly toothed or lobed, and smaller flheads. To 1759m. June. N, S, SF.

4 ADENOSTYLES *Adenostyles alliariae.* Med/tall downy per. Lower lvs triangular heart-shaped to kidney-shaped, coarsely toothed, long-stalked, *downy but green beneath;* upper lvs much smaller, clasping stem. Flheads small, reddish.purple, rayless, 6-8mm long, in dense branched clusters; 3-4 florets to each flhead. Woods, streamsides, scrub and damp rocky places, to 2700m. July-Aug. A,CH,CS, sD, E, c & sF, I, PL, R, YU. **4a** *A.a.* subsp. *hybrida* (= *A. pyrenaica*) has larger flheads, each with 12-15 florets. nE, s & seF, nI, R, YU. **4b** *A. alpina* (= *A. glabra*) is smaller with *kidney-shaped* lvs, hairless or almost so beneath. To 2500m. A, CH, sD, eF, I, nwYU; Alp, Jura and Apennines. **4c** *A. leucophylla* (= *A. tomentosa*) like 4a but shorter, stems and lvs white-woolly, upper lvs stalked. 1900-3100m. A, CH, eF, nI; Alps.

5 YELLOW OX-EYE *Buphthalmum salicifolium* (= *B. grandiflorum*). Short/med softly hairy per, stems branched in the upper half. Lvs oblong to narrow lance-shaped, slightly toothed or untoothed, the lower stalked. Flheads bright yellow, 30-50mm, long-rayed. Damp and stony places, woods, to 2050m. June-July. A, CH, CS, sD, e & seF, H, nI, w & nwYU.

6 ARNICA *Arnica montana.* Short/med downy per, aromatic. Lvs mostly in *basal rosettes* elliptical to oblong, usually broadest above the middle, untoothed; stem lvs few, bract-like, opposite. Flheads large, yellow, 4.5-8cm, long-rayed, usually solitary. Meadows and open woods, to 2850m. T, except Faeroes, GB, c & sI, IRL, IS, nN, nS, SF. May-Aug. **6a** *A. angustifolia* subsp. *alpina* is shorter with smaller fls, 3.5-4.5cm; stem lvs *in pairs.* nN, nS, nSF; Arctic Europe.

7 AUSTRIAN LEOPARDSBANE *Doronicum austriacum.* Med/tall, patch- forming, hairy per. Basal lvs oval-heart-shaped, slightly toothed, stalked; stem lvs clasping, the *lower stalked as* well. Flheads 5-6cm, in *branched clusters* of 5-12. Shady meadows, woods and streamsides, to 2000m. July-Aug. A, CS, D, nE, c & sF, H, nI, PL, R, YU. **7a Leopardsbane** *D. pardalianches* is more hairy, the lower stem lvs stalked, *not clasping.* B (rare), sD, E, F, NL (rare), I (A, CS, GB). **7b** *D. cataractarum* is more robust than 7a but basal lvs hairless or almost so; flheads 4-7cm. A; Koralpe.

8 LARGE FLOWERED LEOPARDSBANE *Doronicum grandiflorum* (= *D. scorpioides*). Low/short slightly hairy per. Basal lvs oval, *narrowed into* the long stalk, toothed; upper lvs lance-shaped, clasping stem. Flheads *solitary,* 3.5-6.5cm; ray florets with a pappus. Stony meadows, rocks and screes, 1300-2900m. July-Aug. A, CH, sD, s & eF, I, YU. **8a** *D. plantagineum* is taller, the ray florets *without* a pappus at the base. Woods. E, F, I (GB, NL). **8b** *D. clusii* has *elliptical,* not oval, basal lvs, densely hairy. A, CH, CS, nE, s & eF, nI, PL, R, YU

9 HEART-LEAVED LEOPARDSBANE *Doronicum columnae.* Short/med patch-forming, hairless or slightly hairy per. Lvs mostly basal, triangular-heart-shaped, stalked, toothed, stem lvs stalkless, clasping. Flheads solitary, 2.5-5cm. Stony places, open woods and scrub, to 2300m. May-Aug. A, seD, I, R, YU. **9a** *D. carpetanum* has the lower stem lvs stalked and *clasping;* flheads solitary or 2-3 together. n & cE.

Daisy Family *(contd.)*

GROUNDSELS or RAGWORTS *Senecio.* Perennials, sometimes annuals with alternate lvs. Flheads, usually with ray florets. A large and difficult group.

1 SOUTHERN RAGWORT *Senecio ovirense.* Variable short/tall grey-downy or greenish per. Basal lvs erect, oval to lance-shaped, *coarsely-toothed,* with broad-winged stalks, withered at flowering time. Flheads *large,* yellow or golden-yellow, 30-40mm, in flat-topped clusters of 3-15, each with 18-21 rays. Damp or shady places, to 2500m. May-July. A, CH, sD, nE, s & eF, H, n & cl, YU **1a S.** *helenites* has lvs untoothed or only slightly so and *smaller* flheads, 20-25 mm. A, B, CH, sD, nE F. **1b S.** *rivularis* like 7 but with *heart-shaped* lvs, the upper half-clasping the stem. s,e,seA. **1c** *S. balbisianus* is stouter than 7 but with broad oval or oblong lvs, the uppermost clasping the stem. seF, nwl; south-western Alps.

2 PINNATE-LEAVED RAGWORT Senecio *abrotanifolius.* Short slightly hairy per. Lvs *2-3-pinnately-lobed,* stalked. Flheads orange-yellow with *brown stripes,* 25-40mm, with 10-12 rays. Rocky slopes, to 2700mm. July-Sept. A, CH, CS, sD, nl, PL, R, nwYU; mainly Alps and Carpathians. **2a** *S. adonidifolius* has *small* yellow flheads, 10-16mm, in dense clusters, each with 3-6 rays. Acid rocks. neE, c, s & eF. **2b Rock Ragwort** S. *squalidus* (= S. *rupestris*). Variable short/med downy or almost hairless ann/bien/per. Lower lvs *pinnately-lobed,* with a broad-winged stalk; upper lvs clasping the stem. Fl heads bright yellow, 15-25mm, each with 10-13 rays; flbracts sometimes black-tipped. Open stony or sandy ground, waste places, to 2300m. A, CH, CS, sD, I, R, YU (DK, F, GB, IRL, H).

3 TOURNEFORT'S RAGWORT *Senecio pyrenaicus* (= *S. tournefortii*). Short/med hairless or slightly hairy per. Lvs crowded in middle of stem, oblong to narrow lance-shaped, lower short-stalked. Flheads yellow, 25-40mm, in flat-topped clusters, *each with* 10-16 rays. Grassy and rocky places, 1300-2000m. July-Aug. E, sF.

4 CHAMOIS RAGWORT *Senecio doronicum.* Variable short/med somewhat hairy per. Lvs elliptical to oval, toothed, stalked, *white-downy beneath.* Flheads large, deep yellow or orange-yellow, 30-60mm, solitary or 2-4, each with 10-22 rays. Grassy and rocky places, often on limestone, to 3100m. July-Aug. A, CH, sD, E, c & sF, I, R, YU. **5a** *S. scopolii* (= S. *lanatus*) has *always solitary,* pale yellow flheads. I, YU.

5 FIELD FLEAWORT *Senecio integrifolius.* Variable short/tall per, greyish- or white-downy at first. Lvs mostly in *flat basal rosettes,* oval to almost rounded, stalked, often untoothed. Flheads yellow or golden-yellow, 15-25mm, in flat-topped clusters of 3-15, each with 12-15 rays. Dry grassy places, to 2200m. May-June. T, except B, E, Faeroes, IRL, IS, NL.

6 ALPINE RAGWORT *Senecio cordatus* (= *S. alpinus*). Med/tall hairless per. Lvs *heart-shaped,* often lobed at the base, coarsely-toothed, stalked, greyish-hairy beneath; upper lvs smaller. Flheads yellow or orange-yellow, 25-40mm, in flat-topped clusters, each with 12-21 rays. Meadows, open woods and damp places, to 2150m. July-Sept. A, CH, sD, eF, n & cl; Alps and northern and central Apennines. **7a** *S. subalpinus* has lvs green beneath, the *upper* pinnately-lobed. A, CS, seD, PL, R.

7 GREY ALPINE GROUNDSEL *Senecio incanus.* Low/short grey- or silvery-white downy per. Lvs broadly oval in outline, long-stalked, pinnately-lobed. Flheads deep yellow, 10-l3mm, in *dense clusters* of 4-10 usually, each with 3-8 rays. Pastures and rocky places on acid soils, 1700-3500m. July-Sept. sCH, swF, nl; southern and south-western Alps and northern Apennines. **7a** *S.i.* subsp. *carniolicus* has narrower basal Lvs than *1, broadest above* the middle. eA. **7b** *S. persoonii* has *lance-shaped* segments to the lower lvs. nel; Maritime Alps. **7c** *S. leucophyllus* is more robust than 7 with larger flheads in clusters of 10 or more, *with 10-16* rays to each flhead. Screes, 1500-2700m. neE, sF; eastern Pyrenees and mountains of central-southern France.

8 ONE-FLOWERED ALPINE GROUNDSEL *Senecio halleri* (= *S. uniflorus*). Low *silvery-white* downy per. Basal lvs oblong, deeply toothed, long-stalked. Fl heads orange-yellow, 20-25mm, *solitary,* with 10-16 rays. Pastures and rocky places on acid soils, 1900-3600m. July-Sept. s & swCH, seF, nl; southern and south-western Alps.

9 WOOD RAGWORT *Senecio nemorensis.* Med/tall densely leafy per. Lvs oval to lance-shaped, upper clasping. Flheads 15-25mm, in loose flat-topped clusters; fl bracts often black-tipped. Damp meadows and woods, to 2200m. July-Sept. B, CH,CS, D, H, nl, NL, PL, R, Yu (sS). **9a** *S.n.* subsp. *fuchsii* is often purple-tinged, the upper lvs short-stalked, not clasping stem. A, CH, E, sF, I, Yu.

Daisy Family *(contd.)*

CARLINE THISTLES *Carlina*. Biennials or perennials with spiny lvs. Flheads large with spiny leaf-like outer bracts and narrow pointed silvery or yellowish inner ones, surrounding a disc of many tubular florets. Flheads closing in bad weather.

1 STEMLESS CARLINE THISTLE *Carlina acaulis*. Low bien/per, stemless. Lvs in a flat rosette, pinnately-cut, spiny, often slightly downy beneath. Flheads solitary, 5-10cm, with *conspicuous* wide-spreading silvery or pinkish inner bracts; disc whitish or purplish-brown. Stony meadows, rocky slopes and open woods, to 2800m. July-Sept. A, CH, CS, sD, n & cE, c & sF, H, I, PL, R, YU. **1a** *C.a.* subsp. *simplex* has a stem up to 60cm *carrying up to 6* flheads. Similar distribution.

2 ACANTHUS-LEAVED CARLINE THISTLE *Carlina acanthifolia*. Low stemless per ratherlike 1 but with broader lvs, *white-velvety beneath*. Flheads solitary, 12-15cm, with wide-spreading, straw-coloured inner bracts; disc lilac. Meadows and stony places, usually on limestone, to 1800m. July-Sept. E, c & sF, I, PL, R, YU. **2a** *C.a.* subsp. *cynara* has narrower lvs and clear-yellow inner flbracts. nE, sF, nI; Pyrenees and northern Apennines.

3 COMMON CARLINE THISTLE *Carlina vulgaris*. Short/med erect per. Lvs short, narrow oblong or oval, spine-toothed, the lower often woolly, *not in* a basal rosette. Flheads *small*, 2-4cm, with straw-coloured inner bracts; solitary or in groups of 2-3. Grassy and stony places, open woods, to 1750m. July-Sept. T, except Faeroes, IS, nN, nS.

4 JURINEA *Jurinea mollis*. Med/tall grey-hairy per, stems unbranched, lower lvs pinnately-lobed with wavy or rolled-under edges; upper lvs often unlobed, linear-lance-shaped. Flheads purple, 2-4.5mm, solitary or several together, all florets tubular; flbracts with a recurved purple tip. Dry grassy and stony places, to 2900m. May-Aug. A, CS, H, nI, nwYU; Alps mainly. **4a** *J. m.* subsp. *moschata* has a leafy much-branched stem; flheads 5 or more together. I; Apennines. **4b** *J. m.* subsp. *transylvanica* is like 4 but lvs and bracts hairless. cR. **4c** *J. humilis* (= *J. bocconi*) is low with stems not exceeding 4cm; flheads reddish-pink, 20-25mm, solitary, *in middle* of a leafy rosette. Dry limestone slopes. June-Aug. E, sF; Pyrenees and Cordillera Cantabrica mainly.

SAUSSUREAS *Saussurea*. Non-spiny perennials. Flheads solitary or clustered, brush-like, rayless; stamens projecting conspicuously.

5 DWARF SAUSSUREA *Saussurea pygmaea* (= *Carduus* or *Cnicus pygmaeus*). Low leafy, tufted, downy per. Lvs linear to narrow-lance-shaped, pointed, usually tufted. Fl heads solitary, violet-purple, 2~35mm. Rocks and screes, usually on limestone, 1800-2550m. July-Aug. A, sD, nI, nwYU, PL; eastern Alps and western Carpathians.

6 ALPINE SAUSSUREA *Saussurea alpina* (= *Serratula alpina*). Short/med erect tufted per; stems often downy. Lvs oval to broad-lance-shaped, narrowed at base, the lower stalked, toothed or untoothed, green above, grey-downy beneath. Flheads closely clustered, purple, 10-l5mm. Meadows, rocky places and screes, 1500-3000m. July-Sept. A, CS, CH, D, nE, F, IRL, I, N, PL, R, S, YU. **6a** *S. a.* subsp. *macrophylla* has *rounded* lvs, not narrowed at the base. eA, neI, nwYU; eastern Alps. **6b** *S. a.* subsp. *depressa* is a *dwarf form* not more than 8cm tall, with lvs grey-hairy above. A, CH, sD, eF, nI, nwYU; Alps.

7 HEART-LEAVED SAUSSUREA *Saussurea discolor* (= *S. lapathifolia* and *Serratula discolor*). Short, erect, downy per. Lvs triangular-lance-shaped, *rounded or heart-shaped* at base, toothed, stalked, green above, white-downy beneath, the upper lvs narrower and clasping the stem. Flheads clustered, bluish- violet, 12-l8mm, fragrant. Rocks and stony places, often on granite, 1400-2800m. July-Sept. A, CH, CS, sD, nI, R, nwYU.

8 STEMLESS COTTON-THISTLE *Onopordum acaulon*. Low stemless bien, greyish or white-woolly. Lvs in a rosette, lance-shaped to elliptical, lobed and spiny-toothed, long-stalked. Flheads white, rayless, 40-60mm, surrounded by numerous narrow spine-tipped bracts, solitary or up to 6 in a cluster. Dry grassland and rocky places, to 1900m. July-Aug. E, sF; Pyrenees, Spanish mountains and Corbieres. **8a** *O. rotundifolium* (= *Berardia subacaulis*) has more rounded, *non-spiny*, scarcely toothed lvs, and solitary whitish or lilac flheads surrounded by long cottony flbracts. Stony places, screes, 1500-2500m. seF, nwI; south-western Alps.

9 COTTON-THISTLE *Onopordum acanthium*. Tall white or greyish-downy bien; stems stout, spiny winged. Lvs oblong-oval to lance-shaped, spiny, stalkless. Flheads purple, sometimes white, 35-50mm, usually solitary. Flbracts numerous ending in yellowish spines. Bare dry and rocky places, to 1500m. July-Sept. T, except Faeroes, IRL, IS (DK, GB, sS). **9a** *O.a.* subsp. *gautieri* has flheads in clusters of 3-5, each 25-40mm across. nE, sF; central and eastern Pyrenees.

Daisy Family *(contd.)*

THISTLES Ca*rduus* and *Cirsium*. Perennials with spiny-winged stems and spine-edged, alternate, lvs. Flheads rayless, rounded and brush-like, often purplish, surrounded by an involucre of many bracts, often spine-tipped. Fr smooth with a feathery pappus in *Cirsium* and one of non-feathery hairs in *Carduus*.

1 MUSK THISTLE Ca*rduus nutans*. Variable med/tall per with *white-cotton* stems. Lvs pinnately-lobed, usually deeply so, with long or short spines. Fl heads bright red-purple, 20-45mm, solitary or clustered, slightly nodding, on spineless stalks; flbracts purplish. Grassy and waste places, to 2500m. June-Sept. A, B, CH, CS, D, E, GB, NL, I, YU (DK, sS).

2 APENNEAN THISTLE *Carduus chryascanthus*. Short/med per with white-cotton stems. Lvs pinnately-lobed, white-cottony beneath. Flheads purple, 30-50mm, borne on spiny stalks; flbracts hairy, long-spined, the lower usually recurved. Dry grassy and stony places, to 2300m. June-Aug. eE, c & sI.

3 GREAT MARSH THISTLE *Carduus personata*. Med/tall per, stems narrowly winged, short-spined. Lvs lance-shaped or oval, softly spiny, white-cottony beneath, the *upper undivided*. Flheads purple-red, 15-25mm, in *tight clusters;* flbracts narrow, not spine-tipped, the outer recurved. Damp meadows and woods, stream banks, to 2300m. July-Aug. A, CS, CH, sD, c & sI, n & cI, PL, R, YU.

4 ITALIAN THISTLE *Carduus litigiosus*. Med bien, stems broadly winged, white-cottony. Lvs pinnately-lobed, white-cottony above and beneath. Flheads purple, 20-30mm, borne in clusters of 2-5; flbracts white-hairy on edges, *not* recurved. Dry grassy and stony places to 1400m. May-July. seF, nI.

5 ALPINE THISTLE *Carduus defloratus*. Med/tall per, stems hairless or slightly white-hairy, wingless and lfless in the upper part. Lvs lance-shaped, more or less hairless, pinnately-lobed, spiny-toothed, Flheads purple to rose-purple, 20-30mm, solitary and *slightly nodding;* flbracts hairless, erect but the outer curled into an *S-shape*. Meadows, stony places and open woods, usually on lime, to 3000m. June-Oct. A, CS, CH, c & sD, H, nI, PL, R, YU; Pyrenean plant is often called C. *medius*.

6 CARLINE-LEAVED THISTLE *Carduus carlinifolius*. Variable low/tall per, stems hairless or white-hairy, *strongly branched* in the upper part, wingless and spineless at top. Lvs thick, pinnately-lobed, more or less hairless. Flheads purple, 20-30mm, usually solitary; flbracts more or less spiny, often recurved. Dry grassy and stony places, screes, to 2500m. June-Oct. CH, n & neE, s & eF, I.

7 WELTED THISTLE *Carduus acanthoides*. Tall bien to 1.5m, stems slightly white-hairy. Lvs pinnately-lobed, with long weak spines, hairless except on the veins beneath. Flheads red-purple, 20-25mm, solitary or clustered *on spiny stems;* flbracts erect or spreading, narrow, long-pointed. Grassy and waste places, hedgerows, to 3000m. June-Sept. T, except E, swF, Faeroes, IS (CH, N). **7a** C. *crispus* has short, narrowly-winged flstalks, up to 8cm long; flbracts all erect. To 1900m. T, except Faeroes, GB, IRL, IS and far north.

8 SOUTH-EASTERN THISTLE *Carduus carduelis*. Med/tall per, stems almost hairless, wingless and spineless at the top. Lvs pinnately-lobed, hairless above, but white-cottony beneath. Flheads purple, 15-30mm, solitary; flbracts slender, the outer curled into an S-shape. Meadows, to 3000m. June-Aug. eA, neI, nwYU; eastern Alps.

Thistledown

Daisy Family *(contd.)*

1 CORYMBOSE THISTLE *Carduus affinis.* Tall per, stems white cottony, with narrow wings. Lvs pinnately-lobed, long-spined, hairy beneath. Flheads purple, 10-25mm, in branched flat-topped *clusters;* flbracts linear, erect, pointed. Grassy places and woods, to 1850m. June-Aug. c & sl; central and southern Apennines.

2 PYRENEAN THISTLE *Carduus carlinoides* (= *C. pyrenaicus*). Short/med *white-downy* per; stems winged and very spiny up to the fls. Lvs pinnately-lobed long-spiny. Flheads rose-red or purplish, sometimes white, 18-25mm, *in tight clusters,* flbracts erect, spine-tipped. Grassy and stony places, screes, to 2200m. July-Sept. E, sF.

3 STEMLESS THISTLE *Cirsium acaule* (= *C. acaulon*). Low/short per, generally stemless but occasionally with a stem up to 15cm. Lvs in a flat rosette, pinnately-lobed. Flheads solitary, red-purple, 30-50mm; flbracts erect, closely overlapping. Dry grassy places, usually on calcareous soils, to 2550m. July-Sept. T, except Faeroes, nGB, IRL, IS, and far north.

4 WOOLLY THISTLE *Cirsium eriophorum.* Tall stout bien to 2m, stems unwinged, white-cottony. Lvs pinnately-lobed, very spiny, white-cottony beneath. Fl heads large red-purple, 40-70mm, *usually solitary;* flbracts spreading, mostly enveloped in white-cobwebby-wool. Grassy and waste places, scrub, on calcareous soils, to 2100m. July-Sept. T, except DK, Faeroes, nGB, IRL, sl, IS, N, S, SF. **4a.** *C. spathulatum* is shorter with slightly smaller flheads, the *flbracts* hairless or white hairy, *not woolly.* sw & sCH, seF, nI. **4b** *C. morisianum* has stems branched in the upper part. Lvs pinnately-lobed half clasping the stem, white-hairy beneath usually, with long spines. Flheads purple, 45-55mm; bracts white-hairy beneath usually, with long recurved spines, 10-30mm long. July-Sept. seF, I; south-western Alps and Apennines. **4c** *C. richteranum* is shorter than 4b, *never more* than 50cm, with crowded flheads in flat-topped clusters, flbract spines 4-8mm long. sF; northern Pyrenees and Corbieres.

5 MELANCHOLY THISTLE *Cirsium helenioides* (= *C. heterophyllum*). Med/tall per, spreading by underground runners; stems leafless towards the top, not winged, white-woolly. Lvs lance-shaped, pinnately-lobed or not, toothed, not *spiny,* white-woolly beneath. Flheads red-purple 30-50mm, solitary or in clusters of 2-4; flbracts erect. Damp meadows and woods, scrub, to 2350m. June-Aug. T, except B, E, Faeroes, sl, NL, YU (IS).

6 BROOK THISTLE *Cirsium rivulare.* Med/tall per, stems leafless above the middle, not winged. Lvs elliptical to oblong, usually pinnately-lobed, but often only at the base, weakly spiny, *green above and beneath.* Flheads purple, sometimes white, 25-30mm, solitary or in clusters of 2-5; flbracts erect. Damp grassy places, on acid soils, to 1750m.June-Aug. A, CH, CS, D, nE, s & eF, H, nI, PL, R, YU (S). **6a** *C. montanum* is taller with broader lvs and *spreading or recurved* flbracts. Damp woods and meadows, to 1500m. seF, n & cI, nYU; mainly southern Alps and Apennines.

7 WALDSTEIN'S THISTLE *Cirsium waldsteinii.* Med/tall per, stems unbranched, leafy to the top. Lvs oval, lobed or deeply toothed, the teeth weakly spiny, white-cottony beneath. Flheads purple, 25-35mm, in clusters of 3-8; flbracts erect but spreading out at tip. Damp and shady places, on acid soils, to 1650m. June-Aug. A, CS, PL, R, YU.

3

Daisy Family (contd.)

1 CARNIC THISTLE *Cirsium carniolicum*. Med/tall slightly branched per; stems with dense long *reddish-brown* hairs. Lvs *flat*, oval to elliptical, lobed and edged with weak spines. Flheads pale yellow, 17-21mm, in clusters of 2-7 or solitary, short stalked; flbracts spreading, weakly spiny. Grassy places and scrub, over limestone, to 1600m. A, neI, nwYU; eastern Alps. **1a** *C.c.* subsp. *rufescens* has slightly larger fl with *at least* 10 lvs immediately below (not 2-5). nE, sF; west and central Pyrenees.

2 PALE YELLOW PYRENEAN THISTLE *Cirsium glabrum*. Short/med per; stems short-hairy. Lvs hairless, oblong, narrowed at base, pinnately-lobed, *undulate, with stout spines*. Flheads pale yellow, 20-35mm, usually solitary, surrounded by lvs; flbracts erect to spreading, short spined. Damp screes and stream sides, to 3000m. July-Sept. nE, sF; Pyrenees.

3 SPINIEST THISTLE *Cirsium spinosissimum*. Rather like 2 but stems with long hairs. Lvs clasping the stem, usually hairy. Flheads pale yellow, 20-25mm, *in clusters* of 2-10, surrounded by long lvs; flbracts erect, long-spined. Damp meadows, stony places and screes, to 3100m. July-Sept. A, CH, sD, eF, n & cl, nwYU.

4 YELLOW MELANCHOLY THISTLE *Cirsium erisithales*. Med/tall per, usually branched, leafless in the *upper part*. Lvs dark green, pinnately-lobed, lobes toothed, scarcely spiny, clasping stem at base. Flheads lemon yellow, *nodding* 20-30mm, solitary or 2-5 clustered; flbracts erect, pointed. Meadows, woods and stony slopes, usually on limestone, to 2000m. July-Sept. A, CH, CS, c & eF, H, n & cl, PL, R, YU.

KNAPWEEDS or CORNFLOWERS *Centaurea*. Perennials, sometimes annuals, with alternate lvs. Flheads with an involucre of many overlapping flbracts, each bract terminated by a scale which may be toothed, spiny, feathery or scale-like; florets tubular surrounded by a ring of conspicuous sterile florets which are deeply lobed and appear 'star-like', as in the Common Cornflower.

5 SOUTH-EASTERN KNAPWEED *Centaurea dichroantha*. Short/med slightly branched per. Lvs green, *hairless*, pinnately-lobed, the lobes linear. Flheads yellow or purple; involucre 10-12mm across, the flbracts with a feathery reddish- brown appendage terminating in a fine spine. Grassy and rocky places on calcareous soils, to 1250m. July-Aug. neI, nwYU; south-eastern Alps.

6 ROCK KNAPWEED *Centaurea rupestris*. Low/med per. Lvs *hairy at first*, 1-2-pinnately-lobed, the lobes narrow, pointed. Flheads pale yellow or orange; involucre 12-15mm across, the flbracts with a feathery brown spine-tipped appendage. Dry meadows and rocky places, to 1100m. June-July. I, YU.

7 LEATHERY KNAPWEED *Centaurea grinensis*. Med/very tall, branched, hairy per. Lvs 1-2-pinnately-lobed, the lobes oblong or lance-shaped. Flheads purple, in *flat-topped clusters* usually; involucre 14-18mm across, the flbracts with a black, brown or yellowish feathery appendage. Dry grassy and rocky places, on calcareous soils, to 1400m. July-Aug. sA, sCH, nl, nwYU; southern Alps. **7a** *C. g.* subsp. *fritschii* is taller, to 2m; flbract appendages with 11-15 long teeth (not 7-11). sCS, H, R.

8 KNAPWEED *Centaurea alpestris*. Med generally unbranched per. Lvs pinnately-lobed, the lobes oval, blunt, toothed. Flheads purple; involucre 20mm across, flbracts *hidden* by their dark brown feathery, non-spiny, appendages. Dry grassy and rocky places, on calcareous soils, to 1600m. July-Aug. A, CS, CH, nE, s & eF, nl, PL, YU; not Apennines.

9 AUSTRIAN KNAPWEED *Centaurea badensis*. Med/tall hairless, unbranched per. Lvs shiny-green, pinnate, the lower with lance-shaped, untoothed lobes, the upper narrower. Flheads purple; involucre 15-18mm across, flbracts brown or black with white feathery appendages. Dry scrubby hillslopes on calcareous rocks, to 1800m. July-Aug. eA, seCS. **9a** *C. sadleriana* has inner flbracts with a white appendage with a *black centre* (not brown or yellow). eA, nH, seCS.

5, colour forms

Daisy Family *(contd.)*

1 ALPINE KNAPWEED *Centaurea alpina.* Short/med, erect, hairless per. Lvs pale green, pinnate, the lobes oblong-lance-shaped, toothed at the apex. Flheads pale yellow, solitary. Involucre 16-20mm across, the flbracts oval with an *oblong or rounded* scale. Woodland and scrub on calcareous soils to 1200m. July-Aug. seF, nI; southern Alps, local. Also in south-eastern Spain.

2 BLUISH KNAPWEED *Centaurea spinabadia.* Med erect bien. Lvs green or greyish-hairy, the lower 2-pinnately-lobed. Flheads purple, solitary. Involucre 10-12mm across, the flbracts with a feathery appendage terminating in a *short recurved spine.* Rocky slopes, usually calcareous, soils to 1100m. May-Aug. n & neE, sF.

3 PANICULATE KNAPWEED *Centaurea paniculata.* Variable med/tall erect, much branched, hairy bien. Lvs green, the lower 1-2-pinnately-lobed. Flheads purple, solitary or in clusters of 2-6. Involucre 3-6mm across, the flbracts with a feathery appendage terminating in a *short straight spine.* Dry grassy and rocky slopes, to 1800m. July-Sept. E, s & seF, I.

4 WHITISH-LEAVED KNAPWEED *Centaurea leucophaea.* Med much branched, hairy bien. Lower lvs pinnately-lobed, at first *whitish or greyish,* later green. Flheads pinkish-purple or lilac, in flat-topped clusters. Involucre 6-13mm across, the flbracts brown, sometimes spotted, or white-hairy, with a pale brown or yellow feathery appendage terminating in a short spine. Dry grassy and rocky slopes, to 1600m. July-Sept. neE, s & seF, nwI. **4a** *C. maculosa* has greenish hairy or hairless lvs and solitary purple flheads. A, Ch, sD, c & eF, nI; Alps mainly.

5 DOUBTFUL KNAPWEED *Centaurea nigrescens.* Very variable short/tall, erect, unbranched or few branched, hairy per. Lower lvs elliptical to lance-shaped or oval, untoothed, toothed or sometimes slightly lobed, the upper narrower, pinnately-lobed or unlobed. Flheads purple, solitary. Involucre 12-l5mm across, the flbracts green with a black or pale brown feathery triangular appendage. Meadows or open woods to 2200m. July-Aug. A, CH, CS, sD, eF, H, I, R, YU. **5a** *C. carniolica* has the lower lvs elliptical or rounded-oval and the upper oval to elliptical, often *partly clasping* the stem. Flheads pink, solitary or clustered. eA, neI, H, R, n & nwYU. **5b** *C. transalpina* is shorter and *more branched* than 5, with solitary or 2-4 clustered pinkish-orange or pink flheads; involucre 12-18mm across. sA, sCH, seF, nI; southern Alps.

6 WIG KNAPWEED *Centaurea phrygia.* Variable med/tall erect, branched or unbranched, hairy per. Lvs green, the lower lance-shaped to oval, toothed or untoothed, the upper ones rounded at base or clasping the stem. Flheads *purple,* solitary. Involucre l5-20mm across, the flbracts with feathery black or deep brown appendages. Meadows, woodland and scrubby places, to 2200m. July-Sept. A, CH, CS, D, DK, H, I, sN, PL, R, SF, YU (sS).

7 PLUME KNAPWEED *Centaurea uniflora.* Short/med, erect, generally unbranched, hairy per. Lvs green or greyish, the lower oblong-lance-shaped or elliptical, toothed, stalked, the upper clasping the stem. Flheads pale violet, *solitary.* Involucre 17-22mm across, the flbracts with a long feathery blackish-brown appendage. Dry meadows, scrub and rocky slopes, to 2600m. July-Aug. A, CH, eF. nI, R, YU; Alps, northern Apennines and southern Carpathians.

8 RHAETIAN KNAPWEED *Centaurea rhaetica.* Short/med, more or less erect, unbranched or few-branched, hairy per. Lvs green, oblong or linear-lance-shaped, toothed or untoothed, the upper almost clasping the stem. Flheads pink-purple, solitary. Involucre 14-20mm across, the flbracts with feathery blackish-brown appendages. Meadows and open woodland, often on calcareous soils, to 2200m. July-Aug. sCH, nI; southern Alps. **8a** *C. procumbens* is shorter, the lower lvs broader, *often* slightly lobed, rather greyish or whitish-hairy. Dry calcareous rocks, to l200m. seF; south-western Alps.

9 MOUNTAIN CORN FLOWER *Centaurea montana.* Variable, short/tall, more or less erect, hairy per with *broadly winged* stems. Lvs greyish, oblong or lance-shaped, untoothed, sometimes slightly toothed. Flheads with blue outer florets and violet inner ones, solitary. Involucre 10-15mm across, the flbracts with a short dark brown comb-like appendage. Meadows and open woods, often on calcareous soils, to 2100m. May-July. A, B, CH, CS, sD, nE, F, n & cl, PL, YU (GB, SF). **9a** *C. triumfetti* has narrowly-winged stems and greener *linear-lance-shaped* lvs. Stony pastures and rocks. A, CH, CS, sD, E, s & eF, H, I, Pl, R, YU. **9b** *C. pinnatifida* is seldom more than 20cm tall with greyish-hairy lvs and violet fls. Alpine meadows. R; southern and eastern Carpathians. The common **Cornflower,** *C. cyanus,* is a greyish-downy *ann* with pinnately-lobed or unlobed lvs. Common cornfield weed to l800m. T, except the far north, but often local or casual.

The genus Centaurea is a large and complicated one with at least 220 species in Europe alone, many in the Mediterranean region. Characters of distinction are not always clear cut but a combination of flower and leaf characters are important diagnostic clues to correct identity. Especially important are the characters of the flower (involucral) bracts which surround the flower heads; these may be simple and fairly plain or more complicated with toothed or feathered apical appendages or wings in pale or dark colours. The accompanying drawings highlight some of these distinctions. The flower bracts are taken from the middle rows of the involucre.

Other important mountain *Centaurea* species found in the region

C. alpestris is a med per with simple or slightly branched stems and pinnately-lobed lvs. Flheads purple with the outer florets longer than the inner; flbracts with a dark brown cut appendage that *completely hides* the bract. A, CH, CS, s & eF, nl, PL, neYU; Pyrenees, Alps, Jura and western Carpathians.

C. atropurpurea a tall per to 150cm; stems somewhat branched and basal lvs pinnately-lobed. Flheads *dark purple*, occasionally yellow, the outer florets only very slightly longer than the inner; flbracts with a black appendage with white teeth, completely hiding the bract. Rocky mountain slopes. R, n & neYU.

C. jacea is a med/tall per with simple or branched stems that are thickened below each flhead. Lvs rough with hairs, the basal lance-shaped pinnately-lobed or undivided. Flheads purple, occasionally white, borne in flat-topped clusters; flbracts with a rounded, pale brown, toothed appendage that hides the bract. Grassy places and open woodland, scrub, sometimes exceeding 1200m. T, except Faeroes, IRL, IS. (GB).

C. kotschyana is like the last species but a shorter plant to 100cm with simple unbranched stems, with the basal lvs simple, *not divided*. R, nYu; mainly in the eastern Carpathians.

C. mollis is like *C. montana* but rarely more than 45cm tall, the stems *scarcely winged or unwinged* and lvs stiffer green above and grey beneath. Flheads violet with the inner florets blue. Mountain meadows. CS, H, PL, R, YU.

C. sadlerana is like the last but a taller plant to 120cm, the flbracts with a black appendage with *white teeth*. Dry hill slopes and shrubberies. eA, seCS, nH.

Centaurea flower bracts, scale all x 4

The flower bracts are very varied in this genus and their various shapes can be useful in accurate identification. Especially important are the various appendages which range from a serrated edge to a comb- or scale-like structures in pale or dark colours. The drawings opposite are of bracts taken from the middle series of the involucre.

1 *C. dichroantha*, p. 308
2 *C. rupestris*, p. 308
3 *C. alpestris*, p. 308
4 *C. alpina*, p. 310
5 *C. badensis*, p. 308
6 *C. paniculata*, p. 310
7 *C. maculosa*, p. 310

8 *C. transalpina*, p. 310
9 *C. nigrescens*, p. 310
10 *C. montana*, p. 310
11 *C. triumfetti*, p. 310
12 *C. cyanus*, p. 310
13 *C. procumbens*, p. 310
14 *C. uniflora*, p. 310

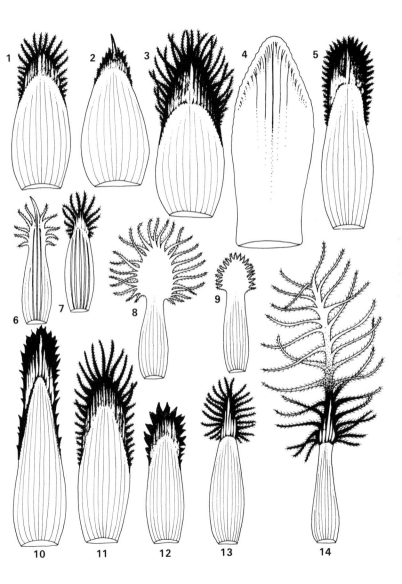

Daisy Family (contd.)

Species 1-4 have thistle-like flheads; 5-9 have dandelion-like flheads, opening in fine weather.

1 SAWWORT *Serratula tinctoria.* Slender short/tall, slightly branched, hairless per, thistle-like but *spineless.* Lvs pinnately-lobed, finely toothed; upper lvs often linear, unlobed. Flheads rayless, purple or whitish, 15-20mm long, short-stalked, *in clusters;* involucre oblong with purplish flbracts. Damp grassy and stony places, open woods and scrub, 1800-2400m. July-Oct. T, except Faeroes, c & sl, IS, nN, nS, SF.

2 SINGLE-FLOWERED SAWWORT *Serratula lycopifolia* (= *Caduus lycopifolius*). Med/tall per, stem usually hairless. Lvs rough-hairy, the lower oval, deeply-toothed, long-stalked; upper lvs pinnately-lobed, stalkless. Flheads *solitary,* purple, 25-40mm long; involucre globular. Meadows and scrub, to 1800m. June- July. A, CS, seF, H, R, YU. **2a** *S. nudicaulis* has most or all lvs in a *basal rosette.* wCH, E, s & eF, I.

3 CARDOON KNAPWEED *Leuzea centauroides* (=*Rhaponticum centauroides*). Tall stout downy per. Lvs pinnately-lobed, toothed, the upper smaller, stalkless, all green above, white-downy beneath. Flheads large, rayless, purple, 50-60mm, brush-like, solitary; flbracts brown, *narrow lance-shaped,* toothed. Meadows and rocky places, to 2000m. Aug-Sept. nE, sF; Pyrenees.

4 GIANT KNAPWEED *Leuzea rhapontica* (= *Rhaponticum scariosum*). Med downy per. Lvs lance-shaped to oval, toothed, stalked, green above, grey-downy beneath. Flheads large, rayless, rose-purple, 60-70mm, solitary; flbracts oval, pointed, hairy-margined. Damp meadows and rocks, on acid soils, 1400-2600m. July-Sept. wA, CH, seF, nI; southwestern and central Alps. **4a** *L.r.* subsp. *heleniifolia* (*P.s.* subsp. *lyratum*) is taller with larger flheads, the lvs *with* a lobe *on each side* at base, white-downy beneath; flbracts blunt. Limestone rocks, 1400-2200m. A, CH, eF, nI, nwYU; Alps. **4b** *L.r.* subsp. *bicknellii* like 4a, but flheads very large, 90-120mm and *stems leafy* to *top,* the basal ones pinnately-lobed. seF, nwI; Maritime Alps and Ligurian Apennines.

5 PURPLE LETTUCE *Prenanthes purpurea.* Short/tall hairless, blue-green per. Lvs elliptical-oblong or fiddle-shaped, toothed, *clasping* the stem. Flheads violet or purplish, 10-20mm long, with 3-6 ray florets; in open, long-stalked, *slightly drooping,* clusters. Woods shady places and streamsides, to 2050m. July-Sept. A, CH, CS, sD, E, c & sF, H, I, PL, R, YU.

6 ALPINE SOW-THISTLE *Cicerbita alpina* (= *Sonchus alpinus, Lactuca alpina*). Med/tall per with milky juice, usually unbranched; stems *reddish-hairy.* Lvs hairless, the lowest pinnately-lobed with a large triangular end lflet; upper lvs smaller, clasping stem. Flheads pale blue or mauvish, 20-28mm, in leafy clusters. Grassy and rocky places, open woods, to 2200m. July-Sept. T, except Faeroes, c & sl, IRL, IS, NL. **6a** *C. plumieri* (= *Sonchus plumieri, Lactuca plumieri*) is hairless. CH, sD, nE, F (GB).

7 MOUNTAIN or BLUE LETTUCE *Lactuca perennis.* Med/tall hairless per with milky juice and branched stems. Lvs grey-green, pinnately-lobed, segments toothed or not, the upper lvs clasping the stem, lower short-stalked. Flheads blue or lilac, 30-40mm, long-stalked, in loose clusters. Open stony and grassy places, on limestone, to 2100m. May-Aug. A, B, CH, CS, D, E, F, H, I, R, YU. **7a** *L. quercina* is ann/bien with less cut, *lyre-shaped lvs* and yellow *flheads.* Woods and scrub. A, CS, D, eF, H, nI, R, sSYU. **7b Edible Lettuce** *L.* sativa is cultivated extensively in the area, to 2500m.

8 GIANT CATSEAR *Hypochoeris uniflora.* Stout short/med roughly hairy per. Lvs pale green mostly basal, lance-shaped, not lobed, toothed; stem lvs smaller. Flheads *yellow,* 40-50mm, solitary on stout stems *swollen at the top;* pappus with one row of hairs. Meadows and open woods, on acid soils, to 2600m. July-Sept. A, CH, CS, sD, I, PL, R, YU. **8a Spotted Catsear** *H. maculata* has slightly branched stems with scale-like lvs. Basal lvs slightly lobed, *purple-black spotted.* Grassy places on calcareous soils, to 1800m. T, except Faeroes, IRL, IS, nN, nS. **8b** *H. radicata* like 8a but lvs more deeply lobed, *unspotted.* To 1800m. T, except Faeroes, IS, SF.

9 CALYCOCORSUS *Calycocorsus* (= *Willemetia*) *stipitatus.* Low/med per, stems densely dark-hairy. Lvs mostly basal, oval or oblong, broadest above the middle, toothed; stem lvs 1-2, linear, or absent. Flheads yellow, 11-14mm, solitary or in clusters of 2-5; flbracts linear, pointed. Wet grassy places, to 2450m. July-Sept. A, CH, CS, sD, s & eF, I, YU.

Daisy Family (contd.)

All species on this page have Dandelion-like flheads (without disc florets).

1 APOSERIS *Aposeris foetida.* Short slender, slightly hairy per; juice foetid. Lvs *all basal*, pinnately-lobed, the lobes rhombic with 1-2 teeth on the *lower margin.* Flheads yellow, 25-30mm, with few florets; pappus absent. Damp meadows, woods and river banks, often on lime, to 2000m. May-Aug. A, CH, CS, sD, seF, nl, PL, R, nw & cYU.

2 BEARDED VIPER'S-GRASS *Scorzonera aristata.* Short/med, slightly hairy, tuberous-rooted, per with leafless stems. Lvs *linear to narrow lance-shaped,* pointed, usually untoothed. Flhead solitary, golden-yellow, 20-40mm, the florets much longer than the sepal-like flbracts. Meadows and grassy places, on limestone, to 2300m. July-Aug. A, nE, s & eF, n& cl, nwYU. **2a. Austrian Viper's-grass** *S. austriaca* has stems with *3-6 scale-like lvs* and pale yellow fls. To 2800m. A, CH, CS, sD, c & eF, H, I, R, YU. **2b** *S. humilis* is like 2a but lower stem lvs *like the basal,* upper scale-like. To 1700m. A, B, CS, CH, D, E, GB (rare), H, I, N, NL, PL, R, sS, YU. **2c** *S. purpurea* has pale lilac or purplish-pink *fls.* Damp and shady places. A, CS, c & sD, eF, H, n &cl, PL, R, YU.

3 GOATSBEARD *Tragopogon pratensis.* Med hairless ann/per. Lvs linear, grass-like, *clasping* stem. Flheads golden-yellow, 40-60mm, opening fully on sunny mornings; flbracts often longer than florets; pappus making a large 'clock'. Meadows and grassy places, to 2600m. May-Aug. T, except Faeroes, IS and far north. **3a** *T. dubius* is taller, the *stems swollen* just below the flheads. To 2150m. A, CH, CS, D, E, F, H, I, R, YU (B).

4 TOLPIS *Tolpis staticifolia* (= *Hieracium staticifolium*). Short/med, almost hairless per. Basal lvs linear to linear-lance-shaped, usually untoothed; stem lvs few, linear. Flheads yellow, 15-25mm; inner florets often *purplish-brown;* flbracts linear to narrow-elliptical, *downy.* Rocky and stony places, usually on basic rocks, to 2500m. A, CH, sD, eF, H, nl, YU.

HAWKBITS *Leontodon* are rosette-leaved pers with solitary yellow flheads.

5 PYRENEAN HAWKBIT *Leontodon pyrenaicus.* Low/short, hairy per. Lvs narrow elliptical to oblong, broadest above the middle, untoothed, stalked; stem lvs small, bract-like. Fl heads 20-25mm, flbracts dark-hairy. Meadows, stony places and scrub, often on acid soils, to 3000m. June-Aug. nE, sF; Pyrenees. **5a Swiss Hawkbit** *L. p.* subsp. *helveticus* is larger in all its parts, to 50cm tall; flbracts white-hairy. A, CH, c & eF, nl, w & nw YU; Alps mainly. **5b Alpine Hawkbit** *L. hispidus* has *toothed or lobed* lvs. T, except Faeroes, IS.

6 MOUNTAIN HAWKBIT *Leontodon montanus.* (incl. *L. montaniformis*) Low hairy per. Lvs linear to oblong, lobed and toothed with a large end segment. Flhead 20-30mm; flbracts with *pale-grey* hairs. Rocky and stony meadows and gravels, often on limestone, to 2900m. July-Aug. A, CH, CS, sD, nE, s & eF, n & cl, PL, R, YU. **8a** *L. autumnalis* is larger with *branched stems* and deep yellow fls; florets red-striped on the outside.

HAWKWEEDS *Hieracium.* Perennials with milky juice and basal rosettes of lvs. Flheads solitary or grouped. Florets usually yellow, sometimes orange or red. A variable and difficult group with many local species.

7 DWARF HAWKWEED *Hieracium humile* agg. Low/short, dark green or blue-green per, *stiffly-hairy.* Basal lvs elliptical, oblong or lance-shaped, deeply- toothed, stalked; stem lvs usually few, small and bract-like. Flheads yellow, 15-25mm, in loose clusters of 4-12. Rocky and stony places, usually on limestone, to 2500m. June-Aug. A, CH, sD, E, F, I, YU. **8 ALPINE HAWKWEED** *Hieracium alpinum* agg. Low/short greenish per, shaggily-hairy. Basal lvs elliptical to oblong or spoon-shaped. Flheads yellow, 25-35mm, *usually solitary*; flbracts blackish. Grassy and rocky places, to 3000m. July-Aug. T, except B, E, Faeroes, IRL, NL. **8a** *H. arolae* agg. has larger stem lvs, similar to the basal and smaller flheads *in groups* of 2-10. A, CH, nl, R, YU. **8b Mouse-ear Hawkweed** *H. pilosella* is white-hairy; flheads soliatry, lemon-yellow, 20-30mm, on *long leafless stalks.* To 3000m. May-Oct. T, except Faeroes, IS and far north.

9 WOOLLY HAWKWEED *Hieracium lanatum.* Short/med per, densely *white-woolly.* Basal lvs oval-elliptical to lance-shaped, stalked. Flheads yellow, 20-30mm, in clusters of 2-8; flbracts white-hairy. Dry grassy and rocky places, to 2100m. May-July. wCH, seF, nwl.

10 ORANGE HAWKWEED or FOX AND CUBS *Hieracium aurantiacum* (= *Pilosells aurantiacum*) agg. Short/med, pale or bluish-green creeping per, very hairy. Lvs few,narrow oblong-lance-shaped; stems with dark blackish hairs and 1-4 lvs. Flheads orange-red, 15-20mm, in tight clusters of 2-8. Meadows and waste places, often on acid soils, to 2600m. June-Aug. T, except Faeroes, IRL, IS). **10a** *H. lactucella* agg. is sparsely hairy with *bluish-green* lvs. Flheads yellow, often red-striped on the outside, in clusters of 2-5. To 2600m. T, except Faeroes, IRL, IS and far north.

Daisy Family *(contd)*

HAWKSBEARDS *Crepis.* Perennials with lvs in basal rosettes and alternate up the stem. Flheads solitary or clustered, dandelion-like, the outer series of flbracts noticeably *shorter* than the inner and often spreading. Pappus white, sometimes yellowish.

1 MARSH HAWKSBEARD *Crepis paludosa.* Med/tall per, stems leafy, slightly hairy, branched above. Lvs *hairless,* lance-shaped, deeply and sharply toothed, the lower stalked; upper clasping the stem with *pointed* basal lobes. Flheads yellow or dull orange-yellow, 15-25mm, in lax flat-topped clusters; flbracts linear with sticky blackish hairs. Damp grassy places, streamsides, to 2150m. July-Sept. T, except Faeroes.

2 NORTHERN HAWKSBEARD *Crepis mollis.* Slender med/tall per, yellow-hairy or hairless. Lvs elliptical to oblong, toothed or not, stalk winged; upper lvs *clasping* the stem with rounded basal lobes. Flheads pale yellow, 20-30mm, few in a loose flat-topped cluster; flbracts linear with blackish or yellowish hairs. Woods and streamsides, to 1400m. July-Aug. A, CS, CH, D, neE, F, nGB, I, PL, R, YU. **2a** *C. lampsanoides* has *lyre-shaped* lower lvs; all lvs toothed. E, c & sF.

3 MOUNTAIN HAWKSBEARD *Crepis bocconi* (= *C. montana, C. pontana*). Short/med per; stem stout hairy. Lvs oblong, broadest above the middle, toothed, the lower with short winged-stalks, the upper *clasping the stem and* untoothed, all hairless except on the edges. Flheads yellow, 40-55mm, solitary; flbracts lance-shaped, green or yellowish hairy on both sides. Meadows, open woods and stony slopes, usually on limestone, 1100-2500m. June-Aug. A, CH, sD, eF, nI, YU. **3a** *C. conyzifolia* (=*grandiflora*) has finely *glandular-hairy* lvs, often more deeply toothed, and with up to 9 flheads on a stem branched above the middle. Meadows, to 3000m. A, CH, CS, sD, E, c & sF, I, PL, R, YU. **3b** *C. pyrenaica* is very variable, low/med, with a single or up to 5 flheads; flbracts *hairless on the inside.* To 2200m. A, CH, sD, n & neE, s & eF, nI, nwYU.

4 ALPINE HAWKSBEARD *Crepis alpestris.* Med hairy per. Lower lvs oblong, broadest above the middle, *deeply toothed to pinnately-lobed* with winged stalks; the upper lvs more or less clasping the stem. Flheads yellow, 20-30mm, *usually solitary;* flbracts lance-shaped, grey or yellowish-hairy. Meadows and stony places, usually on limestone, to 2650m. June-Sept. A, CH, CS, sD, eF, nI, R, YU.

5 PYRENEAN HAWKSBEARD *Crepis albida.* Variable low/short downy per. Lvs *mostly basal,* lance-shaped to oblong, toothed to pinnately-lobed. Flheads yellow, 25-45mm, *solitary or 2* together; flbracts white or yellowish-hairy. Rock crevices, cliffs, usually on limestone, to 2000m. June-Aug. E, s & seF, nwI; mainly Pyrenees and Maritime Alps.

6 PINK HAWKSBEARD *Crepis praemorsa* (= *C. incarnata*). Variable short/tall, hairy or almost hairless per. Lvs usually all in a *basal rosette,* lance-shaped or oblong-oval, broadest above the middle, narrowing into a short stalk. Flheads small, *yellow, pink or white,* 15-16mm, in loose, oblong clusters, the stem *branched near* the top. Dry meadows and stony places, usually on limestone, to 1600m. May-June. T, except B, E, Faeroes, GB, IRL, IS, nN, NL, nS.

7 PYGMY HAWKSBEARD *Crepis pygmaea.* Low/short downy per. Lvs often reddish, *not* in a basal rosette, elliptical to rounded, toothed, with a *wavy winged-stalk.* Flheads pale to golden yellow, 20-25mm, the outer rays often reddish-purple beneath, several on long stalks from the lf joints; flbracts lance-shaped, densely hairy. Damp calcareous rocks and screes, 1600-3000m. July-Aug. CH, E, s & seF, n & sl.

8 TRIGLAV HAWKSBEARD *Crepis terglouensis* agg. (incl. *C. jacquinii*). Low/short slightly hairy per. Lvs *mostly basal,* oblong to linear, pinnately-lobed or unlobed, often hairless. Flheads yellow, 20-45mm, usually solitary; flbracts narrow lance-shaped, *dark-hairy.* Stony places. screes, on limestone, 1500-1600m. July-Aug. A, eCH, sD, nI; central and eastern Alps. Often confused with *Leontodon montanus.* **8a** *C. rhaetica* is smaller with untoothed or slightly toothed lvs, usually hairy; stalks winged. Flheads solitary; flbracts oblong with long *yellowish-hairs.* Limestone rocks and screes, 1950-3000m. A, CH, eF, nI; west, central and southern Alps.

9 GOLDEN HAWKSBEARD *Crepis aurea.* Low/short, slightly hairy per. Lvs *all basal,* oblong. broadest above the middle, toothed or pinnately-lobed. Flheads yellow or orange. 20-30mm, usually solitary, on *long slender* stalks; flbracts lance-shaped. with dark green hairs. Meadows and stony places. often on acid soils, to 2800m. June-Sept. A, CH, sD, eF, nI, nwYU; Alps. **9a** *C.a.* subsp. *glabrescens* usually has *hairless* flbracts. I; Apuan Alps and Apennines.

1

2

3

4

5

6

7

8

9

Daisy Family (contd.)

DANDELIONS *Taraxacum*. Perennials with loose rosettes of rather fleshy lvs; juice milky. Flheads on hollow leafless stems, usually yellow, with ray florets only; flbracts in 2 rows, the outer shorter. Fr a typical 'clock'. A difficult and variable group with many microspecies – the more important montane species groups are described here.

1 *Taraxacum ceratophorum*. Short hairy per. Lvs large dark green, broad lance-shaped, 8-20cm, with large triangular lobes; stalk winged. Flheads 35-50mm on *hairy stems*, rays narrow yellow, striped red, brown or purple, flbracts oval to lance-shaped, green. Grassy and rocky meadows, banks, to 2650m. June-August. A, CH, eF, IS, N, S, SF.

2 MARSH DANDELION *Taraxacum palustre*. Low/short hairless or slightly hairy per. Lvs *linear to narrow lance-shaped*, 5-20cm, finely toothed or with narrow lobes; stalk long and slender, purplish often. Flheads 25-50mm on hairless purple stems, the rays pale yellow, sometimes striped grey or purple; flbracts oval, purple or violet flushed, with a membranous margin. Wet places, stream banks, to 2200m. Apr-Aug. T, except E, sF, Faeroes, IS. **2a Dark Dandelion** *Taraxacum nigricans* has lvs bright to pale green, spoon-shaped, 8-15cm, with variable, often toothed, lobes. Flheads 25-35mm, on slightly hairy stems, the rays dark to orange-yellow, striped grey or purple; flbracts lance-shaped, *dark violet-purple*. Grassy and rocky meadows, to 2200m. June-Sept. A, CH, CS, eF, sD, nI, PL, R, YU. **2a Brownish Dandelion** *T. cucullatum*. Like 2a but lvs larger, dark bright green. Flheads 30-45mm, on hairy stalks, *rays yellow-brown* fading white at edges, sometimes purple striped; flbracts oval-lance-shaped dark green, often flushed purple. Rocky and grassy meadows, to 2200m. June-Sept. A, CH, eF, nI; Alps.

3 ALPINE DANDELION *Taraxacum apenninum* (= *T. alpinum*). Very low, slightly hairy to white-downy per. Lvs in *flat rosettes*, soft, mid-green, lance-shaped, 3-10cm, lobed, or unlobed; stalks long, winged. Flheads 15-20mm, on delicate stems, rays yellow with a grey or brown stripe; flbracts narrow lance-shaped, green. Meadows, rocky debris and by snow patches, 1500-3350m. July-Sept. A, CH, CS, sD, E, s & eF, I, PL, R, YU.

4 BROAD-LEAVED DANDELION *Taraxacum fontanum*. Low/short hairy *per*. Lvs bright green, oval, unlobed or sometimes lobed and toothed; lfstalks widely winged. Flheads 25-35mm, on hairy stalks, rays long and narrow, orange-yellow, striped purplish-brown; flbracts lance-shaped, green with a paler edge. Grassy and rocky meadows, to 2500m. July-Sept. A, CH, CS, sD, eF, nI, PL, R, YU.

5 CUT-LEAVED DANDELION *Taraxacum dissectum*. Low/short per. Lvs numerous, mid to dark green, spoon-shaped, *much cut* into narrow, toothed, lobes, hairy beneath often; lf stalks short, narrow. Flheads 20-30mm, on slender *hairless* stalks, the rays pale yellow, striped grey or red. Rocky and grassy meadows, to 3100m. June-Aug. CH, E, sF, nI; west and central Alps and Pyrenees.

6 BRENNER DANDELION *Taraxacum pacheri*. Low slightly hairy per. Lvs thin, bright green, 3-5cm long, spoon-shaped with shallow blunt lobes. Flheads 20-30mm, the rays yellow, *striped brown or grey;* stems hairy just below flhead; flbracts oval to lance-shaped, black or dark green. Dry pastures and heaths, grassy places, 2000-2900m. July-Sept. A, CH, eF, nI; west and central Alps.

7 GLACIER DANDELION *Taraxacum glaciale*. Low hairless per. Lvs oblong or spoon-shaped, 3-7cm, unlobed to pinnately-lobed. Flheads small 10-15mm, the rays yellow, striped grey or red; flbracts linear, black. Meadows and rocky debris, to 2600m. I; Apennines.

8 *Taraxacum phymatocarpum*. Low *hairless* per. Lvs bright green, narrow spoon-shaped, 2-7cm, unlobed or with shallow triangular lobes. Flheads 15-25mm, rays white or yellow, striped grey, violet or purple; flbracts oval, greyish-green or blackish. A, CH, nN. **8a** *Taraxacum shroeterianum* is somewhat larger the lvs narrow spoon-shaped, 5-15cm, unlobed or shallowly lobed, untoothed, with *long reddish stalks*. Flheads 28-32mm, the rays *plain yellow;* flbracts oval, pointed greyish-green, often red tinged. Grassy meadows and marshes, to 2750m. July-Sept. CH, eF, nI.

9 HOPPE'S DANDELION *Taraxacum hoppeanum*. Short hairy per. Lvs dark olive-green, lance-shaped with long narrow pointed lobes, toothed towards top; stalk winged. Flheads large, 35-45mm, on hairy stalks *red flushed* in the upper part, rays bright yellow striped purple; flbracts oval-lance-shaped, dark green. Dry grassy and rocky places, to 2300m. A, CH, CS, eF, I, PL, R, YU. Not illustrated.

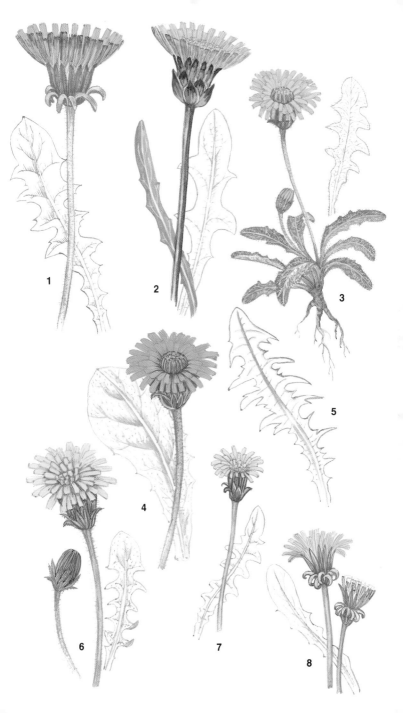

Lily Family Liliaceae

Lvs undivided, usually with long parallel veins. Rootstock a bulb, rhizome or tuber. Fls with 6 tepals (3 sepals and 3 petals - often all looking alike, usually coloured); stamens 6. Fr a three-parted capsule or berry.

1 TOFIELD'S ASPHODEL *Tofieldia calyculata.* Low/short tufted, hairless per; unbranched. Lvs flat, sword-shaped, with 5 or more veins, pale green; stem lvs smaller. *Bracts one-lobed,* papery. Fls tiny, pale yellowish-green, in an elongated cluster. Damp meadows, marshes and damp rocks, to 2500m. June-Sept. A, CH, CS, D, nE, s & sF, nI, PL, R, sS, YU. **1a Scottish Asphodel** *T. pusilla* is dwarfer with 3-4-veined lvs and more rounded fl clusters; bracts three-lobed, green. July-Aug. T, except B, DK, E, c & sGB, c & sI, IRL, NL, R, YU. **1b** *T. p.* subsp. *austriaca* has lvs with 5-7 veins. 1800-2200m. A, neI, nwYU; eastern Alps.

2 BLUE APHYLLANTHES *Aphyllanthes monspeliensis.* Short, tufted, 'rush-like' per. Lvs 'sheath-like', encircling the fl stems. Fls solitary or 2-3 together, open saucers, 20-25mm, tepals bright blue with a darker central stripe. Dry rocky places, to 1400m. Apr-July. E, sF, w & cI.

3 MERENDERA *Merendera pyrenaica* (= *M. bulbocodium, M. montana*). A dwarf hairless bulbous per. Lvs narrow, grooved, appearing in the early spring and dying before fls appear. Fls rosy-pink, the strap-shaped tepals falling apart, *not* hooked together at base. Meadows and screes, 1500-2500m. Aug-Sept. E, sF; Spanish mountains and central Pyrenees.

4 AUTUMN CROCUS *Colchicum autumnale.* Short hairless per. Lvs 2-4 clustered, oblong-lance-shaped, bright shiny green, appearing *in spring* and dying before fls appear. Fls large, 20-45mm, 'crocus-like' but with 6 *stamens,* mauve-pink or white, borne on long whitish tubes. Damp meadows, to 2000m. Aug-Oct. T, except Faeroes, IS, N, nS, SF (DK, sS). **4a** *C. alpinum* is a smaller version of 4 with narrower lvs and tepals; fls 20-30mm. Meadows, often on acid soils, to 2000m. Aug-Sept. sCH, seF, I.

5 SPRING BULBOCODIUM *Bulbocodium vernum.* Low hairless per. Lvs 2-3, lance-shaped, grooved, appearing with the fls. Fls 'crocus-like' but with 6 stamens, rosy-lilac or white, 4-8.5cm, the strap-like tepals *hooked together* at the base. Meadows, to 2000m. Feb-May. sA (rare), CH, nE, s &seF, nI. **5a** *B. versicolor* has *smaller* fls, 2.5-3cm. Dry grassy places at lower altitudes. H, cI, R, YU.

6 ST. BRUNO'S LILY *Paradisea liliastrum.* Short/med hairless per. Lvs linear, basal. Fls trumpet-shaped, 40-50mm, white, fragrant, in loose one-sided racemes. Meadows and rocky places, to 2400m. June-Aug. A, CH, E, s & eF, n & cI, nwYU.

7 ST. BERNARD'S LILY *Anthericum liliago.* Slender, med, hairless per; unbranched. Lvs all basal, linear, grassy. Fls starry white, 30-40mm, in loose racemes. Dry rocks and pastures over limestone, to 1800m. May-July. T, except Faeroes, GB, IRL, IS, N, c & nS, SF; extinct in NL. **7a** *A. ramosum** has *smaller* fls, 20-25mm, borne in branched clusters. To 2000m. June-Aug. Similar distribution.

8 HAIRY GAGEA *Gagea arvensis* (= *G. villosa*). Low, silkily-hairy per. Lvs 2, basal, grassy, grooved, longer than stem. Fls starry yellow, 20-30mm, in clusters with two large bracts below. Meadows and waste ground, to 2200m. Feb-May. T, except Faeroes, GB, IRL, IS, N, n & cS, SF; extinct in B. **8a** *G. lutea* has a single *hairless* basal lf and two stem lvs and smaller fls. Meadows and woods, to 1700m. Mar-May. T, except Faeroes, IRL, IS. **8b** *G. pratensis* like 8a but with a very *long* basal lf and four uneven bracts below the fls. Meadows. Mar-Apr. T, except B, Faeroes, GB, IRL, IS, N, n & cS, SF.

9 PYRENEAN GAGEA *Gagea nevadensis* (= *G. solierolii*). Low hairy per. Lvs 2 basal, grassy, *shorter than stem.* Fls starry yellow, 15-20mm, in loose clusters, each with a *short* bract at base. Meadows and rocky places, to 2500m. Mar-Apr. E, sF. **9a** *G. minima* is similar but usually with a single delicate basal lf, *hooked* at the top. Fls smaller. Meadows, to 1600m. May-June. T, except B, Faeroes, GB, IRL, IS, NL. **9b** *G. bohemica* is like 9 but plant smaller, not more than 4cm tall and basal lvs thread-like and flexuous. Dry grassy places and rock ledges. A, CS, c, e & sD, wF, wGB (Wales, rare), H, I, YU.

10 YELLOW GAGEA *Gagea fistulosa.* Like 8 and 9 but basal lvs *rush-like,* hollow and semi-circular in cross-section. Fls starry yellow, 15-30mm, with two very *large* pointed bracts below. Meadows, 1200-2800m. May-July. A, CH, nE, s & eF, I, R.

Lily Family *(contd.)*

ONIONS AND LEEKS *Allium.* Unbranched hairless, bulbous perennials, smelling strongly of onion or garlic. Fls bell-shaped or starry with separate tepals, borne in umbelled clusters, often mixed with bulbils; enclosed initially by 1-2 papery bracts.

1 CROW GARLIC *Allium vineale.* Med stiff per. Lvs cylindrical, grooved. Fls pink or greenish, 5mm long. bell-shaped, *mixed* with, or entirely replaced by, bulbils; stamens protruding the filaments *with 2-long* projections; bracts shorter than flheads. Cultivated and waste places, to 1900m. June-Aug. T, except Faeroes, IS.

2 ROUND-HEADED LEEK *Allium sphaerocephalon.* Med/tall per. Lvs semi-cylindrical, grooved, hollow. Fls pinkish-purple, 5mm long, bell-shaped, numerous in dense heads; stamens protruding, no bulbils; *bracts short,* papery. Grassy and rocky places, to 2650m. June-Aug. T, except DK, Faeroes, IRL, IS, N, NL, S, SF.

3 STRICT ONION *Allium lineare* (= *A. strictum*). Short/med per. Lvs linear, rounded on back, flat above, borne up to middle of stem. Fls pink or purplish, 4-7mm long, bell-shaped, borne in dense rounded heads, tepals narrow with a purple keel; stamens protruding; bracts as long as flheads. Grassy and rocky places, to 3000m. July-Aug. A, CH, CS, C & sD, nl, PL.

4 MOUNTAIN ONION *Allium senescens* subsp. *montanum.* Short tufted per. Lvs linear, *flat above,* blunt-ended, mostly basal. Fls purplish-pink, 5-6mm long, open bell-shaped, borne in dense heads; stamens protruding; bracts *shorter than* flheads. Dry places and rocks, to 2300m. June-Aug. A, CH, CS, D, E, F, H, I, PL, R, sS, YU (N).

5 FRAGRANT ONION *Allium suaveolens.* Short/med per. Lvs linear, flattish, borne up to middle of stem. Fls purplish, in dense heads, 4-5mm long, bell-shaped; stamens protruding; bracts shorter than flheads, blunt-ended. Grass, scrub, and rocky places, to 1200m. Aug-Oct. A, CH, sD, eF, H, nl, YU.

6 CHIVES *Allium schoenoprasum* (= *A. sibiricum*). Short/med tufted per. Lvs *cylindrical,* fine-pointed, hollow, all borne direct from roots. Fls purple or violet-pink, 9-12mm long, bell-shaped, short-stalked, borne in dense heads; stamens *not protruding;* bracts shorter than flheads. Damp grassy and rocky places, to 2600m. June-July. T, except Faeroes, IS and far north.

7 FIELD GARLIC *Allium oleraceum.* Rather like 1. Med/tall bluish-green per. Lvs semi-cylindrical, grooved, hollow, stems leafy to middle. Fls few, pink, greenish or white, 5-7mm long, bell-shaped, mixed with bulbils; stamens *not protruding;* bracts long-pointed, *much longer* than flheads. Grassy, cultivated and waste places, to 2150m. June- Aug. Probably T, except Faeroes, IRL (IS). **7a Keeled Garlic** *A. carinatum* has *protruding stamens* and the lvs are keeled on the back. T, except Faeroes, IS, N, n & cS, SF (B, GB, IRL, NL).

8 NARCISSUS-FLOWERED ONION *Allium narcissiflorum.* Short tufted per. Lvs linear, flat, green, all basal. Fls purple-pink, 10-l5mm long, bell-shaped, in rather *drooping clusters* of 3-8, but becoming erect; bracts shorter than flheads. Limestone rocks and screes, 1500-2000m. July-Aug. seF, nwl; south-western Alps. **8a** *A. insubricum* has larger fls, 16-18mm long, always borne in drooping clusters. nl; lakes Coma and Garda region.

9 ROCK ONION *Allium saxatile.* Short per. Lvs thread-like. Fls pink or white, 3-5mm long, bell-shaped, borne in dense heads; stamens protruding; bracts pointed, *much longer* than flheads. Rocky places, to 2100m. Aug-Sept. n & cl, R, YU.

10 ALPINE LEEK *Allium victorialis.* Med/tall per. Lvs oblong to elliptical, pleated, stalked. Fls greenish-white to yellowish, 4-6mm long, open bells, borne in rounded heads; bracts as long as flheads. Woods and rocky places, 1400-2600m. June-Aug. A, CH, CS, D, E, F, H, I, PL, R, YU.

11 STRAP-LEAVED ONION *Allium ericetorum* (= *ochroleucum*). Short/med per. Lvs thin and flat, strap-shaped. Fls yellowish or white, sometimes tinged with pink, in dense heads; stamens protruding; bracts about as long as flheads. Grassy and rocky places, to 2000m. July-Aug. A, nE, swF, n& cl, R, YU.

12 YELLOW ONION *Allium flavum.* Short/med tufted per. Lvs thread-like, channelled, bluish-green. Fls clear *yellow,* 4-5mm long, bell-shaped, drooping in fl but later erect; stamens protruding; bracts pointed, much longer than flheads. Dry grassy and rocky places, to 1500m. June-Aug. A, CS, eF, H, I, R, YU.

13 RAMSONS *Allium ursinum.* Short per, often covering large areas. Lvs *broad-elliptical, bright* green, all from roots, smelling strongly of garlic. *Fls white,* starry, 6-10mm, in flat-topped clusters; bracts shorter than flheads. Woods and shady places, to 1900m. Apr-June. T, except Faeroes, IS and far north.

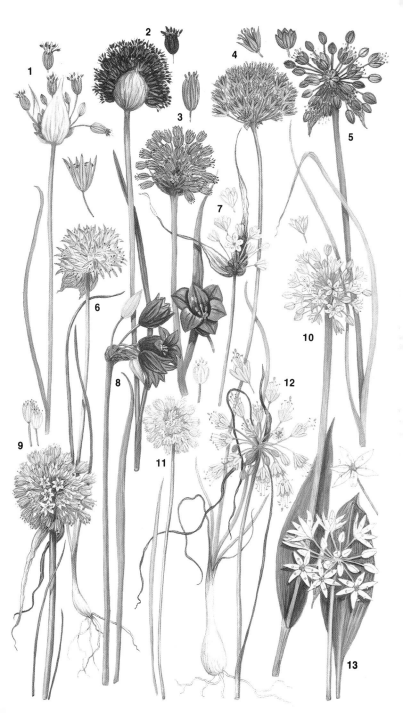

Lily Family (contd.)

1 WHITE FALSE HELLEBORINE *Veratrum album.* Med/tall, robust, hairy per. Lvs broad, oval, pleated lengthwise, downy beneath, sheathing stem at base. Fls starry white, pale green outside *or* all greenish-yellow, 12-15mm, borne in branched spikes. Meadows and woodland clearing, to 2700m. June-Aug. T, except B, Faeroes, GB, IRL, IS, n & cN, NL, S. Poisonous. **1a Black False Helleborine** *Veratrum nigrum* has purplish-black, 10mm flowers. To 1600m. A, CH, CS, eF, H, I, PL, R, YU.

2 ASPHODEL *Asphodelus albus.* Med/tall hairless per. Lvs all basal, strap-like, grooved. Fls large, starry, white or pink-flushed, 40-50mm, borne in dense spikes. Meadows, rocky slopes and thickets, to 1600m. May-July. E, c & sF, H, I, YU.

FRITILLARIES or SNAKESHEAD LILIES *Fritillaria.* Handsome hairless bulbous perennials with thin stems and grassy, rather fleshy lvs. Fls large, *nodding lanterns,* often chequered. Fr a 3-parted erect capsule.

3 PYRENEAN SNAKESHEAD *Fritillaria pyrenaica.* Low/med per with alternate lvs. Fls, 1 (or 2), bell-shaped 25-30mm long, dark-purplish-mahogany with pale yellow and purple chequering, rarely all pale greenish-yellow; inner tepals recurved at tip. Meadows and rocky slopes, to 2000m. May-July. nE, cs & sF; Pyrenees mainly.

4 SNAKESHEAD LILY *Fritillaria meleagris.* Short per with alternate very *slender* lvs, grey-green. Fls 1-2, broad lanterns, 30-50mm long, pale or dark pink, occasionally red-purple with darker chequering. Damp meadows, to 1200m. Apr-May. T, except Faeroes, c & nGB, c & sI, IRL, IS (DK, N, S, SF); extinct in B. **4a** *F. m.* subsp. *burnatii* has *blunt* (not pointed) lower lvs and purple fls. Alpine pastures. swCH, seF, nl.

5 TYROLEAN FRITILLARIA *Fritillaria tubiformis* (= *F. delphinensis).* Low per with alternate lance-shaped lvs, *all on* upper part of stem. Fls solitary, broad lanterns, 32-48mm long, deep reddish-purple with *faint* chequering. Meadows over limestone, 1500-2000m. Mar-June. seF, nwl; south-western Alps. **5a** *F.t.* subsp. *moggridgei* has yellow fls, speckled and chequered brown or purple. seF, nwl; mainly Maritime Alps.

6 SLENDER-LEAVED SNAKESHEAD *Fritillaria orientalis* (= *tenella).* Short/med per with slender *opposite* or *whorled* lvs. Fls small bells, 20-30mm long, dull purple or greenish-yellow flushed purple, often chequered. Rocky meadows, rarely much above 1200m. Apr-May. seF, I, R, YU.

7 THREE-BRACTED SNAKESHEAD *Fritillaria involucrata.* Short/med per with opposite lance-shaped lvs, the uppermost node with *three-leaves* held together above the nodding fl. Fls 1-3, large lanterns, 25-40mm, greenish or yellowish with purple markings. Rocky meadows, to 1500m. Apr-May. seF, nwl.

8 WILD TULIP *Tulipa australis* (= *T. sylvestris australis).* Short/med slender hairless per. Lvs few, linear, rather fleshy, *with no* prominent veins or grooves. Fls large yellow, the outer 3 tepals 25-40mm long, *often* tinged green or reddish-purple and recurved, nodding in bud. Meadows to 2000m. Apr-July. A, CH, E, c & sF, I, YU; possibly in CS, R.

9 RED TULIP *Tulipa gesneriana* (= *T. didieri).* Med hairless or slightly hairy per. Lvs 2-5, rather thick, elliptical to oblong or narrow-lance-shaped. Fls *crimson-orange or orange,* the tepals edged with yellow, 45-75mm long, occasionally all yellow or purplish. Probably not above 1500m. Apr-May. (wCH, E, s & eF, I); origin uncertain.

8

Lily Family (contd.)

LILIES *Lilium*. Med/tall perennials with scaly underground bulbs. Fls showy, borne in erect racemes, or solitary; the tepals often recurved giving a 'turk's-cap' appearance, with prominent anthers and style. Fruit a 3-parted erect capsule.

1 MARTAGON LILY *Lilium martagon*. Med/tall hairless per with red-mottled stems. Lvs in *whorls* up the stem, elliptical, deep green, shiny. Fls in a lax raceme, small turk's-caps, dull pink to purplish with darker spots inside; tepals 28-35mm long; stamens pinkish. Meadows, woods and scrub, to 2800m. June-Aug.A, CH, CS, sD, E, F, H, I, PL, R, YU (B, DK, GB, NL, sN, sS, SF).

2 ORANGE LILY *Lilium bulbiferum*. Med downy per. Lvs alternate, narrow lance-shaped, with blackish bulbils at the base of each lf. Fls 1-5, very large and bowl-shaped, *upward pointing,* bright orange with black spots; tepals 55-85mm long. Meadows, woods and rocky places, to 2400m. May-July. A, CH, CS, sD, nE, H, I, PL, R, nwYU. **2a.** *L.b.* var. *croceum** has *no* stem ¥bulbils. Mainly eF, CH, wA, nl.

3 CARNIC LILY *Lilium carniolicum*. Med per. Lvs alternate, oblong-lance-shaped, spreading to erect, often hair on the veins beneath. Fls few, often solitary, turk's-cap, *bright vermilion or orange-yellow* with light spotting; tepals 30-65mm long; anthers orange. Meadows and scrubland, to 2300m. June-July. A, nel,R, YU; mainly in south-eastern Alps.

4 RED LILY *Lilium pomponium*. Short/med slender per. Lvs *linear,* crowded, silver-margined. Fls 3-8, small turk's-caps, *glistening scarlet-red,* with small black dots inside; tepals 50-65mm long; anthers red-purple. Rocky places, rarely above 1100m. May-July. seF, nwl; Maritime Alps and adjacent region.

5 YELLOW TURK'S-CAP LILY *Lilium pyrenaicum*. *Med/tall* foetid per. Lvs numerous, alternate, narrow-lance-shaped, shiny-green, hairy-edged. Fls in a loose cluster, medium turk's-caps, yellow with brown spots, rarely orange; tepals 50-65mm long; anthers orange. Meadows, clearings and rocky slopes, to 2200m. June-Aug. nE, sF (GB); Pyrenees mainly.

6 DOG'S TOOTH VIOLET *Erythronium dens-canis*. Low/short per. Lvs *two usually,* basal, elliptical or lance-shaped, often mottled. Fls large solitary, bright pink with recurved tepals and prominent stamens; tepals 18-30mm long. Meadows, heaths and woods, to 2000m. Feb-Apr. A, CH, c&sCS, E, F, H, n&cI, R, Yu. **6a** *E. d-c.* var. *niveum* has yellow-spotted lvs and white fls. swR.

2a, var. *croceum*

Lily Family *(contd.)*

1 LLOYDIA or SNOWDON LILY *Lloydia serotina.* Low slender hairless bulbous per. Lvs slender grassy, greyish-green, the stem lvs much shorter than the basal, bract-like. Fls upright 'cups', 10-20mm, white, veined brownish-purple, usually solitary. Rocky places and short turf, often over granite, 1800-3000m. June-Aug. A, CH, CS, sD, F, wGB (north Wales), nI, PL, R, YU.

2 ALPINE SQUILL *Scilla bifolia.* Low/short hairless bulbous per. Lvs *usually two,* narrow strap-shaped, shiny green. Fls starlike, 10-16mm, bright blue, sometimes rose or white, in loose clusters; *no bracts.* Damp meadows and scrub, to 1500m. March-June. T, except DK, Faeroes, GB, IRL, IS, n, S, SF (NL). **2a Spring Squill** *Scilla verna* has 3-6 slender lvs and violet blue fls, each with a *bluish bract* at the base. Heaths, meadows and woods, to 2000m. Mar-June. E, F, Faeroes, GB, IRL, N; western Europe. **2b Siberian Squill** *S. sibirica* with solitary or paired drooping fls, 18-26mm, is naturalised in the region from Russia. (A, CS, NL, R, YU)

3 PYRENEAN SQUILL *Scilla liliohyacinthus.* Low/med rather coarse, hairless bulbous per. Lvs broad strap-shaped, borne in a basal cluster. Fls starry, 16-20mm, blue, in loose racemes on a long stem; bracts greenish, as *long* as flstalks. Meadows and open woodlands, to 2000m. Apr-May. E, c & sF.

4 DIPCADI *Dipcadi serotinum.* Slender hairless bulbous per. Lvs slender, grassy, grey-green, pointed. Fls narrow bell-shaped, 12-15mm, *yellowish-brown,* outer three tepals recurved at tip, borne in loose racemes. Sandy and rocky places, to 2400m. July-Aug. E, sF; extinct in I.

5 STAR OF BETHLEHEM *Ornithogalum umbellatum.* Low/short hairless bulbous per. Lvs linear, grassy, shiny green with a grooved central *white stripe.* Fls starry, 20-30mm, tepals glistening white, with a *green stripe* on the back of each, borne in an *umbel-like* cluster. Grassy places and scrub to 1600m. Apr-June. T, except Faeroes, IS and far north; probably only naturalised in the north of the region.

6 BATH ASPARAGUS *Ornithogalum pyrenaicum.* Med/tall hairless bulbous per. Lvs linear strap-shaped, grey-green, all basal, usually *withering* at flowering time. Fls starry, 10-18mm, greenish outside, yellowish inside, borne in long *spike-like* racemes. Meadows and woods, to 1200m. May-June. A, B, CH, E, F, sGB, I, R, YU. **6a** *O. sphaerocarpum* has pale whitish-green fls, semi-transparent and a rounded rather than oblong ovary. A, CS, sF, H, I, R, YU.

7 PYRENEAN HYACINTH *Brimeura* (= *Hyacinthus*) *amethystinus.* Low hairless bulbous per. Lvs linear, grassy, basal. Fls *tubular-bells,* 7-10mm long, blue, rarely white, in loose racemes. Meadows, stony places and screes, to 1500m. May-July. sF, n & neE; Pyrenees and mountains of north-eastern Spain.

8 GRAPE HYACINTH *Muscari neglectum* (= *M. atlanticum, M. racemosum*). Short hairless bulbous per. Lvs thread-like, grassy, grooved, all from roots and usually *sprawling* on the ground. Fls rounded bells, 4-5mm long, deep violet-blue or black-ish-blue with six white teeth, borne in dense spikes. Cultivated areas and fields, to 1800m. Mar-May. T, except B, DK, Faeroes, IRL, IS, N, NL, S, SF (GB). **8a** *M. botryoides* is similar but with fewer more upright lvs that broaden towards the top, and pale blue or violet fls. Meadows, fields and woods, to 2000m. Mar-May. A, CH, CS, sD, n & eF, H, I, PL, R, YU (B, NL).

9 TASSEL HYACINTH *Muscari* (= *Leopoldia*) *comosum.* Short hairless bulbous per. Lvs long strap-like. Fls bell-shaped, of two types; the lower brownish-green 5-9mm long, the *upper* bright violet-blue, smaller and sterile, more upright. Fields and rocky places, to 1300m. Apr-July. T, except Faeroes, IRL, IS, N, S, SF (B, DK, GB, NL).

10 MAY LILY *Maianthemum bifolium.* Low/short hairless rhizomatous per, forming patches. Lvs two on each stem, *heart-shaped,* shiny. Fls starry, tiny, 2-4mm, white with *4 tepals,* borne in small clusters. Fr a small red berry. Woods on moist humusy soils, to 2100m. Apr-July. T, except c & sE, Faeroes, c & sl, IRL, IS.

2a

Lily Family (contd.)

1 STREPTOPUS *Streptopus amplexifolius*. Short/med hairless rhizomatous per, with erect *zig-zagged* leafy stems. Lvs heart-shaped, *clasping* the stem, unstalked. Fls bell-shaped, nodding, 9-10mm long, greenish-white, solitary, with jointed stalks. Fr a red berry. Damp woods and rocks, to 2300m. July-Aug. A, CH, CS, sD, nE, c & sF, nI, PL, R, YU.

2 WHORLED SOLOMON'S SEAL *Polygonatum verticillatum*. Med/tall hairless rhizomatous per with erect stems. Lvs in *whorls,* of 3-6, narrow lance-shaped, unstalked. Fls bell-shaped, nodding, 6-10mm long, white tipped green, in clusters of 1-4. Fr a red berry. Woods, meadows and rocky places, to 2400m. May-July. T, c & sE, except Faeroes, c & sI, IS, SF.

3 SCENTED SOLOMON'S SEAL *Polygonatum odoratum* (= *P. officinale*). Med hairless rhizomatous per with arching angled stems. Lvs *alternate*, oval or elliptical, unstalked. Fls narrow bells, pendent, 18-22mm long, white tipped green, solitary or in twos, fragrant. Fr a bluish-black berry. Woods and rocky places, to 2200m. May-June. T, except Faeroes, IRL, IS, nN, nS, nSF. **3a. Common Solomon's Seal** *P. multiflorum* has *rounded* stems and greenish-white, unscented, fls *waisted* in the middle. Similar distribution. **3b** *P. latifolium* has lvs minutely hairy on veins beneath; fls in clusters of 1-5, 10-18mm long, unscented. A, CS, H, I, R, YU.

4 LILY OF THE VALLEY *Convallaria majalis*. Low patch-forming, hairless rhizomatous per. *Lvs two*, basal, oblong to elliptical, bright shiny green, stalked. Fls *rounded bells,* 6-8mm long, white, borne in loose one-sided spikes, sweetly scented. Fr a red berry. Woods and scrub, to 2300m. Apr-June. T, except Faeroes, IRL, IS, nN, nS. Poisonous.

5 HERB PARIS *Paris quadrifolia*. Low/short hairless, patch-forming rhizomatous per. Lvs in *a whorl* of 4-5 on otherwise leafless stems, oval, short-stalked. Fls starry, yellowish-green, with 4-8 tepals and prominent stamens, solitary, erect. Fr a black berry. Damp woods, often on limestone, to 2000m. May-June. T, except Faeroes, IS and far north. Poisonous.

Yam Family Dioscoreaceae

Tuberous rooted perennials with heart-shaped lvs and six-petalled fls, male and female parts separate, on the same or different plant.

6 BLACK BRYONY *Tamus communis*. Vigorous hairless climbing per with twining stems. Lvs alternate, dark green, shiny, stalked. Fls tiny starry, pale green; male in slender erect racemes, female in small drooping clusters on a *different plant*. Fr a shiny red *berry*. Woods, scrub and hedges, to 1200m. May-Aug. T, except DK, nGB, N, NL, S, SF (IRL). Poisonous.

7 PYRENEAN YAM *Borderea pyrenaica* (= *Dioscorea pyrenaica*). Low/short hairless, tuberous, per with angular stems branched in the upper half. Lvs clustered or in pairs, long-stalked. Fls tiny greenish, male in loose racemes, female in clusters of one to three, on separate plants. Fr a dry three-winged capsule. Rocky slopes and screes, on limestone, to 2500m, June-Sept. nE, sF; central Pyrenees. **7a** *B. chouardii* has translucent lvs that are narrowed below the apex, *shiny green*; fr capsule 8-9mm long (not 12-20mm). nE; central Spanish Pyrenees.

Arum Family Araceae

With a single species in the area.

8 LORDS AND LADIES or CUCKOO PINT *Arum maculatum*. Short hairless tuberous per. Lvs basal, arrow-shaped, dark green, sometimes spotted, long stalked. Fls tiny, in dense whorls; male above female, topped by a purplish *finger-like* spadix, the whole being surrounded by a pale green, purple marked, *hood* or spathe, open above the fls. Fr a cluster of fleshy bright orange berries. Woods and scrub, shady banks, to 1250m. Apr-May. T, except Faeroes, IS, N, S, SF (DK).

8

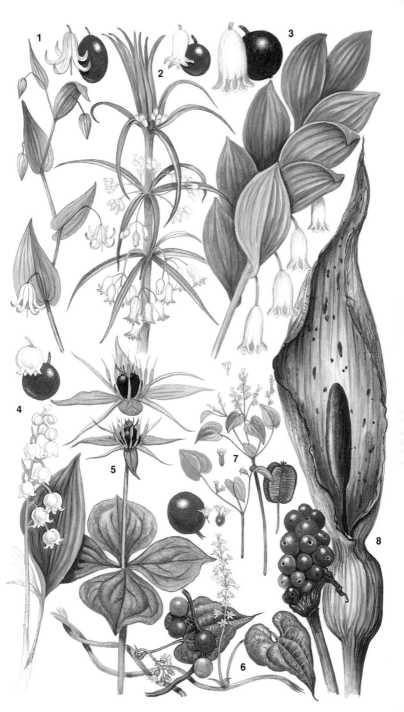

Daffodil Family Amaryllidaceae

Bulbous perennials, hairless, with basal linear lvs and leafless fl stems (scapes), with a bract (spathe) toward the top. Fls with six petal-like tepals (3 sepals and 3 petals), the inner three smaller in snowdrops, with a central trumpet or corona in daffodils. Stamens 6. Fr a capsule, developed below the fl.

1 SPRING SNOWFLAKE *Leucojum* (= *Leucoium*) *vernum.* Short per. Lvs strap-shaped, deep green. Fls nodding bells, 15-20mm long, with 6 *equal* tepals, white tipped green; fls *solitary* or paired. Damp woods and meadows, to 1600m. Feb-Apr. A, B, CH, CS, D, E, F, H, nl, PL, R, YU (GB, DK, NL).

2 SUMMER SNOWFLAKE *Leucojum aestivum.* Short/med tufted per. Lvs long strap-shaped, bright green. Fls nodding bells, 15-18mm long; tepals white tipped green, borne in *clusters* of 2-7 occasionally more. Wet meadows, to 1300m. Apr-June. T, except Faeroes, IS, N, S, SF (DK, E).

3 SNOWDROP *Galanthus nivalis.* Low/short per. Lvs usually two, strap-shaped, grey-green. Fls solitary nodding, 20-25mm long, white, the three *inner tepals shorter* and green tipped. Damp meadows and woods, to 1600m. Feb-Apr. T, except Faeroes, IS and far north; probably only naturalised in the west and north of the region. **3a** *G. elwesii* has base of lvs folded round one another; inner tepals green at base as well as top. cYU, R.

4 POET'S or PHEASANT'S-EYE NARCISSUS *Narcissus poeticus.* Short/med per. Lvs long strap-shaped, upright, grey-green. Fls solitary, large, 4-8cm, with six white rounded-oval tepals and a *small* cup-like orange and yellow trumpet, sweetly scented. Damp meadows, to 2300m. Apr-May. A, CH, E, c & sF, I, YU (B, CS, D, GB). **4a** *N.p.* subsp. *radiiflorus* * has narrower lvs and tepals *narrowed* at the base. H, c & sl, R YU.

5 RUSH-LEAVED NARCISSUS *Narcissus requienii* (= *N. juncifolius*) Low/short delicate per. Lvs thread-like, grassy 1-2mm wide, deep-green, *almost cylindrical*. Fls small, 15-20mm, deep yellow with a short cup-shaped trumpet, sweetly scented, in clusters of 2-5. Short turf and stony places, to 1600m. Apr-May. sF; French Pyrenees.

6 WILD DAFFODIL or LENT LILY *Narcissus pseudonarcissus.* Short/med per. Lvs strap-shaped, grey- or bluish-green, blunt-ended. Fls solitary, slightly nodding, large; tepals pale yellow, oval; trumpet large 25-35mm long, deep yellow or golden, with a frilled and flared edge; flstalk above the spathe, 3-12mm long. Grassy slopes and banks, to 2200m. Mar-June. GB, CH, E, F, NL (A, CS, I, R, YU). **6a** *N.p.* subsp. *abscissus* (= *N. bicolor*)* is readily recognised by its medium sized fls with white tepals and a cylindrical orange-yellow trumpet whose edge is straight, *not flared outwards* as in all the other subspecies; flstalk 15-35mm long. nE, sF; Pyrenees and Corbieres. **6b** *N.p.* subsp. *nobilis* * is taller than 6 with very large fls, often *upward pointing*; tepals pale yellow or creamy-white, the trumpet golden or orange, *flared;* flstalk 8-15mm long. n & nwE; Spanish Pyrenees and Picos de Europa. **6c** *N.p.* subsp. *pallidiflorus is* smaller than 6 with *pale yellow* fls, sometimes bicoloured; flstalk 3-10mm long. nE, sF; Pyrenees and Cordillera Cantabrica. **6d** *N.p.* subsp. *moschatus* (= subsp. *alpestris*) * similar to 6c but with white or creamy-white, *drooping fls*, with a long narrow trumpet; flstalk 10-25mm long. nE, sF; Pyrenees and Cordillera Cantabrica. **6e** *N. p.* subsp. *major* has uniformly deep yellow fls with t*wisted* tepals. E, sF.

7 LESSER WILD DAFFODIL *Narcissus minor.* Low per. Lvs narrow strap-shaped, grey or bluish-green. Fls solitary, slightly nodding, *smaller* than 6; tepals pale to deep yellow, trumpet deep yellow, 16-25mm long, slightly flaired; flstalk 5-20mm long. Grassy places and open scrub, to 2200m. Mar-June. nE, sF (seF); Pyrenees and mountains of northern Spain.

Iris Family Iridaceae

Hairless perennials with bulbs, rhizomes or corms. Lvs flat sword-like, channelled or linear. Fls solitary or several together enclosed by common bracts (spathes), 3-parted, with 3 outer and 3 inner tepals. Fr a 3-valved capsule.

CROCUSES *Crocus*. Low cormous pers, stemless. Lvs linear with a white grooved central stripe. Fls goblet-shaped with six similar tepals (3 sepals and 3 petals), three stamens and a three-parted orange stigma.

1 WHITE CROCUS *Crocus albiflorus* (= *C. caeruleus*, C. *vernus* subsp. *albiflorus*). Corm coat with slightly netted fibres. Lvs green, partly developed at flowering time. Fls pure *white* but often feathered with violet or violet-purple at the base; tepals 15-35mm long. Style *shorter* than stamens. Wet meadows, often by snow patches, to 2700m. Feb-June. A, CH, CS, sD, nE, s & eF, H, I, & nwYU.

2 PURPLE CROCUS *Crocus vernus* (= *C. neapolitanus*, C. *purpureus*). Corm coat with slightly netted fibres. Lvs green, partly developed at flowering time. Fls twice as large as 1, *purple or purple-violet*, often darker at base; tepals 30-55mm long. Styles orange-yellow, longer than stamens. Wet meadows and woods, often by snow patches, to 2500m. Feb-June. I, H, R, YU (GB). **2a** *C. carpetanus* has pale lilac fls with fine darker veins; tepals 20-36mm long; styles whitish or pale yellow. Meadows and open juniper woodland to 2300m. nwE.

3 RIVIERA CROCUS *Crocus versicolor*. Similar in size to 2. Corm coat with parallel fibres only. Lvs grey-green, partly developed at flowering time. Fls white or pale lilac, the outer three tepals *striped* with purple. Meadows and stony places, to 1300m. Feb-Mar. seF, nwI. **3a Leafless Crocus** *C. nudiflorus* has deep purple, not striped, fls on *very long* 10-22cm tubes, flowering before the lvs appear. Grassy and scrubby places, to 2000m. Sept-Nov. nE, swF; west and central Pyrenees, Picos de Europa. **3b** *C. medius* has violet or deep purple fls *with darker veins* and a tube rarely more than 16cm long. Mountain meadows and pastures to 1400m. seF, nwI.

IRISES *Iris*. Rootstock a rhizome or bulb. Fls borne in succession with 3 drooping outer tepals (falls) and 3 upright inner ones (standards), was well as 3 shorter, broad, coloured style arms, each enclosing a single stamen.

4 ENGLISH IRIS *Iris latifolia* (= *I. xiphioides*). Med/tall bulbous per. Lvs long linear, channelled, shiny above. Fls very large, violet-blue or brilliant blue, sometimes white, the falls with a white and yellow/orange zone in the centre, beardless, 60-75mm long. Meadows, to 2200m. July-Aug. nE, sF; Pyrenees and Cordillera Cantabrica.

5 VARIEGATED IRIS *Iris variegata*. Short/med rhizomatous per, stems branched in upper half. Lvs sword-shaped, deep green. Fls yellow or yellowish-white, the falls veined deep violet or brownish-red, bearded, 45-60mm long. Spathes often purple tinged. Rocky and grassy places, seldom above 1200m. June-July. A, c & sD, H, R, YU (CH, I).

6 GRASSY-LEAVED IRIS *Iris graminea*. Short/med rhizomatous per, with *two-winged* flattened stems. Lvs narrow sword-shaped, grassy. Fls with purple standards and falls whitish, veined with violet or pinkish-purple, with a fruity smell; falls 30-50mm long. Grassy and scrubby places, to 1100m. May-June. A, CH, CS, D, nE, sF, H, I, PL, R, YU. **6a** *I. ruthenica* has rounded stems; fls violet the falls *whitish with violet veins*, not scented. c & eR.

7 YELLOW IRIS *Iris pseudacorus*. Med/tall rhizomatous, rather stout per, with branched stems. Lvs sword-shaped, with a raised midrib. Fls yellow, 1-3 together; falls with some green veins or streaks, 50-75mm long. Damp and marshy places, often by streams and ponds, to 1200m. June-Aug. T, except IS.

8 STINKING IRIS *Iris foetidissima*. Med tufted per. Lvs sword-shaped, deep green, with a sickly smell when crushed. Fls straw-coloured, flushed and veined with dull violet or grey-purple, 2-3 together; falls 30-50mm long; style arms pale yellow. Fr splitting revealing *bright orange* seeds. Open woods, shrub and hedgerows, seldom above 1200m. May-July. E, F, GB, I (CH, IRL).

9 GARDEN or FLAG IRIS *Iris germanica*. Med/tall rhizomatous per with branched stems. Lvs broad, sword-shaped, shorter than stems. Fls large, fragrant, bluish-violet or white tinged with blue, 2-3 together; falls with a conspicuous *yellow beard,* 55-90mm long. Dry rocky and grassy places, to 1250m. May-June. Widely cultivated and probably not truly native in the area. (T, except Faeroes, IRL, IS, N, NL, S, SF). **9a** *I. aphylla* is shorter, not more than 30cm tall, with some lvs *longer* than stems; fls smaller, violet or purple. CS, c & sD, seF, H, I, Pl, R, YU. **9b** *I. reichenbachiana* is like 9a but has spathes *strongly keeled* and fls violet, brownish-purple or greenish-yellow. c & nYU, R.

Orchid Family Orchidaceae

Tuberous rooted perennials. Lvs oblong to linear, untoothed. Fls generally in dense spikes with the lowermost petal developed into a lip, often 3-lobed, and spurred. Fruit a 3-parted capsule containing dust-like seed

1 LADY'S SLIPPER ORCHID *Cypripedium calceolus*. Shot/med per; lvs oval to lance-shaped, strongly ribbed, pale green. Fls usually solitary, large, 6-9cm, with spreading reddish-maroon sepals and petals and a prominent pouched yellow lip. Woods and grassy clearings or slopes, usually on calcareous soils, to 2000m. May-July. A, CH, CS, D, DK, neE, s & eF, nGB (northern England, very rare), H, I, sN, PL, R, sS, SF; always very local.

2 LATE SPIDER ORCHID *Ophrys fuciflora* (= *O. holoserica*, *O. holosericea*). Short per. Lvs elliptical, pointed. Fls in short spikes, the sepals pink to white, the petals pink, short; lip *velvety brown* spider-like, quadrangular, patterned with yellowish-green, often with a central blue zone. Grassy places, on calcareous soils, to 1300m. June-July. A, B, CH, c & sCS, sD, E, F, sGB (rare), H, I, R, YU. **2a Bee Orchid** *O. apifera* is taller, fls with pink sepals and short pale green petals; lip rounded, velvety brown with a variable yellow pattern enclosing a red zone - supposedly like the rear of a bumblebee; tip of lip *turned backwards*. Grassy places and thickets, to 1000m. T, except Faeroes, IS, N, S, SF. **2b Early Spider Orchid** *O. sphegodes* like 2a but sepals and petals *yellowish-green* and the lip with a bluish X- or H-shaped zone. Apr-June. T, except Faeroes, IRL, IS, N, NL, S, SF; GB rare and confined to south. **2c Fly Orchid** *O. insectifera* (= *O. muscifera*) has a narrow fly-shaped lip with a forked central lobe and a *central shiny-bluish zone*. Grassy places, scrub and woodland, to 1850m. T, except Faeroes, IS and far north.

3 BUG ORCHID *Orchis coriophora*. Short/med per. Lvs narrow lance-shaped. Fls small in a dense spike, unpleasant smelling; sepals and petals brownish-red, joined into a hood; lip reddish-purple, 3-lobed, 6-10mm long; spur very short, down-pointing. Damp meadows, to 1800m. Apr-July. T, except Faeroes, Gb, IRL IS, N, S, SF; extinct in NL.

4 JERSEY or LAX-FLOWERED ORCHID *Orchis laxiflora*. Med per. Lvs narrow lance-shaped, plain-green; stem and bracts often purplish. Fls in a loose spike, purple, with two spreading sepals and a hood formed from the upper sepal and the two petals; lip 3-lobed, 7-10mm long, the central lobe shorter than the outer; spur short, horizontal, broadened at tip. Damp meadows, to 1150m. Mar-June. T, except Faeroes, all but south-west GB, IRL, IS, N, NL, n & cS, SF. **4a Bog Orchid** *O. palustris* (= *O. laxiflora* subsp. *palustris*)* has a larger lip 9-15mm long with an *equal central lobe*; spur tapered to the tip. Similar distribution, rarer in the south.

5 EARLY PURPLE ORCHID *Orchis mascula*. Short/med per. Lvs usually with *purplish-black spots*. Fls in loose oblong spikes, purple, sometimes pinkish or white, with a cat-like odour, the outer sepals *erect-spreading*, the central sepal and petals forming a hood; lip shallowly 3-lobed, spotted, 8-15mm long; spur long, upcurved. Grassy meadows, scrub and woods, to 2650m. Apr-July. T, except IS. Plants from the central Pyrenees with very dark fls and more erect sepals and petals are referrable to subsp. *hispanica*.

6 SOLDIER or MILITARY ORCHID *Orchis militaris*. Short/med per. Lvs large, broad-oblong, shiny, unspotted. Fls in oblong spikes, greyish or lilac-pink with deeper spots and markings, the sepals and petals *all forming* a close helmet; lip 12-15mm long, with two thin 'arms' and two broad 'legs' with a small central tail in between; spur short, *down-curved*. Grassy and scrubby places, wood and margins, on calcareous soils, to 1800m. April-June. A, B, CS, CH, D, E, F, sGB (rare), H, I, NL, PL, R, sS, YU.

7 GREEN-WINGED ORCHID *Orchis morio*. Variable short/med per. Lvs narrow-oblong, unspotted. Fls in loose oblong spikes, purple, pink or white, fragrant, the sepals and petals all forming a helmet, the sepals (or wings) conspicuously *veined green;* lip shallowly 3-lobed, 7-10mm long; spur long, horizontal or upcurved. Meadows and scrubby places, to 1800m. May-June. T, except Faeroes, IS, SF and far north.

8 PALE-FLOWERED ORCHID *Orchis pallens*. Short/med per. Lvs broad oblong, shiny, unspotted. Fls in egg-shaped or oblong spikes, *usually pale yellow*, rarely purplish-red, the outer sepals spreading upwards, the middle sepal and petals forming a hood; lip 3-lobed, 6-8mm long, *unspotted;* spur horizontal or upcurved, shorter than the ovary. Meadows and woods on calcareous soils, to 2000m. Apr-June. A, CH, CS, sD, eF, H, n & cI, PL, R, YU.

9 PROVENCE ORCHID *Orchis provincialis*. Short per. Lvs oblong-lance-shaped, often brown-spotted; bracts pale. Fls in rather dense oblong clusters, *pale or dark yellow*, the 3-lobed lip *brown* spotted, often orange in the centre, 8-12mm long; spur long, upward pointing. Grassy and shrubby places, to 1300m. Apr-June. s & swCH, E, sF, I, YU.

Orchid Family *(contd.)*

1 LADY ORCHID *Orchis purpurea.* Med/tall per. Lvs broad-oblong, shiny, unspotted. Fls fragrant, the sepals and petals forming *a purplish-green hood;* lip 10-15mm long, whitish or pale pink, darker spotted, lobed, with 2-narrow 'arms' and 2-broad 'legs'; spur short, downcurved. Woods and scrub on limestone, to 1500m. May-June. T, except Faeroes, IS, IS, N, S, SF; GB rare and confined to southern England.

2 MONKEY ORCHID *Orchis simia.* Short/med per. Lvs broad-oblong or lance-shaped, shiny, unspotted. Fls in dense blunt spikes, pale rose or violet, flushed and spotted deeper pink; lip 14-16mm long, with slender 'arms' and 'legs' curved *forward,* with a short central 'tail-like' lobe; spur short, downcurved. Grassy meadows and open scrub, to 1500m. May-June. B, CH, D, E, F, seGB (rare), swH, I, NL, R, YU.

3 TOOTHED ORCHID *Orchis tridentata.* Short/med per. Lvs oblong-lance-shaped, green, unspotted. Fls in *dense rounded heads,* purple-hooded; lip 6-9mm long, whitish, spotted and edged reddish-purple with short broad 'arms' and 'legs' and a short central 'tail'; spur as long as the lip. Grassy places, woods and scrub, to 1500m. Apr-June. A, CS, CH, sD, E, s & eF, H, I, PI, R, YU.

4 BURNT ORCHID *Orchis ustulata.* Low/short per. Lvs oblong, pointed, unspotted. Fls *tiny, fragrant,* in dense conical-heads, the buds and hoods dark brownish-purple, fading with age; lip 4-8mm long, white, dotted with reddish-purple, with very short 'arms' and 'legs'; spur very short. Dry meadows, grassy places over limestone, to 2100m. May-June. T, except Faeroes, IRL, IS, N, n & cS; extinct in NL.

MARSH ORCHIDS *Dactylorhiza.* Like *Orchis* but tubers hand-like, not testicle-like, the lvs usually scattered along the stem; bracts lf-like; sepals spreading; spurs downcurved.

5 ELDER-FLOWERED ORCHID *Dactylorhiza sambucina* (= *Orchis sambucina*). Short per. Lvs elliptical to narrow lance-shaped, shiny pale green, unspotted. Fls in short dense spikes, either pale *yellow* with a purple spotted lip and pale green bracts, or *purple* with reddish bracts; lip rounded, flat, scarcely 3-lobed, 7-8mm long; spur thick, about as long as the ovary. Meadows and woodland clearings, to 2100m. Apr-July. T, except B, Faeroes, GB, IRL, IS, NL and far north.

6 EARLY MARSH ORCHID *Dactylorhiza incarnata.* Variable short/med per. Lvs 4-5, erect, lance-shaped, hooded at tip, usually unspotted. Bracts *longer than* fls. Fls small, variable, purple, pink or whitish, the lip 5-7mm long, slightly 3-lobed with the sides folded backwards; spur half as long as ovary. Damp meadows, marshy places, to 2100m. May-July. T, except IS and far north. **6a Flecked Marsh Orchid** *D. cruenta* is shorter, the lvs *purple spotted;* fls reddish to dark purple.Similar distribution but absent from E, sF, c & sl, YU. **6b** *D. traunsteineri* is like 6 but lvs not hooded at tip; fls purple, the lip 6-9mm long, deeply marked. T, except E, F, H, c & sl, R.

7 BROAD-LEAVED MARSH ORCHID *Dactylorhiza majalis.* Short/med per. Lvs 4-6, *broad,* oblong to broad-lance~shaped, bluish green, *usually brown-spotted.* Lower bracts longer than fls. Fls in dense egg-shaped or oblong spikes, purplish or reddish-purple; lip 9-10mm long, spotted and lined, rounded, 3-lobed. Damp meadows and marshes, to 2500m. May-July. T, except Faeroes, IS, N, nS, SF. **7a** *D. m.* subsp. *alpestris* is shorter the lip scarcely lobed. A, CH, nE, s & eF, nl, nwYU; Pyrenees and Alps.

8 COMMON SPOTTED ORCHID *Dactylorhiza fuchsii.* Variable short/med per. Lvs 7-12, rounded to elliptical, *usually dark spotted.* Lower bracts shorter than fls. Fls pink, pale lilac or reddish-purple; lip 6-9mm long, dotted and lined crimson or purple, *markedly* 3-lobed, the central lobe longer than the outer ones. Grassy places and scrub, usually on limestone, to 2200m. June-Aug. T, except E, sF, Faeroes, c & sl, IS. **8a Heath Spotted Orchid** *D. maculata* has the lip 7-11mm long, shallowly 3-lobed, the central lobe *small and tooth-like.* Heaths and bogs on acid soils. T.

9 BLACK VANILLA ORCHID *Nigritella nigra* (= *N. miniata*). Low/short per. Lvs lance-shaped to linear, pointed. Fls small, fragrant, *blackish-purple* sometimes pinkish, in rounded heads, the petals and sepals all spreading; lip uppermost in fl, 4-5mm long, *like petals.* Meadows, grassy places, to 2800m. May-July. T, except A, CH, D, nE, s & eF, n & cl, N, S, YU. **9a Red Vanilla Orchid** *N. rubra* has rose-pink or flesh-coloured fls with a broader lip. 1600-2300m. A, eCH, nl, R, nwYU.

10 LONG-LIPPED SERAPIAS *Serapias vomeracea.* Short/med per. Lvs lance-shaped, unspotted. Bracts reddish-violet, *longer than* fls. Fls large, sepals and petals forming a pointed violet helmet; lip 30-40mm long, reddish-brown, pointed, curved *under.* Damp grassy places and woods, to 1100m. Apr-June. sCH, E, c & sF, I, YU.

11 MAN ORCHID *Aceras anthropophorum.* Short per. Lvs lance-shaped, keeled, shiny. Fls *greenish-yellow* in long dense spikes; lip 12-15mm long, with long 'arms' and 'legs', often tinged red-brown, *spurless.* Grassy places and scrub, on limestone, to 1500m. May-June. B, CH, sD, E, F, c & sGB, NL, I, YU.

Orchid Family *(contd.)*

1 LIZARD ORCHID *Himantoglossum hircinum.* Short/med pale- or greyish-green per. Lvs oblong-lance-shaped, soon withering. Fls in a long spike, strong-smelling (goat), with a purplish-grey hood; lip *very long*, 30-50mm, purplish, red-spotted, 3-lobed, strap-like, the outer two lobes much shorter; spur short. Grassy banks and slopes, woodland margins and scrub, to 1800m. May-July. T, except DK, Faeroes, nGB, IRL, IS, N, S, SF; GB rare.

2 PYRAMIDAL ORCHID *Anacamptis pyramidalis*, Med per. Lvs narrow lance-shaped, pale green, unspotted. Fls bright pink, rarely white, in a *short pyramidal spike*, foxy smelling, the sepals spreading, petals hooded; lip 3-lobed, 6-8mm long, curved. Meadows and woodland clearings on limestone. to 1900m. MayAug. T, except Faeroes, IS, N, nS, SF.

3 MUSK ORCHID *Herminium monorchis.* Low/med per. Lvs oval-oblong, yellow-green. Fls *tiny*, yellowish-green, in a loose thin spike, *honey-scented*, the sepals and petals spreading; lip 3-lobed, 3.5-4mm long, the middle one longer; spur very short. Dry meadows on limestone. to 1800m. May-Aug. T, except Faeroes, IRL, IS and far north; extinct in H.

4 FALSE ORCHID *Chamorchis alpina.* Low rather insignificant per. Lvs linear, *grassy*. Fls tiny, green tinged purple, with a yellowish-green slightly *3-lobed lip* 4mm long, the sepals and petals spreading, unspurred, few in a loose spike. Damp short grassland, 1500-2700m. July-Aug. A, CH, CS, eF, nI, N, R, S, SF, YU.

5 FROG ORCHID *Coeloglossum viride.* Low/short per. Lvs bluish-green, rounded to oblong or lance-shaped. Fls small, yellowish-green tinged red-brown, in a thin spike, sepals and petals hooded; lip oblong, 6-8mm long, 3-lobed, the central lobe smaller; spur very short. Meadows and scrub, to 2500m. May-Aug. T.

6 SMALL WHITE ORCHID *Pseudorchis albida* (= *Gymnadenia albida, Leucorchis albida*). Low/med per. Lvs oval, the upper narrower. Fls tiny, 2-3mm, greenish-white with a yellow-green 3-lobed lip, the central lobe rather larger, in a dense blunt-spike; spur short and thick. Meadows and pastures, to 2500m. June-Sept. T.

7 FRAGRANT ORCHID *Gymnadenia conopsea.* Med per. Lvs narrow lance-shaped, green, unspotted. Fls purplish-pink, *fragrant*, in a dense cylindrical spike, the sepals spreading, petals hooded; *lip short*, 3.5-5mm long, 3-lobed; *spur long and slender.* Meadows and woodland margins, generally on limestone, to 2500m. June-Aug. T, except Faeroes, IS and far north. **7a** *G. odoratissima* is a frailer plant with greyish-green lvs and pale pink or white, vanilla-scented, fls borne in a short dense spike; *lip* 2-3mm. To 2700m. May-Aug. A, B, CH, CS, sD, E, F, H, I, PL, R, YU, sS.

HELLEBORINES *Epipactis.* Perennials with oval or lance-shaped ribbed lvs, clasping the stem. Fls rather drooping, in one-sided spikes, each fl with a narrow leafy bract at base; petals and sepals spreading; lip short, lobed or unlobed, unspurred.

8 DARK RED HELLEBORINE *Epipactis atrorubens.* Med red-tinged per; stems downy. Lvs large, in two rows up the stem. Fls *dark wine-red or reddish-violet*, fragrant, lip 5.5-6.5mm long, shorter than the sepals. Grassy and rocky places, woods to 2200m. May-Aug. T, except Faeroes, IS and far north. **8a Broad-leaved Helleborine** *E. helleborine* has *spirally arranged* lvs and larger greenish-yellow, red-tinged fls, unscented; lip 9-11mm long, rounded and curled under at tip. Woodland clearings to 1800m. June-Sept. T, except Faeroes, sI, IS and far north. **8b** *E. leptochila* like 8 but shorter, the fls green tinged with white or yellow; *lip pointed*, the same size as the sepals. Beech and coniferous woods, rarely above 1000m. July-Aug. T, except DK, E, Faeroes, I, IRL, IS, N, S, SF. **8c** *E. microphylla* like 8a but with much smaller, more rounded lvs and smaller greenish, purple-margined fls; lip round with a short point. Woods, to 1350m. May-Aug. eP,A,Ap. **8d** *E. muelleri* like 8a, the fls pale green, the inside of the lip cup *reddish*. Forest margins, on lime. A, CH, CS, D, eF, H, NL. **8e Marsh Helleborine** *E. palustris* has reddish or purple-brown fls with a frilly white lip; fr downy. Marshes and damp places. July-Aug. T, except Faeroes, IS and far north. **8f Violet Helleborine** *E. purpurata* like 8 but has *grey-purple lvs* and greenish-white fls flushed purple outside; lip white mottled violet. Woodland, to 1400m. Aug-Sept.

9 VIOLET BIRDSNEST ORCHID *Limodorum abortivum.* Stout med/tall unbranched saprophytic per; stem *violet- or bluish-tinged*. Lvs small, scale-like along stem, violet. Fls in long spikes, large, violet, with spreading sepals and petals; lip yellowish and violet, 16-18mm long, triangular; spur long, pointed. Woodland clearings or shady pastures, to 1200m. May-July. T, except DK, Faeroes, nF, GB, IRL, IS, N, NL, S, SF.

Orchid Family (contd.)

1 RED HELLEBORINE *Cephalanthera rubra.* Short/med slightly purple-tinged per. Lvs narrow lance-shaped, clasping stem at base, strongly ribbed. Fls *bright carmine-pink*, not opening widely, few in a loose spike; lip whitish with a downcurved pointed tip, 15-18mm long, unspurred. Open woods, especially Beech and scrub, on limestone, to 1800m. May-July. T, except Faeroes, n & cB, IRL, IS and far north; rare in GB, extinct in NL. **1a Narrow-leaved Helleborine** *C. longifolia* has longer grassy lvs and *white fls*, the lip ridged with orange-yellow; bracts small and inconspicuous. T, except Faeroes, IS and far north; extinct in NL. **1b White Helleborine** *C. damasonium* like 1a but with broader lvs and large lflike bracts. To 1300m. May-July. T, except Faeroes, IRL, IS, N, & cS, SF.

2 SUMMER LADY'S TRESSES *Spiranthes aestivalis.* Med slender yellowish-green per. *All lvs linear,* grassy, the upper shorter. Fls very small, white, unspurred, borne in a thin *spiralled spike;* lip 6-7mm *long.* Damp meadows and riverbanks, to 1250m. June-Aug. A, B, CH, CS, D, E, F, H, I, NL, YU; extinct in GB. **2a Autumn Lady's Tresses** *S. spiralis* has a basal rosette of oval bluish-green lvs, *withering* before flowering, leaving a few scale-like lvs up the stem. Fls white with a greenish lip, sweetly scented. Dry grassy places, rarely much above 1000m. Aug-Oct. T, except Faeroes, IS, N, S, SF.

3 LESSER BUTTERFLY ORCHID *Platanthera bifolia.* Short/med per. *Basal lvs 2,* oval-elliptical, shiny-green; stem lvs smaller and scale-like. Fls yellowish or greenish-white, vanilla-scented, borne in loose spikes, with spreading sepals and petals; lip 8-12mm long, narrow and undivided; spur long, curved; pollen masses parallel. Meadows, woods and moors, to 2300m. May-July. T, except IS. **3a Greater Butterfly Orchid** *P. chlorantha* is larger with broader lvs; spur swollen towards the tip; pollen masses *diverging.* To 1800m. T, Faeroes, IS.

4 COMMON TWAYBLADE *Listera ovata.* Med per. Lvs a *single pair* at base of the stem, oval, ribbed, dull green. Fls small, yellow-green, unspurred, in long slender spikes; sepals and petals half-hooded; lip 7-15mm long, deeply forked. Woods, scrub and clearings, to 2100m. May-July. T, except Faeroes. **4a Lesser Twayblade** *L. cordata* is smaller, almost insignificant, the single pair of lvs *heart-shaped,* shiny. Fls reddish-green, musky-fragrant, the lip with two short upper lobes and a long forked central one. Wet places and woods, often pine, moors, 1300-2300m. May-Sept. T, except c & sE, H, c & sl.

5 BIRDSNEST ORCHID *Neottia nidus-avis.* Short/med saprophytic per; stem honey-coloured with scale-like lvs. Fls pale brown with a sickly fragrance, unspurred, in broad spikes; petals and sepals small, half-hooded; lip large, 8-12mm long, forked. Beech woods mainly, to 1700m. May-July. T, except Faeroes, IS. Rather like some Broomrapes (p. 268) but these have a 3-lobed lip.

6 CREEPING LADY'S TRESSES *Goodyera repens.* Low/short per with *creeping runners.* Lvs oval, pointed, in a basal rosette; stem lvs smaller, scale-like. Fls tiny, white, fragrant, borne in a slender spiralled spike; sepals spreading, petals hooded; lip short, 3-4mm long, and pointed, unspurred. Woods, especially coniferous, and mossy places on acid soils, to 2200m. May-Aug. T, except Faeroes, IRL, IS.

7 CORALROOT ORCHID *Corallorhiza trifida.* Low/short saprophytic per; stem yellowish-green with *long sheathing* scales. Fls yellowish-green or yellowish-white, unspurred, borne in loose few-flowered spikes; sepals and petals spreading; lip small, 4-5mm long, 3-lobed. Woods, especially coniferous, meadows, 1400-2700. June-Aug. T, except Faeroes, IRL; extinct in NL.

8 GHOST ORCHID *Epipogium aphyllum.* Low/short saprophytic per; stem *mauvish-yellow,* translucent, with long sheathing, pale brown, scales. Fls large, solitary or 2-3 together; petals and sepals yellowish-white, spreading, the *lip pinkish upturned and hoodlike;* spur short, blunt. Beech, oak and pine woods, to 1900m. June-Sept. T, except Faeroes, IRL, IS, NL; often rare, always local.

9 ROUND-HEADED ORCHID *Traunsteinera globosa.* Short/med per. Lvs bluish-green, oblong-elliptic, all on stem. Fls small pale pink, purple-spotted, in dense globular clusters; sepals and petals spreading, the lip short, 3-lobed, 4-5mm long; spur short. Meadows and woods, to 2600m. May-Aug. A, CH, CS, sD, nE, s & eF, H, n & cl, PL, R, YU.

Glossary

Most of the following terms are used frequently throughout the text. Use of the book will be simplified for those unfamiliar with botanical terms such as anther, bract, calyx, corolla, petal, sepal, stamen, stigma, stipule and style, if their meanings are memorised.

Achene: a single-seeded dry fruit, often in clusters as in the Buttercup.

Acid soil or rocks: those having an acid reaction and are hence non-alkaline; rocks such as sandstone and granite may give rise to acid soils. Peaty soils are often acid.

Aggregate: groups of closely related species or microspecies that are often very difficult to distinguish except by very close scrutiny.

Alpine meadows and pastures: those found above the tree line.

Alpines: those mountain plants that occur above the tree line – as defined in the context of this book.

Alternate: leaves placed alternately along the stem, not opposite or whorled

Annuals: plants which complete their whole life cycle, from seed to flowering and fruiting, within the same year. High mountain and scree plants are rarely annual.

Anther: the male organ of the flower which contains pollen.

Berry: a fleshy fruit, usually rounded and containing several hard seeds.

Biennials: plants which germinate in the first year, often surviving the winter as leafy rosettes and flower, seed and die in the second year.

Bog: a habitat on wet peat; an environment for various acid loving plants (see calcifuge).

Boreal: belonging to the north; regions characterised by short summers and long cold winters.

Bracts: small leaf-like or scale-like organs that subtend the flowers – not always present. See also Flower Bracts

Bulbs: underground storage organs consisting of fleshy swollen leaf-bases that closely overlap one another.

Bulbils: small bulb-like organs, found above ground in the axils of leaves or in some instances replacing flowers; bulbils become detach to form new plants.

Calcareous soils: those formed on calcium carbonate rich rock such as limestone or chalk. Lime rich soils have a different and usually a richer association of plants than acid soils.

Calcicole: plants that are tolerant of, and grow happily, in lime-rich soils.

Calcifuge: plants that grow in acid soils and will not tolerate lime.

Calyx: refers to the sepals as a whole – these may be joined to one another in whole or part to form a tube (the sepal tube), or may be separate (free).

Catkin: tight spikes of usually tiny flowers, erect or drooping, often either male or female; male catkins producing copious pollen.

Cluster: a loose group of flowers.

Composite: a collective name used to describe members of the Daisy Family, Compositae; they may have daisy-, dandelion- or thistle-like flowerheads.

Cone: the woody fruit-like structure characteristic of pines, firs and related plants. The cone consists of overlapping woody scales enclosing the seeds.

Corm: 'bulb-like' underground storage organs, consisting of a swollen stem base.

Corolla: refers to the petals as a whole and usually when they are joined wholly or partly into a tube.

Crucifer: a collective name used to describe members of the Cress Family, Cruciferae.

Cushion: plants forming dense rounded tufts, often composed of numerous tight leaf rosettes. A tight cushion form is characteristic of many high alpines; scree and cliff dwellers in particular.

Deciduous: trees or shrubs that shed all their leaves in the autumn.

Digitate: leaves (sometimes bracts) consisting of several similar 'finger-like' leaflets radiating from a central point and joined only at the very base.

Disc florets: of Composites refers to the tubular flowers which make up the central 'eye' of the daisy flowerhead. The flowerhead may sometimes consist solely of disc florets – see also ray florets.

Epicalyx: a secondary calyx located outside the primary calyx; the sepals of the epicalyx may be the same size or smaller than the inner 'true' sepals; common in the Rose Family, in particular the cinquefoils, strawberries etc.

Ericaceous: plants belonging to the Heath Family, Ericaceae.

Falls: the outer drooping petals of the iris flower.

Female flowers: flowers containing only female parts – ovary, style(s) and stigma(s). Female flowers may be found on the same plant as the male flowers (e.g. Hazel) or on separate plants (e.g. willows).

Florets: the individual, often rather small, flowers making up a tight flowerhead.

Flower bracts: as defined in this book refer to the 'bract-like' structures, often numerous and overlapping, which surround the base of flowerheads, as in the Composites or daisies; flower bracts may be small and soft, or large, or spiny (as in many Thistles).

Flowerhead: refers to closely, often tightly grouped, flower clusters, usually terminating the stem(s); typical of members of the Daisy and Scabious Families.

Flower parts refer to all the parts of a typical flower; the sepals, petals, stamens and styles which make up the individual flower, although these may not all be present in a given species. There may be additional organs such as nectaries, epicalyx-sepals and so on. The parts present and their numbers are often characteristic of a particular species and may give a good key to accurate identification.

Follicle: a dry 'pod-like' fruit or carpel, solitary or in clusters, which open along one side and containing several to many seeds (e.g. delphiniums and columbines).

Fringe: refers to the cut margin as in the flowers of the snowbells

Fruit: the seed bearing organ of plants, which may be dry or fleshy, single- to many-seeded, winged or unwinged; they may or may not split to release the seeds.

Glandular hairs: short or long hairs with a gland at the tip; generally seen as a swelling or blob and often giving the plant a sticky feel.

Heath: a habitat on acid soils dominated by heathers and related shrubs.

Helmet: the upper petal, or petal-like structure of a flower, which forms a 'cap-like' helmet, as in the monkshoods.

Hip: brightly coloured false fruits consisting of a fleshy 'urn-like' structure enclosing the seeds and characteristic of roses.

Hood: refers to the upper petals and/or sepals of certain orchid flowers which form a small 'hood-like' cap.

Introduced plants: those plants brought in by man and not native to a particular area; such plants may become widely naturalised.

Keel: the lowest 'petal' of a pea flower which consists of two petals joined together along their lower margins; often boat-shaped.

Labiate: a collective name used to describe members of the Mint Family, Labiatae.

Lance-shaped or **Lanceolate:** spear-shaped, oval but broadest just below the middle, and pointed.

Lax: refers to flowers forming a loose, spaced, cluster.

Legumes: a collective name used to describe members of the Pea Family, Leguminosae.

Linear: refers to long narrow leaves with parallel sides, or almost so; as in many monocotyledonous plants such as the daffodils and scillas.

Lobed: leaves which have lobes but not separate leaflets; the lobes may be toothed or not, deep or shallow, alternate or opposite (see pinnately-lobed).

Male flowers: flowers containing only male parts – stamens; they may occur on the same or on different plants from the female flowers (see also Female Flowers).

Marsh: a wet habitat, but not on peat.

Midrib: the central vein of a leaf, often thickened and raised.

Moraine: the rocks and debris deposited along the sides and at the snout of glaciers and consisting of damp compacted material or an assortment of various sized rocks, acid or alkaline, and with little soil. Moraines often have characteristic plants, though they are seldom rich in species; moraines can be localised or very extensive.

Moor: an upland area, usually covered in heather or related plants.

Nectary: small glandular organ in flowers which secrete a sugary liquid or nectar, attractive to various insects; often located at the base of petals or sepals or in the tips of spurs.

Needle: slender stiff, often leathery leaves, characteristic of pines, firs and related trees.

Net-veined: leaf veins which form an interlacing network, not parallel.

Node: the points on stems where leaves and lateral branches arise.

Opposite: leaves arising opposite each other on the stem, thus appearing in pairs.

Palmate: leaves lobed like a hand as in maples and mallows.

Parasitic plants: are those that live on other plants and have no green pigment (chlorophyll) and are thus entirely dependent on the host plant for their nutrients (e.g. broomrapes). Partial or semi-parasites are only partially dependent on the host plant and have some green pigment (e.g. cow-wheats and rattles).

Peat: deposits of only partially decayed plant material, characteristic of acid moors and heaths and producing distinct plant communities, often with heathers and related plants dominating.

Perennial: plants living for more than two years (often many years), sometimes woody, and flowering each year. Most alpine and subalpine plants fall into this category.

Petals: the innermost floral-leaves of a flower, usually showy and brightly coloured, separate from one another, or joined into a tube and collectively referred to as the corolla. Petals are absent in some species.

Pinnate: a leaf consisting of several opposite pairs of distinct leaflets spaced along a central axis or rachis and with or without an end leaflet.

2-pinnate leaves have the primary leaflets further divided into pinnate structures -*see* figures.

Pinnately-lobed: leaves which have several pairs of shallow or deep lobes, but not distinct leaflets.

Pod: a fruit, long and cylindrical or somewhat flattened, not fleshy and usually splitting into two equal halves when ripe. A characteristic of the legumes or Pea Family, Leguminosae.

Raceme: a flower spike in which the individual flowers are stalked.

Ray floret: the conspicuous outer flowers of a daisy head, with a flat 'strap-like' corolla, tubular at the base and often sterile. Sometimes, as in the dandelions, all the florets in the flowerhead are rayed, in which case at least the central ones have anthers and style. In some instances ray florets are absent (e.g. Thistles).

Rays: in the context of this book refer to the primary branches of an umbel – the spokes in the Carrot Family, Umbelliferae. Secondary rays are the spokes of subordinate umbels.

Rhizome: a fleshy-swollen, horizontal, underground stem bearing leaf scars.

Rhombic: roughly diamond-shaped.

Rosette: a cluster of leaves, usually at ground level and radiating from one point. Cushion plants are usually composed of numerous small, tightly packed, rosettes of leaves.

Runners: slender horizontal above ground stems as in the Wild Strawberry and usually rooting at the nodes to form new plants.

Scale leaves: small appendages, green or sometimes brown or colourless, replacing leaves where they occur on the stem (e.g. broomrapes).

Scree (talus): rock detritus which accumulates at the base of cliffs or steep rocks; screes are often rather dry but have characteristic plants, especially when they have become stabilised.

Sepals form the outer (lower) ring of floral leaves collectively called the calyx. They are usually small and green but are sometimes large and conspicuously coloured like the petals; as in the anemones.

Sepal-tube refers to the tube formed by sepals which are joined together.

Shrub: deciduous or evergreen woody plants branched from the base.

Shrubberies: plant communities dominated by shrubby species, often forming thickets but generally with associated, often rather coarse, herbs.

Species: the basic unit of classification. Species consist of a group of similar looking individuals, distinct, but interbreeding freely with one another.

Spike: a dense elongated group of flowers, often pointed, with the individual flowers unstalked. In the context of this book the term is used loosely to cover spike-like racemes in which the flowers are short-stalked.

Spine: a sharply pointed branchlet or leaf tip.

Spoon-shaped: when referring to leaf or petal shape indicates the general outline, whether or not the surface is convex or concave.

Spreading: standing out horizontally or at a wide angle from the stem or central point; when referring to the petals or sepals of a flower.

Spur: a hollow tubular or sac-like extension to a petal or sepal, and often containing nectar (e.g. columbines and delphiniums).

Stamens: the male organs of a flower consisting of a stalk (the filament) and an anther, which contains the pollen. The number of stamens in a flower is usually characteristic of given species.

Standard refers to the upper petal in the pea flower or the upper three erect petals in an iris.

Starry hairs (stellate): hairs which are branched and in a star shape; often characteristic of certain plants and usually only clearly seen with the aid of a hand lens (x10).

Stigma: the receptive tip(s) of a style which receives the pollen.

Stipules: leaf-like organs, often rather small, located at the base of a leafstalk where it joins with the stem.

Style: the elongated 'stalk-like' organ linking the ovary to the stigma. A single flower may have one or many styles depending on the species; occasionally absent.

Subshrub: a shrub with a woody base and a herbaceous upper part which dies back each year.

Subspecies: the unit of classification immediately below that of species. Subspecies usually differ from one another in one or two characters, such as flower colour or leaf size but inter-breed freely. However, they are normally confined to different geographical, or ecological locations.

Tendrils: fine twisting filaments forming part of a leaf or stem and which enable the plant to climb.

Thorn: sharply pointed straight or curved woody appendage found on the stems or leaf stalks of various plants (e.g. Roses).

Toothed: teeth-like serrations, along the margins of leaves usually.

Tree: a tall, woody plant usually with a single basal stem or trunk, sometimes massive.

Trifoliate (trefoil): leaves with three distinct leaflets, as in the clovers or trefoils.

Two-lipped: corollas or calyces in which the petals or sepals are grouped together into an upper and a lower lobe or lip. Two- lipped flowers are characteristic of the labiates, Labiatae, and related families.

Umbel: a flower cluster in which all the stalks (rays) arise from a central point, like the spokes of a wheel, to give a flat-topped cluster; a characteristic feature of the Carrot Family, Umbelliferae.

Variety: a subordinate rank to species and subspecies consisting of individuals differing from the type by one or two characters such as flower colour or hairiness. Although capable of inter breeding and often occurring in the same geographical locality, varieties often manage to maintain their own identity.

Waste places: places much disturbed by man but not cultivated; frequently inhabited by weedy species, often annuals.

Whorl: a group of flowers or leaves arising from a central point on a stem.

Whorled spike: a spike composed of whorls of flowers rather than alternate or spirally arranged flowers.

Winged: with a flange or flanges running down the stem; as in various vetches.

Wings: the lateral two petals of a pea flower, usually lying on either side of the keel.

Further reading

A Guide to the Vegetation of Britain and Europe, by O. Polunin and M. Walters. A readable and fairly comprehensive guide to habitats found in Europe. Well illustrated.

A Manual of Alpine and Rock Garden Plants, edited by C. Grey-Wilson; covers many of the commoner alpines in cultivation.

Alpenflora, by G. Hegi; good illustrations but far from complete.

Alpine Flora, by H. Correvon and P. H. Robert.

Alpine Flowers in Colour, by T. P. Barneby; many colour photographs, but far from complete.

Alpine Plants of Europe, by H. S. Thompson.

Atlas de la Flore Alpine, by H. Correvon.

Bulbs, the bulbous plants of Europe and their allies, by C. Grey-Wilson and B. Mathew. A comprehensive and well illustrated guide to the bulbous plants of the region. Illustrated by M. Blamey.

Encyclopaedia of Alpines, The Alpine Garden Society; edited by Kenneth Beckett. The most comprehensive work ever produced on alpine plants. Well illustrated.

Europäische und Mediterrane Orchideen, by H. Sundermann; generally good but the nomenclature is muddling.

Field Guide to Orchids of Britain and Europe, by K. P. Butler; probably the best illustrated and most comprehensible guide on the subject currently available

Fleurs Alpines, by E. & O. Danesch; *very* incomplete but with superb photographs.

Flora della Alpi, by L. Fenaroli.

Flora Europaea, edited by T. G. Tutin and others (Cambridge University Press); the standard European flora, in five volumes but not illustrated.

Flora von Mittel-Europa, by G. Hegi; a marvellously detailed work in many volumes.

Flowers of South-West Europe – a field guide, by O. Polunin & B.E. Smythies (Oxford University Press); covers the Pyrenees in part. Designed to be used with *Flowers of Europe.*

Guide du naturaliste dans les Alps, by J.P. Schaer.

La Vegetation alpine des Pyrenees Orientales, by Braun-Blanquet.

Mediterranean Wild Flowers, by M. Blamey and C. Grey-Wilson. Covers some of the mountain species likely to be found to the south of the region covered by this book.

Mountain Flowers, by A. Huxley; a *very* useful guide, mostly illustrated, of many of the alpine and mountain flowers of Europe, including Britain and Scandinavia but not south-east Europe.

Mountain Flowers, by J. E. Raven and M. Walters; although concerned with Great Britain there is a very useful introduction to the subject in Chapter 3.

Orchideen Europas, by E. & 0. Danesch; beautifully illustrated guides to European orchids.

Orchideen (Hallwag Taschenbuch) – a pocket guide; excellent small guide with many photographs in colour.

Quarterly Bulletins of the Alpine Garden Society; many authors. Invaluable articles on alpine and mountain plants and places visited in Europe. Very useful for those wishing to visit mountain areas in Europe. Many illustrations.

Orchids of Europe, A. Duperrex; one of the best and most concise pocket guides to European Orchids. Poorly illustrated.

The English Rock Garden, by R. Farrer; a standard work dealing with the cultivation of alpine, mountain and rock garden plants.

The Illustrated Flora of Britain and Northern Europe, by M. Blamey and C. Grey-Wilson. One of the most comprehensive and fully illustrated floras of the region.

The Wild Flowers of Britain & Northern Europe, by R & A. Fitter & M. Blamey; the companion volume to this book, for Western and Northern Europe, but also for many lowland species outside the scope of this volume.

Unsere Alpenflora (Our Alpine Flora), by E. Landolt.

Index of English Names

Index of Scientific Names

Trinominal names indicate subspecies; for example *Achillea oxyloba mucronulata* is *Achillea oxyloba* subspecies *muronulata* and written throughout the book as *Achillea o.* subsp. *mucronulata* or *A.o.* subsp. *mucronulata*.

NOTES

NOTES

NOTES